Party Politics in Canada

Party Politics in Canada 5th edition

edited by

HUGH G. THORBURN

Department of Political Studies
Queen's University, Kingston, Ontario

PRENTICE-HALL CANADA INC.
Scarborough, Ontario

To my wife, Wendy

Canadian Cataloguing in Publication Data

Main entry under title:
Party politics in Canada

Includes bibliographical references.
ISBN 0-13-652595-4

1. Political parties – Canada – Addresses, essays, lectures. 2. Canada – Politics and government – Addresses, essays, lectures. I. Thorburn, Hugh G., 1924-

JL195.P37 1984   324.271   C84-098813-3

© 1985 by Prentice-Hall Canada Inc., Scarborough, Ontario

PRENTICE-HALL, INC., Englewood Cliffs, New Jersey
PRENTICE-HALL INTERNATIONAL, INC., London
PRENTICE-HALL OF AUSTRALIA, PTY., LTD., Sydney
PRENTICE-HALL OF INDIA, PVT., LTD., New Delhi
PRENTICE-HALL OF JAPAN, INC., Tokyo
PRENTICE-HALL OF SOUTHEAST ASIA (PTE.) LTD., Singapore
EDITORA PRENTICE-HALL DO BRASIL LTDA., Rio de Janeiro
PRENTICE-HALL HISPANOAMERICANA, S.A., Mexico
WHITEHALL BOOKS LIMITED, Wellington, New Zealand

ISBN: 0-13-652595-4

Production Editor: Bruce Erskine
Design: Steve Boyle
Production: Alan Terakawa
Typesetter: ART-U Graphics Ltd.

1 2 3 4 5 IG 89 88 87 86 85

Printed and Bound in Canada

CONTENTS

PREFACE

Materials on Canadian political parties have proliferated in recent years as the picture of Canadian party politics has grown increasingly complex. The task of the fifth edition of *Party Politics in Canada* is to present insightful, up-to-date analyses of the changing party-political picture while continuing to offer the classical background essential to an in-depth understanding of the subject. For the latter purpose I have retained Escott Reid's brilliant article on the rise of national parties in Canada. And I have also kept Gad Horowitz's famous essay on Conservatives, Liberalism and Socialism in Canada. I have also kept my own essay on the development of parties in Canada and, while updating the material substantially, I have kept my article on the interpretations of the Canadian party system. Other veteran articles are Robert Presthus' piece on the process of elite accommodation between the cabinet, the bureaucracy and the interest groups, and the essay on the national party conventions by Professors Lele, Perlin and Thorburn.

W.L. Morton's essay on the Progressive tradition in Canadian politics is another survivor from the past, as is George Perlin's paper on the Progressive Conservatives.

The rest of the book is new or substantially revised. Professor Paltiel has provided an entirely new treatment of Canadian election expenses and Professor Meisel has updated his article on the decline of party in Canada. Dennis Olsen contributed a piece from his book on the state elite, and Kevin Edwards an essay on the problems of policy making for the NDP. William Irvine discusses reforms to the electoral system.

Looking at individual political parties, I have retained Reginald Whitaker's piece, "Party and State in the Liberal Era," which sets the background to the more contemporary analysis of the Liberal party by Christina McCall-Newman and Joseph Wearing. I have been fortunate to be able to include material from the new book by Patrick Martin, Allan Gregg and George Perlin, *Contenders: The Tory Quest for Power.* Alan Whitehorn has written an original essay on the NDP, "The CCF-NDP: Fifty Years After" and M. Janine Brodie has contributed articles on changes in the NDP since the days of the Waffle and on regionalism and party policy.

The section on regional politics is almost entirely new: Raymond Hudon has contributed a new piece on Quebec and J.P. Beaud has written an up-to-date treatment of the Parti Québécois. Nelson Wiseman has agreed to the inclusion of his essay on the underlying pattern of prairie politics, David Smith has updated his essay on Grits and Tories on the Prairies, and Garth Stevenson has allowed me to include his essay "Alberta Politics Today", first written for the *Canadian Forum*. Alan Cairns and Daniel Wong have contributed excerpts from their essay on the party political situation in British Columbia. Robert Williams has written an original piece on Ontario politics and this time the Atlantic provinces are covered in an original paper by Agar Adamson and Ian Stewart.

These substantial additions have, apart from swelling the size of the book somewhat, also forced some pieces out altogether. These have been replaced by up-to-date material in areas which have substantially changed since the appearance of the fourth edition.

The latest of these, the change in government resulting from the 1984 federal election, is examined in the final essay of this collection, which is followed by an appendix of election results, 1878-1984.

I would like to thank the authors and, in cases where their work appeared elsewhere, their publishers, for making their essays available for publication here.

I also wish to express my appreciation to three colleagues who agreed to act as readers of the fifth edition manuscript: Stefan Dupré of the Department of Political Economy, University of Toronto, Professor B. Kymlicka of the University of Western Ontario and Professor Paul Thomas of the University of Manitoba. Their comments and suggestions were very helpful and led to significant changes (and I am sure improvements) in the content of this fifth edition.

I hope the students for whom the book has been prepared will benefit from this collection in achieving a better understanding of the realities of party politics in Canada.

H.G. Thorburn

SECTION ONE

Historical Background

The following essays present different approaches to the growth of national parties in Canada. I have summarized the historical development of our parties from the pre-Confederation period and viewed their platforms as indicators of what they stood for. Escott Reid, in his essay, finds that national parties were slow to develop because parochialism persisted and members of parliament tended to trade their support of the government for local patronage. I have focused on the men and issues at the center of the political system; Mr. Reid is concerned with the country-wide political conditions during the years of slow party growth before the turn of the century.

1 The Development of Political Parties in Canada

HUGH G. THORBURN

The Canadian party system is largely unique and traces its origins to the pre-Confederation legislative assemblies, particularly to that of the United Province of Canada. From an inchoate politics dependent on local patronage and the extent of the governor's powers, it has developed into a stable two-and-a-half party system, in which the two parties of consensus (the Liberals and the Conservatives) receive between them over three quarters of the votes. The remainder go mainly to the third party, the New Democratic Party (NDP) — so far always less than twenty percent — and the rest to other minor parties. We refer to the Liberals and Conservatives as parties of consensus because they are essentially brokerage parties or parties facilitating elite accommodation, which have no ideological perspective deviating from the status quo.

Historical Development

The beginnings of a party system first appeared in the United Province of Canada (now southern Ontario and Quebec) in the period following the Act of Union of 1840. After Confederation and with the addition of the Maritime provinces, this party system was extended to them, and later to the West. However, a national party system did not exist in Canada until the turn of the century.

The pre-Confederation constitutional system was similar in all of British North America: a governor was sent from Britain to exercise the royal prerogative and actively to head the government. He was supported by a council drawn from the leading figures of the colony. The people were represented by a legislative assembly which had the traditional parliamentary budgetary powers to vote or withhold revenues (minus control of such essentials as the civil list and the revenue from crown lands). The elected assemblymen were at first concerned with obtaining their share of local works, especially roads, and came into conflict with the governor and council over the extent of their powers. Their aim was to become another parlia-

2

ment on the Westminster model. Responsible government, according to which the government must resign when it loses the support of a majority of the legislature, came to all the colonies in the 1840s.

Members formed groups around the stronger of their number and developed relations with the other groups — some tending to align themselves with the governor's policy and some against. Weak coalitions were developed, crossing the barrier between English and French. The Baldwin-Lafontaine government brought the Reformers together to face the Conservatives. As this developed, the governor became more of a figurehead and power came to be centered in the assembly and subject to the unstable vagaries of the shifting factions. However, "In spite of the gradual evolution of political groups and the tendency to apply different names to the same political group as it progressed from era to era, there were permanent political parties during the whole Union period (1840-67) and these parties were largely consistent in membership, viewpoint and policy."[1] The government's policies were moderate and there was no "dynamic matter of principle distinguishing the enactments of the Liberal from the Liberal-Conservative governments of the period."[2] The habit of pragmatic moderation, used to appeal to a majority, was formed well before Confederation.

The period of legislative union in the Province of Canada was one of great instability. A more lasting governmental coalition was needed and was supplied by the Liberal-Conservative party, under the leadership of John A. Macdonald. His Tories were the weaker party in Canada West but were more disciplined and cohesive than their Liberal opponents, who were constantly being frayed by new radical movements. The Tories of Canada West and G. E. Cartier's Bleus, along with some moderate reformers from Canada West and big business interests from Montreal, formed the new and lasting coalition that governed both before and after Confederation.

The components of the party were typical of subsequent Canadian parties: Cartier's Bleus, who represented a stable French Canadian majority with the blessing of the hierarchy; the Grand Trunk and other English Canadian business interests, who were seeking an economic empire based in Montreal; Macdonald's Tories with their anti-American bias and including survivors from the old Family Compact; Galt's English-speaking Montreal big business supporters with voting strength in the Eastern Townships; and the Hinkite Reformers from Canada West who had followed Robert Baldwin, and who had established connections with the Grand Trunk.[3] The essential components were sufficient voting strength and sufficient business support to finance the electoral effort.

Pitted against the Liberal-Conservatives were the Clear Grits of Canada West, who drew their voting strength from the Ontario peninsula and their inspiration from George Brown's paper, the *Globe*. They represented frontier agrarian democracy and opposed the Grand Trunk and Galt's protective tariff. In loose association with the Grits were the Rouges of Canada

East, whose anti-clericalism ensured their weakness before a dominating hierarchy. They were the most radical group in the legislature, espousing the republican ideas of France's 1848 revolution and American democracy. They opposed Confederation as "a Grand Trunk job."[4]

This embryonic two-party system was too unstable for orderly government because of the double majority convention, which required the government to command a majority in both Canada East and Canada West. Confederation with the Maritime provinces offered an escape from this trap. The French Canadians would clearly be dominant in the new Quebec legislature, which had control over education, property and civil rights and local matters. English Canadians, on the other hand, had a clear majority in the new parliament, which controlled the major economic areas.[5]

Macdonald's Conservatives dominated parliament for the first thirty years (except for one parliament when his party was defeated because of the revelation of money passing to the party from railway contractors, known as the Pacific Scandal). His coalition was solidified and extended into the Maritimes and the West as the party of Confederation, the party controlling patronage and therefore the party with the most money at election time. It was a party that made the government a partner with business in developing the economic resources of the country. As sponsor of the transcontinental railway, it worked out the philosophy of development that came to be known as the National Policy, which was implemented in the budget of 1878. Under this arrangement, a protective tariff would shelter the infant industries of central Canada from foreign competition and guarantee them a privileged market in Canada. The revenues would support railway expansion, permitting the opening up of new territory and thereby enlarging the market. The railways, in turn, would service the new areas by bringing in settlers and manufactured goods and carrying the grain, timber and other primary products to Montreal for export.

As long as the Liberals continued to represent the farmers of western Ontario and the rural Rouges south of the St. Lawrence, they were no match for Macdonald's business-oriented and development-minded Conservatives. The Mackenzie government (1874-78), which came to power as a result of the disgrace of the Conservatives in the Pacific Scandal, proved to be an upright but immobile holding operation that could not operate on Macdonald's expansionist basis. Mackenzie failed because he could not bring himself to grant the concessions demanded by the business promoters and the representatives of the outlying provinces. Only when the Liberals abandoned their reformist posture as defenders of the agrarian underdog and spokesmen for reform did they succeed; but once they patterned themselves on Macdonald's Conservatives they beat the Tories at their own game — and they are still doing so!

The "credit" for this transformation goes to Wilfrid Laurier, who took over the Liberal leadership in 1895. He turned his back on the Rouge, republican, anti-clerical tradition and declared himself a Liberal in the British, Gladstonian style. He wooed the clergy and won their goodwill. He made peace with the manufacturers and, in effect, accepted the National Policy. This he accomplished with the brilliant stroke of "Empire Preference," which permitted a protective tariff for Canadian manufactures and discrimination in favour of British goods, which appealed to the low-tariff English Canadian farmers. To gain approval from the business community he chose the more tractable W. S. Fielding to replace Sir Richard Cartwright as Minister of Finance. Thus he was able to combine Jeffersonian democratic principles with Hamiltonian business-oriented policies.

Prosperity came at the same time as Laurier's government, permitting economic expansion. He built up railway and banking associations for the Liberals (the Grand Trunk with its western dream, the Grand Trunk Pacific, as well as Mackenzie and Mann's Canadian Northern, and the Bank of Commerce). This proved a match for the Conservatives' Canadian Pacific-Bank of Montreal connection. If imitation is the highest form of flattery, the Conservatives were honored indeed because they remained in opposition for sixty-five of the next eight-seven years. With the change in the Liberal Party, Canada had a two-party system that resembled the American more than the British. Each party mirrored the other closely and sought the support of all classes, religious and ethnic groups by offering prosperity through programs of government support of business. Conflicts between classes and regions were handled quietly within the party rather than openly between parties, both parties recognized the value of secrecy for their internal and financial affairs.

It was during the Liberal years that the Prairies were settled and the provinces of Saskatchewan and Alberta created. Naturally, at first, immigrants were loyal to the party under whose auspices they came to Canada and received their lands. However, it was not long before they came to resent the monopoly position of the railway and the high prices of tariff-protected Canadian manufactured goods. This contrasted sharply with the open world market on which their wheat and other primary products were sold. They began to agitate for reform of these abuses. Laurier began a system of reciprocity in the trading of natural products with the United States. Like the Empire preference device, this appeared to please everyone. The farmers would have an outlet for their produce, yet the eastern industrialists would keep their protected market. Laurier went to the country on this platform in 1911 — and lost.

How? In retrospect, one can say that he broke the basic rule for success in Canadian politics: he gave priority to the outlying areas. The business community feared that reciprocity in natural products would soon be followed by reciprocity in processed goods, and it did not like the party to cater to the farmer. It backed Borden's Conservatives, enabling them to raise the bogey of American domination. "No truck or trade with the

Yankees" was their slogan and they won after an emotional campaign. The Conservative victory was aided by an alliance with Henri Bourassa's Quebec nationalists, who opposed Laurier for not doing more for French Canadian rights. He had opposed the creation of a Canadian navy and favored a bilingual Canada. Opposition to the Liberals meant alliance with the Conservatives. The Tory victory was built on Ontario, Manitoba, British Columbia and Quebec, which provided Borden with twenty-seven of its sixty-five seats.

The election of 1911 marked a turning point in Canadian party politics. The old, simple, two-party system was modified by the complexity of regional discontent in both Quebec and the West: the former for cultural reasons and the latter for economic ones. The empire based on the St. Lawrence valley's great economic interests had matured and was showing signs of strain: there was the beginning of significant class, regional and cultural conflict.

The coming of war in 1914 masked these strains for a time. The patriotic call rallied much of English Canada to the imperial allegiance, but the imposition of conscription alienated French Canada. Laurier opposed conscription and in so doing lost many of his English-speaking Liberals, who joined Borden to form the Unionist coalition. Now the Liberal opposition was predominantly French Canadian and the government English Canadian. The omnibus two-party system appeared to be in ruins.

The end of the war saw a remarkable change. The unionist government suffered from internal strain and the Liberals rebuilt their forces. The Liberal convention of 1919 confronted the party with the basic choice, between Fielding — the Nova Scotian who had gone over to Borden during the war, the older man with the more conservative image — and King, whose absence from the country during the war spared him the need to choose between Laurier and conscription, who was therefore acceptable to both French and English Canadians, yet who appeared to be on the left of the party. In choosing King, the party regained its broad acceptability and made the Conservatives the party of the English and of conscription. In every general election from 1917 to 1958 except in 1930, the Conservatives got fewer than ten seats in Quebec,[6] and the Liberals won absolute majorities every time. It was the same technique used by the Democrats in the United States: "waving the bloody shirt" in the South; and it produced a solid Liberal contingent from Quebec by blaming the Conservatives for conscription. In these eleven elections the Quebec contingent alone constituted more than a third of Liberal representation in the House of Commons every time but one (1935).

King was in the Macdonald-Laurier tradition; he fashioned a party drawing support from all regions, all classes and all cultural groups. As a consequence he succeeded in being Prime Minister longer than anyone else in the history of the Commonwealth: from 1921 until 1948 (except for the depression years 1930-35).

However, it was in the King years that the party system changed from a simple two-party, brokerage system to what has been called a "two-and-a-half party system." The regional, cultural and class disaffection that appeared earlier grew into firmly entrenched third party movements, centered mainly in the Prairies, Quebec and the urban working class. The discontent on the Prairies that Laurier had sought to assuage in 1911 grew into the Progressive party, the Cooperative Commonwealth Federation (CCF) and the Social Credit party.

Unlike his predecessors, King's government did not have a broad national development policy — it was much more of an open brokerage arrangement. These were the years of the opening of the forest and mining frontiers. Investment poured in from abroad (increasingly from the United States) to develop the pulp and paper, base metals and gold mining industries and most important, secondary manufacturing. Branch plants were set up — mostly in the St. Lawrence drainage basin between Windsor and Montreal — to replicate the consumers' durables and other U.S. industries. Ironically, Macdonald's National Policy of tariff protection was created to fend off American economic domination. Now it served to attract American industry to settle behind the wall and sell in the protected Canadian market, and to export to the rest of the Commonwealth and Empire under the Empire preferences system.

The old east-west trading axis based on the timber and wheat economies (which found its markets in Europe and its transportation in the transcontinental railways and the North Atlantic sea route) was challenged by the new north-south axis (based on pulp and paper, minerals and manufacturing, oriented to the United States, and carried by motor vehicle and aircraft, as well as by railway).

The new arrangements, while they "developed" the economy, also inhibited Canada's national independence. Instead of being financed by bonds which, when repaid, would leave a Canadian owned and operated industry, they tended to be subsidiaries wholly owned or at least controlled by the foreign corporation. As these subsidiaries grew and prospered, the Canadian economy fell more and more under foreign domination. At first there was little concern about the new pattern. Development meant jobs, prosperity and the appearance of national maturity. Only later was the country troubled about the dangers of falling into a new colonial status. All this occurred during the Liberal years, when the country was proud of its growing independence and stature in the world. Its active role in the Second World War earned it standing and British power declined at the same time. The British connection grew more tenuous and could no longer be used by Canadian statesmen to fend off American encroachments. The Liberal leadership, perhaps recognizing the inevitable, cooperated with the Americans at home and abroad. The Liberal party, long seen as the champion of Canadian independence against British imperialism, became the party accepting greater continental integration, and the Conservatives under Diefenbaker, the resisters against "Texas buccaneers."

The omnibus character of the two old parties asserted itself as this distinction became clearer. Walter Gordon led a group of Canadian economic nationalists within the Liberal party and was defeated. Diefenbaker was obligated to desist in his anti-American forays and was replaced by the more cautious and compromising Stanfield.

The policy distinctions between the parties are not great or clear. The major difference now is not between the two old parties themselves, but between the two taken together and the third parties. In fact, it is because the two old parties remained so similar during the years when the regional, cultural and economic groups of the country matured and began to demand more of their government, that the third parties appeared. They entrenched themselves as part of the Canadian party system because the old parties did not, or could not, satisfy the grievances they represented. The Progressive party marks the bridge between the two party period before the First World War and the more recent one that includes third parties.

The discontent on the Prairies that led Laurier to offer reciprocity in 1911 increased during the 1914-18 war period, and appeared in the form of a party of political protest among the farmers, not only on the Prairies, but in Ontario as well. In the decade following the First World War, the Progressives or United Farmers formed the government in Ontario, dominated the Prairie provinces and had more seats than any opposition party in parliament, although they refused to become the official opposition. They constituted an agrarian radical reaction against the National Policy and its successors that had built up the commercial empire based on Toronto and Montreal business and given it political power. The revolt lacked discipline and organization and was not agreed on policy or philosophy. Therefore it lacked the staying power to confront the old parties over time. Mackenzie King's flexibility and radical posture succeeded in winning over the key Progressive leaders to the Liberals and the party was largely absorbed.

Western radicalism was not satisfied with Mr. King's blandishments and continued in different forms — but the farmers' movement in the East disappeared. The Cooperative Commonwealth Federation (CCF), a socialist movement drawing support from western farmers, the urban working class and university intellectuals, was formed in the depression of the thirties. It was the first party in Canadian history to build up an organization, a philosophy and a cadre of leaders in order to offer a sustained challenge to the two omnibus parties. It got nine percent of the votes in the 1935 election and grew vigorously during the next decade of depression and war, winning control of the Saskatchewan government in 1944. Postwar prosperity rolled back its advance. To escape from the trap of inadequate campaign funds and a too narrow base, the CCF merged with the labour movement in 1958 to form the New Democratic Party (NDP). The result so far is a more conspicuous because richer, but less doctrinaire, party than the CCF. Whether it will become more conservative in order to defend trade union interests and privileges is yet to be seen. So far the party constitutes the one major challenge to the old parties in both voting strength and intellectual content.

The other outgrowth of Western discontent is the Social Credit movement. When the Alberta variant of the Progressive movement collapsed from incompetence, scandal and the effects of the depression, the province grasped at a magical solution which would defend existing property relationships but infuse effective demand for goods and services into the economic system by issuing "dividends" to enable people to purchase more. While the party was continuously in power from 1935 to 1971, its philosophy was soon forgotten and the party became the most conservative in the country. Its success in both Alberta and British Columbia reveals the combination of western Canadian prosperity-born conservatism and mistrust or jealously of the East, which is presumed to dominate the old parties.

The western parties of dissent have generally been more successful at the provincial than the federal level. Every western province has at one time or another been governed by one of these parties, although no eastern or central Canadian province has (except for the one-shot United Farmers of Ontario government in Ontario in the twenties). Reasons for this are difficult to determine, beyond the obvious fact that to be counted among the government or official opposition one must be either Liberal or Conservative in federal politics. Also, westerners could vote for Diefenbaker from 1957 to 1965, which was not the same as voting Conservative when the leader was close to eastern Canadian business.

The other manifestation of localized dissent — French Canadian nationalism — was even more confined to provincial politics. It too can be traced to the pre-1914 period. The use of troops to suppress the two Riel rebellions and the hanging of the leader, the controversy surrounding the disposal of the Jesuits' estates, the bitterness over the New Brunswick, Manitoba and Ontario school questions all quickened the sensitivity of French Canada to its vulnerable minority situation. Henri Bourassa, politician and founder of *Le Devoir*, became an effective spokesman for French Canadian nationalism in parliament, and did much to bring down Laurier in 1911. However, it was during the Depression that the Liberal establishment was brought down provincially by a new nationalist party under Maurice Duplessis. The *Union Nationale* was built on the electoral organization of Quebec Conservatives, with dissident Liberals and nationalists joining in. Unlike the western third parties, the Union Nationale confined itself to provincial politics and many of its workers remained faithful to the Conservatives federally. Its policies were conservative, with an admixture of nationalist rhetoric. When the nationalist issue sharpened to the separatist option in 1970, the party equivocated and suffered a serious defeat.

In general, French Canadian dissent and western dissent have much in common. Both are reacting to the two-party system, which they see as the instrument of Toronto- and Montreal-based English Canadian and now American business interests. They see the old parties as alter egos of each other; to dissent they must rely on a third party. In the West this party appears in both federal and provincial politics, although it has been more successful in the latter. In Quebec, the Union Nationale and Parti Québécois have so far confined themselves to provincial politics, although Social Credit has achieved its modest successes at the federal level. The province, and particularly its French Canadian majority, has preferred to keep its federal contingent on the government side and its representatives in cabinet — a choice that is not only in its interest but favors national unity. Obviously if there were no influential French Canadians in Ottawa, the separatist cause would have additional serious grievances to feed upon.

ENDNOTES

1. P.G. Cornell, *The Alignment of Political Groups in Canada 1841-1867* (Toronto: University of Toronto Press, 1962), p. 83.
2. *Ibid.*
3. F.H. Underhill, "The Development of National Parties in Canada," *Canadian Historical Review*, Vol. 16, No. 4 (1935), p. 367.
4. *Ibid*, passim.
5. See the article by F.R. Scott in *Evolving Canadian Federalism*, A. Lower, F.R. Scott *et al.*, Duke University Press, 1958, pp. 54-91.
6. Quebec had sixty-five seats until 1949 when it got eight more for a total of seventy-three. It had seventy-five seats from 1953 to 1968, when it lost one, for a total of seventy-four.

2 The Rise of National Parties in Canada*

ESCOTT M. REID

To understand Canadian politics during the first quarter century or so of the country's history one must constantly bear in mind certain differences between the conduct of general elections then and now. The two most important points of difference are that in the first three general elections, those of 1867, 1872 and 1874, voting was open throughout all the provinces and the polling in the various constituencies did not take place at the same time. A Toronto constituency might elect its member one day and the neighbouring York constituency six weeks later. The grosser abuses of the system of non-simultaneous elections were remedied in 1874 but not till 1878 was the ballot used and simultaneous voting established in all but a few of the constituencies of the five eastern provinces. In 1882 Manitoba voted simultaneously with the East and by 1908 deferred elections had been discontinued in the great majority of the remaining western constituencies. It is also worth noting that open voting was resurrected for use in the first two federal general elections held in the North-West Territories, those of 1887 and 1891.

Deferred elections and open voting are important in a study of the rise of national political parties in that they make it possible for government to exercise a great measure of control over the results of elections — and the greater this control of government over elections, the weaker the political parties. Under the old system of open voting, civil servants, contractors — anyone who wanted to obtain favors from the government — could not vote against the candidates it supported without losing their jobs or their expectations of favors should the government be returned to power. On the other hand, if they voted for the government and the opposition were successful their fate would be equally unhappy. As a natural consequence they disliked partisan electoral contests. This dislike was shared by many of their neighbours who, though they did not expect to be the direct recipients

---

*Reprinted from *Papers and Proceedings of the Canadian Political Science Association, IV, 1932.*

of government favors, had the interests of the whole constituency at heart and did not want its chances of obtaining a new post office, wharf or railway spoilt by its unintentional support of the weaker party at an election. Even after vote by ballot was adopted these people continued to disapprove of partisan electoral contests, which committed the constituency to the support of one side or another before they knew which side would constitute the government. The ideal election of these political realists was an uncontested one in which the member was not definitely committed to any party and could therefore make good terms for his constituency in return for giving his support to the strongest party in the House.[1] Such members constituted an important fraction of all the early parliaments; Macdonald called them "loose fish," George Brown, "the shaky fellows" and Cartwright, "waiters on Providence." These appellations are hardly dispassionate enough for us so we shall call them, for want of a better term, "ministerialists," because their politics were not to support a party but a ministry and any ministry would do. These ministerialists were inverted Irishmen. They were always "agin" the opposition. Their counterpart in ecclesiastical politics was the Vicar of Bray.

It was because of the strength of this political realism that non-simultaneous elections threw such power into the hands of the ministry. The government could bring on the elections first in those constituencies in which they were safe, and having carried them, tackle those where they had some chance against the opposition, and leave the dangerous seats till the last. At the close of the election of 1872, The Toronto *Globe* wrote that: "The sole object of this nefarious trickery was to enable the Ministerialists to raise a grand howl over their pretended success and cheat the people into the belief that the Opposition were being awfully beaten."[2]

The *Globe* knew that if the people believed the opposition were being awfully beaten many of them would rally to the government camp and the opposition would be badly beaten. The illusion of victory would create victory. For if the voting in a ministerially minded constituency, in our sense of the word, were deferred until it seemed pretty clear which party would form the government, that constituency need no longer return an avowed "loose fish"; it could return a proper party candidate. Nevertheless that would not mean that it cared at all for parties — that parties had any real existence in that constituency.

National political parties certainly did not exist under the Macdonald government from 1867 to 1873. Confederation saw group government established at Ottawa. The dominant groups or parties in the coalition government were the several branches of Ontario Conservatism under Galt, Macdonald and others, and the French Conservative groups under Cartier. This dual alliance was supported by the Ontario Liberals under McDougall, Howland and Blair, the English minority in Quebec under Galt, and a large group of ministerialists mostly from Eastern Ontario,

Quebec and New Brunswick. The Ontario coalition Liberals and the Cartier followers were not members of a coalition party because they owed their allegiance entirely to their own sectional leaders. They appear to have been willing to support an alternative administration which would have excluded Macdonald and his supporters, and Macdonald in 1871 had to use all his cunning to prevent a successful alliance arising out of the "coquetting", as he called it, which was going on between his French followers and the two wings of Ontario Liberalism.[3] By 1872 the coalition Liberals had returned to the Reform party or had been swallowed up by one of the Conservative groups, and consequently the government followers in Ontario were slightly more homogeneous, though the number of parties which made up Ontario Conservatism was still great if we can judge from the events of 1873. Certainly in that year it appeared as if the Conservative sectional leaders in Ontario could transfer their personal following to the support of another administration at their own mere pleasure. If Galt, for example, had entered Mackenzie's cabinet, as at one time seemed likely, he would have brought over the Conservative members from the Cobourg district and this, according to his adviser (the Conservative editor in Cobourg) would have given him "the strongest personal following of any member of the Cabinet."[4]

The members from New Brunswick in the first two parliaments were either ministerialists or independents. The election of 1867 in that province was fought not between an anti-government party and a pro-government party but between so-called anti-unionists under Smith and Anglin and so-called unionists under Mitchell and Tilley. These terms apparently meant nothing and when the respective groups got to Ottawa the former did not consistently vote with the opposition nor the latter with the government. As a group they gave a "fair trial to the administration" (that over-worked phrase of early Canadian politics) but occasionally they would show their complete independence as, for example, when they voted unanimously in favor of an amendment to the first national tariff debated in parliament.[5] In the election of 1872 only one successful candidate appears to have committed himself to the support of the government or opposition. The others professed varying degrees of independence of party ties.

The Nova Scotians in 1867 constituted a separate political party and its very *raison d'être*, opposition to confederation, signified that it owed no loyalty to any party or leader outside Nova Scotia. According to Howe, even the beaten Tupper party had not taken sides in the party politics of Ontario. "No man in this country," said Howe in the first session of parliament, "went to the hustings pledged to any side of any question in the politics of Canada."[6] When Howe entered the cabinet his followers became still another group within the coalition, for they continued to owe their allegiance to their sectional leader, not to Macdonald. In 1872 in Nova Scotia as in New Brunswick, the issues were mainly personal and the candidates were unpledged to any party. Their general attitude was that they had no affection for the government but that the Reformers were even less likeable for they were a selfish Ontario party.[7]

It follows from this analysis of the government supporters in the first two parliaments that there was then no national Liberal party. The Brownite Liberals of Ontario possessed the unity of adversity — all who were not truly loyal had deserted to join the winning side — but they, like the Conservatives, did not even extend over the whole province, for Ontario east of Kingston was a hotbed of ministerialism. Members from that district might call themselves Liberal or Conservative but they almost unanimously supported the government. There was also a Liberal or Rouge party in Quebec but the Ontario and Quebec Liberal parties were not united. There was between them little more than an entente cordiale, at most a dual alliance. Not until 1872 were they able to draw close enough together to choose a common leader in parliament. This dual alliance of Ontario and Quebec Liberals did not even have an entente with the New Brunswick independents or the Nova Scotian party. The leaders of the Liberals, Mackenzie and Dorion, tried to cooperate with the maritimers but they could carry only about half their supporters with them on a division.[8] The Liberals did not even possess enough cohesion to pursue a tactically sound policy.

The election of 1872 increased the number of votes the Liberal alliance could muster on a division but it did this by increasing the number of groups (and perplexed ministerialists who attached themselves to its standard) rather than by adding to the strength of the real party. The reason for ministerialists supporting an opposition party was that as the returns came in during the long six weeks of polling they were so close that both parties claimed the victory and the ministerialists were not certain on which side of the fence to jump. The wiser of them concluded that even if Macdonald had won, his was but a temporary triumph and his tenure of office would be brief. Consequently it was good policy to support the opposition so that they would be remembered when the opposition came into its own. In Quebec there were interesting developments which showed how thin was the veneer of party unity which had covered the fissures between the various groups under Cartier, now weakened by the intrigues of church politics, by the Riel rising and the New Brunswick school law. He lost support on the right to the Ultramontanes or Programmists, and on the left to the Parti National, and both dissident groups attached themselves to the Rouges. Thus the Quebec oppositionists constituted no longer a fairly united party but a heterogeneous collection of groups. The parallel with 1896 is interesting.

After the downfall of Macdonald over the Pacific scandal one coalition government succeeded another. The dominant groups in the new coalition were the Ontario Liberals and the Quebec Rouges. They were supported by a few Ontario Conservatives who had left their party because of the scandal, by the Parti National and the Programmists, and by the usual assortment of ministerialists from eastern Ontario and Quebec and by almost unanimous ministerial groups from the Maritimes and the West. The personnel of the cabinet gives convincing evidence of the coalition's heterogeneity. The Ontario members were Mackenzie, Blake, Cartwright, D.A. Macdonald, Scott and Christie. Of these, Cartwright and Scott had been avowed Conservatives as late as two years before and D.A. Macdonald was an eastern Ontario "wobbler." The original Quebec representation of three were all Rouges but not one of the five maritime members could have been called a Mackenzie supporter in the previous election. A.J. Smith of New Brunswick had declared at his nomination meeting that he had said to Sir John Macdonald and Sir George Cartier, that even if he had the power he would not turn them out for the sake of office, for he thought no other could do any better than they.[9] Burpee, the other cabinet minister from that province, had denounced the Liberal opposition because they were engrossed by the sectional interest of Ontario.[10] Ross of Nova Scotia had not even supported the remonstrance to the Governor General on August 12, 1873, when a dozen of the usual government supporters had bolted, and though Coffin of Nova Scotia had joined in the remonstrance he had previously supported Macdonald in the two party divisions on the charges of corruption. Laird of Prince Edward Island had not taken part in the campaign of 1872 since the Island was not then a member of Confederation. Thus even counting D.A. Macdonald as Liberal, the Liberals constituted only half the Mackenzie cabinet.

It was only by 1878 that the Ontario-Quebec parties had conquered most of eastern Canada. That was the election, it will be remembered, in which the ballot was introduced and elections were held simultaneously in all but four of the eastern constituencies. Of the 141 eastern members of parliament who sought re-election all but one did so as supporters of that leader whom they had supported in the first session of the parliament of 1874, and the great majority of the other candidates committed themselves in their election speeches to following one of the two party leaders. The result was that the Toronto *Globe* and the Montreal *Gazette* disputed over the party affiliations of only five members-elect instead of the thirty-five of 1872, and it was possible to discover the approximate strength of the parties in the House as soon as the ballots were counted, whereas previously that knowledge could only be gained after the first party division had taken place. There flowed from this the establishment of a constitutional precedent, for Mackenzie resigned before meeting the new parliament. This break with tradition did not go uncondemned. The *Dominion Annual Register* for that year summed up the criticism which was directed against his action: "To count up the results of an election according to the success of certain candidates who were represented to hold certain views on public affairs and to accept that results as the will of the people constitutionally expressed was...a dangerous approach to the plebiscite."[11]

The critics were right. General elections were becoming dangerously like plebiscites but the reason was not Mackenzie's break with constitutional precedent but the establishment of the two-party system in eastern Canada. Every advance towards national political parties was to mean a further step towards making general elections plebiscites.

We must not think of the two parties as being as firmly established in eastern Canada in 1878 as they were by 1896. The Conservative party in Quebec in 1878 was still made up of a union of groups and it is possible that the only loyalty which a member of one of these groups owed was to his own sectional leader. Certainly in 1887 the ultramontane members did not seem to experience any violent conflict of loyalties when they broke with Macdonald and sought to destroy him in revenge for the murdered Riel; they were so nearly successful that Macdonald was only saved by the extra seats his gerrymander had given him in Ontario. It would appear, however, that from 1891 on the federal Conservative party did possess a measure of sovereignty in Quebec, for Chapleau was not certain enough of the loyalty of his followers to risk an open break with Macdonald. Instead he kept one foot in each camp.

Partisanship had been making no progress in the western provinces in the 1870s. The politics of Manitoba and British Columbia in the three general elections of that decade can be explained as the result of two forces: their desire for the Pacific Railway and the holding of their elections some weeks after the results in the East had been declared. Until the railway was completed the West could not afford the luxury of party politics. It had to be ministerialist. And as it always knew which party had been sustained by the East, it could be ministerialist without difficulty. All parliamentary candidates in the West in the seventies were unanimous in their opposition to the opposition. Opposition candidates did not appear in Manitoba until 1882 nor in British Columbia until 1891. Western ministerialism was, however, of a different nature from the *politique de pourboire* of the eastern ministerialists. The westerners did not sell their support in return for the petty favors of the patronage machine and the pork barrel but only in return for the railway, the whole railway and nothing but the railway. This attitude of political realism, dictated by the economic needs of the frontier, did not triumph in Manitoba without a struggle against the partisan political attitudes of the Ontario settlers. The struggle was short and not severe. The economic necessities of the present triumphed over the political institutions of the past.[12] The British Columbians had no such struggle, for few of them had any interest in the party politics of the East until the completion of the railway in 1885 brought eastern immigrants and with them eastern political ideas. This difference in the composition of the population of the two provinces meant that Manitoba declared its allegiance to the eastern parties as soon as it was safe for it do so, that is in 1882 or 1887, while British Columbia delayed till 1891 or 1896. The North-West Territories did not swear loyalty to the parties till 1896 in spite of a false appearance of partisanship in 1887 — the result of perplexed ministerialism. The *Globe* told them that the Liberals had won and the *Gazette* that the Conservatives had again triumphed.

With the conquest of the West completed in 1896 the Conservative and the Liberal parties had at last become national and thus a national two party system was established in Canada for the first time. In becoming national the two parties did not lose all their old characteristics. 1878 and 1896 do not mark breaks in the evolution of political parties in Canada, for the development of such extra-legal political institutions is a gradual process. Consequently it is not surprising to find today sectionalism in parties, heterogeneity in cabinets and ministerialism in constituencies — veiled and modified as they are by the party system. Bargaining between sectional groups still takes place but nowadays more often in caucus and cabinet than on the floor of the House of Commons. In caucus the party is sectional. In public it is homogeneous. In reality it is federal.

What is the force which has made out of the loose coalitions of Macdonald and Mackenzie the federated unions of sectional groups that have constituted the national parties from 1896 to the present day? The loose coalitions had as their core dual alliances of Quebec and Ontario groups. Whichever of these alliances proved to be the more powerful ruled with the assistance of the maritime and western groups, which remained neutral until the struggle in the central provinces had been resolved and then made as good terms as possible with the victors. There came a time when the neutral groups had to choose before the struggle of the rival dual alliances which one they would support. As some chose one and some another, the dual alliances would have become quintuple had not other forces been working to make them two federations of five or more groups. For when allied and associated powers are fighting a war for supreme power — and political combinations are always fighting a war for supreme power — the alliance tends to itself become the direct object of the devotion and loyalty of the citizens of the separate powers or, in other words, there is a tendency for the alliance to acquire sovereignty and so become a super or federal state. The other force making for closer union is the result of the actions of the leaders of the groups who find from bitter experience that an alliance is most effective in attack or defence when it is united under a supreme command. These two forces meet, the force of individual devotion pushing up from the bottom and the force of political strategy pushing down from above, and what was once a loose dual alliance is compressed into a federal union. The cement which made this union durable is furnished from non-political sources. Better means of communication bind the sections together; inter-migration breaks down sectional differences; new territories are settled as a common enterprise; a national feeling struggles into existence. Out of the alliances of sectional parties are created the federations of sectional groups — the national Conservative and the national Liberal parties.

ENDNOTES

1. An example of such an election is that in the constituency of Cornwall (eastern Ontario) in 1872. Candidates of both parties were nominated but the Conservative, who was a son of John Sandfield, withdrew and allowed the nominal Liberal, Bergin, to be elected by acclamation. In withdrawing, Macdonald said that "he believed that when Dr. Bergin got into Parliament he would throw over all ties and follow the crowd if the Government had a majority in the House. He thought that he would show good judgment in doing so, because he would get more favours by going with the majority than he could from the minority." The Toronto *Globe,* August 24, 1872.
2. *Ibid.,* August 8, 1872.
3. Sir John Macdonald to Hon. Alex. Morris, April 21, 1871, in Sir Joseph Pope, *Correspondence of Sir John Macdonald* (Toronto: Doubleday & Co., Inc., 1921), p. 145.
4. H.J. Ruttan to Sir Alex. Galt, November 17, 1873, in O.D. Skelton, *Life and Times of Sir. A.T. Galt* (Toronto: Oxford University Press, 1920), pp. 465-466.
5. Amendment of McDonald (Lunenburg) of December 14, 1867, "for the purpose of placing wheat and rye flour, cornmeal and corn in the free list," *Journals of the House of Commons* (Canada), 1867-68, p. 92.
6. *House of Commons Debates* (Canada), November 8, 1867.
7. For example, Killam, the member of Yarmouth from 1867 to 1882, said in his campaign, according to an editorial in the *St. John Daily Telegraph,* August 17, 1872: "I have not had much confidence in the Government in many respects; but am sorry to say that I have no confidence in the Opposition. They...have attempted to treat the interests of these Maritime Provinces as mere makeweights in the scale, to further the selfish aims of great parties in Ontario."
8. Examples of such divisions are those on the amendment of McDonald (Lunenburg) of December 14, 1867, mentioned above, and on the Holton amendment of April 29, 1868, moving the House into Committee of the Whole "to consider the alleged grievances of [Nova Scotia]". *Journals of the House of Commons* (Canada), 1867-68, pp. 92, 249.
9. *St. John Daily Telegraph,* August 6, 1872.
10. *Ibid.,* August 5, 1872.
11. H.J. Morgan, *Dominion Annual Register 1878* (Montreal: Dawson Brothers, 1879), p. 211.
12. This struggle is reflected in the editorials of *The Manitoba Free Press,* January 10, 17 and February 7, 1874.

The Canadian Party System

In this section we deal with the dominant elements of the political power structure in Canada: the ideological bases of the major parties and the interests they stand for, the elites they relate to, the choosing of party leaders, the federal-provincial dimension, the financing of election campaigns and the bias of the electoral system. The picture emerges of a liberal, business oriented society that has built up large bureaucratic structures that have taken on a life of their own, and grown ponderous, complex and unresponsive. Interests that once dominated have grown increasingly frustrated as they observe the parties they influence fumbling with the new and complex issues that confront government. Overwhelmed by fiscal crisis, chronic unemployment and threatening inflation, the political parties soldier on, unable to innovate or deal effectively with mounting problems. The federal system and electoral arrangements combine to sustain this situation. However, recent developments suggest a decline in the salience of parties themselves, as the society grows more bureaucratic and complex. The important decisions tend to be taken by cabinet in consultation with senior bureaucrats and interest group representatives. The amateur politician is becoming a thing of the past.

3 Interpretations of the Canadian Party System

HUGH G. THORBURN

Over the years the Canadian party system has been interpreted in innumerable ways by many observers: party activists, historians, political scientists, sociologists, journalists and interested laymen. Most have been casual, simplistic views, but a few have been stimulating and insightful interpretations. Of the significant analyses, two basic approaches stand out. One sees the system shifting around a basic norm of two rather similar parties. This is examined first under the title "Two-Party System". The other, which sees the norm as one dominant party with other parties jostling about it is discussed under "One-Party Dominance". Lastly, I examine the party system today as I see it.

The Two-Party System

Tories versus Reformers

The oldest perception of the Canadian party system dates back to the early nineteenth century colonial period when our forebears struggled over responsible government. This dispute was most clearly fought out in Upper and Lower Canada, where it culminated in rebellion. The governmental system relied upon the British governor for leadership and control, and he, in turn, worked through a small elite of placemen or patronage appointees and privileged economic and social leaders assembled into the Executive Council of the colony. The Legislative Council or upper house also included most of the same Tory faces of the governing clique. The government was a highly restricted power monopoly, which no doubt was acceptable to those of conservative and loyalist mind who feared the rise of popular power lest it lead to revolution, as had recently occurred in the southern colonies, now independent as the United States of America. However, many of the excluded people resented their situation and they elected members to the Legislative Assembly who were pledged to reform. In these early days before responsible government was conceded, there was a political party system in embryo, which was to grow into the two-party system of the post-Confederation period.

At first the governor, most conspicuously Sir Francis Bond Head of Upper Canada, openly campaigned against the reformers, thereby putting the state apparatus, including the crown, on one side of a political dispute. The reformers were then led to rebel not only against the Family Compact but also against the governor and the imperial system for which he stood. Therefore the demands of the reformers took on a seditious appearance, and open armed rebellion, albeit on a small scale, was the result. While the rebels were easily scattered, the British government sent Lord Durham ("Radical Jack", as he was familiarly known in England) to investigate the affairs of British North America. Lord Durham recommended responsible government for the colonies, which would mean the governor would take advice from his council only so long as it was supported by a majority in the assembly, and the combining of the two colonies of Upper and Lower Canada into one to assure an overall British majority.

Once responsible government was conceded, the governor was largely removed from the political arena, leaving the politicians to settle matters between themselves. While different groups appeared in the assembly of the United Province of Canada and in the other colonies, the basic division between Tories and Reformers of earlier times remained in the mind of all as the basic touchstone of political distinction.[1] When the party system settled down to the classic Anglo-Saxon two-party dichotomy after Confederation, this older distinction between the parties was not forgotten: the Liberals continued to remind the electorate of their heroic antecedents and depicted the Conservatives as the successors of the Tories of the Family Compact and the Château Clique. One still encounters this interpretation of the party system, especially from Liberal campaign orators, long after it has lost all relevance to Canadian political life.

The Ins versus the Outs

The most widely accepted of the older interpretations of the Canadian party system is the one which sees two similar parties, each seeking to appeal to the many interests, classes, regions and ethnic groups that make up the country. The parties are depicted as Tweedledum versus Tweedledee, the Ins versus the Outs: two brokerage parties or teams of office-seekers who rival one another in mounting and presenting programs calculated to attract the support of a majority of the electorate. Alexander Brady describes the relationship:

> Each party is loosely attached to formal attitudes and ideas, and is supported by the social groups and regions which, out of long habit or temporary interest, favour the stand taken...Within a decade the parties may unblushingly interchange programmes. Sir John Williston wrote out of an extensive if cynical knowledge of Canadian affairs that "no man in Canada has been more inconsistent than the man who has faithfully followed either political party for a generation." This circumstance derives inexorably from the internal

necessity of the parties to make a universal appeal, to dramatize the fact that they stand for a synthesis of interests within the nation, and to alter their programme with the shifts of opinion throughout the country. As one party or the other manoeuvres into a fresh position, the partisan battleground changes. The leaders who succeed in making the widest national appeal are those who rule. This is the bedrock of democratic politics in a country constituted like Canada. From it there can be no escape as long as the parties seek to win office by the liberal procedure of debate and persuasion.[2]

Professor Brady admits that the parties have their differences, especially in their traditional supporters. "The social groups least interested in close relations with the United States are most commonly Conservatives; those least sympathetic to an imperial outlook are usually Liberals."[3] He cites Lord Bryce approvingly: "In Canada ideas are not needed to make parties, for they can live by heredity and, like the Guelfs and Ghibellines of Medieval Italy, by memories of past combats."[4]

One can discern a mixture of two interpretations in Brady and the other prewar writers on the two-party system:[5] a system of two identical parties, totally devoid of theory, that alter their policies like shopkeepers changing their window displays; and a system of a liberal or progressive party versus a conservative or traditional one that exchange office as the mood of the country shifts, from for example, optimism to pessimism, imperialism to continentalism, free-trade to protectionism. In the latter case, each party has a traditional rhetoric and engages in opportunistic posturing (which often contradicts its theory) in the scramble to out-maneuver its rival. These two interpretations are vastly different, but there is much evidence in the history of the Liberal and Conservative parties to support each of them. Most casual observers have settled for a mixture of both as the best explanation of the two old parties and most academic observers start with this as the basic set of assumptions from which subsequent refinements can be drawn.

The Shifting National Mood Theory

Professor J.R. Mallory sees the parties as the Ins versus the Outs; yet he explains:

What is important is that at any given time only one party is in tune with a national mood — and that party is likely to stay in power until the mood changes and leaves it politically high and dry. Macdonald was, in his way, the perfect expression of the national spirit in the nineteenth century — raffish, careless, tough and pliable. Laurier expressed the character of the new Liberal Party which he was able to create out of what had been merely a series of doctrinaire and local provincial parties. Laurier combined an elegant and eloquent idealism with the embodiment of a spirit of compromise — of healing the scars of conflicts of race, religion and region which had grown up since the seventies. The time came when much of the glamour of the Liberal position wore off, when compromise appeared merely the inaction of old, tired men in office. The earnest, precise Borden represented the reaction in a time of deep national trial. Again Mackenzie King, with his earnest preaching about the virtue of conciliation, represented the tortured doubts of an age of national frustration; when constitutional difficulties, the baffling new problems of an industrial age and a shattered world combined to create an atmosphere of cautious despair. With Louis St. Laurent a new look came to the Liberal Party: tough-minded, bland, sophisticated and confident in managing a growing society bursting at the seams with growth. But mere prosperity and competent government is not enough. There is plenty of evidence that the pace of modern living produces a host of frustrations and a mixture of guilt and insecurity. Into this atmosphere was skillfully projected the personality of John Diefenbaker, solemnly intoning evangelical phrases about a national vision and a national dedication. It does not matter whether these 'thoughts' have much meaning — they did catch a mood.[6]

Interest Group Theory

This interpretation suggests that major interest groups, particularly business, are largely determinant in the formulation of policies of the major parties, especially when in office.

Professor Frank Underhill was the Toronto historian who provided much of the intellectual backing for the early CCF, but who later served as the curator of Laurier House, where Mackenzie King lived, and where his memorabilia are kept.

In a well-known article, Underhill wrote:

The real function of the two-party system since the Laurier era has been to provide a screen behind which the controlling business interests pull the strings to manipulate the Punch and Judy who engage in mock combat before the public. Both parties take for granted that their first duty in office is to assist the triumphant progress of big business in the exploitation of the country's resources....A party system which depends for success (i.e. for office) upon the different and often contradictory appeals which it must make to different sectional interests will inevitably in course of time become mainly dependent upon and responsible to those interest groups which are themselves best organized and most strategically located for applying effective pressure upon party leaders. In Canada there are two such groups who have always held a dominating position in our politics because of their superior internal organization — the French Catholic Church in Quebec and the interlocking financial, industrial, commercial interests which we usually refer to nowadays as big business...Big business depends primarily upon campaign contributions, also upon constant official and unofficial lobbying, and upon the complex economic and social relationship between business and political leaders.[7]

With the increasing costs of modern elections, the parties are becoming more dependent upon wealthy interests for funds to finance the campaigns, which in turn, rely more on costly image-building in the media than on rational argument. While the public benefits from a modern social security system, the corporate interests have retained much of their influence, although deepening problems are preventing governments from responding as they used to in prosperous times. The largest and most dynamic sector of the business community is under foreign control, and this makes the previously harmonious relationship of elite accommodation between business and government more difficult. Foreign head offices find their interests more likely to clash with Canadian governmental priorities, leading at times to plant closures and the shifting of production out of Canada. Since both leading Canadian political parties have long-standing relationships with the major business interests, they now find themselves torn between this loyalty and the pull of events suggesting policies that some of these interests will oppose. Even the third party, the NDP, is caught in a cross-fire between the international trade union movement which, since its founding in the early sixties, has provided much of its funding and campaign workers, and the recently expanded, purely Canadian unions based mainly in the recently organized public service sector.

The Two-and-a-Half Party System

A more contemporary interpretation takes the minor parties, and particularly the radical CCF-NDP, into account. This party's spokesmen accept the Tweedledum versus Tweedledee theory and see the NDP as the party offering the only real alternative to the Canadian people. This view holds that the Liberals and Conservatives are the agents of the giant corporations and that the NDP is the voice of the people struggling to be heard over the din of the old parties' expensive advertising campaigns.[8] T.C. Douglas has argued that both old parties' are "committed to maintaining our present unregulated and unplanned economy"[9] with consequent poor economic performance and the permitting of the takeover of the Canadian economy by giant U.S.-controlled corporations. Solutions to the nation's unemployment problem that might adversely affect business are ruled out.[10] The NDP has come to a more nationalistic position than the others because of its opposition to big business, which in Canada is largely controlled from abroad.

Essentially this interpretation seeks to convert the Tweedledum vs. Tweedledee party system into one in which the two old parties merge into one defender of big business while the NDP takes up the position of advocate of the ordinary citizens — a familiar analogy is the Conservative versus Labour situation which prevails in Great Britain.

There is an important consequence of the working of this system. If the two brokerage parties monopolize office and the official opposition, the reformers and persons with new ideas will tend to be drawn off to the NDP and other minor parties, where they have virtually no chance of participating in government. Therefore the implementation of reforms is even more remote than if reformers had to remain in the two omnibus parties, although the public agitation for reform will be substantial. People will therefore be led to expect changes that are not forthcoming — a situation that is bound to engender frustration and cynicism among the electorate.

In addition, the NDP (unlike its predecessor, the CCF) is not a pure party of reform. It depends heavily for financial and other support on one of the vested interests of the country: the Canadian Labour Congress, and is therefore in many ways a conservative force[11] This fact is enhanced by its affiliation, or rather that of its member unions, with the American labour movement, the AFL-CIO. The importance of this connection was especially obvious at the time of the leadership conventions at both the federal and Ontario levels in the early seventies.

A less partisan variant of this theory is that since the two old parties offer so little choice to the disenchanted elector, the third parties supply the needed breadth of choice. Professor Mallory argues:

> The innovator role is explained by the state of monopolistic competition which confronts major political parties — similar to that facing the industrial giants which produce soap or motor cars. Like them, the parties adhere to the principle of minimum differentiation of the product, warily peddling the same set of ideas and policies which have worked for them in the past. They are disposed to be afraid of new ideas, for fear of making costly mistakes which may lose support they already have, without making compensating gains.
>
> Third parties, with nothing to lose, can afford to experiment with new ideas, for ideas are the only working capital they have. In the process the public will be gradually educated to an awareness of the need for a new policy or a new program. Then, in the fullness of time, the larger parties will take over the more durable of the reforms advocated by third parties and enact them into law.[12]

This is the notion of a two-and-a-half party system in which the minor party (the half) supplies the innovating quality to an otherwise static system.

The Communist View: Parties in the Interest of Big Business

Another partisan perspective that is given relatively little attention is the Communist one, for which Tim Buck, long-term leader and virtual personification of the Canadian Communist party, is the best source. In his view, "the actual competition between Liberals and Tories...was solely as to which party could serve Canadian capitalism best. There was no difference in their attitudes towards the profit system."[13]

Elsewhere Buck states:

> The traditional terms and slogans which until recently distinguished the two parties of Canadian capitalism, have lost their original meanings. In the past the Liberal and Conservative parties represented the competing interests of different sections of capitalism and the rival imperialist interests of Britain and the U.S. Those differences are now completely over-shadowed.[14]

Far from being considered the left-wing innovator, the CCF-NDP is viewed as sharing the same anti-Communist, pro-capitalist goals as the other parties. In reference to J.S. Woodsworth, Tim Buck pointed out:

> His aim was a reform party — a party which could secure support from sections of the capitalist class, from well-to-do farmers and urban middle-class people, and from some workers. He did not pretend that he advocated social-ism. His political philosophy was summed up in the following sentences which he repeated hundreds of times: "The state should own and control certain essential public utilities. That is all".[15]

Buck goes on to note NDP retreats from the 1933 CCF Regina Manifesto, which stood forcefully against "participation in imperialist wars," to a position of support for the government "in its preparation for an aggressive imperialist war — to make the world safe for capitalism."[16] In short, the Communist critique sees both the major parties and the minor parties (including, in a qualified sense, the NDP) as the servants of the capitalist system and of reactionary positions generally. It proposes itself as the real alternative.

> To stop U.S. domination of our country and to bring about the sort of policies that are needed now in domestic affairs requires the bringing together of a political force which is not hamstrung by ties with U.S. imperialism, as both the Liberal and Tory parties are. It must represent the interest of the masses of the people and be able to unite them at the polls.[17]

The Complex Cleavages Trap Theory[18]

Professors F.C. Engelmann and M. Schwartz present an interesting interpretation in their study of the Canadian party system.[19] They emphasize the role of the media in party politics:

> Technological innovations increase the media's capacities for spreading vast amounts of information to more people more quickly, thus altering the style in which party politics is conducted. Among the consequences is a need for extensive financial resources in order to fully use the media. Parties with insufficient funds from membership contributions must thus rely on large donations from a few contributors. By doing so, they make themselves vulnerable to the pressure which such contributors are then able to exert, a

consequence which the new Election Expenses Act hopes to avert. A further consequence has been the utilization of personnel skilled in the exploitation of the media, which tends to turn parties away from volunteer workers and party strategists concerned with issues, to highly paid experts primarily concerned with techniques for electing candidates, regardless of the issues involved. These trends further contribute to the professionalization and rationalization of politics."[20]

While the increased role of the media affects all parties, it most affects those receiving large donations from wealthy corporate interests, which are also the ones least concerned with policy or doctrine. The electorate is skillfully manipulated through the media by the gimmickry of the professional public relations and advertising counsel, drawing their attention away from the serious problems, the solution to which would be against the interest of their clients and their backers.

Engelmann and Schwartz predict the continuation of the "two parties plus" system in which "electoral success, rather than fixed principles has been the focus of so much of Canadian party politics." The many cleavages (generally regional-ethnic and regional-class) in Canada would break up a party that tried to commit itself to broadly-based principles "unless it switches its focus to the attainment of office as an end in itself." In short, we are stuck with a politics based on opportunism because our problems are too complex for a principled party or parties to succeed and tackle them seriously.

We might call this the "complex cleavages trap" theory of Canadian parties. It has been applicable from Mackenzie King's time to the present, but it has not been proven that the reason for obfuscation by politicians is in the cleavages themselves; it may be in the nature or character of the men directing the governing parties. Does the situation really demand that there be more brokers or compromisers than problem-solvers?

One-Party Dominance

The Centrist Party Theory

Professor Frank Underhill commented in 1958: "What Mackenzie King established was a one-party domination at Ottawa with two or three splinter parties posing as opponents of the leviathan in office." His party, "which called itself Liberal," monopolized the center of the political spectrum and "spread out so far both to the left and to the right, that the opposition groups seemed to become more and more ineffective." The Liberal defeat in 1957 did not signal the end of this situation but its continuance under new auspices, as the Progressive Conservatives sought to continue the formula with themselves playing the leading role.[21]

The Conservatives were not successful in the long term. The long tenure of the Liberals in office had attracted competent talent, especially of an administrative and business kind, whereas the Conservatives' lengthy period in opposition had made them a pole which attracted the protest vote. The business community, which finances victory, remained largely pro-Liberal, leaving the Tories vulnerable unless they followed a narrowly pro-business line — a course that essential parts of the party, notably Diefenbaker's western supporters, would not countenance. The party lost in 1963 and has remained in opposition ever since, except for the nine month Clark interval in 1979-80.

The Quasi-Party Theory

Professor C.B. Macpherson presents a variant of the one-party dominance theory with his theory of the quasi-party system, a conclusion to his study of Alberta under Social Credit (which he suggests may be applied to Canadian federal politics).[22] Stated briefly, the theory is that a community like Alberta with a homogeneous population of petit-bourgeois independent producers in a quasi-colonial relationship to, and forming a subordinate part of, a mature capitalist economy, will normally reject the orthodox (two) party system in favor of a "quasi-party" system, i.e., one in which there is a dominant local party outside the two orthodox parties which attract majority support in the country. This system "can, to a limited degree, express and moderate the conflict of class interests in which such a society is involved." Here "the conflict of class interests is not so much within the local society as between that society and the forces of outside capital."[23] The system is essentially a plebiscitary one as "the independent producer resists the subordination imposed upon him by the capitalist economy, yet accepts the fundamentals of its property institutions."[24] In short, he accepts the private property basis of society "because he is himself a small proprietor, yet he supports the local quasi-party to resist the domination of powerful outside interests." However, this resistence is *within* the established economic system, and does not challenge it. The quasi-party system does not provide fully democratic government but does offer means of covering over class conflict and of preventing or attenuating the arbitrary use of power.

Professor Macpherson suggests that this theory has some applicability at the federal level, where some parallels to the Alberta quasi-party situation are evident. (He was writing in 1953 and noted that opposition parties appeared to be developing into regional parties.)" As Canada becomes increasingly over-shadowed by the more powerful economy of the United States, her position approximates the quasi-colonial; the characteristics of independent-producer assumptions about the nature of society are very widespread in Canada."

These, he sees, are the basic preconditions for a quasi-party system, which offers "the most satisfactory answer to the problem of maintaining the form and some of the substance of democracy".[25] It is "either the final stage in the deterioration of the capitalist democratic tradition, or a way of saving what can be saved of liberal-democracy from threatening encroachment of a one-party state."[26]

In the thirty years since the writing of *Democracy in Alberta* the two orthodox parties have moved in the direction of their older relationship of alternative governments to each other. However, the conditions of the quasi-party system are even more applicable now than in the past. The theory of the quasi-party system remains a stimulating tool for the analysis of the Canadian party system. Events suggest that the Liberal party has come to occupy a position between that of the leading party in the orthodox two-party system, and that of a quasi-party à la Social Credit in Alberta in the past. In the eye of the Canadian voter it is the former; for the American corporate investor it is probably the latter.

One-Party Dominance as a Cause of the Rise of Third Parties

Another stimulating interpretation of one-party dominant situations is offered by Professor Maurice Pinard.[27] His analysis centers on Quebec and deals with the rapid rise of Social Credit prior to the 1962 federal election. Quebec was in a situation of one-party dominance in federal politics; the Conservatives had received an average of only 7.8 percent of the votes from 1917 to 1957. Because they were not a realistic alternative to the Liberals, disgruntled voters would be inclined to support another party if one existed.

There were other factors which favored Social Credit, including what Pinard calls "strain within the system" (large-scale unemployment and privation, especially in the rural areas), plus the fact that the leaders of the protest chose to organize their own party rather than to support the Conservatives.

In summary, when a conventional two-party system is subjected to structural cleavages within the society, or when attachments arise linking one party to the local community, or when flagrant corruption discredits one of the two parties (especially under a single-member constituency electoral system), there is alienation from one of the two parties and the emergence of a one-party dominance system. When the voters seek an alternative to the party in power, the opportunity arrives for the rise of a third party.

Pinard does not suggest the applicability of his theory to the Canadian federal government. Indeed, he points out that Social Credit is likely to decline because it has no prospect of winning a national election. "The voters do not want to exchange their vote for nothing, and there is not much of a return if the party has no chances of forming a government."[28] However, if Canadian federal politics is, in fact, in the situation of the one-party dominance Pinard refers to, or drifts into it, then the road should be open to the rise of a third party, provided the existence of the other conditions of stress and conduciveness.

Ideological Continuum Theory

While seldom elaborated in detail, some writers make an analogy between the Canadian party system and a continental European one of an ideological continuum from left to right: Communist, NDP, Liberal, Conservative, Social Credit. While it is easy to agree to put the NDP on the left, the rest of the construct rests on flimsy, if not contradictory, evidence. There is virtually no communist party, and the evidence of an ideological difference, in a left-right sense, between the Liberals and Conservatives is confused. Indeed, if preference by the business or capitalist interests is a guide, then the federal Liberals are the more right-wing party. As for Social Credit, its distinctive ideology does not fit the left-right continuum, although its period in office in Alberta would align it with the Liberals and Conservatives as a party commanding the confidence of business. Nevertheless, this view of a left-right dichotomy has been put forward, either as fact or desideratum, by such leading students of Canadian politics as Professors Alan Cairns, Gad Horowitz, John Porter and John Wilson.[29] However, Canadian political dynamics continues, as far as the parties with any chance of governing are concerned, to be a scramble for the center.

The Party System Today

Generally, we can hypothesize that Canada has three types of parties at the federal level: the normal government party (Liberal), the normal opposition party (Conservative), and the third party that has virtually no chance of forming the government or official opposition, but has continuing strength (NDP). The election results support this. Since 1921 the Liberals have been in power 50 years, the Conservatives twelve and all others none. Since 1896 the Liberals have won 18 out of 25 elections: losing only in 1911, 1917, 1930, 1957, 1958, 1962, 1979. Hypothesizing further, we can say that the Liberals are perceived to be the successful party, and therefore draw to themselves those people who most want to be on the winning side, to be close to power, and who are most prone to accept the *status quo*. Conversely, the federal Tories draw those people who seek to take issue with the government in an ideologically conformist manner, and who are prepared to be on the losing side most of the time (in federal politics). This hypothesis about recruitment suggests that early Liberal successes made later ones more likely; the party attracts the most ambitious young people to work for it, and has come to be the accepted governing party by the electorate. For the Conservatives the opposite would be true, and the party would be issue- rather than power-oriented, because issues are the instruments for winning power away from an incumbent government. People, however, disagree about issues; the party would, therefore, be prone to factionalism.

Extending the hypothesis further, one can say that the third parties will attract those who are reconciled to being on the losing side for the present and foreseeable future, and who take their critique of the *status quo* beyond the point of ideological conformity. The NDP supporter is obviously prepared to accept and advocate a greater degree of ideological deviance (socialism) than the Liberal or Conservative supporter. The third parties should, according to this theory, be less success- and power-oriented than both old parties, and more prone to factionalism.

The Canadian party system works as well as any and better than most as a device for providing cohesive governmental majorities in parliament, while encouraging innovation and legitimating moderate dissent. Canada is a large and disparate country; if it is to continue to function as a cohesive political unit, it requires a mechanism which will permit the expression of the view of its various elements, and enable them to work out their differences. The classical two-party system proved inadequate to the task, but formed the basis from which the current system is adapted: the addition of the third parties added a necessary, but still limited, flexibility.

If we look at the governing party, we find that it attracts talent of the sustaining kind: people who benefit from the system, who approve of it and wish to continue it with only moderate adaptations. This includes the dominant business community and the professionals that serve it (particularly lawyers, accountants, notaries, engineers). Since these people represent the wealth of the country, they guarantee that the Liberal party will be generously supported financially and in terms of manpower, particularly at election time. In addition, while in power, the Liberal party has had the additional advantage of access to, and the right to utilize, the civil service, plus the right to choose election dates. Given modern survey research techniques, the latter is an immense advantage.

The Liberal party has thus become the vehicle of ruling elites and those aspiring to elite status. As a result, its policies are conservative and conventional. They reflect the interests of the party's supporters, both voters and financial backers. But since the party normally wins elections and receives over forty percent of the total vote cast, its policies will be acceptable to a majority or near-majority.

The role of the Conservative party is an intermediate one between the Liberals and the third parties. In the old two-party system, it was *the* alternative to the Liberals. Its existence is a guarantee against any show of Liberal arrogance. The Conservatives are close enough to the Liberals, ideologically and in the interests they represent, that, should the Liberals become excessively corrupt, susceptible to minority pressures or incompetent, they provide a ready alternative. One need not move beyond the ideologically conventional to replace the old government with a new one.

The party is also a bulwark against ideological deviation. Conservative interest will sustain the party to ensure an acceptable opposition to the government, instead of allowing the deviants to preempt this role.

However, the Conservatives have an innovative, as well as a sustaining role in the system. In a rapidly changing society experiencing technological advancement, urbanization and secularization in a localized or "lumpy" fashion, some parts of the country will develop increasingly different wants and needs. If the Liberals are more susceptible to the demands of modern, urban Canada and French Canadians and Catholics, the Conservatives have benefited from the discontent of the rural areas, the outlying provinces (especially the Prairies and the Maritimes), the "loyalist" or traditional Anglo-Saxons and the protestants. Mr. Diefenbaker's government gave farmers (especially on the Prairies) real benefits, and provided the traditional WASP with a psychological advantage.

The Conservatives also offer an opportunity for the support and implementation of innovative ideas relating to national policy. Mr. Diefenbaker's "vision of the north" and his call to halt the influence of the "Texas buccaneers" are well-known examples, although his follow-through may have been weak. His policy of aid to small business is another example — although it is related to the demands of the Conservative constituency outlined above. Mr. Clark's government set about a program of "privatizing" crown corporations, beginning with Petro-Canada — the government oil company — a policy that may have contributed to his government's subsequent defeat in the 1980 election.

The Liberals and Conservatives between them constitute the power component of the political system. However, the function of offering new ideas and new solutions for national problems has been fulfilled largely by the third parties, and especially by the NDP. This may be a thankless task, but it is an important one. Many (some say most) reforms were mooted first by the CCF or NDP and, when they appeared to appeal to the electorate, were implemented, often in a diluted fashion, by the Liberals. This is the case with much of our social security legislation, for example. The third parties have made their major contribution to the system as innovators and promoters of these reforms to the electorate. Now, with the trend against enlarging social security coverage, this role appears to be diminishing.

Third parties also play a role as legitimators of dissent. People who are too radical to be content with the old parties usually turn to them. There they may be able to work for their ideas, often very effectively, although they must accept that it is unlikely that they will be elected to a legislative assembly, unless they represent one of the few areas of their party's strength. The party thus legitimates dissent, offers it an outlet and harnesses it to the governing system.

If the success of third parties was measured solely by their impact at the national level, they might be considered a failure. However, they have been successful in forming provincial governments and implementing their ideas there. The Progressives formed governments in Ontario and the Prairies for a short time in the twenties and early thirties. The CCF-NDP governed Saskatchewan for a generation, and recently again formed the government of that province. The NDP also governs Manitoba and has governed British Columbia in recent years. Social Credit governed Alberta for thirty-five years and has governed British Columbia for twenty-five. The Union Nationale has three times formed the government of Quebec. Now the Parti Québécois governs that province. These substantial attainments have made third parties successful, enabling them to recruit supporters and maintain party organizations. Attaining power provincially has sustained the legitimate dissident role of third parties in Canadian politics.

Related to this is the third party's role of representing minority positions, whether they be ideological, ethnic-cultural, religious, class or other — what Georges Lavau calls the "fonction tribunitienne" (after the Roman institution of the tribune of the plebs).

Political parties that happen to be "manifestly" opposed to the system will thus be able to fulfill in a latent way this function of tribune. This will involve several factors for them: first, that they have, in fact, ceased to be revolutionary parties; then, that they have acquired sufficient power and representativeness to enable them effectively to block or hobble the functioning of the system, without the latter daring to respond by repression or declaring the parties illegal; and finally, that they have sufficient authority, over the groups whose [representative] they mean to be, to prevent them from resorting to desperate acts or taking refuge in withdrawal or boycott.[30]

He sees this as a contribution to the political system

...in the sense that it deflects the revolutionary tendency, and that it is, in certain explosive situations, a means of living with cleavages. For the parties that accommodate themselves to this role, it involves the advantage of providing a favourable area for growth by the systematic exploitation of discontent, but it also involves the risk of making them lose their revolutionary character, of committing them to a sometimes unstable clientele, and finally of leading to their permanent or prolonged exclusion from the exercise of responsibilities and therefore from the fruits of office.[31]

In Canada, this role has been played by the CCF-NDP, with its moderate but nonetheless deviant ideology, its identification with the labour unions and dispossessed elements of society, and its social welfare and "progressive" policies. Through the NDP the bulk of Canadian radicals of the left find a means of expression within the system, and are able to exercise a kind of teaching role for society and the establishment parties.

However, in recent years the NDP has grown more like the two old parties. Its association with the Canadian Labour Congress has assured it of financial security and a cadre of effective party workers. Therefore it has become more of a party and less of a movement, more success-oriented and less ideologically committed. Also the power of the mainly urban labour movement has caused resentment among the committed agrarian supporters of western Canada, causing regional tensions within the party. Now, with huge government deficits diminishing the appeal of additional social security measures, the NDP, held to a narrow ideological range by its trade union attachments, finds its attractiveness attenuated by its failure to come up with ideas to attract or keep support. The anti-union bias of a majority of the electorate also limits its hope of broadening its support.

The Canadian party and political system is both narrowly controlled by a fairly closed elite of office-holders and their associates and susceptible to influence from a broad spectrum of opinion. This apparently contradictory situation may be the reason for its strength and durability. Power is concentrated, within the two old parties, in a select group of MPs, senators, party office-holders and fund-raisers who are drawn from the professions (mainly law) and business, enjoy relatively high incomes, live in the major cities, and come disproportionately from the British and French charter groups of the Canadian population. From such an oligarchy, with its close connections with the influential business-oriented interest groups and its inevitable associations with the civil service "mandarins," one would expect a style of government and a pattern of legislative output favouring the classes "in power." Yet if one examines the Canadian policy output and compares it with other advanced countries with a larger left-wing power component, the difference is not great, as far as social security, civil rights, labour and trade union rights, progressive taxation and educational services are concerned. The parties representing privileged interests do implement measures popular with and beneficial to the general citizenry and, in some cases, the less advantaged members of society. Why?

While a portion of the highly privileged party elite clearly objects to the "socialistic" measures that have been implemented by both Liberal and Conservative governments mainly since 1945, more consider that they represent the price that must be paid to remain in power. While the benefits going to the masses have been comparable to those granted by frankly social-democratic governments, the capitalist structure of economic life has been retained, and the party system with this elite in command has survived unscathed. This is a considerable "accomplishment" in a mass democracy with universal suffrage. Of course it would not have been possible if Canada were not a fairly wealthy country. Indeed the current fiscal crisis is threatening to challenge this arrangement, as governments are beginning to cut back on social security expenditures in an attempt to reduce massive government deficits.

This flexibility is traceable, in part, to the party system which, through the third parties, popularized ideas for reform to the point where the old parties either saw the expediency of implementing them or became convinced of their value and justice.

Are we to conclude that Canada has developed the flawless party system, permitting both political stability and policy flexibility? Certainly it worked well enough in an earlier period, when both old parties were acceptable in English Canada. Then all regions returned enough government supporters to offer the Prime Minister an adequate supply of able men for his cabinet, and the government caucus contained enough representatives of all regions (Quebec was almost always overwhelmingly on the government side) so that all significant interests and all regions were well represented. The system permitted inter-regional compromises to be hammered out behind closed doors in the congenial atmosphere of a one-party caucus and cabinet.

This system came unstuck during the Trudeau years, although strains began to appear in the Diefenbaker and Pearson periods. The Liberals have fallen so out of favour in the west that, as of 1984, no Liberal members represent constituencies west of Winnipeg. The Liberal caucus can no longer represent the west or legitimately speak for it, and the cabinet has only one elected western representative. The Liberals have caught the Tory disease; they are rejected in one of the country's major regions. However, in the Liberal case it is more serious, because they are the government party. The result is that the incumbent government of Canada is rejected in the west — whereas in the past it was only a case of the opposition party being rejected in Quebec. Since the Liberals have been in office about four years out of five the government was still, until recently, spared the regional rejection that undermines authority.

The present situation is more serious than is generally recognized. While the problems in Quebec and western Canada are known to all, few recognize the seriousness of their effect on the party system, and through it on governmental authority. Professor William Irvine, in Chapter 12, discusses this situation and offers institutional reforms that would greatly alleviate the situation — reforms which have not, however, been taken up by either major political party. Pending change, therefore, Canada is stuck with a parliamentary system that merely reflects in an exaggerated form the national divisions, but is powerless to bridge them, and a cabinet which lacks the needed authority to make policy for the whole country. Power therefore passes to the provinces, which are inclined to press for their own sectional interests at the expense of pan-Canadian priorities.

The government, lacking nation-wide electoral support as demonstrated by regional representation in parliament from across Canada, is forced back upon favourable elements in the business community, and an inevitable reliance upon the public service. Elections in Canada have long been a means of combining the financial and moral support of business with electoral strength drawn from voters across the country. When the latter falters in one or more regions, the government's reliance on business for its legitimacy can be expected to grow. Our present experience, however, does not confirm this expectation precisely. In fact western business interests, dominated by the energy industries, seem at one with the western electorate in seeing the Liberals' policies, particularly the Natural Energy Policy, as serving eastern Canada. Recent Progressive Conservative flirtations with the neo-conservatism popular in the United States has appealed to right-wing elements in the business community. The Liberal government therefore has not inspired general support either from the national electorate or from the business community. It has been inclined to go on the defensive and rely upon the policy proposals of the civil service and its own brain trusts in the Privy Council Office, the Prime Minister's Office, and even the Liberal Party itself. Perhaps the selection of John Turner as party leader will improve its appeal to business and western Canadian voters.

The business community is not homogenous in outlook. Each group pushes for its own interest, which can readily conflict with other business interests. Recently the question of petroleum pricing ranged the Alberta producers behind Premier Lougheed against the eastern consumers behind Premier Davis of Ontario, with the federal government caught in the middle, opting finally to side with the more numerous consuming interests. Business influence can thus be destabilizing for the political system.

The undue influence that the Canadian business community (and especially the larger interests) have in a system in which the parties raise their money from private business sources gives businessmen an entrée to government policymakers not enjoyed by ordinary citizens or less wealthy groups. The worst effects of this arrangement are countered by the need to secure election by the mass electorate, combined with the situation of party competition, which includes the third parties that are generally ideologically opposed to the influence of wealthy business interests. However, intense party competition can, at times, make the government extremely vulnerable to business pressure when elections appear to be close.

There are great problems posed by the federal system for our political parties. Since the Second World War the federal government has greatly enlarged its role as equalizer of revenues between the provinces, and this has affected intra-party relations. In the Atlantic provinces, to which the largest per capita transfers are made, there has grown up a feeling of dependence among politicians at the provincial level which has served to enhance the integration between the two levels of both major political parties. It is in the interest of the region for politicians at the provincial level of a party to get on well with those at the federal level, and vice versa; therefore, relations have tended to be good between provincial and federal organizations of the same party in the Atlantic provinces.

The same cannot be said for the other provinces. There the federal government, far from being perceived as a benefactor, appears as a taker of benefits and/or as a challenger. In Quebec, the federal government is the force opposing the enlargement of provincial rights — and therefore the federal level of the same party is a threat to the interests defended by the provincial level. The Liberal Party of Quebec, therefore, was the first to form a separate organization from its federal counterpart. This example was following shortly after in Ontario.

Indeed, relations between the federal and provincial wings of the Liberal Party in Ontario are especially instructive. The bitter confrontation in the 1940s between the province's Liberal Premier, Mitchell Hepburn, and Mr. MacKenzie King, the federal Liberal leader, had a dramatic effect on the internal workings of the party. With the defeat of the Hepburn government, the provincial organization of the party virtually collapsed, and the party has been out of office for forty years.

The federal Liberal party, far from supporting its provincial counterpart, has stood aside while the provincial party floundered for want of financial support and high quality personnel. Why? No doubt in part this is a result of the inevitable dynamics of politics. Losers attract neither members nor contributions. However, the weak condition of the provincial party in a sense favoured the governing federal party, because in the adversarial federal-provincial negotiations the federal Liberals preferred to confront their political adversaries, rather than their political kith and kin, in situations where the two levels of government were rivals for tax resources and political credit for government services. It is striking that in the relatively prosperous part of Canada west of the Ottawa River there is not one viable Liberal provincial party; whereas in the five poorer eastern provinces the Liberals are the official opposition in competitive two-party systems, with clear possibilities of forming the government in all five provinces.

There is a new "confederalizing" of the political party structures in Canada, that is to say the provincial party organizations are inclined to go their own way, parting with their federal component on key policy issues. For example the Conservative governments of Ontario and New Brunswick sided with the federal Liberal government against the federal Conservatives and the other provinces (including four with Conservative governments) in the 1981 and 1982 discussions on constitutional change. At the same time the provincial Liberal party of Quebec under Claude Ryan criticized Mr. Trudeau's amendment proposals. Even the NDP, a more programmatic party and therefore presumably less susceptible to division, encountered assaults on the policy of its federal wing when it backed the Trudeau amendment proposals, especially parts of the Charter of Rights and Freedoms. This new tendency reflects the appearance of issues which are regionally very divisive, so that regional or provincial interest exercises a stronger pull than does that of party solidarity. This is especially true in a time of "decline of ideology." There is no longer sufficient ideological consensus within a party to stand up to the regional pull. This has reached the point where, at the provincial level, the Liberal party has been reduced to third party status in the party system of all four western provinces. Indeed in Alberta and British Columbia it scarcely exists at all. Similarly in Quebec politics the Conservatives have not been a factor since the early thirties.

With this growing dissidence between federal and provincial wings of the parties, the way has been opened for the provincial wings of the Conservative party in western Canada to take over the earlier function of regional protest parties (such as the Progressives, Social Credit and the Saskatchewan C.C.F.). This is particularly true of Peter Lougheed's Conservatives in Alberta — an example for Premier Devine of Saskatchewan. This shift, in turn, has created tension within the federal Conservative caucus, ranging western Tories against eastern Tories.

Another serious problem for party politics is that of leadership selection. As one influential party member commented in an interview: "Our greatest shortcoming is the fact that to be party leader you have to be rich or beholden to people that are — that is the worse of the two." This is not to say that leadership candidates pay all their own expenses, although some pay very large sums. But to be serious contenders they have to be acceptable to the party backers, and have the independence, strength, and standing conferred by private means. They also require the assurance that their campaign will not falter before the end because of a shortage of funds.

Not all leadership candidates are rich men — although normally most of the serious ones are. However, there have been times when men of modest means not only were serious contenders, but won the nomination: Diefenbaker and Pearson are examples. However, both were men who were in fact nominated before the convention, having been deemed the inevitable leader because of special attributes. On the other hand, the conventions since the 1950s have been genuinely open and competitive, fought in the costly days of television, jet air travel, public relations and expensive entertainment.

Both old Canadian parties still attract small memberships. While amendments to the Canada Elections Act and its provincial equivalents, which provide subventions from the public treasury to parties and allow the deduction of a major part of individual donations from income tax might be expected to draw the parties closer to the voters, this has not occurred. Public cynicism to parties may well have increased, as parties grow more opportunistic, following opinion polls and "smart" public relations counsel in search of election-winning formulas, instead of being agents for the substantial interests that once were their chief financial backers at election time. And with small membership the parties are ripe for capture by those interested in manipulating them. The Conservative Party, during the leadership campaign of 1983, experienced the concerted attempt of Amway distributors to take over local associations, as well as the embarrassment of having the agents of the foremost leadership aspirants round up children and derelicts to become instant party members who could vote for delegates committed to a candidate. The Liberal convention of 1984 was preceded by another such abuse: the rounding up of recent immigrants by organizers who paid their membership fees making them "instant Liberals," able to vote for delegates to the leadership convention. Constituencies with small party memberships were particularly susceptible to being swamped in this way.

The old parties remain small, vulnerable organizations standing for little of substance beyond "free enterprise." Collectively they are the vessels into which money, organizational talent and public relations expertise are poured to enable political activists to conduct electoral battles to choose political office holders. They rarely offer clear policy options, and when they do, they may not deliver on their undertakings (e.g., the Liberal election campaign against wage and price controls of 1974 was followed the next year by the implementation of controls by the re-elected Liberal government). The politicians at the elite (cabinet) level and the ordinary candidates serve very brief terms — so seldom make much of an impression (there are, of course, exceptions — Pierre Trudeau, for instance). Policy therefore owes what stability it has largely to the public service mandarinate.

The country has yet to face the full implications of these serious structural and attitudinal shortcomings in its parties. However, it may soon be compelled to, if the present crises of national unity and the economy deepen. These crises are at least in part traceable to a party system that does not permit the electorate to make hard policy choices and does not encourage the government to follow policies dictated by rational analysis of the long-term national interest. Instead, governments spend their time reconciling various pressures from powerful interest groups.

ENDNOTES

1. For a discussion of these events, consult any good history of Canada, notably A.R.M. Lower, *Colony to Nation* (Toronto: Longmans, Green & Co., 1946); D.G. Creighton, *The Commercial Empire of the St. Lawrence, 1760-1850* (Toronto: Ryerson, 1937), pp. 302-303, 331, 336; D.G. Creighton, *Dominion of the North* (Toronto: Macmillan, 1962).
2. Alexander Brady, *Democracy in the Dominions* (Toronto: University of Toronto Press, 1947), p. 94.
3. *Ibid.*, p. 97.
4. *Ibid.*, p. 103.
5. See the writings of R.A. MacKay, R. MacG. Dawson and H. McD. Clokie.
6. J.R. Mallory, "The Structure of Canadian Politics," in *Canadian Politics*, Mount Allison University Publications, No. 4, Sackville, N.B., 1949.
7. Frank Underhill, "The Party System in Canada," *In Search of Canadian Liberalism* (Toronto: Macmillan, 1961), p. 168.

8. See, for example, the speech by T.C. Douglas in Windsor, Ontario, May 25, 1962, as reported in NDP press release in Documents Department, Douglas Library, Queen's University.

9. Text of broadcast "The Nation's Business," January 8, 1962, CBC television, *ibid.*

10. Michael Oliver, President of NDP, Halifax, N.S., April 26, 1962, *ibid.*

11. See speech by Ed Finn, "Nationalism and the NDP," to the National Party Convention, Winnipeg, October 28-31, 1969, *ibid.*

12. J.R. Mallory, *The Structure of Canadian Government* (Toronto: Macmillan of Canada, 1971), pp. 201-2.

13. Tim Buck, *30 Years: The Story of the Communist Movement in Canada* (Toronto: Progress Books, 1952), p. 106.

14. Tim Buck, *Our Fight for Canada: Selected Writings, 1923-1959* (Toronto: Progress Books, 1959), p. 191.

15. Buck, *30 Years*, p. 112.

16. *Ibid.*, p. 115.

17. Tim Buck, *Our Fight for Canada*, p. 185.

18. This awkward title is mine.

19. F.C. Engelmann and M. Schwartz, *Canadian Political Parties: Origin, Character, Impact* (Scarborough: Prentice-Hall of Canada Ltd., 1975).

20. *Ibid.*, p. 137-38.

21. Frank H. Underhill, "The Revival of Conservatism in North America," *Transactions of the Royal Society of Canada*, LII, Series 3 (June 1958), pp. 1-19.

22. C.B. Macpherson, *Democracy in Alberta* (Toronto: University of Toronto Press, 1953).

23. *Ibid.*, p. 246.

24. *Ibid.*, p. 247.

25. *Ibid.*, p. 249.

26. *Ibid.*, p. 250.

27. Maurice Pinard, *The Rise of a Third Party: A Study in Crisis Politics* (Englewood Cliffs, N.J.: Prentice-Hall, Inc., 1971).

28. *Ibid.*, p. 253.

29. R. MacG. Dawson, *The Government of Canada*, 5th ed. (Toronto: University of Toronto Press, 1970), p. 414.

30. Georges Lavau, "Partis et Systemes Politiques: Interactions et Fonctions," *Canadian Journal of Political Science*, II (March 1969), pp. 18-44. (Translation by H.G. Thorburn).

31. *Ibid.*, p. 39.

4 Conservatism, Liberalism and Socialism in Canada: An Interpretation*

G. HOROWITZ

Introduction: The Hartzian Approach

In the United States, organized socialism is dead; in Canada, socialism, though far from national power, is a significant political force. Why this striking difference in the fortunes of socialism in two very similar societies?

...It will be shown that the relative strength of socialism in Canada is related to the relative strength of toryism, and to the different position and character of liberalism in the two countries.

In North America, Canada is unique. Yet there is a tendency in Canadian historical and political studies to explain Canadian phenomena not by contrasting them with American phenomena but by identifying them as variations on a basic North American theme. I grant that Canada and the United States are similar, and that the similarities should be pointed out. But the pan-North American approach, since it searches out and concentrates on similarities, cannot help us to understand Canadian uniqueness. When this approach is applied to the study of English Canadian socialism, one discovers, first, that like the American variety it is weak, and second, that it is weak for much the same reasons. These discoveries perhaps explain why Canadian socialism is weak in comparison to European socialism; they do not explain why Canadian socialism is so much stronger than American socialism.

The explanatory technique used in this study is that developed by Louis Hartz in *The Liberal Tradition in America* [1] and *The Founding of New Societies*.[2] It is applied to Canada in a mildly pan-North American way by Kenneth McRae in "The Structure of Canadian History," a contribution to the latter book.

The Hartzian approach is to study the new societies founded by Europeans (the United States, English Canada, French Canada, Latin America,

*Reprinted from the *Canadian Journal of Economics and Political Science*, XXXII, no. 2, May, 1966.

Dutch South Africa, Australia) as "fragments" thrown off from Europe. The key to the understanding of ideological development in a new society is its "point of departure" from Europe: the ideologies borne by the founders of the new society are not representative of the historic ideological spectrum of the mother country. The settlers represent only a fragment of that spectrum. The complete ideological spectrum ranges — in chronological order, and from right to left — from feudal or tory through liberal whig to liberal democrat to socialist. French Canada and Latin America are "feudal fragments." They were founded by bearers of the feudal or tory values of the organic, corporate, hierarchical community; their point of departure from Europe was before the liberal revolution. The United States, English Canada and Dutch South Africa are "bourgeois fragments," founded by bearers of liberal individualism who have left the tory end of the spectrum behind them.

The significance of the fragmentation process is that the new society, having been thrown off from Europe, "loses the stimulus to change that the whole provides."[3] The full ideological spectrum of Europe develops only out of the continued confrontation and interaction of its four elements; they are related to one another, not only as enemies, but as parents and children. A new society which leaves part of the past behind it cannot develop the future ideologies which need the continued presence of the past in order to come into being. In escaping the past, the fragment escapes the future, for "the very seeds of the later ideas are contained in the parts of the old world that have been left behind."[4] The ideology of the founders is thus frozen, congealed at the point of origin.

Socialism is an ideology which combines the corporate-organic-collectivist ideas of toryism with the rationalist-egalitarian ideas of liberalism. Both the feudal and the bourgeois fragments escape socialism, but in different ways. A feudal fragment such as French Canada develops no whig (undemocratic) liberalism; therefore it does not develop the democratic liberalism which arises out of and as a reaction against whiggery; therefore it does not develop the socialism which arises out of and as a reaction against liberal democracy. The corporate-organic-collectivist component of socialism is present in the feudal fragment — it is part of the feudal ethos — but the radical-rationalist-egalitarian component of socialism is missing. It can be provided only by whiggery and liberal democracy, and these have not come into being.

In the bourgeois fragment, the situation is the reverse: the radical-rationalist-egalitarian component of socialism is present, but the corporate-organic-collectivist component is missing, because toryism has been left behind. In the bourgeois fragments "Marx dies because there is no sense of class, no yearning for the corporate past."[5] The absence of socialism is related to the absence of toryism.

It is *because* socialists have a conception of society as more than an agglo-meration of competing individuals — a conception close to the tory view of society as an organic community — that they find the liberal idea of equality (equality of opportunity) inadequate. Socialists disagree with liberals about the essential meaning of equality because socialists have a tory conception of society.

In a liberal bourgeois society which has never known toryism the demand for equality will express itself as left-wing or democratic liberalism as opposed to whiggery. The left will point out that all are not equal in the competitive pursuit of individual happiness. The government will be required to assure greater equality of opportunity — in the nineteenth century by destroying monopolistic privileges; in the twentieth century by providing a welfare "floor" so that no one will fall out of the race for success, and by regulating the economy so that the race can continue without periodic crises.

In a society which thinks of itself as a community of classes rather than an aggregation of individuals, the demand for equality will take a socialist form: for equality of condition rather than mere equality of opportunity; for cooperation rather than competition; for a community that does more than provide a context within which individuals can pursue happiness in a purely self-regarding way. At its most "extreme", socialism is a demand for the *abolition* of classes so that the good of the community can truly be realized. This is a demand which cannot be made by people who can hardly see class and community; the individual fills their eyes.

The Application to Canada

It is a simple matter to apply the Hartzian approach to English Canada in a pan-North American way. English Canada can be viewed as a fragment of the American liberal society, lacking a feudal or tory heritage and therefore lacking the socialist ideology which grows out of it. Canadian domestic struggles, from this point of view, are a northern version of the American struggle between big-propertied liberals on the right and petit-bourgeois and working-class liberals on the left; the struggle goes on within a broad liberal consensus, and the voice of the tory or the socialist is not heard in the land. This pan-North American approach, with important qualifications, is adopted by Hartz and McRae in *The Founding of New Societies*. English Canada, like the United States, is a bourgeois fragment. No toryism in the past, therefore no socialism in the present.

But Hartz notes that the liberal society of English Canada has a "tory touch," that it is "etched with a tory streak coming out of the American revolution."[6]

Take as an example the central concern of this study — the differing weights of Canadian and American socialism... The CCF failed to become a major party in urban Canada, but it succeeded in becoming a significant minor party — a success denied to the American socialist...

The most important un-American characteristics of English Canada, all related to the presence of toryism, are: (a) the presence of tory ideology in the founding of English Canada by the Loyalists, and its continuing influence on English Canadian political culture; (b) the persistent power of whiggery or right-wing liberalism in Canada (the Family Compacts) as contrasted with the rapid and easy victory of liberal democracy (Jefferson, Jackson) in the United States; (c) the ambivalent centrist character of left-wing liberalism in Canada as contrasted with the unambiguously leftist position of left-wing liberalism in the United States; (d) the presence of an influential and legitimate socialist movement in English Canada as contrasted with the illegitimacy and early death of American socialism; (e) the failure of English Canadian liberalism to develop into the one true myth, the nationalist cult, and the parallel failure to exclude toryism and socialism as "un-Canadian;" in other words, the legitimacy of ideological diversity in English Canada.

The Presence of Toryism and its Consequences

Many students have noted that English Canadian society has been powerfully shaped by tory values that are "alien" to the American mind. The latest of these is Seymour Martin Lipset, who stresses the relative strength in Canada of the tory values of "ascription" and "elitism" (the tendency to defer to authority), and the relative weakness of the liberal values of "achievement" and "egalitarianism."[7] He points to such well-known features of Canadian history as the absence of a lawless, individualistic-egalitarian American frontier, the preference for Britain rather than the United States as a social model, and generally, the weaker emphasis on social equality, the greater acceptance by individuals of the facts of economic inequality, social stratification, and hierarchy,...belief in monarchy and empire unity, greater stress on "law and order", revulsion against American populistic excesses, different frontier experiences and so on. One tory touch in English Canada...is the far greater willingness of English Canadian political and business elites to use the power of the state for the purpose of developing and controlling the economy....Canada is not a feudal (tory) fragment but a bourgeois (liberal) fragment touched with toryism....

Let us put it this way: pre-revolutionary America was a liberal fragment with insignificant traces of toryism, extremely weak feudal survivals. But they were insignificant in the *American* setting; they were far overshadowed by the liberalism of that setting. The revolution did not have to struggle against them; it swept them away easily and painlessly, leaving no trace of them in the American memory. But these traces of toryism were expelled into a *new* setting, and in this setting they were no longer insignificant. In this new setting, where there was no pre-established overpowering liberalism to force them into insignificance, they played a large part in shaping a new political culture, significantly different from the American. As Nelson wrote in *The American Tory*, "the Tories' organic conservatism represented a current of thought that failed to reappear in America after the revolution. A substantial part of the whole spectrum of European...philosophy seemed to slip outside the American perspective."[8] But it *reappeared* in Canada. Here the sway of liberalism has proved to be not total, but considerably mitigated by a tory presence initially and a socialist presence subsequently....In Canada, the Family Compacts were able to maintain ascendancy and delay the coming of democracy because of the tory touch "inherited in part from American Loyalism, which restrained egalitarian feeling in Canada."[9] The early power of whiggery serves to emphasize the importance of the Tory touch in English Canada....

In the United States, the masses could not be swayed by the Federalist-Whig appeals to anti-egalitarian sentiments. In Canada the masses *were* swayed by these appeals; the role of the Compacts was to save "the colonial masses from the spectre of republicanism and democracy."[10] What accounts for this is the tory presence in English Canadian political culture — the "greater acceptance of limitation, of hierarchical patterns."[11]

The next step in tracing the development of the English Canadian political culture must be to take account of the tremendous waves of British immigration which soon engulfed the original American Loyalist fragment.... These British immigrants had undoubtedly been heavily infected with non-liberal ideas, and these ideas were undoubtedly in their heads as they settled in Canada. The political culture of a new nation is not necessarily fixed at the point of origin or departure; the founding of a new nation can go on for generations. If the later waves of immigration arrived before the *point of congealment* of the political culture, they must have participated actively in the process of culture formation....

Between 1815 and 1850 almost one million Britons emigrated to Canada. The population of English Canada doubled in twenty years and quadrupled in forty. The population of Ontario increased ten-fold in the same period — from about 95,000 in 1814 to about 950,000 in 1851.[12]...Is it not possible that the immigrants, while they were no doubt considerably liberalized by their new environment, also brought to it non-liberal ideas which entered into the political culture mix and which perhaps even reinforced the non-liberal elements present in the original fragment? If the million immigrants had come from the United States rather than Britain, would English Canada not be "significantly" different today?

The difficulty in applying the Hartzian approach to English Canada is that although the point of departure is reasonably clear, it is difficult to put one's finger on the point of congealment. Perhaps it was the Loyalist period; perhaps it was close to the mid-century mark; there are grounds for arguing that it was in the more recent past. But the important point is this: no matter where the point of congealment is located in time, the tory streak is present before the solidification of the political culture, and it is strong *enough* to produce *significant* "imperfections", or non-liberal, un-American attributes of English Canadian society. My own opinion is that the point of congealment came later than the Loyalists....

The indeterminate location of the point of congealment makes it difficult to account in any *precise* way for the presence of socialism in the English Canadian political cultural mix, though the presence itself is indisputable. If the point of congealment came *before* the arrival of the first radical or socialist-minded immigrants, the presence of socialism must be ascribed primarily to the earlier presence of toryism. Since toryism is a significant part of the political culture, at least part of the leftist reaction against it will sooner or later be expressed in its own terms, that is, in terms of *class* interests and the good of the community as a corporate entity (socialism) rather than in terms of the individual and his vicissitudes in the competitive pursuit of happiness (liberalism). If the point of congealment is very early, socialism appears at a later point not primarily because it is imported by British immigrants, but because it is contained as a potential in the original political culture. The immigrants then find that they do not have to give it up — that it is not un-Canadian — because it "fits" to a certain extent with the tory ideas already present. If the point of congealment is very late, the presence of socialism must be explained as a result of *both* the presence of toryism and the introduction of socialism into the cultural mix before congealment. The immigrant retains his socialism not only because it "fits" but also because nothing really *has* to fit. He finds that his socialism is not un-Canadian partly because "Canadian" has not yet been defined.

Canadian liberals cannot be expected to wax enthusiastic about the non-liberal traits of their country. They are likely to condemn the tory touch as anachronistic, stifling, undemocratic, out of tune with the essentially American ("free", "classless") spirit of English Canada. They dismiss the socialist touch as an "old-fashioned" protest, no longer necessary (if it ever was) in the best (liberal) of all possible worlds in which the "end of ideology" has been achieved. The secret dream of the Canadian liberal is the removal of English Canada's "imperfections" — in other words, the total assimilation of English Canada into the larger North American culture. But there is a flaw in this dream which might give pause even to the liberal. Hartz places special emphasis on one very unappetizing characteristic of the new societies — intolerance — which is strikingly absent in English Canada. Because the new societies other than Canada are unfamiliar with legitimate ideological diversity, they are unable to accept it and deal with it in a rational manner, either internally or on the level of international relations.

The European nation has an "identity which transcends any ideologist and a mechanism in which each plays only a part."[13] Neither the tory, nor the liberal, nor the socialist, has a monopoly of the expression of the "spirit" of the nation. But the new societies, the fragments, contain only one of the ideologies of Europe; they are one-myth cultures. In the new setting, freed from its historic enemies past and future, ideology transforms itself into nationalism. It claims to be a moral absolute, "the great spirit of a nation."[14] In the United States, liberalism becomes "Americanism"; a political philosophy becomes a civil religion, a nationalist cult. The American attachment to Locke is "absolutist and irrational."[15] Democratic capitalism is the American way of life; to oppose it is to be un-American.

To be an American is to be a bourgeois liberal. To be a French Canadian is to be a pre-Enlightenment Catholic; to be an Australian is to be a prisoner of the radical myth of "mateship"; to be a Boer is to be a pre-Enlightenment bourgeois Calvinist. The fragments escape the need for philosophy, for thought about values, for, "where perspectives shrink to a single value, and that value becomes the universe, how can value itself be considered?"[16] The fragment demands solidarity. Ideologies which diverge from the national myth make no impact; they are not understood, and their proponents are not granted legitimacy. They are denounced as aliens, and treated as aliens, because they *are* aliens. The fragments cannot understand or deal with the fact that *all* men are *not* bourgeois Americans, or radical Australians, or Catholic French Canadians, or Calvinist South Africans. They cannot make peace with the loss of ideological certainty.

The specific weakness of the United States is its "inability to understand the appeal of socialism" to the Third World.[17] Because the United States has "buried" the memory of the organic medieval community "beneath new liberal absolutisms and nationalisms"[18] it cannot understand that the appeal of socialism to nations with a predominantly non-liberal past (including French Canada) consists precisely in the promise of "continuing the corporate ethos in the very process" of modernization.[19] The American reacts with isolationism, messianism and hysteria.

English Canada, because it is the most "imperfect" of the fragments, is not a one-myth culture. In English Canada ideological diversity has not been buried beneath an absolutist liberal nationalism. Here Locke is not the one true god; he must tolerate lesser tory and socialist deities at his side. The result is that English Canada does not direct an uncomprehending intolerance at heterodoxy, either within its borders or beyond them. (What a "backlash" Parti-Pris or PSQ-type separatists would be getting if Quebec were in the United States!) In English Canada it has been possible to consider values without arousing the all-silencing cry of treason. Hartz observes that "if history had chosen English Canada for the American role" of directing the Western response to the world revolution, "the international scene would probably have witnessed less McCarthyite hysteria, less Wilsonian messianism."[20]

Americanizing liberals might consider that the Pearsonian rationality and calmness which Canada displays on the world stage — the "mediating" and "peace-keeping" role of which Canadians are so proud — is related to the Un-American (tory and socialist) characteristics which they consider to be unnecessary imperfections in English Canadian wholeness. The tolerance of English Canadian domestic politics is also linked with the presence of these imperfections. If the price of Americanization is the surrender of legitimate ideological diversity, even the liberal might think twice before paying it....

Non-liberal British elements have entered into English Canadian society *together* with American liberal elements at the foundations. The fact is that Canada has been greatly influenced by both the United States and Britain. This is not to deny that liberalism is the dominant element in the English Canadian political culture; it is to stress that it is not the sole element, that it is accompanied by vital and legitimate streams of toryism and socialism which have as close a relation to English Canada's "essence" or "foundations" as does liberalism. English Canada's "essence" is both liberal and non-liberal. Neither the British nor the American elements can be explained away as "superstructural" excrescences.

Un-American Aspects of Canadian Conservatism

So far, I have been discussing the presence of toryism in Canada without referring to the Conservative party. This party can be seen as a party of right-wing or business liberalism, but such an interpretation would be far from the whole truth; the Canadian Conservative party, like the British Conservative party and unlike the Republican party, is not monolithically liberal. If there is a touch of toryism in English Canada, its primary carrier has been the Conservative party. It would not be correct to say that toryism is *the* ideology of the party, or even that some Conservatives are tories. These statements would not be true even of the British Conservative party. The primary component of the ideology of business-oriented parties is liberalism; but there are powerful traces of the old pre-liberal outlook in the British Conservative party, and less powerful but still perceptible traces of it in the Canadian party. A Republican is always a liberal. A Conservative may be at one moment a liberal, at the next moment a tory, and is usually something of both.

If it is true that the Canadian Conservatives can be seen from some angles as right-wing liberals, it is also true that figures such as R.B. Bennett, Arthur Meighen and George Drew cannot be understood simply as Canadian versions of William McKinley, Herbert Hoover and Robert Taft. Canadian Conservatives have something British about them that American Republicans do not. It is not simply their emphasis on loyalty to the crown and to the British connection, but a touch of the authentic tory aura — traditionalism, elitism, the strong state and so on. The Canadian Conservatives lack the American aura of rugged individualism. Theirs is not the characteristically American conservatism which conserves only *liberal* values.

It is possible to perceive in Canadian conservatism not only the elements of business liberalism and orthodox toryism, but also an element of "tory democracy" — the paternalistic concern for the "condition of the people" and the emphasis on the tory party as their champion — which, in Britain, was expressed by such figures as Disraeli and Lord Randolph Churchill. John A. Macdonald's approach to the emergent Canadian working class was in some respects similar to that of Disraeli. Later Conservatives acquired the image of arch-reactionaries and arch enemies of the workers, but let us not forget that "Iron Heel" Bennett was also the Bennett of the Canadian New Deal.

The question arises: why is it that in Canada the *Conservative* leader proposes a New Deal? Why is it that the Canadian counterpart of Hoover apes *Roosevelt?* This phenomenon is usually interpreted as sheer historical accident, a product of Bennett's desperation and opportunism. But the answer may be that Bennett was not Hoover. Even in his "orthodox" days Bennett's views on the state's role in the economy were far from similar to Hoover's; Bennett's attitude was that of Canadian, not American, conservatism. Once this is recognized, it is possible to entertain the suggestion that Bennett's sudden radicalism, his sudden concern for the people, may not have been mere opportunism. It may have been a manifestation, a sudden activation under pressure, of a latent tory-democratic streak. Let it be noted also that the depression produced two Conservative splinter parties, both with "radical" welfare state programs, and both led by former subordinates of Bennett: H.H. Stevens' Reconstruction party and W.D. Herridge's New Democracy.

The Bennett New Deal is only the most extreme instance of what is usually considered to be an accident or an aberration — the occasional manifestation of "radicalism" or "leftism" by otherwise orthodox Conservative leaders in the face of opposition from their "followers" in the business community. Meighen, for example, was constantly embroiled with the "Montreal interests" who objected to his railway policies. On one occasion he received a note of congratulation from William Irvine: "The man who dares to offend the Montreal interests is the sort of man that the people are going to vote for."[21] This same Meighen expressed on certain occasions, particularly after his retirement, an antagonism to big government and creeping socialism that would have warmed the heart of Robert Taft; but he combined his business liberalism with gloomy musings about the evil of universal suffrage[22] — musings which Taft would have rejected as un-American. Meighen is far easier to understand from a British than from an American perspective, for he combined, in different proportions at different times, attitudes deriving from all three Conservative ideological streams: right-wing liberalism, orthodox toryism and tory democracy.

The western or agrarian Conservatives of the contemporary period,

John Diefenbaker and Alvin Hamilton, who are usually dismissed as "prairie radicals" of the American type, might represent not only anti-Bay Street agrarianism but *also* the same type of tory democracy which was expressed before their time by orthodox business-sponsored Conservatives like Meighen and Bennett. The populism=(anti-elitism) of Diefenbaker and Hamilton is a genuinely foreign element in Canadian conservatism, but their stress on the Tory party as champion of the people and their advocacy of welfare state policies are in the tory democratic tradition. Their attitudes to the monarchy, the British connection and the danger of American domination are entirely orthodox Conservative attitudes. Diefenbaker Conservatism is therefore to be understood not simply as a western populist phenomenon, but as an odd *combination* of traditional Conservative views with attitudes absorbed from the western Progressive tradition.

Another aberration which may be worthy of investigation is the Canadian phenomenon of the red tory. At the simplest level, he is a Conservative who prefers the CCF-NDP to the Liberals, or a socialist who prefers the Conservatives to the Liberals, without really knowing why. At a higher level, he is a conscious ideological Conservative with some "odd" socialist notions (W.L. Morton) or a conscious iedological socialist with some "odd" tory notions (Eugene Forsey). The very suggestion that such affinities might exist between Republicans and Socialists in the United States is ludicrous enough to make some kind of a point.

Red toryism is, of course, one of the results of the relationship between toryism and socialism which has already been elucidated. The tory and socialist minds have some crucial assumptions, orientations, and values in common, so that from certain angles they may appear not as enemies, but as two different expressions of the same basic ideological outlook. Thus, at the very highest level, the red tory is a philosopher who combines elements of socialism and toryism so thoroughly in a single integrated *Weltanschauung* that it is impossible to say that he is a proponent of either one as *against* the other. Such a red tory is George Grant, who has associations with both the Conservative party and the NDP and who has recently published a book which defends Diefenbaker, laments the death of "true" British conservatism in Canada, attacks the Liberals as individualists and Americanizers and defines socialism as a variant of conservatism (each "protects the public good against private freedom").[23]

The Character of Canadian Socialism

Canadian socialism is un-American in two distinct ways. It is un-American in the sense that it is a significant and legitimate political force in Canada, insignificant and alien in the United States. But Canadian socialism is also un-American in the sense that it does not speak the same language as American socialism. In Canada, socialism is British, non-Marxist and worldly; in the United States it is German, Marxist and other-worldly.

I have argued that the socialist ideas of British immigrants to Canada were not sloughed off because they "fit" with a political culture which already contained non-liberal components, and probably also because they were introduced into the political culture mix before the point of congealment. Thus socialism was not alien here. But it was not alien in yet another way; it was not borne by foreigners. The personnel and the ideology of the Canadian labour and socialist movements have been primarily British. Many of those who built these movements were British immigrants with past experience in the British labour movement; many others were Canadian-born children of such immigrants. And in British North America, Britons could not be treated as foreigners.

When socialism was brought to the United States, it found itself in an ideological environment in which it could not survive because Lockean individualism had long since achieved the status of a national religion; the political culture had already congealed and socialism did not fit. American socialism was alien not only in this ideological sense, but in the ethnic sense as well; it was borne by foreigners from Germany and other continental European countries. These foreigners sloughed off their socialist ideas not simply because such ideas did not "fit" iedologically, but because as foreigners they were going through a general process of Americanization; socialism was only one of many ethnically alien characteristics which had to be abandoned. The immigrant's ideological change was only one incident among many others in the general process of changing his entire way of life. According to David Saposs, "the factor that contributed most tellingly to the decline of the socialist movement was that its chief following, the immigrant workers,...had become Americanized."[24]

A British socialist immigrant to Canada had a far different experience. The British immigrant was not an "alien" in British North America. The English Canadian culture not only granted legitimacy to his political ideas and absorbed them into its wholeness; it absorbed him as a person into the English Canadian community, with relatively little strain, without demanding that he change his entire way of life before being granted full citizenship. He was acceptable to begin with, by virtue of being British. It is impossible to understand the differences between American and Canadian socialism without taking into account this immense difference between the ethnic contexts of socialism in the two countries.

The ethnic handicap of American socialism consisted not only in the fact that its personnel was heavily European. Equally important was the fact that it was a *brand* of socialism — Marxism — which found survival difficult not only in the United States but in all English-speaking countries. Marx has not found the going easy in the United States; but neither has he found

strict, authoritarian, concerned with theory

the going easy in Britain, Canada, Australia or New Zealand. The socialism of the United States, the socialism of De Leon, Berger, Hillquit and Debs, is predominantly Marxist and doctrinaire, because it is European. The socialism of English Canada, the socialism of Simpson, Woodsworth and Coldwell, is predominantly Protestant, labourist and Fabian, because it is British.

The CCF has not been without its other-worldly tendencies: there have been doctrinal disagreements and the party has always had a left wing interested more in "socialist education" than in practical political work. But this left wing has been a constantly declining minority. The party has expelled individuals and small groups — mostly Communists and Trotskyites — but it has never split. Its life has never been threatened by disagreement over doctrinal matters. It is no more preoccupied with theory than the British Labour party. It sees itself, and is seen by the public, not as a coterie of ideologists but as a party like the others, second to none in its avidity for office. If it has been attacked from the right for socialist "utopianism" and "impracticality", it has also been attacked from the right and left for abandoning the "true" socialist faith in an unprincipled drive for power.

collection

/ desire for

Canadian Liberalism: The Triumphant Center

Canadian Conservatives are not American Republicans; Canadian socialists are not American socialists; Canadian Liberals are not American liberal Democrats.

The un-American elements in English Canada's political culture are most evident in Canadian conservatism and socialism. But Canadian liberalism has a British color too. The liberalism of Canada's Liberal party should not be identified with the liberalism of the American Democratic party. In many respects they stand in sharp contrast to one another.

The three components of the English Canadian political culture have not developed in isolation from one another; each has developed in interaction with the others. Our toryism and our socialism have been moderated by liberalism. But by the same token, our liberalism has been rendered "impure", in American terms, through its contacts with toryism and socialism. If English Canadian liberalism is less individualistic, less ardently populistic-democratic, more inclined to state intervention in the economy and more tolerant of "feudal survivals" such as monarchy, this is due to the uninterrupted influence of toryism upon liberalism, an influence wielded in and through the conflict between the two. If English Canadian liberalism has tended since the depression to merge at its leftist edge with the democratic socialism of the CCF-NDP, this is due to the influence which socialism has exerted upon liberalism, in and through the conflict between them. The key to understanding the Liberal party in Canada is to see it as a *center* party, with *influential* enemies on both right and left.

In English Canada, Liberal Reform, represented by King's Liberal party, has had to face the socialist challenge. Under socialist influence, it abandoned its early devotion to "the lofty principles of Gladstone, the sound economics of Adam Smith, and the glories of laissez faire."[25] King's *Industry and Humanity* and the Liberal platform of 1919 mark the transition of English Canadian Liberalism from the old individualism to the new Liberal Reform.

King's Liberal Reform, since it had to answer attacks from the left as well as from the right, projected a notoriously ambivalent conservative-radical image:

> Truly he will be remembered
> Wherever men honor ingenuity
> Ambiguity, inactivity and political longevity.

When he faced Bennett and Meighen, King was the radical warrior, the champion of the little people against the interests. When he turned to face Woodsworth and Coldwell, he was the cautious conservative, the protector of the status quo. He

> ...never let his on the one hand
> Know what his on the other hand was doing.[26]

Hartz points out that the "pragmatism" of the New Deal enabled it to go farther, to get more things done, than European Liberal Reform. "The freewheeling inventiveness typified by the TVA, the NRA, and WPA, the SEC"[27] was nowhere to be found in Europe. Defending itself against socialism, European Liberal Reform could not submerge questions of theory; it had to justify innovations on the basis of a revised liberal ideology; it had to stop short of socialism openly. The New Deal, since it was not threatened by socialism, could ignore theory; it "did not need to stop short of Marx openly"; hence it could accomplish more than European Liberal Reform.

King had to face the socialist challenge. He did so in the manner of European Liberal Reform....The similarity of socialism and Liberal Reform could be acknowledged; indeed it could be emphasized and used to attract the socialist vote. At the same time, King had to answer the arguments of socialism, and in doing so he had to spell out his liberalism. He had to stop short of socialism openly. Social reform, yes; extension of public ownership, yes; the welfare state, yes; increased state control of the economy, yes; but not too much. Not socialism. The result was that King, like the European liberals, could not go as far as Roosevelt....Like the European liberals, and unlike Roosevelt, he had to defend private property, he had to attack excessive reliance on the state, he had to criticize socialism as "impracticality" and "utopianism." "Half radical and half conservative — a tired man who could not make up his mind" — is this not the living image of Mackenzie King?

"In America, instead of being a champion of property, Roosevelt became the big antagonist of it; his liberalism was blocked by his radicalism."[28] In Canada, since King had to worry not only about Bennett and Meighen and Drew, but also about Woodsworth and Coldwell and Douglas, King had to embark upon a defence of private property. *He* was no traitor to his class. Instead of becoming the antagonist of property, he became its champion; his radicalism was blocked by his liberalism.

An emphasis on the solidarity of the nation as against divisive "class parties" of right and left was "of the very essence of the Reformist Liberal position in Europe." "Who," asks Hartz,"would think of Roosevelt as a philosopher of class solidarity?"[29] Yet that is precisely what Roosevelt would have been if he had had to respond to a socialist presence in the American political culture. And that is precisely what King was in fact in Canada. His party was "the party of national unity". One of the most repeated charges against the CCF was that it was a divisive "class party"; the purpose of the Liberal party, on the other hand, was to preserve the solidarity of the Canadian people — the solidarity of its classes as well as the solidarity of French and English....

The Liberal party has continued to speak the language of King: ambiguous and ambivalent, presenting first its radical face and then its conservative face, urging reform and warning against hasty, ill-considered change, calling for increased state responsibility but stopping short of socialism openly, speaking for the common people but preaching the solidarity of classes.

In the United States, the liberal Democrats are on the left. There is no doubt about that. In Canada, the Liberals are a party of the center, appearing at times leftist and at times rightist. As such, they are much closer to European, especially British, Liberal Reform than to the American New Deal type of liberalism.

In the United States, the liberal Democrats are the party of organized labour. The new men of power, the labour leaders, have arrived politically; their vehicle is the Democratic party. In English Canada, if the labour leaders have arrived politically, they have done so in the CCF-NDP. They are nowhere to be found in the Liberal party. The rank and file, in the United States, are predominantly Democrats; in Canada at least a quarter are New Democrats, and the remainder show only a relatively slight, and by no means consistent, preference for the Liberals as against the Conservatives.

In the United States, left-wing "liberalism," as opposed to right-wing "liberalism," has always meant opposition to the domination of American life by big business, and has expressed itself in and through the Democratic party; the party of business is the Republican party. In Canada, business is close to both the Conservatives and the Liberals. The business community donates to the campaign funds of both and is represented in the leadership circles of both.

The Liberal party in Canada does not represent the opposition of society to domination by organized business. It claims to be based on no particular groups, but on *all*. It is not against any particular group; it is for *all*. The idea that there is any real conflict between groups is dismissed, and the very terms "right" and "left" are rejected. "The terms 'right' and 'left' belong to those who regard politics as a class struggle....The Liberal view is that true political progress is marked by...the reconciliation of classes, and the promotion of the general interest above all particular interests."[30]

A party of the left can be distinguished from parties of the center and right according to two interrelated criteria: its policy approach and its electoral support.

Policy Approach

The policy approach of a left party is to introduce innovations on behalf of the lower strata. The Liberals, unlike the liberal Democrats, have not been a party of innovation. As a center party, they have allowed the CCF-NDP to introduce innovations; they have then waited for signs of substantial acceptance by all strata of the population and for signs of reassurance against possible electoral reprisals, before actually proceeding to implement the innovations. By this time, of course, they are strictly speaking no longer innovations. The center party recoils from the fight for controversial measures; it loves to implement a consensus. Roosevelt was the innovator *par excellence*. King, though he was in his own mind in favor of reform, stalled until public demand for innovation was so great and so clear that he could respond to it without antagonizing his business-sponsored right wing. He rationalized his caution into a theory of democratic leadership far different from Roosevelt's conception of the strong presidency:

> Mackenzie King's conception of political leadership, which he often expressed, was that a leader should make his objectives clear, but that leadership was neither liberal nor democratic which tried to force new policies...on a public that did not consent to them.[31]
>
> He believed that nothing was so likely to set back a good cause as premature action.[32]

This was the official Liberal explanation of King's failure to embark on any far-reaching program of reform until 1943. King himself undoubtedly believed that his caution was based at least in part on a "democratic" theory of leadership. But his diaries suggest that the reforms came when they did because CCF pressure became so threatening that it could no longer be ignored by King's right-wing colleagues, so threatening that King felt able to surrender to it without jeopardizing the unity of his party. The bare facts are these: In August 1943, the CCF became the official opposition in Ontario. In September 1943, the CCF overtook the Liberals in the Gallup poll (Canada: CCF 19 percent, Liberals 28 percent; Ontario: CCF 32 percent, Liberals 26 percent; The West: CCF 41 percent; Liberals 23 percent).[33] King's reaction is summed up in the following quotation from his diary: "in my heart, I am not sorry to see the mass of the people coming a little more into their own, but I do regret that it is not the Liberal party that is winning the position for them....It can still be that our people will learn their lesson in time. What I fear is we will begin to have defections from our own ranks in the House to the CCF."[34] Almost immediately after the release of the September Gallup Poll, the Advisory Council of the National Liberal Federation, meeting at King's request, adopted fourteen resolutions "constituting a programme of reform...of far reaching consequences".[35] King wrote in his diary: "I have succeeded in making declarations which will improve the lot of...farmers and working people....I think I have cut the ground in large part from under the CCF...."[36]

The Liberal slogan in the campaign of 1945 was "A New Social Order for Canada." The election of June 11 returned King to power with a drastically reduced majority. The CCF vote rose from 8.5 percent to 15.6 percent, and its representation in the Commons from 8 to 29. But King's swing to the left had defeated the CCF's bid for major party status. The CCF's success was much smaller than it had expected. The success was actually a defeat, a disappointing shock from which socialism in Canada has not yet recovered.

The Liberal-CCF relationship in 1943-1945 is only the sharpest and clearest instance of the permanent interdependence forced upon each by the presence of the other, a relationship which one student describes as "antagonistic symbiosis." The Liberals depend on the CCF-NDP for innovations; the CCF-NDP depends upon the Liberals for implementation of the innovations. When the left is weak, as before and after the Second World War, the center party moves right to deal with the Conservative challenge; when the left is strengthened, as during the war and after the formation of the NDP, the center moves left to deal with the challenge.

In a conversation between King and Coldwell shortly before King's death, King expressed his regrets that Coldwell had not joined him. With Coldwell at his side, he would have been able to implement reforms which were close to his heart; reforms which had either been postponed until the end of the war or not introduced at all. He said the CCF had performed the valuable function of popularizing reforms so that he could introduce them when public opinion was ripe. Coldwell replied that it was impossible for him to join King, especially in view of the people who surrounded King.[37] There, in a nutshell, is the story of the relationship between the Liberal party and the CCF-NDP. The Liberals, says King, are too conservative because the left has not joined them. The left has not joined them, replies Coldwell, because they are too conservative.

King wanted to show the people that he was "true to them." He was saddened that the CCF and not the Liberals were fighting the people's battles. But he could not move from dead center until CCF power became so great that the necessity of moving was clear, not only to himself but to all realistic politicians. King's best self wanted to innovate; yet he saw the Liberal party not as a great innovating force but as the party which would implement reforms once they had been popularized by the CCF. Yet he wanted to absorb the CCF. The lot of the centrist politician is not a happy one.

The absence of Lockean "monotheism" strengthened socialism in Canada. Socialism was present in the political culture when liberalism began to concern itself with the problems of the industrial age; liberalism was therefore forced to react to the socialist challenge. In doing so, it was cast in the mold of European Liberal Reform (center) parties — ambivalent, radical and conservative, alternating attacks on the status quo with defence of the status quo. Socialism had sufficient strength in English Canada to force liberalism into the European rather than the American position — center rather than left. King's liberalism was therefore not capable of reacting to the depression in the Rooseveltian manner. As a result, socialist power grew.

Socialism was not powerless, so there was no New Deal. There was no New Deal, so socialism grew more powerful. Socialism grew more powerful, so King reacted with "A New Social Order for Canada." The center and the left dance around one another, frustrating one another and living off the frustration; each is locked into the dance by the existence of the other.

I have been stressing the strength of Canadian socialism in order to make clear the differences between the Canadian and the American situations. Of course this does not mean that the differences between Canada and Europe can be ignored. Canadian socialism has been strong enough to challenge liberalism, to force liberalism to explain itself, and thus to evoke from it the same sort of centrist response as was evoked in Europe. But socialism in Canada has not been strong enough to match or overshadow liberalism. The CCF became a significant political force but, except for the years 1942-45, it never knocked on the gates of national power.

In Europe, the working man could not be appeased by the concession of Liberal Reform. The center was squeezed out of existence between its enemies on the right and on the left. In Canada, the center party's concessions were sufficient to keep the lower strata from flocking en masse to the left. The concessions were not sufficient to *dispose* of the socialist threat, but they were sufficient to draw the socialists' sharpest teeth. In Canada the center party emerged triumphant over its enemies on the right and on the left. Here, then, is another aspect of English Canada's uniqueness: it is the only society in which Liberal Reform faces the challenge of socialism *and* emerges victorious. The English Canadian fragment *is* bourgeois. The tory-ism and the socialism, though significant, *are* "touches."

Electoral Support

There is a dearth of information about the influence of class on voting behavior in Canada, but there are strong indications that the higher strata are more likely than the lower to vote Conservative, the lower strata are more likely than the higher to vote CCF-NDP, and that both groups are about *equally* attracted to the Liberals. This would, of course, confirm the picture of Conservatives as the right, NDP as the left and Liberals as the "classless" center. This is in sharp contrast to the situation in the United States, where the lower strata prefer the Democrats, the higher prefer the Republicans and there is no center party.

Although this picture of the relationship between class and voting is broadly true, it is also true that class voting in Canada is, generally speaking, overshadowed by regional and religious-ethnic voting. In some parts of Canada, e.g. Ontario, class voting is as high as in the United States or higher. Nevertheless, in Canada *considered as a whole* class voting is lower than in the United States; non-class motivations appear to be very strong.[38] Peter Regenstrief suggests that one factor accounting for this is the persistent cultivation by the Liberal party of its classless image, its "abhorrence of anything remotely associated with class politics,"[39] its refusal to appeal to any class *against* any other class.

What this points to again is the unique character of English Canada as the only society in which the center triumphs over left and right. In Europe the classless appeal of Liberal Reform does not work; the center is decimated by the defection of high-status adherents to the right and of low-status adherents to the left. In Canada, the classless appeal of King centrism is the winning strategy, drawing lower-class support to the Liberals away from the left parties and higher-class support away from the right parties. This forces the left and right parties themselves to emulate (to a certain extent) the Liberals' classless strategy. The Conservatives transform themselves into Progressive Conservatives. The CCF transforms itself from a "farmer-labour" party into an NDP calling for the support of "all liberally minded Canadians." The Liberal refusal to appear as a class party forces both right and left to mitigate their class appeals and to become themselves, in a sense, center parties.

Class voting in Canada may be lower than in the United States, not entirely because regional-religious-ethnic factors are "objectively" stronger here, but also because King Liberalism, by resolutely avoiding class symbols, had *made* other symbols more important.

> He blunted us.
> We have no shape
> Because he never took sides,
> And no sides,
> Because he never allowed them to take shape.[40]

ENDNOTES

1. Louis Hartz, *The Liberal Tradition in America* (New York: Harcourt, Brace and World [Toronto: Longmans], 1955).

2. —, *The Founding of New Societies* (New York: Harcourt, Brace and World [Toronto: Longmans], 1964).

3. *Ibid.*, p. 3
4. *Ibid.*, p. 25.
5. *Ibid.*, p. 7.
6. *Ibid.*, p. 34.
7. Seymour Martin Lipset, *The First New Nation* (New York: Basic Books, 1963), esp. chap. 7.
8. William Nelson, *The American Tory* (Oxford: Clarendon Press, 1961), pp. 189-90.
9. Hartz, *New Societies*, p. 91.
10. *Ibid.*, p. 243.
11. Lipset, p. 251.
12. Hartz, *New Societies*, p. 245.
13. *Ibid.*, p. 15.
14. *Ibid.*, p. 10.
15. Hartz, *Liberal Tradition*, p. 11.
16. Hartz, *New Societies*, p. 23.
17. *Ibid.*, p. 119.
18. *Ibid.*, p. 35.
19. *Ibid.*, p. 119.
20. *Ibid.*, p. 120.
21. Roger Graham, *Arthur Meighen*, vol. II (Toronto: Clarke, Irwin, 1963), p. 269.
22. *Ibid.*, vol. III (Toronto: Clarke, Irwin, 1965), pp. 71-4.
23. George Grant, *Lament for a Nation* (Toronto: McClelland and Stewart, 1965), p. 71.
24. David Saposs, *Communism in American Unions* (New York: McGraw Hill, 1959), p. 7.
25. Bruce Hutchison, *The Incredible Canadian* (Toronto: Longman's, Green and Co., 1952), p. 6.
26. F.R. Scott, "W.L.M.K., "*The Blasted Pine*, ed. F.R. Scott and A.J.M. Smith (Toronto: Macmillan, 1962), p. 28.
27. Hartz, *Liberal Tradition*, p. 271.
28. *Ibid.*, p. 267.
29. *Ibid.*
30. J.W. Pickersgill, *The Liberal Party* (Toronto: McClelland and Stewart, 1962), p. 68.
31. *Ibid.*, pp. 26-27.
32. J.W. Pickersgill, *The Mackenzie King Record* (Toronto: University of Toronto Press, 1960), p. 10.
33. *Globe and Mail*, Sept. 29, 1943.
34. Pickersgill, *Record*, p. 571.
35. National Liberal Federation, *The Liberal Party*, p. 53.
36. Pickersgill, *Record*, p. 601.
37. Interview with M.J. Coldwell, March 28, 1962.
38. R. Alford, *Party and Society* (Chicago: Rand McNally, 1963), chap. 9.
39. "Group Perceptions and the Vote," in Meisel, ed., *Papers on the 1962 Election*, p. 249.
40. Scott, *The Blasted Pine*, p. 27.

5 The Consequences of Elite Accommodation between the Cabinet, Bureaucracy and Interest Groups*

ROBERT PRESTHUS

The present centralization of decision-making in the hands of the cabinet, higher bureaucrats and functionally-relevant interest groups leads to a neglect of comprehensive, long-range social and economic planning in favor of case-by-case, uncoordinated, incremental policy-making. There tend to be few, if any, overarching priorities for ordering the system in directions that will permit industrial rationalization to overcome inapposite claims of protectionism. The going assumption is that the claims of virtually all major articulate groups are equally legitimate and should be honored, a consequence encouraged by the fact that such claims, as we have seen, tend to appear in substantively and administratively watertight compartments. Governments everywhere, of course, are organized essentially along functional lines, so it is quite understandable that accommodation will proceed in this segmented fashion. Political incentives aggravate the resulting fragmentation and proliferation, as ministers, senior civil servants and interest group leaders indulge their natural enthusiasm for growth within their respective sectors. Party ideologies such as the well-known Liberal managerial style are also germane.

The larger outcome is a relatively uncontrolled expansion of activities, without much qualitative differentiation among the competing claims of major social interests. Theoretically, the Cabinet is supposed to provide the ultimate synthesizing force, but such hardly seems the case. Efforts are made to ease the resulting proliferation by task force surveys and management studies, often motivated by "efficiency" incentives. But these, however useful some of their recommendations, are beside the point in this context. It is the larger, overall programmatic aspects of government that

*Reprinted from Robert Presthus, *Elite Accommodation in Canadian Politics*, Cambridge University Press, 1973.

requires rationalization, not the management aspects of existing programs. Perhaps here, however, one is being equally beside the point in contemplating rational solutions for a governmental process powered essentially by brokerage incentives. If parties gain and maintain office by expanding their distributive parameters, it is probably useless to insist that the uncoordinated reconciliation of most group claims result in collective hypertension.

A second consequence of the going system of elite accommodation is a reinforcement of the status quo in terms of the existing pattern of distribution of public largesse and political power. Functional ties and established clientele relationships tend to crystallize existing power relationships. As we have seen, it is understandably difficult for new or substantively weak interests to penetrate the decision-making process. Inertia also plays a part as the influence of those groups which have gained legitimacy in their various sectors is reinforced through sustained contact and the weight of cumulative loyalties. The perhaps inevitable inequalities in political resources among interest groups mean that government, to some extent, is pushed into the anomalous position of defending the strong against the weak. While the governmental elite plays an equilibrating role in welfare areas, much of its energy is also spent reinforcing the security and growth of interests that already enjoy the largest shares of the net social product. Here again, the fundamental problem is the unequal distribution of political resources that characterizes all societies. But some easing of its consequences might occur if governmental elites played a more qualitative role in resource allocation, based upon broader criteria than those now in effect. Conforming to established influence structures is, to some extent, the understandable but easy way out.

The tendency of governmental elites to reinforce the going distributive system also reflects, as we have shown, the socioeconomic, interactional and (to a lesser extent) ideological continuities existing between them and politically-active interest group leaders.

Meanwhile, another fillip to the status quo follows as the major parties are necessarily (again from the standpoint of pragmatic politics) constrained to listen most closely to those groups in Canadian society who can contribute the most generous shares of financial support and respected public endorsement of their policies. As long as parties require huge amounts of money to compete successfully in national and provincial political arenas, it is difficult to see how the existing system can be modified. Perhaps the growth of latent, mass-oriented consumer groups is one answer, but here the incentives for organizational viability and continuity are rarely as strong as those enjoyed by groups organized around producer interests. To some extent, a fuller understanding that modern governments tend *not* to play an equilibrating role in the contest among badly matched publics may have an effect. Such an appreciation, however, depends upon greater educational opportunity at the advanced levels to enable more citizens to comprehend the going system of elite accommodation and to develop the resources required to participate in it. From such sources may come the incentives and knowledge required to stimulate a more competitive, and hence more democratic, interest group politics.

Such a development bears directly upon a third consequence of the existing process of accommodation, the extent to which it tends to restrict meaningful participation to those with a direct substantive interest. Here again, while desires of the political elite for dispatch and expertise provide eminently desirable incentives, the perhaps unanticipated consequences include a heavy reliance upon consultation with interested groups and a tendency to define problems as essentially technical, with the implication that "political" considerations are probably illegitimate and certainly devisive. Here again, the "Old Tory" theory of authority is germane, since it aggravates the technological drift, while at the same time it encourages the constriction of the boundaries of participation in policy-making. The assumptions of cabinet government and the jejune policy role of backbenchers are among the institutional factors that reinforce the traditional and somewhat astounding assumption that the major policies of government are properly formulated in secret.

Given the weight of such elements of Canadian political culture, some long-term resocialization regarding leadership and rank-and-file participation will be required before traditional models of policy-making can be modified. Such again is a long-range solution requiring both time and increased equality of educational opportunity, buttressed by a realization among young people that the higher learning has other objectives than occupational success. These ends, in turn, will probably require some modification of elitist conceptions of higher education which still enjoy considerable support among advantaged social groups, as seen in current fulminations about the high costs of university expansion and successful attempts to cut back graduate education. Given the small proportion of university graduates in Canadian society, and the technical and scientific manpower required to sustain a modern industrial economy, this policy seems anomalous indeed. Whether Canada can, or should, continue to rely so heavily upon immigration for its supply of highly skilled and professional manpower is of course a moot point.

In sum, while the going success of elite accommodation has much to commend it, it tends to result in an incremental, uncoordinated expansion of governmental and private programs, without adequate direction by the only institution possessing the legitimacy and authority to do so, government. A crystallization of existing patterns of resource allocation follows, which makes the introduction of new scientific, technical and economic directions difficult as they strike against established influence structures, based largely upon long-standing, functionally-determined, agency-clientele relationships. The rational consideration of policy alternatives is correspondingly inhibited so that, despite the flurry of plans and programs, task forces and reorganization schemes announced by ministers naturally anxious to be regarded as innovative, the more things seem to change, the more they remain the same. Power continues to meet with power, through the process of elite accommodation.

Finally, the going system has significant implications for those who take democratic participation seriously. Symbolized by the tradition of governmental secrecy, cabinet hegemony and the weakness of backbenchers in the formulation of policy, the consequences include a virtual monopoly of access by established groups which tend to enjoy major shares of political resources. One by-product is a built-in disposition toward inequity, which only the governmental elite can ease by widening the channels of participation. It is clear that some governmental leaders are aware of this problem and are attempting to liberalize the system. But their own advantaged positions in the social structure and their preferences for going values make it extremely difficult to interact with representatives of less-advantaged groups. There is also some evidence that political elites sometimes obfuscate the substance of policy issues for tactical reasons. Such stratagems, which are surely encouraged by the complexity of many public issues yet deny the essential educative function of parties, are part of the quasi-participative ethos.

In addition to such social, ideological and tactical restraints, there is the vital issue of practical politics which, all else being equal, compels governmental elites to defer to those who command the most powerful institutional structures in finance, industry and the mass media. Indeed in some cases, they are the same individuals. Meanwhile, elections require vast amounts of funds and support from those who can provide them. Thus the barriers to a more participative political culture include social and ideological discontinuities between political elites and ordinary citizens, as well as the brute economic calculus of successful party politics. Equally important is the lack of political sophistication and interest on the part of large proportions of Canadians, again reinforced by residues of elitist values, the assumptions of the parliamentary system and limitations of the opportunity for higher education which is critical in distributing larger shares of political resources among more citizens.

6 The Political Elite*

DENNIS OLSEN

...Behind the façade of a multi-ethnic democracy the old elite alliance between British and French Canadians remained strong at the federal level. The 1960s saw this alliance shift *slightly* in favour of the French, backed up by the political and social movements in the province of Quebec. The number of French-Canadian ministers began to increase with the Liberal cabinet of 1965, and their gains solidified with the Trudeau government of 1968. But the numerical increase of ministers tells only part of the story; continuity in elite position is another important dimension of power, and French Canadians improved in this regard as well. During the Diefenbaker regime and the first half of the 1960s, the average length of stay of French-Canadian ministers in the federal cabinet was only about three years. By the end of 1973, the average length of stay (or continuity) of French-Canadian ministers had risen until it exceeded five years. By 1979, British-Canadian dominance of the cabinet had been firmly re-asserted. The incoming Clark cabinet was 67 percent British Canadian, 20 percent from non-charter group backgrounds, and only 13 percent French Canadian.

In general, the more powerful positions within the state tend to be held by persons with higher-ranking background characteristics. For example, the educational credentials of the politicians tend to be of higher standing as one shifts attention from a provincial legislature up to a provincial cabinet, from a smaller province to a larger province, or from any of these to the federal cabinet. In short, there are more university degrees higher up in the system. Ethnicity follows a similar path. The two charter groups dominate the more powerful positions in the state system, and the non-charter groups tend to be found in less powerful positions. The two charter groups, for example, tend to be numerically dominant in the federal cabinet and the cabinets of the two most populous provinces....

Compared with the Canadian working population as a whole, the political

*From *The State Elite*, by Dennis Olsen. Used by permission of the Canadian publishers, McClelland and Stewart Ltd., Toronto.

elite is strikingly exclusive in occupational backgrounds. Of more than 22,000 occupational titles used by the Canadian census, only a small handful can be attributed to the elite. Practice of law is the most common occupation in the background of elite members. In the present study 58 percent of the elite were lawyers; previously the figure was even higher at 64 percent. Of the thirty-member Clark Cabinet of 1979, fourteen were lawyers. Why does this one occupation monopolize so many positions in the elite? Unlike most wage workers and salaried employees, lawyers are available for politics because of the way they have traditionally organized themselves in law partnerships and law firms. They can free their time for politics through arrangements with their partners and after serving their stint in politics can expect to return to an enhanced and profitable practice. Law is also one of the few occupations that involves its students in formal training in rhetoric and the persuasive pleading of causes, a training that is useful for politics.

The former occupations of federal cabinet ministers were not concentrated quite so heavily in this profession. Lawyers made up only 41 percent of this sub-group of the elite, a figure which was down 20 percent from the Porter study. The vacancies were taken up by businessmen, who rose from 19 to 27 percent of the elite, and by teachers, academics, and journalists, who rose from 5 to 16 percent. The great expansion of education in the 1960s helps explain the increase of teachers and academics as the growth of television and advertising, and their increased importance for politics, helps explain the increase of journalists. Both these occupations develop skills in public speaking that are necessary for politics. None of the federal cabinet ministers came from an occupation that one could call working class. Very few of the businessmen who entered the political elite were previously part of the Canadian corporate elite....

In general, the economically powerful have not had to seek political office directly. Their interests are usually served by those who are already there. As Porter remarked, "in the corporate world both major political parties, the Liberals and the Conservatives, are seen as being favourable to the interests of corporate power," which is to say that both parties are viewed as being willing to provide the function of stabilizing "the field for corporate activity."[1]

The corporate elite, of course, make up only a very small group of the economically powerful in Canada. Below them is a larger stratum of those who operate substantial but not dominant business corporations and those who are personally wealthy. What is the relationship between having wealth and being a member of the political elite? The evidence is that the corporate world and the wealthy, in general, have had a fairly stable core of representation in the political elite, well able to look after their common interests. At the same time, it is not necessary to be wealthy to be part of the political elite, although with the high cost of political campaigns and advertising it must certainly help. Moreover, having wealth is not alone a sufficient condition....

Some federal cabinet ministers possessed considerable inherited wealth before they entered politics. Among these one would almost certainly have to include James Richardson, Pierre Trudeau, Charles M. Drury, Walter L. Gordon, and George Hees. Others were connected to substantial family fortunes through marriage before entering politics. This group would include William Benidickson, Donald Fleming, and John Turner. Fleming, Gordon, and Turner were all ministers of Finance in the federal government. Among them they held this very important economic post for eleven of the eighteen years between 1957 and 1975....

The typical member of the political elite comes from a middle- or upper-middle class background; hence he is not usually among the very wealthy in Canada. Nevertheless, a conservative estimate would locate at least 16 per cent of the provincial premiers and federal cabinet ministers studied among those few Canadians who have inherited wealth or have access through marriage to family fortunes or are wealthy through their own efforts in previous careers. If more information were available on this carefully guarded subject the figure would probably be closer to 20 percent. Together these people held a number of important positions that enabled them to exercise a great deal of control over economic decisions within the jurisdiction of the state. While the wealthy do not constitute the norm in the Canadian political elite, there are enough of them, with enough continuity, to ensure that the institutional arrangements that protect the private ownership and control of wealth are safely preserved.

Our next question concerns changes in the social class origins of the political elite....They are the sons of lawyers, small businessmen, bank managers, teachers, and so on. The Canadian state recruits primarily from the middle class, a middle class that was quite small, perhaps 15 to 20 percent of the population, in the time of the current elite's fathers. So the elite are the sons of the middle class, but they are also middle class by virtue of their own occupations before entering politics....

This middle class is not really a class for itself in a national sense, that is, one that aspires to be a ruling class and produces a national program and ideology to that end. There is no real attempt on its part to build a lasting alliance with the larger Canadian working class. This is the reason there are so few members of the elite with working-class backgrounds. It is a middle class that is generally content to leave the small upper class dominant in society, while elite members themselves *individually* aspire to move up the ladder....Absorption of the middle class through state recruitment helps keep political peace by giving it a share of power, but the Canadian state nevertheless remains a state *of* the middle class rather than a state *for* the middle class because the absorption produces an *alliance* between the middle class and the small but dominant upper class. In return for places in the state, the middle class pays the price of compromising its own long-term interests in favour of those of the upper class.

It is the middle class that provides most of the key personnel of politics in Canada because it is this class, rather than the upper class, that must struggle and engage in politics in order to secure favourable policies from the state or to secure positions within the state. Canadian politics during the 1965-75 period was dominated by regional factions of the middle class struggling for power. Members of the political elite who made their political debut in that decade were more middle class than was the norm.

Their family backgrounds also provided many members of the elite with certain political advantages. At least 25 percent of the elite came from families in which an earlier member had served in politics. In these cases, political attitudes and party loyalty are passed along, together with the necessary connections that get the younger member off to a headstart in the political game....

It is clear that there are marked patterns of continuity in the social background characteristics of the political elite considered as a group. The patterns of persistence in the social composition of the elite should not, however, be confused with the individual politician's personal continuity in office. The political elite as a *group* retains its characteristics simply by recruiting similar social types with the same background characteristics, even though the individual members do not usually stay in office very long. What are the career patterns of individuals in the elite?...

Of the sixty-six federal cabinet ministers appointed between 1961 and 1973, only 12 percent had previously served in municipal politics compared with 16 percent reported in the previous study. Experience in provincial legislatures has declined even more, from 20 percent in the earlier study to 8 percent. Porter reported that about 14 percent of the cabinet ministers he studied had moved from provincial legislatures to service in the federal cabinet. In the present study only 5 percent have done so. Clearly, then, there has been a marked decline in personnel moving from municipal or provincial politics to federal politics. This is probably another facet of the strengthening of the provinces as power bases. Provincial parties and elites are better able to attract and keep the men they want. They even manage to pull a few people away from federal politics. Seven percent of the provincial cabinet ministers studied had previously served in federal politics as members of the House of Commons. So there is a small outflow of personnel from federal politics to the provinces, and the House of Commons apparently serves as a training ground for a few provincial elites. Being a federal M.P. increases the probability of reaching the very top positions in the provinces. Six of the twenty-eight provincial premiers (21 percent) had experience in the federal parliament *before* becoming premiers, while only 7 percent of the remaining provincial cabinet ministers had this advantage.

The vast majority of both federal and provincial cabinet ministers remain with the one level of government rather than using one as a stepping-stone to the other or alternating back and forth between both levels. In this sense federal and provincial cabinets are more sharply separated in terms of personnel exchanges than they were in 1960, when a fifth of the federal ministers had provincial experience as well. An absence of persons with political careers spanning more than one level of government is another part of the general fragmentation of the Canadian state system that has occurred during the last several decades.

The lack of political experience among the ministers is indicated by the proportion of political "outsiders" recruited to cabinet. Ten percent of the ministers in the previous study were classified in this way because they had never had a real political career before becoming a minister. In the present study nearly 20 percent, double the previous proportion, are "outsiders."...

The recruitment of outsiders has been used, especially by the Liberals, to put together inside cabinet a coalition that represents what the political elite views as the significant power groups in society and to ward off potential threats to their rule through co-optation. Of the thirteen outsiders in the present study, six were French Canadians, most of whom were active in trying to prevent the perceived threat of Quebec separatism during the 1960s. Another three of the thirteen represented constituencies in western provinces where the Liberals have been unable to make political headway. (The co-optation of Jack Horner from the Conservative Party in 1977 was another example of this.) Apart from this, the practice is used to acquire expertise for the cabinet, to attract prestigious personnel to politics, and to guarantee the personal loyalty of ministers to the "chief," on whom their political careers depend to a very great extent. There is a self-fulfilling-prophecy aspect to the practice inasmuch as the recruitment of outsiders downgrades parliament as the conventional method of entry and downgrades parliamentary expertise as a requirement for cabinet office, which means that top-notch people tend not to try to use political office as the route to the highest positions. The political elite is consequently able to argue that it is necessary to look outside the parliamentary backbenches to find the calibre of people that cabinet requires. As Porter remarks, the process is in this sense a vicious circle.

If politics is considered to be one part of a society that has institutionally separate spheres and elites, the practice of recruiting outsiders appears to be an abnormality or a pathology. Like patronage, bribery, or political corruption, it downgrades the institutional autonomy of the political sphere. Having said this, however, one can view these pathological phenomena as being fairly "normal," given a model of a broader ruling power structure, which necessarily involves a coalition of elites and classes in a complex society. Transactions that appear in the one view as "bribery," "corruption," or "patronage," including the recruitment of "outsiders," are simply part of the overall co-ordination and perpetuation of power that is carried on by both open and hidden means. Many of the so-called outsiders recruited to political cabinets were very definitely "insiders" within the broader Canadian power structure. This fact is especially evident in the case of the recruitment of top-level federal bureaucrats or leaders from the world of private corporations. In these cases, we have election from above rather than election from below and consequently a circumvention of democracy.

Cabinet ministers in Canada do not remain in office very long. In comparison with the higher civil servants, the Supreme Court justices, and the corporate and labour union leaders, the political elite has the highest turnover of personnel. In fact, the turnover in political careers of all kinds appears to be very high in Canada; on the average, 40 percent of members of the House of Commons do not return after each election.[2]

Fifty-two percent of the federal ministers who left office between 1961 and 1973 served less than five years in office. Ninety-five percent had gone before they had completed ten years of service, up 16 percent over the previous study. Thus the probability of a politician remaining in the federal cabinet for at least ten years seems to be decreasing, there being only five chances in a hundred in the present study. Despite the apparent stability of the Trudeau regime, the turnover of *individual* ministers was high. Of the thirty cabinet ministers in office in January 1974, six — that is, 20 percent — were not in office one year later in January 1975. One had retired, one was defeated at the polls, and the other four were demoted to the backbenches....

It follows from this that most of the important jurisdictions in Canadian politics are characterized by party stability but *not* by personal career stability. The important exceptions are a very few key figures, such as the prime minister, a few provincial premiers, and a handful of cabinet ministers. What this smacks of is government by a series of cliques. Small wonder that Porter said that Canadian politics is characterized by "chieftainship," since the continuity seems to be provided by a few chiefs, each with his own small band of followers....

It would be difficult, in light of the career evidence presented above, to argue that Canada has a cadre of professional politicians, or that politics as a career is any more of a reality now than it ever has been. The evidence suggests the opposite conclusion in each case. If the political system appears weak and fragmented we should remember that this does not necessarily imply that the state system as a whole is in quite the same condition. It does suggest, however, that the political arena is perhaps more vulnerable to penetration by other spheres of power than need be the case. It has been particularly vulnerable — probably "receptive" is the better word — to influence from the corporate and business sphere in the last fifteen years....

The final question to be addressed with regard to the career paths of the political elite is to ask what they do after holding an elite position and what form their exit from cabinet takes. The long-term trend, from 1940 through to the end of 1973, is that one-third of the federal cabinet ministers pick up a political appointment of some kind when they leave the cabinet. These patronage appointments include the bench, the Senate, the lieutenant-governorship of a province, and bureaucratic posts such as an ambassadorship or the chairmanship of a state regulatory board. Sixty-nine federal cabinet ministers left office for one reason or another between 1961 and 1973. Of these, twenty-four took a patronage exit, fourteen going to the Senate, five to bureaucratic posts, three to lieutenant-governorships, and two to the bench. Compared with findings in the previous study, exits to the bench were down while those to the Senate and bureaucracy were up.

Forty-three did not take patronage exits. Of these, only sixteen (37 percent) remained active in political roles after leaving office, and could seriously be said to be following politics as a career or vocation....

But the majority of ministers who did not get patronage appointments left politics for good. Most of them went to business careers. One of the noticeable differences between the present and the previous studies is the increase in the proportion who took up business as a career after politics. Thirteen ministers took this route in the present study. Of these thirteen, ten had come from business before politics, one was a lawyer with strong business connections, and two had little or no previous business experience. In some cases the stint in politics gave the individual a sharp boost in his business career by helping him into the boardrooms of dominant corporations....

There were fourteen federal cabinet ministers who went to the Senate on leaving the House. At least five of these took up corporate directorships in addition to the senatorship....

The overall volume of circulation between business and the political elite has increased from one study to the next, as is also the case between the federal bureaucracy and the political elite. In the previous study, 19 percent of the political elite came from business, and of those who left office 9 percent went directly to business. In this study, 27 percent of the elite came from business and 19 percent of the exits were directly to business. Thus there are two *trends* whose logical extension might eventually mean the monopolization of positions in the political elite by bureaucrats and businessmen. The figures actually understate the extent of the relationship between politics and business because they do not take into account those who went to law firms or the Senate and subsequently took up corporate directorships. As mentioned above, if all the elected members of the political elite who eventually take up corporate directorships are included, the exits to roles that involve corporate decision making increase from 19 percent to 27 percent, which is exactly the same as the inflow percentages from business. In short, about 27 percent of the volume of circulation through the political elite involves those who have had, or will have, business or corporate roles. This volume appears to be half again as much as in the previous study. From the other side of the relationship, Clement reports that the corporate elite now contains a greater proportion of ex-bureaucrats and ex-members of the political elite: "In 1972 it was found that 17 [members of the corporate elite previously] had their main careers in the political elite with another 18 in the bureaucratic elite, more than double the numbers from 1951."[3] Taken together, the results of this study and Clement's mean that there was in the last twenty years an increased inter-penetration and drawing together of these three key elites in Canada — the corporate, the political, and the bureaucratic....

It is clear, then, that the Canadian political elite changes very slowly and not at all in some respects. The elite is still dominated by male lawyers and businessmen of French- and British-Canadian origins who come from middle- or upper-middle-class families. Most spend a relatively short time in politics, and, apart from a few individual "chiefs," few turn it into a regular lifetime career. The continuity of class and ethnic backgrounds suggests that the Canadian state creates, internally, a structured alliance between the two charter ethnic groups and between the middle and upper classes. This being the case, very little effective state power accrues to other ethnic groups or to the working classes.

ENDNOTES

1. John Porter, *The Vertical Mosaic* (Toronto: University of Toronto Press, 1965), p. 296.
2. Roman R. March, *The Myth of Parliament* (Scarborough: Prentice-Hall Canada, 1974), pp. 41-42.
3. Wallace Clement, *The Canadian Corporate Elite* (Toronto: McClelland and Stewart, 1975), p. 258.

7 Tensions from Within: Regionalism and Party Politics in Canada

M. JANINE BRODIE

Introduction

Conventional wisdom has been that our two major parties do not offer the electorate distinct policy options, especially in economic matters, because they are too preoccupied with mediating the often intense regional and ethnic divisions in Canadian society. Recent developments in federal party politics, however, may call this conventional wisdom into question. The dual federal elections of 1979 and 1980, as well as the 1983 Progressive Conservative leadership campaign, suggest that there is a growing cleavage in party positions on such fundamental questions as the power of the federal state and the proper role for government in the economy. The Progressive Conservative party appears to be staking out a unique position on the right of the political spectrum through its advocacy of greater provincial power and greater reliance on the private sector for economic growth. The Liberals, in contrast, have maintained their commitment to a strong federal state and, if anything, envision a greater activist role for the state than they have in the past. The present period, therefore, represents one of the rare instances in Canadian party politics when the electorate has been asked to choose between quite distinct party platforms.

Two questions about the apparent diversity in the platforms of the major federal parties will concern us here. The first is whether the interparty debate on federalism and economic strategy which was so clearly evident in the campaign rhetoric and party platforms of the late 1970s was reflected in the electorate. Second, if Canadian voters were divided over these issues, did their party loyalties or their regional orientations underlie their disagreement? These questions will be examined below with survey research data collected from Canadian voters in the spring of 1979. First, however, we will briefly trace the history of Liberal-Conservative consensus and disagreement on the questions of federal power and economic strategy.

Federal Parties and Development Strategies

Fundamental disagreements between the Liberal and Progressive Conservative parties over questions of state power and economic development have been relatively rare in our political history. The BNA act provided for a strong federal government and from the beginning, it was an active participant in Canada's economic development. For example, under the so-called "National Policy," first unveiled by Macdonald's Conservative party, the federal government underwrote large, capital-intensive infrastructural projects, such as a national railroad system; it also sponsored immigration and discouraged the free-flow of continental trade by placing prohibitive tariffs on imported manufactured goods.

While in opposition in the early years of Confederation, the Liberals were viewed as the party of provincial rights and sometimes toyed with a free trade platform. Nonetheless, when the Liberals replaced the Conservatives as the dominant federal party in 1896, the distinctions between their platforms gradually disappeared. Except for a brief and unsuccessful flirtation with trade reciprocity in 1911, the Liberals also adhered to the economic development strategy designed by their Conservative predecessors. Both parties offered the electorate an essentially similar policy of developing a national economy through tariffs, though the Conservatives broke ranks briefly in the 1930s and again, in 1942, after the Port Hope conference.

The apparent consensus on economic policy among federal party elites during Canada's first half-century was not, however, clearly reflected in the electorate. Voters in the prairie provinces, especially farmers, grew increasingly disaffected with the economic policies of both federal parties. They argued that tariffs on manufactured goods such as farm machinery were excessive, and freight rates, which imposed a higher toll on goods shipped in the West than in the East, were discriminatory. Farmers' organizations pressed both parties to reconsider their economic platforms, but neither responded favourably. The economic alternatives advocated by the western farmers' movement were not voiced in the federal party system until it launched its own political party, the Progressives, in 1921.

The typical practice in federal politics has been that alternative economic development strategies have been introduced to the electorate by third parties rather than by one of the two major parties. The Progressives faded from the federal political landscape in the mid-1920s after they had extracted a few concessions from a minority Liberal government. They were quickly succeeded in 1933 by the Cooperative Commonwealth Federation (the CCF) which advocated a radically different role for the state. As a self-defined socialist party, it raised the option of direct state participation in the marketplace through public ownership of key sectors of the economy. More important, it advocated state economic planning to ensure economic stability and a wide net of social legislation for the general welfare. Each of these goals became part of the postwar Keynesian consensus.

The CCF's strong showing in the public opinion polls during the war years may have encouraged the Liberals and later the Conservatives to adopt a new perspective on economic policy. Both parties maintained an overriding commitment to capitalism in their postwar economic platforms, but both advocated state intervention and social welfare programmes. The "new national policy" was based squarely on the Keynesian imperative that the chief economic role of the national government was to ensure appropriate levels of aggregate demand through fiscal and monetary policies and through lowering barriers to international trade and investment.[1] Taken together these currents in economic thought provided the foundations for the contemporary Canadian state and the integration of the Canadian economy into the greater North American one.

With the possible exception of the Diefenbaker years, the two major parties offered the electorate essentially the same development strategy throughout the 1950s, 1960s and most of the 1970s. Thus, it is hardly surprising that survey research conducted during the period found that the public perceived only minor, if any, differences between the two. Analysis of voter perceptions indicated that the electorate tended to place both the Liberals and Conservatives at the centre of a left-right continuum while the NDP was perceived to be to the left of both.[2] The conclusion drawn from these studies was that the two major parties simply did not conform to the conventional classificatory schema of parties of the left and parties of the right.

It has been argued that the late 1970s witnessed an uncharacteristic, if incomplete, polarization in Canadian party politics. The Progressive Conservatives became the party of free enterprise and decentralization while the Liberals became the party of state intervention in the economy and federal power.[3] We cannot be certain whether the current debate in federal partisan politics constitutes the long-term agenda in Canadian politics. At the very least, however, the 1979 and 1980 federal elections represent one of the rare periods in Canadian history when the two major parties offered the electorate different economic development strategies.

The Liberals and Progressive Conservatives appear to be in fundamental disagreement over three broad policy questions. The first is whether the federal or provincial governments should have more power in the determination of economic priorities and policy. The postwar interparty consensus was that the federal government should have priority in setting economic policy. In many ways, the new consensus necessitated an overarching federal power because the key governing instruments of the Keynesian state, money supply and taxation, rested within federal jurisdiction. Moreover, the federal government had both the will and the requisite spending power to initiate a welfare state when most of the provinces did not.

The movement for decentralization of federal power did not come initially from the federal Tories but rather from western provincial governments which throughout the 1970s came in conflict with the federal government in their attempts to gain control over economic development and diversification within their respective jurisdictions. In 1979, however, the federal Conservatives, perhaps reflecting the influence of their western support base, raised the option of provincial power with the rather ambiguous phrase, "community of communities." They argued that federal programmes and constitutional powers involving lotteries, fisheries, resources, culture and communications should be turned over outright to the provinces or shared by both levels of government. That Canada should draw its strength from building strong provinces was anathema to the Liberals, who stressed that Canada was more than the sum of its parts and that the strategic role of the federal government in economic and other policy fields should not be relinquished to the provinces.[4]

The proper role for government in the economy was the second point of dispute between the two major federal parties during the late seventies. The Liberals and New Democratic parties did not deviate much from the postwar consensus about the propriety of an activist state in the social and economic policy fields. The Progressive Conservatives, however, increasingly adopted the "buzz-words" of neo-conservatism, a philosophy which already had attracted adherents not only in the United States and Britain, but also in the western provinces and among members of the Canadian business community. At the heart of the neo-conservatives' analysis of the ongoing economic malaise was the proposition that the postwar state had failed to nurture economic stability and growth. It was too large, wasteful, inflationary, overly burdensome on the average taxpayer and restrictive of free enterprise. Reflecting this new orthodoxy, the Conservatives argued that the state should not participate directly in the economy but simply provide favourable conditions for the private sector to achieve. The new direction of Conservative economic policy would place far greater faith in the free market and put more onus on individual Canadians' own initiatives to create a better life for themselves.[5] The Conservatives, therefore, offered to cut taxes, reduce the size of the federal civil service, minimize government regulatory activity and turn numerous crown corporations over to the private sector.[6] The Conservatives promised nothing short, in the words of John Crosbie, of "a new era in the economic and financial affairs of this country — an era of new realism and an economic climate to provide improved opportunities and incentives for Canadians."[7]

The PetroCanada issue, in particular, demonstrated the fundamental differences in the economic approaches of the parties. PetroCan had been established by a minority Liberal government under pressure from the NDP, which proposed that a public corporation in the petroleum industry was a necessary counterbalance to the power of giant multinational oil companies and a means to achieve Canadian ownership in a vital resource sector. While at first resisting the idea, the Liberals became increasingly reliant on the crown corporation as a means of penetrating the provincial jurisdiction over petroleum resources and opening new projects for the possible participation of Canadian capital. These goals were later firmly enshrined in the National Energy Programme. For the Conservatives, however, PetroCanada seemed to embody all that was wrong with the drift in postwar economic strategy — federal dominance over provincial jurisdiction and an unnecessary intrusion by the state into a field best left to the private sector. Thus, even though public opinion polls favoured the retention of the corporation in the public sphere, the Tories were determined to "privatize" it.

In addition to federal power and state intervention, the PetroCanada issue also reflected the third major area of interparty disagreement — the issue of economic nationalism. For most of the postwar period the Liberals had actively encouraged foreign, especially American, investment in Canada. This policy had facilitated the growth of a branch-plant manufacturing sector in central Canada and large scale ownership of key resources by U.S. interests. The Liberal party's continentalism was opposed by the NDP and by the Tories under the leadership of John Diefenbaker. By the late 1970s, however, the Liberals appeared to reverse their familiar continentalist orientation in favour of economic nationalism. Whether because of pressure from the political left, the force of public opinion or, more likely, the failure of the branch-plant economy to sustain employment, they adopted policies and established agencies designed to improve investment opportunities for Canadian capital. In contrast, the Conservatives perceived such regulatory instruments as the Foreign Investment Review Agency (FIRA) as unnecessary restrictions on the private sector. Discouraging foreign investment, they argued, was a luxury the economy could ill-afford.

Political parties constantly sort through issues, championing some and ignoring others, in order to gain electoral advantage. It is more difficult to explain why political parties change their orientations on such fundamental questions as the proper balance of federal power, the role of the state and economic nationalism. In the case of the Progressive Conservatives, their new direction may be viewed as part of the revival of conservatism in many western democracies and the rejection of the Keynesian state because of its apparent failure to live up to its promise of economic growth. This shift, however, cannot be separated from the politics of Canadian regionalism and the party's western support base. Western premiers, in recent years, have been major proponents of decentralization of the federal state's economic prerogatives, the free market system and foreign investment. The "twinned moods" of regionalism and conservatism have been manipulated by many western politicians, especially in Alberta, to protect provincially-oriented and often provincially-directed development strategies, strategies which often relied heavily on American investors and consumers, from the advances of the federal government.[8] Indeed, the Liberals were not beyond intimating that the new economic orientation of the federal Tories was simply a capitulation to the demands of the province-builders and resource exporters.

It is not uncommon for political parties to give greater weight in their policy calculations to regions or groups from which they draw their electoral strength. The Liberal party, for example, is careful to adopt platforms which, at the very least, do not alienate their Quebec support base. Similarly, the Conservatives' new orientations may reflect their reading of the demands and aspirations of what is increasingly their bastion of electoral support, the prairies. The question is whether the partisan policy differences observed at the elite level in recent years also characterize the electorate.

Policy Cleavages Between and Within the Major Federal Parties

There is little research examining the policy preferences of the Canadian electorate. Perhaps this is because early voting studies found the electorate confused about the respective policy positions of the federal parties and far less issue-oriented than political elites.[9] These findings, however, may have reflected the lack of coherent policy options presented to the electorate in a typical federal election. A more recent analysis of public opinion polls in the 1949-1975 period indicates that policy cleavages exist in the Canadian electorate and, more relevant to our present discussion, partisan disagreement over economic and social policy has increased during the postwar period while regional differences have declined.[10]

In this brief analysis of Canadian public opinion we will be concerned with the questions of whether the current debate over economic strategy among party elites is reflected in the electorate and second, whether mass policy preferences are primarily partisan or regional in origin. These questions are explored with survey data collected from 3475 Canadians in the period between April and July of 1979.[11] The questionnaire incorporated a number of items which relate to the issues discussed above. In particular, a question concerning whether the federal or provincial governments should have more power in Confederation addresses directly the issues of decentralization of federal powers. Two questions pertaining to inflation and two questions referring to government intervention in the private sector tap the neo-conservative undercurrents of the 1979 and 1980 federal campaigns. Finally, there is an item concerning American investment which will serve as a partial measure for the economic nationalism issue.

The degree to which Liberal and Conservative voters disagree on each of these issues is displayed in Table 1. The survey results indicate a substantial

TABLE 1   **Partisan Differences in Mass Attitudes Toward Selected Economic Issues
(% in Agreement)**

	(Federal Party Support)	
	Liberal	*Conservative*
1) Provincial governments should have more power.	31.5% (346)	43.8% (345)
2) Inflation is most serious economic problem.	34.9% (434)	46.0% (403)
3) Government policies cause inflation.	39.7% (459)	57.4% (467)
4) Government should leave big business alone.	22.3% (251)	28.7% (229)
5) Government should leave energy to the private sector.	28.0% (323)	36.6% (295)
6) Foreign investment is good for the economy.	52.2% (597)	44.0% (362)

degree of conformity between the positions put forward by party elites at the end of the decade and the policy preferences of their supporters.[12] While the depth of the policy cleavages among the voters vary by issue, those favouring the Progressive Conservatives in 1979 were more likely than Liberal voters to agree that provincial governments should have more power, that inflation is the most serious economic problem and that government policies are inflationary. They also were more likely to adopt a free enterprise position, agreeing that government should leave big business alone and energy in the hands of the private sector. The only inconsistency with expectations was that Liberal voters were more likely than Conservatives to agree that foreign investment is good for the economy. The Liberal party's recent foray into the unfamiliar terrain of economic nationalism, it would seem, was not clearly reflected in its electoral constituency in 1979.

The survey results indicate an approximate organization of Canadian voters along a left-right continuum with the Liberals to the left of the Conservatives. The fit, however, is not perfect. While Conservative voters were more likely than Liberals to endorse positions consistent with the political right, the majority of Conservative voters do not appear to accept the fundamental tenets of neo-conservatism. For example, only 29 percent of Conservative voters rejected outright government regulation of big business and a minority, 37 percent, felt government should withdraw from the energy sector. Similarly, less than half felt provincial governments should have more power. These findings, then, lend some support to the argument that the Clark administration did not have a solid electoral foundation from which to pursue some of its more conservative policy initiatives, especially those with a free enterprise orientation.[13]

TABLE 2 **Strength of Partisan and Regional Differences in Mass Attitudes Toward Selected Economic Issues (Cramer's V)**

Issues	Party	Region	Issues	Party	Region
1) Provincial Power	.14*	.21*	4) Free Business	.13*	.09
2) Inflation	.09	.29*	5) Energy	.08	.11*
3) Government Inflationary	.12*	.14*	6) Foreign Investment	.11*	.12*

*p. < . 05

We have found that Conservative voters tend to take more conservative postures than Liberal voters in the issue areas examined here, areas where one might expect more Conservative support. Our previous discussion, however, suggests that voters in different regions of the country might also take different positions on these items. To what extent, then, is region more important than party preferences in determining the policy preferences of Canadian voters? The relative importance of region and partisanship in explaining variations in policy preference can be inferred from the measures of association displayed in Table 2. Their magnitude indicates the degree of disagreement among the sample on each item: first, on the basis of their party preference, and second, on the basis of their region of residence.[14] While neither party nor region explain a great deal of the variation in the sample, region appears to take precedence over party in most cases. Party preference is marginally more important than region in explaining which voters are most likely to endorse a free enterprise orientation, but region is more important in understanding the sample's disagreement over the question of provincial power, inflation and government activity in the energy sector. Thus, while the statistics are not as conclusive as we might like, these findings suggest that there are regionally-based cleavages within both parties.

The measures of association in Table 3 are approximate indicators of the degree to which each party's electoral support base is riddled with regional policy cleavages. Liberal supporters are more divided among themselves

TABLE 3 **Regional Divisions within Partisan Electorates on Selected Economic Issues (Cramer's V)**

Issues	Party Supporters		Issues	Party Supporters	
	Liberal	P.C.		Liberal	P.C.
1) Provincial Power	.20*	.17*	4) Free Business	.05	.09
2) Inflation	.34*	.20*	5) Energy	.10*	.12*
3) Government Inflationary	.11*	.12*	6) Foreign Investment	.11*	.10*

*p. < . .05

than Conservative voters on the question of whether inflation is the most serious economic problem facing Canada and slightly more divided on the provincial power option. Regional cleavages within each party's electorate are more or less of equal strength with respect to government as a source of inflation, government involvement in the energy sector and foreign investment. Both parties, in short, house regional policy cleavages.

Space does not permit us to examine the region by region responses of both party electorates on these issues. On the question of increased provincial power, however, voters from Quebec and the prairie provinces, regardless of party preference, were more likely to endorse the provincial power option. Western voters were more likely to worry about inflation and see government as inflationary while Quebec voters were least likely to agree that government should not intrude on big business or the energy sector. Overall, the orientations of Quebec voters and, to a lesser extent, prairie voters, account for much of the regional variation within each party's electorate.

Since regionalism is a pervasive force in Canadian politics, it is hardly surprising to note that the electorate houses geographically-based policy cleavages. Nevertheless, the nature of these cleavages pose unique dilemmas for the strategists of each party. The different policy orientations of Quebec voters, for example, are not too threatening to the Progressive Conservatives, at least in the short run, because of the party's electoral weakness in the province. Parties can and often do "write off" the demands of regions which hold no promise of electoral momentum. Party unity and electoral fortunes can be jeopardized, however, when two or more regions from which a party draws the bulk of its electoral strength disagree about fundamental policy objectives. To what extent, then, do the regional constituencies upon which each party is dependent for electoral survival disagree in their policy preferences?

In order to address this question, we will exclude Liberal voters in the prairie provinces and Conservative voters in Quebec from our calculations. Table 4 shows how much, on average, (in percentage) Liberal and Conservative voters residing in regions where their party is electorally competitive

TABLE 4 **Mean Regional Variations in Partisan Attitudes Toward Selected Economic Issues (In Percentage)**

Issues	Party Supporters		Issues	Party Supporters	
	Liberal	P.C.		Liberal	P.C.
1) Provincial Power	9.9	5.7	4) Free Business	1.8	1.2
2) Inflation	12.6	5.3	5) Energy	3.7	3.7
3) Government Inflationary	8.2	4.9	6) Foreign Investment	7.0	5.3

disagree among themselves on key policy issues. The results of this analysis give us a quite different impression of the nature of regionally-based policy cleavages within each party's electoral constituency. Progressive Conservative voters in regions of that party's strength are quite similar in their policy preferences. P.C. voters in the prairie provinces differ from those in Ontario, in particular, on the question of provincial power, but the average deviation in percentages across all regions excluding Quebec is only 5.7 percent.[15] Most of the remaining issues examined here have been interpreted as a basis for conflict between Ontario and the West. It is noteworthy, therefore, that Conservative voters do not demonstrate much disagreement on them cross-regionally. Although we found little basis for a rigid neo-conservatism among Conservative voters in 1979, clearly there are electoral foundations in the electorate outside Quebec for a moderate cross-regional conservative coalition.

Liberal voters are more deeply divided among themselves than Conservatives on each of the six policy questions even when the responses of prairie Liberals are excluded. As might be expected, the source of this disagreement is Quebec. Liberals in that province were much more likely than their counterparts elsewhere to support the options of provincial power and foreign investment but less likely to be concerned about inflation or see government as its cause. These findings point to a strategic dilemma for the Liberal party. Quebec is unique in its ethnic composition and cultural concerns and the party often makes appeals to it on that basis. However, it also differs from other regions in terms of its policy preferences. The Liberal party in the late 1970s appears to have been in the rather difficult position of countering the Progressive Conservatives' policies favouring decentralization and foreign investment even though their major voting block favoured these options.[16] Nevertheless, Quebec voters, regardless of party preference, were discernably further to the left than voters elsewhere on the remaining issues. The Tories' package of decentralization and conservatism did not fit the pattern of decentralization and liberal policy orientations in Quebec.

Summary

This analysis of public opinion data indicates that the electorates of the Liberal and Progressive Conservative parties in 1979 were marginally divided on the questions of federal power and the proper role of the state in the economy. Overall, Conservative voters were more likely to endorse decentralist and conservative policy options. The data, however, do not demonstrate that the Progressive Conservative party had cultivated a solid electoral constituency for its more conservative, anti-Keynesian policy initiatives. The majority of Conservative voters surveyed did not believe that government should leave big business alone or vacate the energy sector. Moreover, the majority did not think that provincial governments should have more power within Confederation. The Clark government, therefore, may have misread its mandate in 1979.

Our analysis also indicates that region is more important than party preference in explaining, if only partially, the different positions of Canadian voters on these issues. In this respect, the new policy orientations of the Conservative party were more compatible with the preferences of its prairie electoral support base.[17] Studies of Canadian voting behaviour have not ruled decisively on how heavily issues weigh in the calculus of federal elections, especially those in which the major parties appear to offer fundamental policy alternatives. If they do count, however, our findings suggest that the Tories will have to change more than their leadership in order to make significant inroads in Quebec. While Quebec voters favour decentralization, they also are in substantial agreement about the propriety of government intervention. The complex task of resolving the conflicting policy orientations of the West and Quebec under the umbrella of a single federal party has proved increasingly problematic for the Liberal party in recent years. The results presented here indicate that the task will be no less difficult for the Conservatives.

ENDNOTES

1. Donald V. Smiley, "Canada and the Quest for a National Policy," *Canadian Journal of Political Science*, Vol. III, No. 1, p. 47.
2. For a discussion see Rick Ogmundson, "On the Measurement of Party Class Positions: The Case of Canadian Federal Political Parties," in R. Schultz, O. Kruhlak and J. Terry, *The Canadian Political Process*, 3rd ed. (Toronto: Holt, Rinehart and Winston, 1979) pp. 192-203, especially 194.
3. James Laxer, *Canada's Economic Strategy* (Toronto: Lorimer, 1980), p. 9.
4. John Courtney, "Campaign Strategy and Electoral Victory: The Progressive Conservatives and The 1979 Election," in H. Penniman, ed., *Canada at the Polls, 1979 and 1980: A Study of the General Elections* (Washington: American Enterprise Institute for Public Policy Research, 1980), p. 148.
5. Michael Prince, "The Tories and the NDP: Alternative Governments or Ad Hoc Advocates," in B. Doern, ed. *How Ottawa Spends: The Liberals, the Opposition and Federal Priorities* (Toronto: James Lorimer, 1983), p. 45.
6. William Irvine, "Epilogue: The 1980 Election," in Penniman, *Canada at the Polls*, p. 342.
7. John Crosbie, Budget Speech, as quoted in Jeffrey Simpson, *Discipline of Power* (Toronto: Personal Library, 1980), p. 19.
8. Laxer, *Canada's Economic Strategy*, p. 21.
9. John Meisel, *Working Papers in Canadian Politics* (Montreal: McGill-Queens University Press, 1972), Chap. 2.
10. R. Simeon and D. Blake, "Regional Preferences: Citizen Views of Public Policy," in R. Simeon and D. Blake, eds., *Small Worlds: Provinces and Parties in Canadian Political Life* (Toronto: Methuen, 1980), pp. 77-105.

11. A complete description of the data collection project is in Bryn Greer-Wootten and Bharat Patel, *Sampling the Quality of Life in Canada: A Design Report for the National and Panel Studies* (Toronto: Institute for Behavioural Research, York University, 1978). The survey was administered by the Survey Research Centre of the Institute for Behavioural Research at York University in cooperation with the Centre de Sondage at the Université de Montréal.

12. Party supporters were determined by the following question: If a federal election were held today, which party's candidate do you think you would favour?

13. Simpson, *Discipline of Power*, xii, *passim*.

14. The sample was divided into five regions - Atlantic, Quebec, Ontario, Prairies and B.C.

15. Some 50.7% of P.C. voters in the prairies endorsed provincial power compared to 34.4% in Ontario.

16. Among Quebec Liberals, 43.1% favoured provincial power and 57.8% saw foreign investment as good.

17. Among prairie P.C.s, 51% supported the option of provincial power; 53% saw inflation as the most serious economic issue and 56% saw government as inflationary. Some 43% thought government should leave energy to the private sector.

8 Limits on Policy-Making by Social Democratic Parties*†

KEVIN EDWARDS

North American politics is dominated by what have come to be known as brokerage political parties. A brokerage party attempts to present as non-ideological an appearance as possible, occupying the middle ground of the political spectrum. Such a middle-of-the-road party has no clear ideological position: it may lean to the left on one issue and to the right on another, with both positions being variable over time. By promoting and presenting such an image the brokerage party hopes to draw majority support; then it hopes to attract a great enough proportion of these interests to defeat the other contending parties.

There are two basic arguments for why brokerage political parties have developed. The first says such parties exist because the North American economic elite finds them a useful tool for breaking down class barriers, thereby having elections, and politics generally, fought on other than class lines. The contrary argument suggests that the growth of brokerage political parties is simply a pragmatic response to the needs of a diverse electorate, an electorate that includes not only economic interests, but also linguistic, ethnic, religious and, perhaps most significantly, geographical interests. The truth probably lies somewhere between these two positions.

The third party cannot ignore the brokerage tradition, and it remains an important political consideration. This can best be seen in the growth of social democratic parties (CCF/NDP). There is a need for the third party to pick up the opposition slack, so to speak.[1] The fact that a third party is able to become "a real contender" does not mean the end of the brokerage party system, for these third parties have often drawn support from a wide base and have in fact acted as brokerage parties. Support may come from the generally disaffected, but they represent many different groups. Third party movements do not threaten the brokerage party tradition, they simply become an adjunct to it.

---

* Reprinted from *Provincial Policy-Making: Comparative Essays*, by permission of the editor, Donald C. Rowat, Department of Political Science, Carleton University, ISBN, 07709-0112-3.

† This essay was written while Kevin Edwards was a graduate student at Carleton University.

Social democratic parties stand in contrast to this, apparently because they claim a class base of support. Thus, it is hard for them to reconcile themselves with the brokerage party tradition which denies a class basis to politics. However, a closer examination of social democratic parties reveals that they do come to terms with brokerage politics.

While a social democratic party may maintain its policy distinctiveness in opposition the question of what happens to it once it gains power must inevitably be asked. Does a social democratic party maintain this policy distinctiveness or does it alter its position and, if so, why? The only evidence of this is provided by the various provinces which have elected social demo- cratic governments. We will examine this evidence later, but first let us look at social democratic parties as they rise to power and the effect the achievement of such power has on their policy positions.

Historically, the social democratic movement in Canada has had to alter its ideological position in order to gain support. This was certainly the case with the CCF. Between 1936 and 1938 the CCF dropped all use of the word "socialism" from its campaign literature in an attempt to appear less radical.[2] As the CCF moved closer to the ideological middle it ceased to be the butt of attack from all other parties.[3] It was as if, in the eyes of its opponents, it had crossed the threshold to acceptability.

By 1944 the CCF in Saskatchewan was arguing for the nationalization of natural resource industries only, whereas previously it had held that it was necessary to socialize the banking, credit and financial systems as well.[4] Among other things, the party dropped the idea of land nationalization, increased its emphasis on social security, scrapped plans to eliminate class biases in the educational system, and developed a complete "labour and trade union policy."[5] In 1944, the CCF gained power for the first time — largely, it would seem, on the basis of its compromised position. In other words, a social democratic party that is successful is one that does not challenge the brokerage party system but simply becomes part of it. The CCF could no longer carry on a systematic attack on capitalism and all its institutions. The party had become largely a farmers' pressure group seek- ing to win agrarian reforms.[6]

This analysis is also applicable to the Saskatchewan NDP today; indeed, it could even be extended. Looking at the joint venture approach to resource development, it becomes apparent that the NDP government has actually aligned itself with the multi-national enterprises which it strove in its early years strictly to control.

Clearly this role for a social democratic party involves many contradic- tions, the most obvious being its alignment with the financial interests it was supposed to shackle. However, it also represents part of a shift to the middle of the road in ideological terms. There is certainly nothing unique about limited government involvement in an extractive industry. The Con- servatives in Alberta and the Liberals in Ottawa are directly involved in various such projects (i.e. the tar sands and Petro-Canada in its exploration ventures).

The NDP government in Manitoba (1969-77) also made it clear that a social democratic party has to compromise its ideological position once it gains power. In an examination of NDP expenditures in Manitoba, James McAlister found that there were no significant differences from the pattern of expenditure of the previous Conservative government; even though the size of the budget increased, the growth rate was not significantly larger than that under the Conservatives.[7]

In all, NDP governments have shown a tendency, once they gain power, to become more conservative. This is not to say that they completely abandon their social democratic ideals. It is simply that socialist parties often compromise in an effort to gain the acceptance and support of as many sectors of society as possible. In other words, they come to terms with the realities of the brokerage politics tradition in Canada.

Of course, it should be realized that social democratic governments do not move into the "mainstream" purely of their own accord. It is not simply that they feel this would advance their position in electoral terms. Much of the move is in response to factors in their environment, factors which they must deal with. Since brokerage politics is the norm, it sets basic intangible boundaries within which political activity and policy-making are judged acceptable. Working within these boundaries, social democratic parties cease to be the butt of attack by all other political actors as they shift from radical positions to ones within acceptable limits.

Social democratic governments are forced to conform, and are limited in their policy-making, by both the structure of federal-provincial financial arrangements and the nature of the financial system itself. When the federal government introduces a shared-cost programme or makes funds available for any particular area, it necessarily shapes provincial policy. For example, if the federal government were willing to pay fifty per cent of the cost of schooling in bilingual districts, it would be difficult for a province to refuse, even though this might divert funds from an area which was a priority of a social democratic government. Of course, such effects are the same for all provincial governments, but they are likely to affect a social democratic government more, particularly if it is committed to policies of radical reform.[8]

The social democratic government is also in a dependent position within the financial system. A provincial government does not have control of its own money supply. Thus, if it wishes to raise short-term financing it must go to the financial markets: Bay and Wall streets. If the government hopes to secure such financing it must maintain its credit rating with these institutions.[9] Given this dependence it is difficult for any social democratic government to move in radical policy directions, for to do so could jeopardize the short-term financing it requires to carry out its day-to-day business. This is so because those same financial interests would be the ones hurt most by any radical schemes.

Given its dependence on federal and financial market revenue sources, it is clear that a social democratic government becomes severely restricted in its policy options. Of course, it should be remembered that it still has the option of not "playing ball" with these interests, but that would probably spell suicide for the party, as most government services would deteriorate and give the opposition ample fuel with which to fight an election.

Another factor restricting a social democratic government's policy options is the bureaucracy with which it must deal. Without bringing about wholesale personnel changes, the social democratic government must deal with the bureaucracy established by its predecessors, which is usually conservative in outlook.[10] The most important group within the bureaucracy as far as policy development goes is obviously the bureaucratic elite. If it is not substantially changed, one could expect little change in the policy options that would be placed before a minister, however radical that minister might be.

A social democratic government is also limited by its identity. Where a Liberal, Conservative or Social Credit government would not flinch at taking certain actions, a social democratic government must be aware that adverse reaction may result, simply because the act was carried out by a "social democratic" government. This could easily be exploited by the party's opponents; for instance, by means of "red scare" tactics, though such an attack might be totally unwarranted.[11]

In the final analysis what emerges is a picture of social democratic parties gaining support within society once they have conformed to the basic limits of the political system. Such a party is then able to grow in prestige and credibility in the eyes of the electorate and may finally achieve power. However, all the time it is gaining support among the electorate it is becoming entangled in the system, owing more and more individuals and groups for their support. This debt necessarily limits the policy options open to a social democratic government. It has surrendered, to a greater or lesser extent, its policy distinctiveness. The party becomes locked into the whole structure of the economic and political system and cannot move without losing its base of support. It is thus brought within the fold of brokerage political parties.

ENDNOTES

1. M. Pinard, *The Rise of a Third Party* (Montreal: McGill-Queen's University Press, 1975).
2. S.M. Lipset, *Agrarian Socialism* (Berkeley: University of California Press, 1959), pp. 109-110.
3. *Ibid.*, p. 113.
4. *Ibid.*, p. 132.
5. *Ibid.*, p. 151.

6. *Ibid.*, p. 113.
7. J.A. McAlister, "The Fixed Analysis of Policy Outputs", *Canadian Public Administration* Vol. 23, no. 3 (1980), p. 466.
8. J.A. McAlister, *Social Democracy: The New Democratic Party Government of Manitoba, 1969-1977*, Ph. D. Thesis, Carleton University, Dept. of Political Science, 1979, p. 291.
9. *Ibid.*, p. 295.
10. *Ibid.*, p. 234.
11. *Ibid.*, p. 339.

9 The National Party Convention

J. LELE, G.C. PERLIN AND H.G. THORBURN

The respective leadership conventions of the Progressive Conservatives in 1967, the Liberals in 1968 and the New Democratic Party in 1971 have all been cited as evidence of progress toward more open and democratic intra-party politics in Canada. Proponents of this view may be found among experienced journalists, dedicated party politicians and academics alike. Their argument focuses upon the democratic forms of leader selection by convention. They emphasize the election of constituency delegates, the efficacy of the secret ballot in freeing delegates from exposure to manipulative pressures and the openness and genuine competitiveness of the convention campaign in which candidates seek to win votes by exposing their personalities and views, not just to the voting delegates during the convention itself, but to the electorate at large.

This argument can be challenged on at least three important grounds. First, the delegates at each of the three conventions were representative of the more privileged groups in Canadian society. They resembled neither the mass of Canadian society nor the respective party's supporters in the 1968 general election. Second, convention rules continued to afford a position of relative advantage to the elite representing the establishment within each party. Third, up until the moment of balloting, opportunities for widespread manipulation were utilized by candidates and their agents.

We shall attempt to demonstrate these three points with evidence we have gathered in studying each of the three party conventions. Our research data consists of more than 3,000 completed questionnaires gathered in post-convention mailings, personal interviews with more than 100 senior party members and key informants, and an analysis of documents related to each of the conventions.

The Background

All three of these conventions were, at least in part, the result of the declining power and effectiveness of party leaders both within and outside their parties. The Progressive Conservative convention was held in September of 1967 after four years of open controversy in the party over the leadership of John Diefenbaker. Following the defeat of the Progressive Conservative government at the polls in 1963, unrest with Diefenbaker's leadership, previously confined largely to the federal cabinet, spread to the party outside parliament and resulted in a succession of attempts to oust him. In 1966, Dalton Camp, President of the National Progressive Conservative Association, campaigned for re-appraisal of the leadership, with the result that after a deeply divisive internal conflict, the 1966 annual meeting of the Association directed the national executive to call a leadership convention before the end of 1967.

The convention met in Toronto and, after five ballots, chose Robert Stanfield, the Premier of Nova Scotia. Stanfield's opponents included John Diefenbaker himself, who withdrew after three ballots, Duff Roblin, the Premier of Manitoba, and six former members of the federal cabinet: E.D. Fulton, George Hees, Alvin Hamilton, Wallace McCutcheon, Donald Fleming and Michael Starr.

The Liberal convention of 1968 was held under less controversial circumstances. Lester B. Pearson, who had served as leader since 1958 and as Prime Minister since the Liberal win in the 1963 election, announced in December 1967 that he wished to retire as party leader. Accordingly, a convention was called to be held in Ottawa during the first week of April 1968. Pierre Elliott Trudeau, Pearson's Justice Minister, won on the fourth ballot. Trudeau defeated six cabinet colleagues: Robert Winters, John Turner, Paul Hellyer, Paul Martin, J.J. Green, Allan MacEachen and a former Quebec minister, Eric Kierans. Another candidate, Mitchell Sharpe, then Minister of Finance, withdrew before the convention and announced his support for Trudeau.

The New Democratic Party convention was called in April 1971 on the retirement of T.C. (Tommy) Douglas, who had been elected the first leader of the party in the 1961 convention. In the election of 1968 that swept the Liberal government of Pierre Trudeau to power with a strong majority, Douglas lost his seat in the Commons. He later gained a seat in parliament through a by-election. Although Douglas received a vote of confidence from the delegates to the NDP national convention in Winnipeg in October 1969, he indicated before the next regular national meeting in Ottawa in 1971 that he would not run again.

Five candidates contested the party's leadership at the Ottawa gathering. There was little doubt, however, that David Lewis was the front-runner. He had been a member of the National Executive of the CCF for more than 20 years and an NDP member of parliament for more than six years at the time of his election. Two of his opponents, Ed Broadbent and Frank Howard, were also members of parliament. The other two candidates, John Harney and James Laxer, had never contested public office for the party. Despite Lewis' edge, it took him four ballots to win. His main rival was Laxer, leader of the radical Waffle faction.

Delegates: Socioeconomic Base

Delegates to each of the three conventions were drawn from a strikingly narrow socioeconomic base. Not one of these three delegations is representative either of the Canadian population as a whole or of those persons claiming to identify with each respective party. This fact holds true over each of the three standard measures of socioeconomic status: income, education and occupation (see Table 1).

Almost 60 percent of the New Democrats and 70 percent of each of the Liberals and Progressive Conservatives reported family incomes exceeding $10,000 a year. This income group constituted only 16 percent of the sample interviewed in Professor John Meisel's survey of the national electorate in 1968. More than 40 percent of the Liberals and Conservatives reported incomes of $15,000 or more and almost 30 percent of the NDP delegates showed similar incomes. In contrast, just five percent of the Meisel sample fell in this income bracket. What is perhaps more remarkable is that this high income group represents only five percent of the Liberal and Progressive Conservative identifiers and only one percent of the NDP identifiers.

If we look at the income data from the other end of the scale the results are equally striking. Although 40 percent of the Meisel sample reported earnings of less than $5,000 in 1968, only eight percent of the Liberal and Conservative delegates and just 12 percent of the New Democrats placed themselves in this group.

The occupational distribution of the delegate samples reflects a similar bias. Compared to the Canadian population (in the Meisel survey) professional or executive occupations are over-represented among NDP delegates by 24 percentage points and among Liberal and Progressive Conservative delegates, by 46 and 48 percent respectively. The middle-class bias of each party is further demonstrated by the under-representation of workers. Even among NDP delegates, both skilled and unskilled workers are under-represented, albeit not nearly so badly as among the delegates of the other two parties. The under-representation of skilled and unskilled laborers among the New Democrats contrasts both with the party's image as a working-class party and with the substantially higher working-class representation among its identifiers.

Not surprisingly, the delegates reported a significantly higher level of education than the Canadian population as a whole. About 60 percent of the Liberals and Conservatives and about 50 percent of the New Democrats reported some education past high school. Over 40 percent of the Liberals and Conservatives and just over 30 percent of the New Democrats held at least one university degree. Available data suggest that the proportion of the general Canadian population that had post-high school training at that time was only about 14 percent. The proportion that held a university degree was only seven percent. Furthermore, only ten percent of the Conservative identifiers in 1968, 14 percent of the Liberal identifiers and 14 percent of the NDP identifiers had received any education beyond the high school level. Not more than seven percent of these people reported having university degrees.

While not denying the relative differences that exist between the parties, these collective characteristics of the delegates are consistent with our expectations. Studies of American convention delegates have repeatedly shown that the degree of political activism varies directly with socioeconomic status. Thus our data show that each of these three sets of convention delegates is weighted away from both the population as a whole and their respective party identifiers in the general electorate. Our major concern at this stage is to deal with the claim that the convention process effects broad participation, either from party supporters or the society at large. It is clear that it does not. In short, if the openness of these conventions is to be judged by their effectiveness in providing proximate representation to the main body of interests in Canadian society, they were clearly unsuccessful.

Rule-making for the Conventions

Our second point is that convention rules and practices both ensure a position of advantage to party elites. The evidence suggests that each of the three political parties has built rules and procedures into the process of delegate selection that give a disproportionate influence to the party establishment.

Historically, as Senator Richard Stanbury, past president of the Liberal Federation of Canada has pointed out, this was the accepted practice in the Liberal party. Up until 1958, "the Party was a Cabinet-run party, with Cabinet Ministers having complete responsibility for organization, policy and finance. Conventions during that period were made up of delegates who were generally named by the leaders or their local agents, so that the results of the conventions generally depended upon sub-alliances of leaders at the conventions."[1] In 1965 the Liberal party passed a new constitution and formulated new rules for conventions. In light of this document, Stanbury claimed that, since 1968, the Liberal Federation of Canada had become substantially participatory and democratic. However, the party constitution still retains a substantial role for the party elite[2] at conventions.

Major officers of federal and provincial party associations, women's organizations and university clubs, MPs, senators and provincial MLAs are assured delegate status at all conventions as *ex officio* delegates. In 1968 they made up 35 percent of the total delegate body at the convention. Furthermore, ex officio delegates enjoy an advantage because of their continuous and intense participation in party affairs. The disproportionate role of the party elite has not gone unnoticed. In 1968, for example, the Hull Federal Liberal Association moved an amendment to the federation's constitution, which read in part: "whereas, the number of ex-officio delegates is too numerous compared to elected delegates; whereas, certain federal districts have a very large membership; it is proposed that the number of elected delegates be twenty per federal electoral district...."[3]

While the Liberals wrote the rules for convention representation into their constitution, the calling and administration of conventions in the Progressive Conservative constitution was, until 1967, left entirely to their national executive. According to the Progressive Conservative constitution, in effect in 1967, the members of the national party elite who sat on the executive were empowered to set the time and place for the convention, to establish rules for its conduct, to decide how delegates would be apportioned and to adjudicate the credentials of delegates. In other words, the executive, acting through the authority of the Convention Committee, had the specific power to define the scope of mass participation at the convention. Following the precedents of every other convention in the party's history,[4] it used this power to protect the position of the party establishment by creating a broadly defined category of ex officio delegates, and a category of elite-appointed delegates-at-large. Some 23 percent of the total delegate body was made up of ex officio delegates and 23 percent was made up of delegates-at-large. Thus, elected delegates accounted for only 54 percent. (Subsequent revisions to the constitution have established specific rules of representation but ex officio delegates and delegates-at-large still constitute a substantial minority.)

This tempering of intra-party democracy met with very little opposition within the Conservative Convention Committee in 1967. No one questioned or apparently thought to question the creation of ex officio delegates,[5] while such discussion as there was of delegates-at-large focused mainly upon the method of their selection.[6]

The appointment of delegates-at-large is certainly not unique to Canadian leadership conventions. They have been widely used at American national party conventions where, as David, Goldman and Bain observe, they "often represent a special form of patronage and recognition...[and] provide leaders who can represent [state delegations] in negotiations with other delegations, convention managers and candidates".[7] Informants claim that these delegates play a similar role in the structure of the Progressive Conservative party. Fundraisers, substantial contributors to the party and very active members without official positions could be assured of participation as delegates-at-large. Furthermore, such appointments were used to find positions on the convention floor for key members of candidates' organizations.[8]

The New Democratic Party has made the national convention and regular leadership selection a fundamental cornerstone of its constitution. The

NDP has often pointed out proudly that the party in convention is the "supreme governing body" by constitutional provision. The party holds a convention every two years, at which time policy is determined, the constitution confirmed and the leader selected for a further two-year term.

About 16 percent of the 1971 convention delegation was made up of ex officio delegates holding positions comparable to their counterparts in the other two parties. These were members of the federal council of the party, members of the caucus, NDP Youth representatives and appointees of central labor bodies. Affiliated local groups accounted for nearly 500 of the 1,740 accredited delegates. This latter group of delegates falls into a class somewhere between ex officio and delegates-at-large. They are representatives of groups which hold affiliate memberships under the provisions of the constitution. Informants report that the selection of these delegates often reflected the will of local union leaders and those above them in the union hierarchies. Together, ex officio and affiliated local representatives constituted some 44 percent of the total delegate registration.[9]

The presence of a large proportion of ex officio delegates or delegates-at-large does not in itself constitute evidence of elite control of the convention outcome (at least in terms of who will win). We have not attempted to argue that there is an absence of competition among the members of the Canadian party elites. We do assert, however, that if party elites wish to influence the selection of the convention winner they are well placed to do so. But the fact still remains that somewhere between 60 and 70 percent of the respective conventions were chosen at the constituency level. It is at this level of the grass roots of the party constituency associations that elitism and privilege must be demonstrated in order to sustain our argument.

Constituency Delegations: Elite Manipulation

The guarantee of an independent mass voice in each convention was assumed to be afforded by the "election" of a majority of the delegates at meetings in constituencies. In fact, the extent to which this guarantee was honored varied widely from constituency to constituency because the rules under which the elections were conducted exposed them to manipulation.

The sole requirement for participation in a constituency election in the case of the Conservatives was the possession of a party membership card. These were supposed to have been purchased for one dollar, but often were made available free. There was no other prerequisite, not even a minimum length of time set on membership. Thus new voters could be (and were) marshalled even as a meeting was in progress. In some ridings, candidate organizations took advantage of this situation to ensure the election of committed delegates. More commonly, local party notables were able to ensure that they themselves were chosen as delegates.

In the case of the Liberal party, the qualifications for participation in constituency elections varied from riding to riding. Some required at least 90 days of party membership, while in others there was no minimum condition of any sort. This lack of consistency does not seem to have deterred candidate organizations in their efforts to pack constituency meetings. The practice actually appears to have been more widespread in the Liberal party. As one of the organizers for Hellyer put it, "The general technique was to study the rules and to figure out how to get around them.... One came to expect this sort of thing, the packing of meetings in politics and we didn't get too shocked about it." Evidence from key informants suggests that successful efforts to manipulate constituency elections in this way were made by every major candidate's organization. This is not to suggest that members of the national party elite (as members of candidate organizations) directly packed these meetings themselves. Information from interviews suggests that this was done through local party elites who were "familiar with the territory".

In the New Democratic Party the regulation of the constituency meetings choosing delegates to the national convention is up to the provincial party. The practices of delegate manipulation and the packing of meetings at the constituency level appear to be least widespread in the New Democratic Party. However, almost half of the delegates in our sample reported that less than one third of the members of their constituency association or affiliated group were in attendance when they were selected. In the NDP, poorly publicized meetings seem to have been more common than in the other two parties, with somewhat the same result as the Liberal and Conservative practice of packing meetings. Informants suggest that this is particularly so in the case of the affiliated groups, which sent almost a third of the total delegates to the convention. Furthermore, more than half of the delegates elected by constituency and affiliate meetings reported that they were officers of their associations. In this respect the NDP closely resembles the Liberals, who reported over 60 percent of their constituency representatives as office-holders.[9] The fact that the Waffle group's substantial anti-establishment bid for the party leadership met with some success suggests that the NDP delegate selection process at the constituency level was equally open to manipulation by a well-organized group.

The evidence for all three parties is insufficient to permit accurate measurement of the number of genuinely open constituency elections, but the main point is clear: the election of constituency delegates could be and was, in a number of identifiable instances, an ineffective instrument of popular control of the party leadership. We have been able, in fact, to point to some evidence which suggests that quite the opposite is true. Constituency elections afford the elite an opportunity to effectively control the party rank and file. The rules are not structured in order to ensure the success of a particular establishment candidate so much as they work to minimize the probability that radical elements will mount a successful challenge to the establishment itself.

Summary

In summary, we hold that there are at least three reasons for doubting the claim that the leadership conventions are indicative of substantial progress towards a more open and participatory kind of party politics in Canada.We have been able to present some evidence to suggest that party elites protected their position at the conventions through their control of the convention rules and that both in terms of numbers and activism they were able to exercise disproportionate influence upon the convention process. We have also shown that the election of constituency delegates was subject to considerable manipulation, either by national or local elites.

Finally, our data demonstrate that the delegates to each convention substantially over-represented the most privileged socioeconomic groups in Canadian society. In response to this point, it may be argued that this simply reflects the basic cultural context of the Canadian political system. Lack of political participation by lower status groups may be explained by the culture factors of their lower sense of political efficacy, lower sense of satisfaction with the responses of governments and lower affect for the symbols of the system. It may be argued that within the limited context of the conventions there is very little that political parties can do to encourage greater participation by these groups. Defenders of these arguments claim that parties have made substantial efforts to overcome the problem by such devices as offering travel subsidies to delegates. In many cases, however, these expenses only cover a small portion of the cost. As one informant put it, "For a fisherman from New Brunswick, the cost of attending the Progressive Conservative convention would amount to a month's wages."

It seems clear to us that if the parties are sincere in their claims to want to open their decision-making processes, they must make far more radical reforms in their organization and procedures. Furthermore, they must accept the fact that more intra-party democracy entails a fundamental challenge to the interests and positions of the party establishment.

ENDNOTES

1.   R.J. Stanbury, *Liberal Party of Canada* (mimeo June 15, 1969), p. 3.
2.   We use the term "elite" to refer simply to those who hold power. Operationally, we define the elite in a party as those who hold party office or those who hold public office as a consequence of their party role. It may be argued that the

operational definition excluded the "power-holders" who have no formal organizational role. In the context within which this paper is set, such power-holders, meaning fundraisers and providers of similar resources, could affect the outcome of the conventions only through the operationally defined elites.

3. Liberal Federation of Canada, *Constitutional Amendment* (no date), p. 20.

4. A thorough exposition of organization and procedure at earlier conventions is presented in Ruth M. Bell, "Conservative Party National Conventions 1927-1956," (Unpublished M.A. thesis, Carleton University, 1965).

5. Flora MacDonald, whose memorandum on the practice of past conventions was the basis for the delegate apportionment proposals made to the committee, says the suggestion that there should not be ex officio delegates, to her knowledge, was never considered. Miss MacDonald and other key informants who were asked about this point took the position that there were certain members of the party who, by virtue of the importance of their positions or the nature of their service were entitled to an assured place at the convention.

6. In an address to the opening of the Montmorency Conference in August 1967, E.A. Goodman, chairman of the 1967 convention executive committee, announced that all participants had been invited from outside party ranks, a point not lost on those opposing the delegate-at-large category. The party's national director, James Johnston, later wrote that he disapproved of the convention committee's practice of "assuming the right not only to set the rules of the game but then to try to play in the game itself." He went on to voice discontentment over "the establishment of the party having this power to perpetuate itself...." See James Johnston, *The Party's Over* (Don Mills: Longmans of Canada, 1971), p. 221.

7. Paul T. David, Ralph M. Goldman and Richard C. Bain, *The Politics of National Party Conventions* (Washington: Peter Smith, 1960), p. 194.

8. For example, Fulton's campaign manager, Lowell Murray, was appointed as a delegate-at-large from Ontario, although, except for the fact of living in Ottawa, he was not directly involved with the Ontario party.

9. John C. Courtney, *The Selection of National Party Leaders in Canada* (Toronto: Macmillan of Canada, 1973), p. 93. Courtney reports that 68 percent of the Liberal delegates in his sample had been or were currently holders of party offices.

10 The Decline of Party in Canada*

JOHN MEISEL

Some years ago, the Royal Winnipeg Ballet gave a command performance at the National Arts Centre in Ottawa to honor the King and Queen of Belgium. Balletomanes found it hard to buy tickets, however, because a very large proportion had been obtained by the Canadian and Belgian governments for free distribution to special guests. The *Globe and Mail's* comment on this event struck a note which is increasingly evident in Canadian coverage of politics:

> The ballet gala...provided an unintended demonstration of who really rates around Ottawa. The elected politicians — Canadian MPs and visiting legislators were invited to come (in lounge suits) for the ballet....Guests invited by External Affairs and the Governor General — mostly bureaucrats and diplomats — were invited to come in black tie and dinner jacket and stay for a champagne party.[1]

The incident is trivial and may be explainable in terms of an administrative slipup or in some other harmless way, but it does provide a picturesque reminder of the declining role of parliament and hence of party politics in Canada's political system.

Anthony King, in a searching paper analyzing the role of parties in liberal democracies, summarizes much of the relevant literature by listing six usually cited functions of parties: (1) structuring the vote; (2) integration and mobilization of the mass public; (3) recruitment of political leaders; (4) organization of government; (5) formation of public policy; and (6) aggregation of interests.[2] He notes that there is a good deal of imprecision in the manner in which political scientists deal with the roles of parties and that the importance of their functions tends to be exaggerated. Nevertheless, he concludes, parties are critical components of the political process and they need to be studied, albeit with greater precision than is often the case.

---

* This is a slightly revised version of a paper which appeared in the fourth edition of *Party Politics in Canada*.

This article shares King's view and, although it focuses on the relative decline of political parties in Canada, it should not be interpreted as arguing that the parties and the party system are insignificant. Parties clearly still influence critical aspects of politics and, most notably, they influence who occupies the government benches in parliament and who heads the various departments and ministries. The emphasis in this article is on federal politics, although many of the observations also apply to the provincial arena.

Parties still perform the first function listed: they structure the vote in most elections, except at the municipal level. They, to some measure, present options to the electorate about current issues and so can be said to organize mass opinion, although one is often tempted to conclude that they disorganize it. As for the related role of mobilizing the public, a remarkably high proportion of Canadians participates in elections in one way or another, and by no means just by voting. The preparation of electoral lists, staffing the polling booths, and organizing the campaigns on a polling division by polling-division basis all takes a great deal of effort, most of which is provided by volunteer activists. This not only enables the electoral process to function, it increases the public's knowledge of political questions and facts. It is well-established that a greater sense of partisan attachment is associated with a greater knowledge of politics.

Nevertheless, an increasing number of Canadians have sought to participate in politics and public life outside the framework of parties — in tenants' or neighborhood organizations or through voluntary associations, from unions to environmental or anti-nuclear groups. There was an upsurge of such "unconventional" politics in the sixties in the United States and to a lesser extent in Canada, but there is some uncertainty about the degree to which non-partisan politics has continued to flourish in North America in the seventies. Although the situation in Canada is a little ambiguous, there is no doubt that the proportion of people in the United States who identify with political parties in the sense that they think of themselves as Democrats or Republicans is steadily declining.

Parties also recruit politicians, although many question whether, in general, politics attracts a sufficiently high calibre of individuals. Data are unavailable on this point but some speculate that other careers appeal to the ablest Canadians and they conclude that we could do with a good deal more talent in the parties. This question raises another, also imperfectly understood puzzle: what characteristics make for a good politician? Indeed, what is a good politician?

By deciding which partisan team forms the government and who is in opposition, parties do organize government in an important way. But there is little doubt that a great many decisions about what is placed on the public agenda and at what time, are forced on political parties by events, non-political decision-makers and very often the preferences of powerful civil servants, whose responsibility to the politicians is increasingly more formal than real. Even the organization of the government — the way in which legislation is drafted and considered by the cabinet and its committees, the extent to which outside interests are consulted, the manner in which policies are administered — is more likely to reflect the wills of a small number of senior civil servants than the decision of senior party officials, including the ministers. It is indeed questionable whether the government party leader — the prime minister — continues to function as a party person after accession to power or whether the party role and influence are maintained as a successful administration becomes accustomed to power and develops close relationships with senior civil servants.

In short, one must ask whether the parties really play the central role liberal democratic theory ascribes to them in organizing government and in the formation of public policy. And, given the changes in communication and the importance of voluntary associations and interest groups, one wonders about the relative unimportance of parties in the processes which aggregate the interests of various individuals and groups into satisfactory policies.

In seeking to identify the main manifestations of, and reasons for, the decline of party, relative to other political factors, this essay distinguishes between long-run factors, most of which are universal in liberal democracies and appear to a greater or lesser extent in most highly industralized and post-industrial societies, and those which are of more recent origin and uniquely Canadian.

Long-run Reasons for Party Decline

Rise of the Bureaucratic State

Modern political parties evolved from small cliques of power-wielders when the extension of the franchise necessitated the organization of mass electorates. The greater participation of the public in political life led, in conjunction with other factors, to the emergence of the positive state — one which increasingly participated in virtually every aspect of the human experience. But the "ancestors" of our political institutions and the political parties serving them evolved at a time when governments were dealing with a limited range of problems, and when only a small minority of the population was politically active. Under these conditions parties were able to act as suitable links between the small electorate and the even smaller number of political decision-makers.

The continuous expansion of governmental activities has created mounting problems for the legislative and representative system. Up until the First World War, the Canadian parliament dealt with only a small number of issues, met seldom and required little specialized and technical knowledge to operate. Now the number and complexity of the areas in which the federal government operates are so vast that it is quite impossible for MPs to be abreast of what is going on. At best, each can become reasonably well-informed about one or two areas.

The expansion of government activities and the increasingly complicated nature of government decisions have reduced the capacity of elected officials to deal with many important public issues and necessitated the restructuring of many governmental institutions. Thus MPs and even cabinet ministers are often incapable of fully understanding the problems and options confronting them, and the normal structures of ministries is being supplemented by a large number of quasi-independent administrative, regulatory and judicial boards and commissions not directly responsible to the elected representatives of the public or to party politicians. In short, an important shift has occurred in the locus of power of liberal democracies, from elected politicians to appointed civil servants, whose links to political parties are indirect and increasingly tenuous. This means that parties, supposedly in control of the political process and responsible to the public for its performance, are often little more than impotent observers of processes they cannot control and the results of which they can only rubber stamp.

A good illustration is the case of irregularities in the sale of reactors by Atomic Energy of Canada Ltd., a crown corporation, to Argentina and Korea. There were strong suspicions that bribes had been paid and that the foreign exchange regulations of some countries had been violated. Enormous commissions were also allegedly paid to shadowy foreign agents. One of the reactors was sold at a loss of over 100 million dollars. The Public Accounts Committee of the House of Commons held extensive hearings and questioned closely Mr. J.L. Gray, president of Atomic Energy of Canada at the time of the sales. His stonewalling of the issue, and that by everyone else connected with the matter, was so effective that the House of Commons committee failed to shed light on the sales and finally had to let the case rest.

Pluralism and the Rise of Interest Group Politics

Before the expansion of governmental activities and the increase in their complexity, the usual pattern of lawmaking was relatively simple. Ministers or the whole cabinet, with or without prompting by their civil servants, decided on the broad outlines of what needed to be done. Civil servants, drawing on expert knowledge and advice, prepared the necessary background papers and draft proposals. These were discussed by the ministers, in the absence of their civil servant advisors,and ultimately presented to parliament for enactment. The basic decisions were essentially those of politicians and their officials. More recently, a more involved process of legislation has evolved, partly because of the need to deal with problems having enormous ramifications, partly in an effort to make government more participatory, and partly in response to the claims of a market-oriented, pluralist society in which political parties depend on the financial support of powerful economic interests or of unions. Before any law or important administrative decision is decided upon, an intense consultation between officials and representatives of various vested interests takes place. There has been a striking increase in lobbying by interest groups who have the resources and capacity to do so. Many important decisions are arrived at through private consultations between civil servants and spokesmen for various vested interests, during which politicians play no role. By the time ministers enter the decision-making process, the die is cast and only minor changes, if any, can be made. The *general* interest, therefore, as aggregated by political parties, tends to receive scant attention and parties are left with little choice but to approve what has already been decided by others. The process of consultation is for the most part totally non-partisan and most ministers engaged in it act as governmental decision-makers, far removed from their party personas. For the government party caucus to disown government policies already decided on after considerable negotiations would be politically harmful and is hardly ever heard of. Convincing testimony to the relative impotence of parties is found in Robert Presthus's study of Canadian interest groups, which shows that the latter spend considerably more time and effort lobbying bureaucrats than members of parliament.[3] Furthermore, it is clear that having recourse to pressure group participation in policy-making is not a feared or temporary phenomenon. The Canadian government, like many others, has institutionalized the practice by appointing large numbers of advisory committees and other bodies designed to ensure the pressure of interested parties in the policy process.

Incipient Corporatism

A related phenomenon received wide attention during the ill-fated, mid-1970s anti-inflation program of the federal government. Although the case is derived from Canadian experience, the phenomenon is not unique to this country. Efforts to control prices and wages required the cooperation of both management and labor. The idea was that federal economic policy would emerge from regular consultations between the government and representatives of labor, industry and business and that a group comprised of these interests would become institutionalized as a permanent consultative body. In the end, this structure was never established. It is difficult to see how this kind of change in the governmental process could have been made without undermining the power of parliament and hence of political parties. Compromises delicately wrought by a tripartite council would not likely be upset by the House of Commons even if members of the majority party wished to repudiate the deals made by their leadership.

Recourse to the tripartite consultative process reflects a tendency toward a new form of corporatism — a process of arriving at collective decisions through the efforts of representatives of the main "functional" interests in the country rather than of its territorial delegates. Because corporatism is usually associated with fascism, it is viewed with suspicion; but there is nothing inevitably authoritarian in it. There are corporatist elements in the usually highly regarded Swedish politico-economic system. But whatever its general merits, corporatist institutions supplement legislature and reduce the importance of political parties.

A more recent example of a variant of the corporatist approach concerns the Trudeau government's so-called "Six and Five World." This policy designed to reduce inflation was conceived and launched entirely without any involvement of the Liberal party and its success depended very heavily on the government's ability, in private conversations and negotiations with industry, to ensure voluntary compliance by the private sector with the guidelines. While decidedly non-partisan, it diverged from the corporatist model by not resting on the collaboration of government, business and industry, as well as labour. The latter was bitterly hostile to the program and vigorously repudiated it. It should, however, be noted that in the execution of the scheme, Senator Keith Davey, the quintessential Liberal party activist, played a key role on the committee guiding the implementation of the "Six and Five" program. But he was asked to perform this task because of his personal qualities and not because of his party connections.

Federal-Provincial Diplomacy

Another and increasingly threatening cause of the decline in the importance of parties lies in the changing nature of Canadian federalism. Accommodation between the various regions of the country (and to some extent, between special interests which happen to be in part regionally based) is taking place more and more through two mechanisms which are largely unrelated to party politics. The first of these is the federal-provincial prime ministerial conference, where Ottawa and the provinces hammer out compromises touching virtually every aspect of human experience. Most of these are the result of delicate bargaining on the part of eleven governments which sometimes cannot help but take positions imposed by other negotiators and which therefore cannot be anticipated by legislative caucuses, let alone by party supporters.

The second procedure through which policies are agreed upon by the federal and provincial governments is the regular meeting and consultation among federal and provincial officials. There are now thousands of such encounters annually and hundreds of formally established committees, task forces and work groups in which decisions are made which bind the participating governments. As with prime ministerial meetings, these encounters reach decisions which can be reversed or altered only at great cost — one not likely to be risked by rank-and-file members of political parties.

It can be argued that governments, at the ministerial level, are composed of leading party politicians and that their actions are in a sense those of political parties. This is technically correct, but the infrequent and unfocused expression of party opinion and the almost nonexistent party activity between elections deprive elected officials of any viable contact with their party organisms. There is, in contrast, a striking frequency and intensity of contacts between office-holding politicians and civil servants and spokesmen for vested interests. It is no exaggeration to argue that although ministers, and through them, the officials who serve under them, formally reflect party interests, they do not do so in any meaningful way. Between elections, except for occasional and exceedingly rare party gatherings, the cabinet *is* the party, insofar as the government side of the equation is concerned. Thus, such major policy changes as the introduction of wage control in the 'seventies and Trudeau's 1983 resolve to play a mediating role between the superpowers were introduced without any party involvement of any sort.

The Rise of Electronic Media

Until the advent of radio and particularly of television, politicians were the most effective means through which the public learnt about political events. In many communities across the country the political meeting was not only an important means of communication but also prime entertainment. Political issues were personalized by politicians who, in addition to adding colour to the consideration of matters of public policy, lent the political process a gladiatorial dimension that heightened its public appeal.

Television has, to a great extent, changed all that. The average Canadian spends several hours a day watching all manner of programs among which political material plays a relatively minor role. The entertainment value of face-to-face politics has declined since there are so many other exciting things to watch. And the public perception of the political process and of political issues that remains is derived from television treatment of the news and of political personalities. Public taste and public opinion on almost everything is being shaped by television programs and television advertising. Politics and politicians are filtered by a medium in which the primary concern is often not enlightenment, knowledge or consciousness-raising but maximal audiences and profits. This has meant that even major political events like the choosing of national party leaders are dominated by the requirements of television. The organization and scheduling of meetings are arranged so that the most appealing events occur during prime time, when they are broadcast, and all other aspects, even the quality of discussion and the time spent on critical issues, are made subservient to the demands of the electronic media.

Television has to some extent wrested the limelight from party politicians; but, on the other hand, it provides a matchless opportunity for the public to witness the party game. Its coverage of the most colourful political events — leadership conventions, .elections, and so-called debates between party leaders — furnishes unprecedented opportunities for parties to be seen in action. The problem is, of course, that the exposure is chosen by the media largely for entertainment value, rather than as a continuous in-depth exploration of the dominant political issues and partisan strategies. The focus tends to be on the people who report and comment on political news rather than on the political actors themselves. One result of this tendency is that public opinion on political matters is shaped as much by media intermediaries as it is by the protagonists representing the various parties. Furthermore, the key role of television is changing the character of political leadership. It is now virtually impossible for anyone who is not "telegenic" to be chosen as party chief. His or her presence and style on television can make or break a politician; yet, these are only some (and not the most important) attributes of an effective political and governmental figure.

Investigative Journalism

Although television has come to occupy a key position in the manner in which the public perceives political and party life, it has not eclipsed the more traditional ways of reporting and analyzing news and of entertaining the public. Newspapers and periodicals still receive considerable attention, particularly among the politically most active members of the public. Partly, no doubt, in response to the competition provided by TV and partly because of the intense rivalry among some of the major printed media, newspapers and magazines have recently resorted to numerous ploys designed to attract attention and a wider audience. Among these, investigative journalism — a return of sorts to the old muckraking days — has been particularly important. Many of the major papers and some of the periodicals have sought to discover governmental lapses and to reveal wrongdoing on the part of local, provincial and federal authorities. These efforts at exposing flaws and shortcomings, errors, dishonesty and inefficiency perpetrated by governments have often led to the establishment of judicial and quasi-judicial inquiries and to the corroboration of the sins unearthed by the sleuthing journalists. The watch-dog function of the print and electronic media is important to the present argument because it can be seen as an encroachment upon, or at least a complement to, the role of opposition parties. They, of course, are the agents par excellence, according to conventional theory, for keeping governments on their toes and for publicizing their misdeeds.

Although opposition politicians and investigative journalists no doubt derive mutual benefit from one another's activities, the recent increase in the role of the media as agents unearthing governmental malfeasance, regardless of how beneficial it may be, detracts from one of the most essential roles of opposition parties — that of criticizing the government. This is not to say the activities of the journalists inhibit or hamper opposition politicians; on the contrary, the latter exploit them; but the relative importance of government debate is reduced when much of the combat occurs outside the party arena — on the printed page or the television screen. One of the questions presented by the new or perhaps revived emphasis in the media on tracking down governmental errors of commission or omission is in fact whether the often vigorous reportorial initiative of the media does not reflect a decline in the energy and resourcefulness of opposition parties. Like many of the arguments presented above, this is a question requiring systematic research.

Whatever the reasons, a considerable challenge of, and check on, governments today originate outside the realm of political parties and tend to reduce the effectiveness of the party system. The media may be able to report governmental failings, but they cannot provide alternative governments — one of the functions of opposition parties. By sharing with others the task of exposing and criticizing official actions (and by often being outdone by them), opposition parties lose some of their credibility as alternatives to the current power-holders.

Opinion Polling

Increasingly widespread use of opinion polls by the small groups of officials and cronies working with the party leader has diminished the need to rely on the knowledge of public attitudes by local militants and elected politicians. The vast, sensitive network of contacts, reciprocal favours, and exchanges of information which characterized the relationship between party leaders and their followers has to some extent been attenuated by the use of scientific sampling, sophisticated interviewing techniques and subtle statistical analyses. While the results are in some respects more reliable, there is also a decided loss: the interplay between public opinion and the leadership exercised by politically informed and concerned activists is substantially reduced. There is likely less debate and argument, since local party people are no longer encouraged to take the pulse of their "parishioners" and to mediate between the grass roots and the leadership. Public opinion, as defined by pollsters, guides political decisions more and political decision-makers are less involved in forming public opinion. Two consequences, at least, are relevant for our purposes: the character of political leadership and of political styles has changed and the party organization is no longer needed as an essential information network.

The Domination of Economic Interests

There is little agreement among scholars about the exact role of economic factors in the sociopolitical realm. Are the forces and relations of production basic causes of all other aspects of social organization or can social organization be manipulated through political means? Whatever one's judgment, one does not need to be an economic determinist to acknowledge that governments have frequently found it difficult to resist certain kinds of economic pressures or to work against certain economic realities. This vulnerability is enhanced by the greatly increased number and power of multinational corporations. These vast, globe-girdling enterprises are rarely dependent on their operations in any one political jurisdiction and are adept at playing one interest against another. The behaviour of the oil companies before, during and after the oil crisis of the seventies is a case in point. Even those who doubt that Canadian industry and business can withstand governmental pressure cannot ignore the fact that the multinationals, recognizing no loyalties other than to their balance sheets, can obviate, ignore, influence and even dominate Canadian governments. A striking example came to light in the autumn of 1977 when Inco, a Canadian-based multinational, which has benefited from lavish tax and other concessions, announced that it would lay off 3,000 employees in Canada. Against arguments to the effect that the company was at the same time using funds provided by Canadian taxpayers to expand productive capacity overseas, a senior vice-president indicated that "fears of government takeover and other economic recriminations in Indonesia and Guatemala forced Inco…to cut back production in Canada where massive layoffs could be made with little prospect of serious political interference."[4] This episode provides an illuminating vignette illustrating the impotence of the Canadian government[5] and of Canadian political parties, in the face of economic pressure from industry. This subservience of the political realm to the economic is related to the prevailing value system and dominant ideologies: when parties and governments buckle under economic pressure, they do so because they do not believe in interfering with private enterprise.

One-Party Dominance

Finally, among the long-run, general factors leading in the decline of party in Canada is the very nature of the Canadian party system. Its chief feature during this century has been that it is a one-party dominant system, in which the important alternation is not between different parties in office but between majority and minority Liberal governments.[6] Increasingly, the line between the government and the Liberal party has become tenuous, leading Liberals have become ministerial politicians and the opposition parties have been out of office for so long that they are seldom perceived as being capable of governing, sometimes (according to one scholar) even by themselves.[7]

Canada has long been in a situation in which there has been a serious loss of confidence in the government and in the government party and at the same time no corresponding or compensating sense that the opposition might do better. The latter was perceived as inexperienced, fragmented and disposed to attack on principle everything and everyone who had anything to do with the government. Public opinion polls taken after the 1975 Conservative leadership convention showed a major decline in Liberal support and a corresponding upsurge in Conservative fortunes, but the election of a Parti Québécois government in November 1976 reminded Canadians of the woefully weak position of the Conservatives in Québec and of the fact that, in the past, only the Liberals (among the major parties) have tried to find a satisfactory accommodation between French and English Canada. The fear of national disintegration drove many voters back towards the Liberals, albeit with very little enthusiasm. Despite extensive doubt about the Liberal's capacity to provide adequate government (particularly west of the Ottawa River), the Conservatives were able, after the 1979 election, to form only a minority government which was toppled a few months after coming to power by the combined vote of the Liberals and the NDP.

This reinforced the already strong sense, among most leading Liberals, that they are indispensable and (since the Canadian public seems to recurrently favour them), nearly infallible in dealing with Canadian problems. The sense of self-assurance — an increasingly important element in the party's physiognomy[8] — has itself contributed a great deal to the decline of party in Canada.

Among the many other consequences of one-party dominance, one requires special notice in the present context. The less favoured parties (unless they are essentially doctrinaire organizations which attract ideologues regardless of electoral opportunities) experience great difficulty in attracting candidates of top quality. Highly successful and ambitious individuals do not, for the most part, wish to foresake promising careers in exchange for a difficult electoral campaign and, at best, an almost permanent seat on the opposition benches. In a system in which parties in power alternate, able deputies know that part of their career is likely to be spent in the cabinet and they may therefore be attracted to a political career even if their preferred party does not, in the short run, seem to stand a good chance of election.

Short-run Causes: The Liberal Style

Disdain of Parliament

Prime Minister Trudeau is not, as has often been noted, a House of Commons man. He seems to hold parliament in low esteem and is on record as questioning the intelligence of his opponents. He seldom uses parliament as the platform for important pronouncements, preferring to deliver policy statements or general reflections on the state of the country in public speeches, television interviews or press conferences. Having entered politics relatively late in life, and having been strongly critical of the Liberals, Pierre Trudeau's personal circle appears to be outside the ranks of the party he now leads, and outside of parliament. The two intimate colleagues who entered politics with him, Jean Marchand and Gérard Pelletier, were also not at home in the House of Commons milieu and have retired from it.

A significant decision of Mr. Trudeau, in the present context, was his move in 1968 to establish regional desks within the privy council office, which were designed to keep abreast of developments and ideas in the regions. A more party-oriented prime minister would have relied on his party contacts and on colleagues in the House of Commons rather than on civil servants, and there was much criticism of the prime minister's move in the House of Commons and privately, among Liberal back-benchers. The desks as such have been abandoned but the government continues to bypass the House of Commons on some critical issues.

Examples abound of the Trudeau government wishing to bypass parliament, presumably so as to escape unfavourable or contentious publicity. After the first election of the Parti Québécois, for instance, opposition spokesmen sought an extensive House debate and the establishment of a parliamentary committee which would engage in a searching and continuous consideration of Canada's crisis of unity. The government provided for a three-day parliamentary debate and refused to establish the requested committee. Instead, the prime minister created special national unity groups of officials in the privy council office and established a task force on national unity under Jean-Luc Pépin, a former cabinet minister, and ex-Premier John Robarts of Ontario. Important government decisions, like those dealing with the testing in Canada of the Cruise missile or with the abandonment of Via railway lines, are announced when the House is recessed, and frequently news which is likely to embarrass the government is released late on Friday, thereby precluding its receiving the immediate attention of the House. These moves bespeak a lack of enthusiasm for using parliament as an instrument for fashioning — as distinct form merely legitimizing — national policy. And to play down parliament is to play down political parties, since their chief national arena is the House of Commons.

Confusing the Public

A certain amount of sophistry is indigenous to politics when it comes to governments justifying their failure or unanticipated changes in their policies and strategy. But the public is not likely to maintain respect for either its government or the whole political system when it is confronted by an administration which, after an election, completely repudiates a major policy stand or when it welcomes into its ranks a former opposition member who has been a vociferous leader against one of its most important pieces of legislation. The Liberal party has done both, thereby weakening confidence in the integrity of our political parties and of their practitioners.

One of the principal differences in the platforms of the Liberal and Conservative parties in the 1974 election was the question of how to combat inflation. The Conservatives advocated a temporary price and wage freeze (pending the development of a permanent policy), for which the Liberals excoriated them, arguing that the public would never accept such controls. Having done much to undermine confidence in officially sanctioned constraints, and having given the impression that Canadians could not be trusted to cooperate in such a program, the government in 1975 introduced its own anti-inflation program, which froze wages and tried (unsuccessfully) to control prices. Not surprisingly, the government that campaigned on a vigorous anti-controls platform encountered considerable opposition when it tried to apply them.

The general language policy of the Official Languages Act of 1969 is one of the most important Liberal government attempts to promote national unity. Robert Stanfield, then Conservative leader, succeeded in persuading his party to follow him in supporting the language bill, but he was challenged and about twenty of his followers broke party ranks. None of them was more implacably opposed to efforts designed to assure that both French and English speaking Canadians could deal with the federal government in their own language than Jack Horner, the member for the Crowfoot constituency in Alberta. Mr. Horner had consistently been one of the most savage opponents of efforts to protect the French language and to create in Canada an ambience agreeable to francophones. However, after unsuccessfully contesting the Tory leadership, Mr. Horner became disillusioned with the leadership of his successful rival, crossed the floor of the House, and ultimately became a Liberal cabinet minister.

It is not always easy to distinguish between our two old parties but some basic diverging orientations do in fact divide them.[9] One is the attitude they adopt towards French Canada. Although the official leadership of the Conservative party has, under Robert Stanfield, Joe Clark and Brian Mulroney, been sympathetic to the aspirations of French Canada, the party has always been plagued by a bigoted wing of members who lacked comprehension of and sympathy for Quebec. Mr. Horner, as a leading member of this group, was a strange bedfellow for the Liberal MPs, the former targets of his venom. While this move gave the Liberals a much needed prairie seat and Mr. Horner a cabinet post long before he might otherwise have received one (if ever), it made a mockery of what our political parties allegedly stand for.[10]

Decline in Ministerial Responsibility

It has been a cardinal principle of the cabinet system of government that individual ministers are responsible for anything that is done by the ministries and departments for which they are responsible. The civil service is supposed to be an anonymous body without political views, obediently carrying out the commands of its masters, the politicians. This has always been something of a fiction, of course, since senior civil servants must provide useful advice and so there is no point in their totally ignoring the partisan and political constraints impinging on the ministers. The tendency for ministers and deputy ministers to see the world in like fashion is particularly pronounced in a one-party dominant system in which the collaboration between a minister and his or her deputy may continue for many years. All this notwithstanding, the principle of ministerial responsibility has had a long and respected tradition in Canada, at least in the sense that ministers, as politicians, have assumed complete responsibility for the actions of their civil servants and their departments. The political party in office has thus been the beneficiary of all the popular things done by the public service and the victim of its failings.

Recent developments have altered the once well-established principle of ministerial responsibility. First, there is a rapid turnover in the various ministries. The result is that few ministers have a chance to master the complex business of their ministry before they are assigned a new portfolio. While an alert and hard-working minister can be briefed fairly quickly by his new subordinates, it takes a prodigious amount of work and insight, and a great deal of time, to be able to become the effective head of a department and to lead it. Until this happens — and many ministers of course never gain the upper hand — the politicians are in a sense the captives of their officials. Ministers may, under these conditions, take formal responsibility for what is done in their name but the real power lies elsewhere.[11]

The Trudeau government has gone further than any of its predecessors in accepting ministerial *lack* of responsibility for the actions of officials and in so doing has brought about an important revision in our constitutional practice. Trudeau's ministers have steadfastly refused to resign when consistently harrassed by opposition members, sometimes for the excellent reason that the bloodthirsty cries of their opponents were unjustified and irresponsible. But there have been several instances when, under previous custom, ministers would have backed down, whereas members of the Trudeau cabinet, supported by their leader, refused to assume responsibility for the actions of people working under them. The most notorious, and on other grounds, exceedingly troubling, case of this concerns revelations, made in 1977, about RCMP break-ins and other illegal acts in 1972 and 1973. The government's cavalier manner of responding to this situation need not detain us here, although it is another instance of the government undermining public trust in the political process. The relevant point is that the government defence was simply that the then solicitor-general (the "responsible" minister) had not been informed of the RCMP's actions and since the particular minister had been moved to another department, the principle of ministerial responsibility was no longer applicable. The former solicitor-general at first failed even to make a statement to the House about the whole affair, although he later did deliver one. Members of the RCMP repeatedly broke the law and no minister took responsibility for these extremely serious transgressions. If a party holding office is no longer accountable for what is being done by officials under one of its ministers, the party system cannot ensure that governments are responsible to the electors. This state of affairs makes a mockery of democratic procedures and further diminishes the credibility of political parties.

Plebiscitary Tendencies

All of the short-run causes for the decline of party mentioned so far were laid at the doorstep of the Liberals. While that party has been an important cause of the process of party attenuation, it should not, of course, be assumed that it is the sole culprit. The opposition parties have been unable to present an acceptable alternative and have failed to convince the public that they could remove some of the ills currently afflicting the country. Nor can party politicians of any stripe be held responsible for the fact that much of the political decision-making has shifted from the conventional sites to federal-provincial negotiations, where parties do not fit neatly.

A recent factor that might possibly further impair the viability of parties is also not the Liberal's making, although Mr. Trudeau's reaction to it might exacerbate its effect on the place of parties in our system. The Parti Québécois' insertion of the referendum into our political process takes away from the monopoly enjoyed by parties in deciding certain issues. The PQ is of course not the first to introduce direct consultation of the public to Canadians. W.L. Mackenzie King had recourse to this device during the conscription crisis in the Second World War, and two referenda were held before Newfoundland became part of Canada. But the commitment of the PQ government to conduct a referendum to decide whether Quebecers wish to break or redefine their relationship with the rest of the country has brought forth an indication that Ottawa might itself conduct a similar vote.

Referenda normally ignore political parties and emphasize policy options, thereby diminishing the importance of parties in the political process. If they are held very infrequently, and only with respect to such fundamental issues as the nature of the country and its constitution, then they are unlikely to do much damage to the role of parties. But once they are used in one case, it may be impossible to prevent them from being applied to other issues — for example, the reintroduction of capital punishment, or language legislation — and they might slowly usurp some of the functions performed by parties. Any federal recourse to referenda is therefore seen by some opposition members as a potential further encroachment on the traditional role of parties.

Conclusion

The above catalogue of factors and developments reducing the relative importance of parties touches only some of the highlights; it is a partial and superficial look at a very complex phenomenon. This article's emphasis on federal politics has, for instance, led it to neglect the all-important provincial sphere and the interaction between federal and provincial party organizations. And our skimming of the high points has led to a neglect of some serious questions posed by these developments. We might have asked, for instance, whether the reason for the Liberal party's role in reducing the importance of parties is to be found in the fact that it is a quasi-permanent government party or in some special characteristics associated with Canadian Liberalism at the federal level. Does the Ontario Conservative party play a similar role in the decline of party in that province?

Our purpose here is not to answer these kinds of questions, important though they are, but to indicate that significant changes are occurring which alter the role played by political parties. If a series of limited advantages is allowed to reduce the overall effectiveness of a major mechanism for decision-making without producing at least an equally useful alternative, then the cost to society may be unexpectedly high. One is reminded in this connection of one of R.K. Merton's celebrated "theories of the middle range:"

> Any attempt to eliminate an existing social structure without providing adequate alternative structures for fulfilling the functions previously fulfilled by the abolished organization is doomed to failure.[12]

Now it is true that no one is consciously trying to eliminate Canadian parties or even to reduce their importance, and that Merton was thinking of the return or rebirth of a structure whose function was needed. But the parties' sphere of influence and effectiveness is being reduced, by design or not. It may be to the country's advantage to reassign the functions of parties if they are being neglected: society might find other ways of performing these needed functions. There is a danger, however, that the alternatives may be less satisfactory and in other respects — in the field of individual freedom, for instance — potentially very harmful.

The Canadian party system is far from being perfect, but the world is full of examples showing how appalling some of the alternatives can be. That considerable reform is needed is clear. We can benefit from some of the changes occurring now and from ones which could be instituted. Students of Canadian parties need to decide which features deserve preservation and which require change. And before they are in a position to do that, they must undertake more extensive study of the issues raised here.

ENDNOTES

1. "Getting in Cheap with the Aristocrats," *Toronto Globe and Mail*, September 26, 1977, p. 8. See also "Another Chapter in the Propaganda War," *Toronto Globe and Mail*, October 3, 1977.

2. Anthony King, "Political Parties in Western Democracies," *Polity*, Vol. II, No. 2, (Winter 1969), pp. 111-41.

3. Robert Presthus, *Elite Accommodation in Canadian Politics* (Toronto: Macmillan, 1974).

4. Roger Croft, "Safer to Fire Canadians Inco Admits," *The Toronto Star*, October 29, 1977, p. A3.

5. There is little difference between the federal and provincial spheres here: The *Globe and Mail*, October 28, 1977, p. 3, ran a story entitled "Davis Cautions Critics of Inco Layoffs," with a sub-head reading "Cites threat to investment climate". Similarly, even more reform-minded regimes have floundered in the face of industrial pressure.

6. For a fuller description and analysis, see John Meisel, "The Party System and the 1974 Election," in Howard R. Penniman, ed., *Canada at the Polls* (Washington: American Enterprise Institute for Public Policy Research, 1975).

7. For a recent analysis of this phenomenon within the Conservative party see George Perlin, *The Tory Syndrome* (Montreal: McGill-Queen's University Press, 1980).

8. See John Meisel, "Howe, Hubris and '72," in J. Meisel, *Working Papers on Canadian Politics* (Montreal: McGill-Queen's University Press, 1975).

9. See John Meisel, "Recent Changes in Canadian Parties," in H.G. Thorburn ed., *Party Politics in Canada* 2nd ed. (Scarborough: Prentice-Hall, 1967).

10. Horner's subsequent career is instructive. He was repudiated by his electors in 1979, but not abandoned by the Liberal government. In 1982 he was appointed Chairman of the CNR by the Trudeau government.

11. An interesting and possibly path-breaking departure from the traditional pattern occurred when Ian Stewart, the then Deputy Minister of Finance, resigned and in a letter to the Prime Minister took responsibility for Allan MacEachen's ill-fated 1980 budget. See J.E. Hodgetts, "The Deputies' Dilemma", *Policy Options*, Vol. IV, No. 3, (May/June 1983), pp. 14-17.

12. R.K. Merton, *Social Theory and Social Structure* (Glencoe, Illinois: The Free Press, 1949), p. 79.

11 The Control of Campaign Finance in Canada: A Summary and Overview

KHAYYAM Z. PALTIEL

More than two decades have passed since the movement for the reform of party and election finance was launched in the province of Quebec by the quiet revolutionaries led by Jean Lesage. The exposure of the notorious system of *ristournes* developed by the Union Nationale political machine under Maurice Duplessis and the reforms which followed heralded similar revelations of election fund scandals in other provinces, as exemplified by the Fidinam Affair in Ontario, and at the federal level (the Rivard Affair). The investigations which followed laid the basis for the adoption of changes in the electoral laws of Canada (enacted by the federal parliament), and seven of its provinces (passed by their legislatures), aimed at regulating the raising and spending of campaign and organizational funds during and between elections (including the reimbursement or assumption of certain costs by the public treasury and tax incentives for donations to party and campaign funds.)

At the outset these measures were rationalized and legitimized as attempts to foster integrity and fairness in the campaign process. Probity was to be encouraged by imposing stringent reporting, disclosure and audit procedures to increase openness and eliminate the secrecy surrounding the sources and use of campaign funds; some provinces sought to check the undue influence of large contributors by placing restrictions on the size of donations which may be accepted by parties or candidates. A liberal concern for equality of opportunity among electoral competitors and growing dismay at escalating costs prompted the various attempts to impose limits on total spending by parties and candidates, together with monetary or time restraints on particular types of expenditure, particularly on advertising and the electronic media. Equity, the professed desire to make for a more open campaign process and reducing dependence on large contributors, provided arguments justifying subsidies in the form of monetary reimbursements to parties and candidates, as well as for the adoption of a tax credit system for donations to campaign funds. The fact that the subsidies reduced demands on party war chests, party members and supporters, and, along with tax credits, transferred the financial burden of elections to the state, was noted but scarcely highlighted.

This summary review of Canadian federal and provincial legislation in the field of election expenses emphasizes the principal features of the measures adopted in the various jurisdictions. It concludes with a preliminary assessment of the impact of these reforms on the Canadian electoral process and offers some conjecture as to their consequences for the Canadian party and political systems generally; particular attention is paid to the recent amendments to the federal law embodied in Bill C-169, adopted in November 1983.

Party and Candidate Agents

Seven of the ten provinces have adopted the federal doctrine of agency first employed in the reforms which followed the Pacific Scandal of the 1870s. An eighth, Newfoundland, is currently considering a reform bill. Accordingly, all contributions and payments to or on behalf of a party or candidate must be made through their respective agents, who are legally responsible for the receipt, expenditure and reporting of these funds. The names of these agents must accompany the applications for official registration of the parties and the nomination papers of each candidate. In the provinces these agents go by various titles such as "official representative" in Quebec and New Brunswick, "business manager" in Saskatchewan, or "chief financial officer" in Alberta and Ontario; in British Columbia and Prince Edward Island a candidate can act as his own agent. At the federal level corporate bodies can serve as the agents of registered parties. The virtue of this doctrine lies in the fact that it fixes responsibility for the financial aspects of campaigns and subjects the persons and bodies involved to supervision and control. However, only Manitoba, New Brunswick, Quebec, Ontario and Alberta call for the registration of local constituency associations of the registered parties and subject them to supervision and control on a continuing basis. This glaring gap in federal law means that an essential link in the party and electoral system escapes accountability for its financial activities while benefitting directly and indirectly from tax incentives and reimbursements from the public treasury.

Only those parties which have been duly registered, authorized, or recognized may raise and spend monies for electoral purposes. Such permission is granted only to those groups which apply to the appropriate control body or official, setting out their full name and abbreviation, the names and addresses of the party leader, chief agent, auditor and other officers together with the addresses of party offices, the location of records and, in the case of some provinces, statements of the party's financial position at the time of registration. To maintain party status the various provincial jurisdictions have imposed additional conditions concerning the number of seats parties must hold in the legislature, or the number of candidates they must have presented in the previous or ongoing general election. In Nova Scotia and Quebec these parties include those of the current Premier and Leader of the Opposition or any party which fielded at least ten candidates at the preceding or current general election; New Brunswick follows a similar pattern. Ontario recognizes those parties which were represented in the Legislative Assembly by at least four sitting members; or, which entered candidates in at least half the electoral districts in the preceding or current general election; or, a party which in the inter-election period supported its application for registration by depositing a petition signed by at least 10,000 eligible electors. Alberta and Manitoba requirements follow the Ontario model.

Federally, the Canada Elections Act requires that a registered party have at least 12 members in the House of Commons prior to dissolution, or present at least 50 candidates at a federal general election. While this appears equitable, closer examination demonstrates that the latter provision would effectively preclude the establishment of Atlantic, Prairie or Western regional parties. Only Ontario and Quebec regional formations would be capable of authorization. Had such provisions been in force in the 1930s it is doubtful whether the CCF or Social Credit could have gained a toehold on Parliament Hill. Since history has demonstrated that such regional movements have been among the most innovative forces on the Canadian political scene, the stringency of this requirement (which some would like to be made more severe) is deplorable. In the absence of a provision parallel to the Ontario registration by petition, federal law appears to reduce the opportunity for participation in the electoral process and runs counter to the claim that the election expense provisions were adopted in order to "open up" the process.

The Reporting of Party and Candidate Expenses

Federal and provincial laws generally stress the disclosure of sources and amounts of party funds. Nevertheless, great weight is given to the reporting of party and candidate spending through the imposition of specific and over-all limits as a basis for determining the subsidies to be granted in the form of state reimbursement of a portion of campaign costs. Most provinces define illegal expenses in their statutory provisions dealing with corrupt practices. By contrast British Columbian and federal law attempt to detail the kinds of expenditures which candidates and parties may make legitimately in the course of a campaign.

Candidates and their agents in Canada and the nine provinces must submit campaign expense declarations within periods ranging from two to six months from polling day or the return of the election writs. These declarations must be accompanied by supporting documents and in many cases by an auditor's report. After transmission to the appropriate control body or official they are generally available for public scrutiny and summaries are published in newspapers circulating in the relevant constituencies. Newfoundland and Prince Edward Island have yet to recognize formally the existence of parties; British Columbia and Nova Scotia take note of their financial activities only during election campaigns. By contrast New Brunswick, Ontario, Manitoba, Alberta, Saskatchewan and the federal government pay heed to the ongoing functions of political parties. For British Columbia a party is simply an electoral association which expends funds on behalf of particular candidates. The party is only required to submit an unverified statement of expenses at the end of the campaign. Quebec, New Brunswick, Manitoba and Nova Scotia require detailed campaign expense reports subject to public scrutiny, summaries of which are published in the official *Gazettes,* or reports published by the appropriate commissions or electoral officers. Canada, Ontario, Manitoba and Saskatchewan also require some form of audited annual report of expenses by the parties, the contents of which are subject to public scrutiny and disclosure.

Quebec, which has undertaken a programme of support for the ongoing organizational expenses of parties represented in the National Assembly, requires annual statements of maintenance costs, which, however, are not disclosed. In Ontario, Quebec and Alberta registered local constituency associations must also submit annual expense statements.

Expense Ceilings

Qualitative, quantitative and monetary limits of various kinds have been imposed on campaign spending at the federal and provincial levels. Certain practices have been banned as corrupt and illegal. In addition, non-party groups such as trade unions, interest groups, and single issue organizations have been forbidden or severely restricted from spending money aimed at opposing or supporting political parties and candidates during the campaign period, in Canada and several provinces. Ontario purports to limit costs by subjecting advertising alone to a specific monetary limit per voter at the party and candidate level during the campaign period. Saskatchewan and Manitoba seek to check the advantages of incumbent parties by cancelling and forbidding all paid government publicity during the electoral period except for emergency announcements.

Under the Canada Elections Act, advertising is limited to the four weeks prior to polling day. Paid publicity on radio and television is further restricted to a total of six and one-half hours on any broadcasting station or network, to be allocated for sale amongst the registered parties in proportion to the number of seats won and votes received in the previous election (a further thirty-nine minutes is available for allocation for sale among

newly registered formations). Similar proportions are fixed for the allocation of "free time" among the political parties by the electronic media.
Federal and provincial statutes also permit the print, broadcasting and other
mass media to charge parties and candidates no more than the lowest rates
charged generally for similar space and time.

Canada, Manitoba, Nova Scotia, New Brunswick, Quebec and Saskatchewan attempt to limit costs by placing comprehensive restrictions on the
spending of parties and candidates. Saskatchewan's registered parties may
each spend a maximum of $250,000; Nova Scotia and Quebec authorize a
party to spend up to 40 cents and 25 cents respectively per elector in the
aggregate of districts in which they present candidates. New amendments
to the federal law allow the party limit of 30 cents per elector to be adjusted
by reference to the annual rise in the consumer price index since 1980; the
limit by April 1984 will be thirty percent higher than the 1980 figure.

At the candidate level, the federal ceiling and those of three provinces
are based on sliding scales linked to the number of eligible voters and the
geography of the constituencies. The basic federal ceiling, adjusted by the
rise in the consumer price index since 1980 (30% higher by 1984) is $1 for
each of the first 15,000 names on the electoral list, 50 cents for the next
10,000 and 25 cents for each elector in excess of 25,000; constituencies
whose electorate is below that of the average for all constituencies are
calculated to have a higher number of voters, equal to half the difference
between their actual and the average eligible voting population per constituency; also, candidates in extremely large constituencies with sparse populations may spend an additional 15 cents per square kilometre to cover their
higher traveling and communications costs. During by-elections, several
provinces permit additional spending, either at the party or candidate level.
The generosity of these limits may be seen in the official statistics covering
the 1980 federal general election. A federal party which fielded a full slate
of 282 candidates was permitted to spend $4,546,192 at the party level and
its candidates a total of $7,840,987: over $12,300,000 in all. As it was, the
Liberals spent just under $10,000,000, the Progressive Conservatives
somewhat over that figure, the New Democrats well over $6,000,000 and
Social Credit more than $400,000. All five other registered parties, their
candidates and independents spent no more than $420,000. If the limits
were a brake on costs, the only ones affected were the two traditional
major parties and their standard-bearers.

Given the recent amendments to the Canada Elections Act tying spending limits to the rise in the Consumer Price Index, removing the limit on a
candidate's personal expenses, and granting more generous geographic
allowances (and taking into account that the next election will be fought on
the basis of the 1971 census, meaning no rise in the number or boundaries
of constituencies) it can be estimated that party and candidate spending

limits in the next election will rise by at least one-third with a corresponding rise in actual spending, especially as the two old parties always spend close to the ceiling.

As a final note, it bears considering that inter-election party spending has yet to be limited at any level.

Candidate and Party Subsidies

Nova Scotia, New Brunswick, Quebec, Ontario, Manitoba, Saskatchewan, and the federal government provide help to qualifying parties and candidates by reimbursing a portion of their permitted monetary expenditures (Newfoundland proposes to do so). Federal law also requires the allocation of free broadcasting time to registered political parties on the national radio and television networks. At the candidate level, all those who win or have gained at least 15 percent of the votes cast are eligible for reimbursements in four of the provinces and federally; in New Brunswick, the law favours candidates who receive one-fifth of the votes and in Quebec, it favours those who ran under the banner of parties whose local nominees gained the greatest or next-to-greatest number votes in the previous election, regardless of current results. Manitoba sets this threshold at 10 percent of votes cast.

New Manitoba legislation would permit the reimbursement of half the permitted campaign costs of registered parties, provided they receive at least 10 percent of the votes cast in the aggregate of seats in which they present candidates. A newly introduced Newfoundland bill would provide financial assistance to a party which won at least 15 percent of the popular vote in an election, elected two members to the Legislature and fielded candidates in at least three-quarters of the province's 52 electoral districts. Amendments to the federal law have transformed the former reimbursement of half the permitted and actual broadcasting time costs into a general subvention of 22.5 percent of total campaign expenditures of registered political parties which have spent at least 10 percent of their permitted election expense limit.

The actual subventions to qualifying candidates are calculated on a flat rate or sliding scale basis. Reimbursements to Quebec candidates are at the rate of 15 cents per listed elector, plus one-fifth of actual costs between 15 and 40 cents and all expenditures over 40 cents per elector to the allowable expense ceiling; payments to party scrutineers at the polls benefit the two largest parties. The Ontario subsidy provisions make for the repayment of actual expenses or the sum of 16 cents and 14 cents multiplied by the first 25,000 names and those above that number respectively. New Brunswick pays out 35 cents plus the cost of a one ounce first class postage stamp per elector to eligible candidates. The new federal bill C-169 transforms the old sliding scale system to a reimbursement of half the actual, or a maximum of half the permitted, costs for local candidates. In addition, Ontario, Saskatchewan and the federal government reimburse auditing fees for the reports required of all candidates at elections. Quebec assures similar payments to the auditors of registered parties for their annual reports.

Quebec remains the only jurisdiction which provides assistance to political parties for their annual organizational and maintenance costs. However, it should be noted that where annual tax credits have been instituted, all registered parties benefit from this tax incentive. This is in addition to the assistance provided at both the federal and some provincial levels to the parliamentary caucuses of parties for research and other expenses.

Control of Party and Candidate Income

The federal government and the majority of the provinces attempt to assure the disclosure of the amounts and origins of funds raised by parties and candidates. Donations to parties and candidates must be made through the official agents and details must be provided to the electoral officers and/or commissions regarding the sums received by category and amount of gift. A strict definition of membership dues, a low threshold (usually $100) for the reporting of sums received from individuals, businesses, trade unions, or other bodies and the requirement that such sums be paid by cheque and backed by appropriate receipts and vouchers, help assure the accuracy of the audited reports which must be submitted to the election authorities by parties and candidates and made available for public inspection annually and immediately after a campaign period.

Alberta, Ontario, New Brunswick and Quebec legislation differ from other control mechanisms in Canada in that their laws place emphasis on the revenues rather than the expense of the parties (although the latter two, as we have seen, seek to regulate expenses as well.) New Brunswick, Ontario and Alberta limit the amounts which parties and candidates may accept during campaign and inter-election periods. Only individuals, trade unions and businesses domiciled in these provinces may contribute through the official agents; intra-party transfers from the federal to provincial level or vice versa are severely restricted. In Ontario annual gifts from a particular source may not exceed $2,000 to a registered party or $500 to any one local constituency association to an aggregate of $2,000 to the local entities of any one party; during an election year these sums may be doubled. In Alberta, the parallel figures are $10,000 or $20,000 for the parties, and $500 or $1,000 for local party associations or candidates to a maximum of $2,500 or $5,000 in a non-election or campaign year respectively. Payments by candidates in their own behalf and gifts in kind or services exceeding $100 in market value are treated as reportable contributions subject to full disclosure. All monetary gifts must be made by cheque to depositories registered with the election officials. Trade union check-off funds are subject to stringent regulation so as to bear most heavily on the New Democratic Party, which relies on such support. On the other hand, Alberta and Ontario law allows the ruling Progressive Conservative Parties to conceal the source and amounts of funds raised before disclosure legislation became effective, funds which are held in trust and may be used for campaign purposes.

By contrast, the federal act places no ceiling or prohibitions on the amounts or sources of party and candidate funds. The annual and post-election reports required of federal parties must reveal the number, amounts and identity of all gifts in excess of $100 by class of giver: individuals, businesses, commercial organizations, trade unions, corporations without share capital, unincorporated organizations and associations. A similar report is required of a candidate's agent after each election; where the sums come from a local party association, a similar detailed breakdown must accompany the candidate's audited statement. These statements may be copied for a nominal fee and are available for public inspection. Summaries of the candidate's declaration must be published in a newspaper circulating in the constituency concerned.

The efficacy of the regulation of election finance in Canada and its provinces rests primarily on disclosure, the doctrine of agency which fixes responsibility for the collection and expenditure of funds, and the quality and alertness of the control body or official charged with the enforcement of the regulations and their sanctions.

Fiscal Incentives for Political Funding

Alberta, Manitoba, Ontario and Quebec have followed the federal initiative by adopting a system of tax credits to encourage individual donations to candidates, parties and their local associations. Alberta has extended the system to cover corporate gifts, while Ontario permits such donations to be deducted from taxable income in determining corporate taxes due. The Canadian, Alberta and Ontario income tax acts respectively allow a person to claim a credit for contributions to federal or provincial parties or candidates, amounting to 75 percent for gifts up to $100; $75 plus 50 percent for aggregate gifts from $100 to $550; and $300 plus one third of gifts over $550 to a maximum tax credit of $500. Annual tax credits of $1,000 are thus available to Alberta and Ontario residents who contribute at both levels. In addition, Ontario corporations may deduct a maximum of $4,000 annually from the provincial share of their taxable income in calculating the provincial corporation tax for gifts to Ontario parties and candidates. Quebec law permits an individual elector to claim a credit against his provincial income tax due equal to 25 percent of his contributions to a maximum of $100 for campaign and party donations. Newfoundland is considering the introduction of a tax credit system for political donations.

Although the tax credit system is not universal, there is considerable evidence that some provincial affiliates of federal political parties have taken advantage of the opportunities made available by the federal act through intra-party transfers.

Control Systems

The regulatory procedures adopted by parliament and the various provincial legislatures have had a profound effect on the Canadian party system and the internal articulation of the established political parties. Elaborate record-keeping and reporting procedures have encouraged the formalization and professionalization of party structures. While the process is uneven there is evidence that the control systems have done little to foster a more open party system. Indeed the opposite appears to be the case. The laws, regulations and administrative procedures adopted have tended to inhibit and even to prevent the emergence of new formations. The Commissions and ad hoc advisory bodies which administer the controls or are consulted in the framing of policy are overwhelmingly composed of persons directly or indirectly affiliated with the existing established legislative and parliamentary parties. In many instances it is a case of those who are to be regulated actually formulating the regulations; such examples are common in other spheres as well.

Federal election expense legislation is administered by the Office of the Chief Electoral Officer, which is a model for systems in Alberta, Manitoba, Saskatchewan, Quebec and Nova Scotia. Ontario has established a Commission on Election Contributions and Expenses made up of a Chairman — usually a person prominent in the governing party — representatives of the registered parties with seats in the Legislative Assembly, a Bencher of the Law Society and the provincial chief electoral officer; this pattern has been adopted in New Brunswick. At the federal level and in Alberta the Chief Electoral Officers have established extra-legal ad hoc advisory committees made up, usually, of non-elected paid officials of the parliamentary and legislative parties. The new Manitoba act sanctions such bodies. These informal groups have become the main source of changes in the respective acts but, as might be expected of such groups, their proposals (even when they appear as suggestions of the Chief Electoral Officer) are largely designed to benefit the incumbent and established institutionalized parties.

The legal accountability of parties, candidates and their agents for their financial practices has been reinforced in most Canadian jurisdictions, but the efficacy of the legislation has yet to be fully proved (witness the recent scandals and court cases in Nova Scotia). Complaisant or co-opted control bodies, no matter what their formal authority, can well undermine the intent of the legislation by restricting their criticisms to the endorsements of big-name hockey players, trade union leaders, occasional dissident groups and disaffected individuals while allowing the use of public facilities and the abuse of government advertising by incumbents to escape scrutiny and censure.

Concluding Observations

At the outset it was argued that probity, equity and a concern to set a limit on the escalation of the costs of participation in the electoral process lay behind the movement for the control of election contributions and expenses in Canada. There is no doubt that much has been done in many Canadian jurisdictions to remove the mystery surrounding party funding and campaign war chests through the enactment of detailed reporting and disclosure provisions. But there are still gaps. Only Quebec has, in any meaningful way, tackled the problem of funds from non-domestic sources, by limiting the acceptance of donations to individuals duly inscribed on the provincial electoral list. Quebec and, to a limited extent, Alberta, Ontario and Saskatchewan, have also confronted the problem of funds derived from foreign sources. However, parties at the federal level, notably the Liberals, seek large contributions from foreign-based multi-national corporations. The NDP is known to get financial support from U.S. based trade unions and ideological allies.

Federal law purportedly attempts to inhibit the swamping of the electorate by advertising on the electronic media, but the 1983 amendments to the procedures governing the allocation of broadcasting time simply further the institutionalization of the party system by confirming the advantages accruing to the present parliamentary parties. The Ontario ceilings on advertising expenditures during the campaign period are simply a bad joke. Only Saskatchewan and Manitoba have attempted to cope with the abuses of government advertising (to the obvious advantage of the governing party) during the campaign period.

The changes in the Canada Elections Act (adopted in 1983 without public discussion and debate) demonstrate that the aim of reducing election costs has been effectively abandoned. The indexing of party and candidate spending limits, and the linking of reimbursements to these rising ceilings, means a steady escalation of expenditures which will escape public scrutiny inasmuch as neither the parties, the candidates nor the Chief Electoral Officer will have to request authorization for such increases in the future. The proposals adopted were the product of the informal ad hoc committee of party officials with no standing in the law, accountable to no one, for whom the Chief Electoral Officer simply acted as a figurehead. The House of Commons simply adopted its recommendations, which were aimed principally at benefitting those already represented on Parliament Hill. Included in the package was an amendment of doubtful constitutionality which will effectively prevent non-party groups from participating in the campaign process. Aimed ostensibly at abuses of the campaign activities of single-issue organizations and interest groups, including trade unions, concerned with some aspect of public policy, the amendment removed the defence that the person or organization concerned incurred expenses solely for the "purpose of advancing its "aims" or "gaining support for views held by him." The amendment originated from the left as well as the right; the N.D.P. sought this change because of activities of anti-abortion groups and the Liberals because of their embarrassment at the hands of the anti-cruise missile and peace groups.

This amendment is clearly subject to constitutional challenge and a suit has been launched by the right-wing National Citizens' Coalition and its leader Colin Brown asking that the Courts declare the relevant sections of the Canada Elections act as amended *ultra vires* of the Parliament of Canada. The grounds for the challenge are that the amendments infringe the freedoms guaranteed by the Canadian Charter of Rights and Freedoms and the principles of parliamentary democracy contained in the preamble to the Constitution Act.

On June 26, 1984, Mr. Justice Donald Medhurst of the Alberta Court of Queen's Bench ruled the clause invalid. This decision, unless overturned on appeal, means that interest groups and individuals will be free to spend any amount of money to promote or oppose political parties and candidates during federal election campaigns. In effect this means that the limits imposed by the 1974 legislation on election spending, as amended, no longer apply. New, constitutionally valid legislation will have to be introduced to address the issue of restraints on campaign spending.

Only the registered parties and candidates would be subject to restraints. Money would dominate the campaign scene. The removal of the defence contained in the original legislation was clearly an error, inasmuch as it deprives legitimate, ongoing groups from expressing their views. It has also opened the way for a specious challenge by those who wish to circumvent the intent of the original legislation which was to pinpoint the responsibility for the financial aspects of the campaign process, introduce a measure of equity, check the escalation of costs and reduce the influence of those with access to the "big money", not to speak of the masking of special interests. How much better would it have been if the press, parliament and observers of the political scene had engaged in a public debate on the implications of these amendments. As it is, the Chief Electoral Officer, his *ad hoc* committee, and the Government and parties which sponsored this amendment may be hoist by their own pétard.

What is particularly shocking about the recent amendments is that nothing has been done to strengthen the control measures. In fact they have been weakened. At the federal level, local constituency associations are still not accountable for their financial activities, though all the evidence shows that many are in possession of large surplus funds stemming from the reimbursement provisions and tax credit stimulus now afforded to the candidates. Secondly, the responsibility of the auditors has been diluted. The original act required the candidate's auditor to vouch that the reports submitted by the official agent conformed to the requirements of the Act; the new provision only requires the auditor to state that these declarations reflect the state of the candidate's records. Even on the question of costs a new loophole has been opened. There will no longer be a limit on the amount of "personal expenses" which a candidate may incur, nor will these be counted as "election expenses", they will only have to be "reasonable." However, no definition is provided for the latter term; all that will be required is a statement of such costs.

Publicity, therefore, remains the principal control measure and to the extent that disclosure fosters honesty, then probity has also been advanced. But it can scarcely be said that the federal act as amended has worked to reduce costs or make the electoral system more equitable and open to potential competitors. In addition, the fact that federal and provincial rules diverge is bound to have the effect of strengthening the distinctive features of federal and provincial party politics.

ENDNOTES

1. Khayyam Z. Paltiel, *Political Party Financing in Canada* (Toronto: McGraw-Hill, 1970).
2. Khayyam Z. Paltiel, "Contrasts among the Several Canadian Political Finance Cultures," in Arnold J. Heidenheimer, ed., *Comparative Political Finance; The Financing of Party Organizations and Election Campaigns* (Lexington, Mass.: D.C. Heath & Co., 1970), pp. 107-134.
3. Khayyam Z. Paltiel, "Election Expenses," in D.J. Bellamy, J.H. Pammett and D.C. Rowat, eds., *The Provincial Political Systems: Comparative Essays* (Toronto; Methuen 1976), pp. 161-176.
4. Khayyam Z. Paltiel, "Improving Laws on Financing Elections," in K.M. Gibbons and D.C. Rowat, eds., *Political Corruption in Canada: Cases, Causes and Cures* (Toronto: McClelland & Stewart, 1976), pp. 295-299.
5. Khayyam Z. Paltiel, "The Impact of Election Expenses Legislation in Canada, Western Europe and Israel," in Herbert E. Alexander, ed., *Political Finance,* Sage Electoral Studies Yearbook, Vol. 5, (Beverly Hills, London: Sage, 1979), pp. 15-39.
6. Khayyam Z. Paltiel, "Campaign Finance: Contrasting Practices and Reforms," in David Butler, Howard R. Penniman, and Austin Ranney, eds., *Democracy at the Polls: A Comparative Study of Competitive National Elections* (Washington, D.C.: American Enterprise Institute, 1981), pp. 138-172.
7. F. Leslie Seidle and Khayyam Zev Paltiel, "Party Finance, the Election Expenses Act, and Campaign Spending in 1979 and 1980," in Howard R. Penniman, ed., *Canada at the Polls, 1979 and 1980: A Study of the General Elections* (Washington, D.C.: American Enterprise Institute, 1981), pp. 226-279.
8. *Report of the Committee on Election Expenses* (Ottawa: Queen's Printer, 1966). (Barbeau Commission report).

9. Khayyam Z. Paltiel, ed., *Studies in Canadian Party Finance* (Ottawa: Queen's Printer, 1966).

10. *Bill C-169, An Act to amend the Canada Elections Act (No. 3),* received Royal Assent on November 17, 1983, First Session, Thirty-second Parliament, 29-30-31-32 Elizabeth II, 1980-81-82-83.

12 Reforming the Electoral System*

WILLIAM IRVINE

...Our parliament...represents all parts of Canada, but neither our government, nor our opposition, does. This poses problems, primarily for the legitimacy of the federal government, but also for the capacity of the opposition to take over the government.

At the level of conflicts of interest, this means that the caucus of the governing party is unable to fulfil its primary function. It cannot report to ministers how their plans will affect and be perceived in all parts of the country. It cannot offer a voice to important interests in different sections of the country. It cannot speak authoritatively, either for or to all sections of the country.

This has never been clearer than in the results of the [1979 and 1980] elections. In May of 1979, it seemed that Canada would have to deal with a Quebec referendum with a federal government having only two elected members from Quebec. The situation was different, but no happier, after the February 1980 election. Western alienation has been mounting for years, and our federal government will have to deal with that. And again, the federal government has been virtually shut out of a crucial region.

There are optimists who feel that this situation is episodic. Indeed, some feel that both problems — the weakness of the Liberals in the west and the weakness of the Conservatives in Quebec — will be solved at one stroke, by the retirement of Prime Minister Trudeau. This is simply not so.

It is true that the Progressive Conservative party has in the past been able to win seats in Quebec. In 1958. Mr. Diefenbaker won 50 seats there. It is also true that the Liberals have been able to win seats in all the western provinces. In 1968, Prime Minister Trudeau did just that — winning 27 seats, four of them in Alberta.

These are very attractive trees and worthy of note, but the forest remains dark and foreboding for both parties. Surely, what is most striking

---

*Exerpted from *Policy Options*, Vol. 1, #4, December 1980.

is the inability of the parties to consolidate their victories. It is striking, but it is not inexplicable.

Our present electoral system produces a very weak relationship between the votes cast for a party and the seats won by that party. In translating votes into seats, it over-represents the leading party in any area placed second and third.

The under-representation is increasingly sharp as a party gets weaker. The Liberals get well over one-fifth of the votes cast west of Ontario but win only two of the 80 seats — less than three percent. The progressive Conservatives have retained the support of thirteen percent of the Quebec electorate but get only slightly more than one percent of Quebec's seats.

Liberals are weak in the west. No monkeying with the electoral system will change that. But a person now has to be close to a masochist to campaign as a Liberal in the west. Trying to build a local organization, to encourage good candidates to come forward, and to attract people to participate in policy discussion within the party may be equally fruitless, and even more thankless. The same situation holds for the Progressive Conservative party in Quebec. Both parties do find good people to run under their banners — but only once.

This is the explanation for the parties' inability to consolidate their breakthroughs. There is no incentive for particularly able people to devote themselves to political careers within the party and nurture local roots for it.

The effect of the electoral system is aggravated by the images of the parties. They are seen by many potential candidates as hostile environments. They feel that even if they do get elected, in some 1958 or 1968-type sweep, it will take them a while to be able to influence their parties. The "while" just isn't there. They will probably lose at the next election. It is vital that someone represent the west in the Liberal caucus and Quebec in the Conservative caucus. Acquiring influence to represent effectively takes time. It requires commitment from the potential representative. Such a commitment is presently irrational.

Its absence is equally unfortunate. There is a feedback mechanism at work. Inability to elect a significant number of members regularly means few people to tend the party organization. It means, for those who are elected, near isolation within the caucus. The lack of influence means that regionally attractive policies are less likely to be forthcoming, and that regionally-sensitive ministerial talent is rare. The lack of organization means that even the good policies may not earn their reward.

Lack of influence and organization make it difficult for a party to attract votes in its region of weakness. Without votes, and votes which must be bunched in particular constituencies, caucus influence will decline further. So will commitment to organizational development. The cycle begins again.

Weakness breeds weakness. There is the danger that parties could eventually lose further electoral support and not just parliamentary support.

From analysts of the American Civil War to the Task Force on Canadian Unity, writers have commented on the danger of having political parties confined to a single region of a large country. Canada has been, and continues to be, fortunate in having nationally oriented parties at the federal level. They find it increasingly difficult, however, to maintain this orientation given the contrary incentives of the electoral system.

Moreover, they find it difficult to persuade Canadians that they are national parties. Most observers see only the party caucuses. It is easy for them to conclude that the Liberal party is the spokesman for Quebec and has no western support. It is easy to draw the opposite conclusion about the Progressive Conservatives. These are the parties as they appear on the top of figure 1.

The bottom is generally unseen. Canadians might be surprised to discover that more than one vote out of every ten cast for the Progressive Conservative party was cast by a Quebecker, and that there are more Progressive Conservatives in Quebec than in Manitoba and Saskatchewan combined. Similarly, one Liberal voter in every seven lives west of Ontario, and there are more Liberals, almost 700,000, in the west than in Montreal.

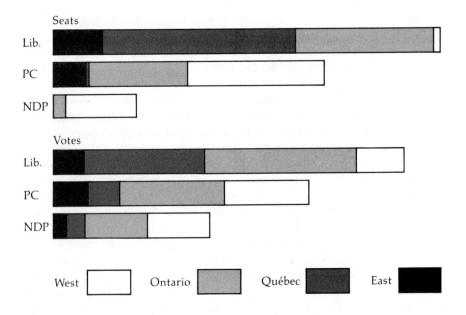

Figure 1 Seats and Votes of Major Parties, by Region

There are more in Alberta and British Columbia than there are in Toronto.

The problem is to increase their visibility. This means changing the electoral system — the set of rules that determines how votes cast get translated into parliamentary seats.

Many people and groups have suggested possible reforms. The Task Force on Canadian Unity briefly outlined one approach in its report, *A Future Together*, before the 1979 election. I published a book (*Does Canada Need a New Electoral System?*) shortly after that election. The 1980 results stimulated the NDP to renew a proposal made a couple of years before. The Canada West Foundation also recently produced another design for electoral system reform....

The four proposals all preserve the single member constituency that we now have. The authors seem to agree with the general view that having a single member of parliament responsible to a defined body of electors offers certain advantages. My own proposal would have reduced our present number of constituencies by one third. The Canada West Foundation proposal includes a 10 percent reduction in the number of constituencies, while the NDP and Pepin-Robarts approaches both leave the present constituencies untouched.

In order to correct the over-and-under-representation of the present system, all four proposals must add a number of non-constituency seats — that is, seats whose occupant is decided on a different basis than are occupants of constituency seats. The proposals differ somewhat in allocating the non-constituency seats. The NDP proposal gives ten to each of five regions: British Columbia, the Prairies, Ontario, Quebec, and the Atlantic Provinces. The task Force on Canadian Unity proposed that its additional seats should first be divided among the political parties according to the proportion each received of the national vote. In 1980, for example the Liberals would receive 27 of the 60 additional seats for their 44.3 percent of the national vote. The Progressive Conservatives would receive 19, having won slightly less than one-third the national vote and the NDP would obtain 12 for about one fifth the national vote.

My own proposal, and that of the Canada West Foundation, divided the additional seats on a territorial basis, assuring that each province's total parliamentary delegation remains proportionate to its overall share of the Canadian population.

These differences in initial allocation have potential constitutional implications which I shall address later.

The four proposals differ in their secondary allocations as well. The NDP proposal is to allocate the regional seats according to proportions garnered of the regional vote. The Canada West proposal is very similar. Since it operates at a provincial level, it allocates additional seats according to proportions of the provincial vote.

Quebec, which is both a region and a province, may serve as an example. Of the ten seats it would get under the NDP proposal, seven would go to the Liberals, and one each to the Progressive Conservatives, the NDP and Socreds. The 15 seats for Quebec under the Canada West system would also be allocated proportionately to the vote; 10 for the Liberals, 2 for the Progressive Conservatives, 2 for the NDP and 1 for the Social Credit party. The general philosophy behind each proposal is that in each region, a vote is a vote for purposes of the additional seats.

The Pepin-Robarts philosophy is different. It allocates seats to parties in the first step. For that allocation, a vote is a vote wherever it is cast. At the second stage, it allocates the parties' additional seats to provinces. At this stage, its philosophy is "a vote for party X is a vote for party X, whether it is cast in Alberta or in Quebec or anywhere else." That manifestly is not true in our present constituencies: 176,000 Liberals in Alberta get no representation; 1,675,000 Liberals in Ontario, about 10 times as many, get 52 representatives.

Treating each party successively, the Pepin-Robarts system distributes the additional seats to correct these distortions. After dealing with the malrepresentation of Liberals exemplified above, it would correct the similar distortions in representing Progressive Conservative or NDP voters. (We have already seen that 373,000 Conservatives in Quebec get one MP; 357,000 in Manitoba and Saskatchewan combined get 12 MPs. Similar distortions for the NDP could also be reported.)

My own proposal was based on the most radical of the philosophies of representation: A vote is a vote, no matter where it is cast and no matter for whom it is cast. It would work to correct the distortions at the constituency level by over-representing at the provincial level those parties who have the hardest time translating votes into seats. It thus shares elements of all the above systems.

In Quebec, for example, the Liberals got almost 99 percent of the seats with 68 percent of the votes, and the Conservatives got just over one percent of the seats for 13 percent of the votes. I proposed a large number of additional seats for Quebec, 44 against 50 constituencies. I would then allocate the provincial seats disproportionately to the Progressive Conservatives to assure them 13 percent of Quebec's overall parliamentary representation, and also over-represent other parties at the provincial level to bring them to the parliamentary strength warranted by their vote.

The consequences of these proposals for the present House of Commons (assuming that the votes continued to be cast in the same proportions) are shown in tables 2 to 5, and may be compared with the current patterns in table 1. Table 3 is taken from the draft paper for the Canada West Foundation. The others are my calculations; since the NDP proposal is on a regional basis, I have had to guess at the allocation of seats among the Atlantic and Prairie provinces.

TABLE 1 **The Actual Distribution of Seats in the House of Commons after the 1980 Election**

	Liberal	*P.C.*	*NDP*	*Other*	*Total*
Newfoundland	5	2	0	0	7
Prince Edward Island	2	2	0	0	4
Nova Scotia	5	6	0	0	11
New Brunswick	7	3	0	0	10
Quebec	74	1	0	0	75
Ontario	52	38	5	0	95
Manitoba	2	5	7	0	14
Saskatchewan	0	7	7	0	14
Alberta	0	21	0	0	21
British Columbia	0	16	12	0	28
Yukon Territory	0	1	0	0	1
Northwest Territories	0	1	1	0	2
Total	147	103	32	0	282
Percent Liberal	52				

A number of things are immediately apparent. First, the Liberals would still form a majority government under all proposals but the completely proportional one I have suggested. In all cases, however, that majority is reduced and becomes quite precarious (one seat) under the NDP proposal. Secondly, all proposals do change the regional complexion of the party caucuses, but in quite varying amounts.

One can do a rough "cost-effectiveness" analysis of the four proposals. Any listener to open-line shows will know what the primary cost is. A

TABLE 2 **The 1980 Distribution of Seats in the House of Commons under the NDP Proposal**

	Liberal	*P.C.*	*NDP*	*Other*	*Total*
Newfoundland	6	3	1	0	10
Prince Edward Island	2	2	0	0	4
Nova Scotia	7	7	1	0	15
New Brunswick	8	5	0	0	13
Quebec	81	2	1	1	85
Ontario	56	42	7	0	105
Manitoba	3	7	7	0	17
Saskatchewan	1	9	7	0	17
Alberta	1	22	2	0	25
British Columbia	2	20	16	0	38
Yukon, Northwest Territories	0	2	1	0	3
Total	167	121	43	1	332
Percent Liberal	50				

TABLE 3 **The 1980 Distribution of Seats in the House of Commons under the Canada West Foundation Proposal**

	Liberal	P.C.	NDP	Other	Total
Newfoundland	5	3	1	0	9
Prince Edward Island	3	2	0	0	5
Nova Scotia	6	6	1	0	13
New Brunswick	7	4	1	0	12
Quebec	80	3	2	1	86
Ontario	58	44	8	0	110
Manitoba	3	6	8	0	17
Saskatchewan	1	8	8	0	17
Alberta	2	22	1	0	25
British Columbia	2	17	14	0	33
Yukon, Northwest Territories	0	2	1	0	3
Total	167	117	45	1	330
Percent Liberal	51				

common reaction to electoral system change is "We already have too many MPs who don't do anything." Whether such low esteem of our parliamentarians is general or justified will not be discussed here, but it is a fact that most schemes of electoral system reform would increase numbers in the House, implying increases in salary, overhead for space, support staff and office expenses, and so on.

The additional number of MPs, then, could be taken as a rough index of the cost of electoral system change. The proposals range from a net increase of 48 for Canada West to a net increase of 72 for my proposal.

TABLE 4 **The 1980 Distribution of Seats in the House of Commons under the Pepin-Robarts Proposal**

	Liberal	P.C.	NDP	Other	Total
Newfoundland	5	2	0	0	7
Prince Edward Island	2	2	0	0	4
Nova Scotia	5	6	1	0	12
New Brunswick	7	3	0	0	10
Quebec	74	12	3	2	91
Ontario	59	46	12	0	117
Manitoba	4	5	7	0	16
Saskatchewan	3	7	7	0	17
Alberta	6	21	1	0	28
British Columbia	9	16	12	0	37
Yukon, Northwest Territories	0	2	1	0	3
Total	174	122	44	2	342
Percent Liberal	51				

TABLE 5 **The 1980 Distribution of Seats in the House of Commons under the Irvine Proposal**

	Liberal	*P.C.*	*NDP*	*Other*	*Total*
Newfoundland	4	3	2	0	9
Prince Edward Island	3	2	0	0	5
Nova Scotia	6	5	3	0	14
New Brunswick	6	4	2	0	12
Quebec	64	12	9	9	94
Ontario	50	43	26	0	119
Manitoba	5	7	6	0	18
Saskatchewan	4	7	7	0	18
Alberta	6	17	3	0	26
British Columbia	8	15	12	0	35
Yukon, Northwest Territories	2	1	1	0	4
Total	158	116	71	9	354
Percent Liberal	45				

To measure the effectiveness we have to specify exactly what is wrong with the present electoral system. The defects are numerous. There is the pure insensitivity to voter preferences, since many candidates get to parliament with the support of less than half their constituents. There is the exaggeration of voter shift. From 1979 to 1980, Progressive Conservative support fell from 36 to 33 percent of the electorate, but that party's seats in parliament fell from 136 to 103, a decline of 12 percent of the House.

British students have claimed that this tendency of our electoral system encourages short-run coping rather than long-run problem solving. In this regard, we may note research suggesting that few governments manage to resist temptation to inflate their economies before elections and deflate them afterwards; Edward Tufte (*Political Control of the Economy*: Princeton University Press) could find only eight democracies where such a cycle was not in evidence. All have highly proportional electoral systems.

However, the present debate in Canada focusses on one particular defect of the electoral system: its tendency to produce party caucuses unrepresentative of the party vote. Let us then take this as the measure of benefit from any reform proposal. The following may be defined as the representation gaps: Liberal seats from Manitoba westward, Progressive Conservative seats in Quebec, New Democratic seats from Quebec eastwards. Additional seats in these categories may be rated as benefits.

The tables show that the proposals have quite different representational payoffs. The NDP proposal produces only 2 Conservative seats in Quebec (a gain of one), three NDP seats in the east, and seven Liberal seats in the west (a gain of five). Overall then, the NDP proposal increases the size of the Commons by 50, but improves representation by 9, a benefit to cost ratio of .18. Similar calculation shows the Canada West proposal to have a ratio of .27, the Pepin-Robarts proposal to have a ration of .58, and my own proposal to have a ratio of .69.

It must be said that, in this calculation, the measure of benefit is unsophisticated, and many will protest that my suggested measure of cost is inadequate. They see the biggest cost of electoral system reform as governmental instability or indecisiveness.

Let us agree in the first place on the limits of institutional tinkering. Electoral system reform will no more turn Canada into Weimar Germany or Fourth Republic France or present-day Italy than it will turn us into present-day Germany or France. How an institution works depends very much on the history of conflicts in the host society. The cases of system instability are marked by much more profound class and/or religious cleavages than any that have marked Canadian history. Moreover, in the 1920s German and present Italian cases, important sectors of society had a very short history of participating in the political process, and the party systems did not have histories as long as those on the major Canadian parties.

Secondly, we must note that only a fully proportional electoral system is likely to make minority government more probable than it already has been in Canada. Whether this should be counted as a cost or not would require a long discussion and analysis.

Thirdly, while our present electoral system works against the representation of political forces that are small and evenly spread, it is quite vulnerable to a regionally concentrated protest movement. In 1962, Social Credit support was primarily concentrated in Quebec. In that province, the party took 35 percent of the seats with 26 percent of the votes....Any new party or leader that could put together 35 to 40 percent of the vote in some province like Quebec or Saskatchewan or Alberta could win a very large share of the seats in that province.

This, not the Rhinoceros or a Marxist Party, is the most probable threat to the present federal party system. Against such a threat the present electoral system offers *less* protection than would a more proportional one. Therefore, I do not think that I have understated the cost of the proposed reforms.

Given the immediacy of the need for action, particularly action to rebuild the legitimacy of central institutions, electoral system reform has the advantage of being the most quickly accomplishable. Speed here is to be assessed in terms of the number of governments that must agree. Since the Supreme Court judgement on the Senate reference, changing that institution now requires a formal amendment. Change in the Supreme Court itself might be within the sole competence of the federal government, but this is not entirely clear.

Electoral system reform, by contrast, is likely to be within the sole competence of the federal parliament. This does not mean that decision will be quick. Any new system should have broad legitimacy and support from all parties. But it does mean that electoral reform could be brought about more quickly than changes in other institutions.

A possible stumbling block to electoral system change is section 52 of the British North America Act, which provides that provinces are to be represented in the House of Commons in proportion to their populations....

The proposed provincial members would not represent particular constituencies, but are meant to represent whole provinces. They would, of course, be elected by provincial voters. The more votes cast for the Progressive Conservative party in Quebec, for example, the more members it would be assured from that province. Reform simply tries to ensure that Conservative voters in Quebec can get representation even if they are not bunched in one or two constituencies.

Reform would mean, however, that we have to pay close attention to the process of selecting these provincial members. In many of the proposals, their nomination will be crucial. The nomination process may decide, in part at least, who is successful.

This is not, however, very different from the present situation. Present nomination processes may account for the under-representation of women in the House of Commons.

In any case, how provincial representatives are nominated will affect their status and legitimacy. It will determine whether a member is seen as a representative from the west to the Liberal caucus or as a representative of the Liberal caucus to the west.

There are two general ways to make the choice of candidate: let the voters do it, or let the party do it. Some have suggested that the additional seats be filled by the highest runners-up in constituency contests. Others propose province-wide primaries with seats to be filled in order of preference with the primaries. One could adopt a multimember constituency with the single transferable vote method of election as another way of letting voters choose which of several party representatives might be returned to parliament.

There is a general difficulty with all of these. Each leads members of the same party to compete against each other. Indeed, this intra-party competition will be much stronger than inter-party competition. With a highest-runner-up or single-transferable-vote system, candidates will feel it unlikely that they could replace a partisan opponent but will try to get an advantage on co-partisans. They might try to do so by assiduously courting a single-issue group (a pro-capital punishment group for example, or an anti-immigrant group). They might try to do so by espousing the policy line of the locally popular party. It is as if the NHL scoring championship were decided solely on the basis of goals scored. Members of a forward line would start stealing the puck from each other as they got into the opponents' end.

The purpose of the reform exercise is to strengthen parties as organizations that can embrace Canadians from 11 provinces. It should not be coupled with a method that would serve to destroy the organization. Both coordination and leadership require a party to be able to do some things on its own responsibility. Deciding on who might be provincial representatives, to my mind, is one of those things.

The alternative, therefore, is to have provincial members elected from lists chosen by the political parties. But who is the party? The answer to this question goes a long way to deciding who is being represented. Leaving list-making solely to the national leader might look too much like an avenue for cronyism. It would, in any case, be a system most likely to be seen as representing the party to the region, rather than the other way.

Still, the leader cannot be left out. When Mr. Stanfield excluded Leonard Jones in 1974 he was exercising his prerogative to protect what he believed the Progressive Conservative party stood for. We need to balance the interests of the national party and of its provincial organization.

My preference is for the selection of provincial lists to be predominantly up to provincial party organizations. How they would proceed could be left to the parties, but there is no reason that lists could not be drawn up well in advance of elections and, perhaps, even ratified by party conventions in each province.

Some principles would have to be established spelling out a role for the national leader. A number of avenues might be followed. The national leader might be allowed to veto names from the list but not to insert names. He could be allowed to pick the first name but have no voice on the rest. He could be allowed to rearrange order on the list by one or two ranks but not to delete names.

Whatever one's own preference, list-formation is a most important matter. The parliamentary committee, proposed in the 1980 Throne Speech, is the logical body to decide the question. It may be sufficient to say simply that the national leader of the party must sign the lists submitted to the chief electoral officer. This would allow the parties to choose their own internal procedures. Parliament might want to go farther, however, and state explicitly a role for provincial associations of the federal parties. To do this would be further encouragement for parties to maintain vital associations in all provinces.

Any new electoral system has to be accepted by Canadians, and particularly by the areas now most under-represented in major party caucuses. A reform not seen as helping to resolve the representation problem is probably worthless. The parliamentary committee, through public hearings and consultation with national organizations and their provincial affiliates, is the best forum to work out a broad consensus on such a reform.

Political science is a "soft" science, and "legitimacy" may be one of its softest concepts. We are not quite sure how to measure legitimacy, but there would be little dissent from the following proposition about its source: a government or decision-making body is accepted as legitimate if a group is confident that its interests are heard within it. If public opinion polls show greater feeling of closeness to provincial governments than to the federal, it is because such governments are seen as closer to the people. For the federal government, the problem of sheer distance has recently been complicated by the problem of under-representation and mis-representation.

Electoral system reform would make a marginal but still important contribution to rectifying this. Even the most effectively redistributive electoral system would not dramatically change the picture shown in our figure one. It would not alter the fact that the Liberal caucus draws it largest contingent from Quebec. Under the present electoral system, Quebec supplies half the Liberal caucus.

Even under the Pepin-Robarts proposal Quebec would make up more than 42 percent of the caucus; but the west would make up almost 13 percent, ten times the weight it has now. This is good for the west; it would have its share of Ministers, parliamentary committee chairmen, all of whom would add to the sensitivity of the executive. It would also be good for the Liberal party; no longer would it be seen in the west as "them."

Exactly the same could be written for the Progressive Conservative party. It would still be a strongly western caucus under the Pepin-Robarts formula: 42 percent as opposed to the 50 percent drawn from there now; but 10 percent of its caucus would represent Quebec — again, ten times the weight that Quebec has now.

Provinces have, and will continue to have for the foreseeable future, important roles in defining the national interest of the country. Electoral system reform would allow a national government, of whatever party, to have an independent conduit to opinion in all segments of the country. Nationally based parties could seek to amalgamate these opinions into their own versions of national interest. These versions would attach less weight to the institutional interests of provincial governments, but still might be sold to residents in all parts of the country. A national party caucus might compete more effectively with the federal-provincial conference or the inter-provincial conference as a forum for working out national policies. Competition among representative bodies could only be in the interests of the represented.

The Two Old Parties

In this section, the results of recent research show the Liberal party as *the* government party at the federal level, deploying its appeal so as to attract sufficient voter support to retain power and the necessary financial support from dominant corporations to finance its campaigns. This has been so successful that it is easy for the party to attract able and ambitious people as candidates and party workers at all levels. Long tenure of office has served to merge the party with the higher echelons of the public service, especially for purposes of policy-making. Effective networks of party elite members have developed, linking the body of the party with the essential advertising, polling and policy-making groups. But the system has gone on too long and is becoming deadened by long service in power.

The Progressive Conservative party, while in some ways the mirror image of the Liberal party, is in other ways its obverse. Like the Liberal party, it is an elite-dominated brokerage party that finances itself by appealing to wealthy and mainly corporate interests. On the other hand, its long years of electoral reverses have created a pattern of expectations on the part of both its supporters and the public. They see the party as a permanent minority party, shut out of Quebec, with little chance of forming the government. As a result, the party has attracted people who are prepared to dispute policy in internecine struggles. The party has become fractious and insubordinate to its leader, which diminishes its appeal as a governing party and further contributes to its failure. This makes it difficult to recruit able and upwardly-mobile people, undermining public confidence in the party and contributing to its position as a permanent minority. It is this situation that the selection of Brian Mulroney as leader is calculated to correct. He is perceived to be a winner who can so convince the party of his capacity that it will unite to defeat the Liberals and assume power.

13 Party and State in the Liberal Era*

REGINALD WHITAKER

Environmental Constraints

The environmental constraints on the Liberal party would appear to have been dominated by three factors. The Canadian political system is liberal-democratic, which, as C.B. Macpherson has ably argued, is a system characterized by a fundamental or structural ambiguity: the coexistence of the democratic and egalitarian values of the political institutions based on universal adult suffrage and the inegalitarian nature of the liberal capitalist economic structures upon which the political structures arose historically. The Liberal party was operating in an environment in which two sometimes contradictory forces were at work in shaping the party's role. On the one hand, the party had to finance its operations as a party as well as to manage a capitalist economy as a government, both of which left it vulnerable to the demands of the corporate capitalist world. On the other hand, the party had to get votes, which left it vulnerable to the demands of public opinion. Contradictions were not always in evidence between these two forces, but when they were, the party was in a state of crisis. Crisis can mean not only danger but opportunity. The Liberal party demonstrated superior skill at calling in one of these forces to redress the balance when the other became too dominating. In the King period this often meant calling in the force of the voters to compensate for the opposition of the private economic interests, but in the St. Laurent period it more often meant calling in the force of corporate capitalism to restrain and manage public opinion. In either event, both the political power of the voters and the economic power of corporate capitalism were in effect resources with which the party, as an intermediary force, could bargain. The ambiguity of this role was heightened, and even cultivated, by the ambiguous ideological role of the party fashioned by Mackenzie King. That the party never

*Reprinted from *The Government Party*, by Reginald Whitaker, by permission of the University of Toronto Press. ©University of Toronto Press, 1977.

rejected the support of the vested capitalist interests, while at the same time never entirely losing its credibility with the voters as a party of democratic reform, left it precisely the flexibility and freedom of action to "wheel and deal" in the center of the political spectrum and to make the kind of practical accommodations necessary to maintain its hold on power.

The third environmental factor, this somewhat more specific to Canada, was the regional diversity and political fragmentation inherent in a federal society as decentralized as Canada. This factor is at the same time so obvious as to be almost taken for granted, and yet so important that it can scarcely be overestimated. The relatively weak impact of the dominant *class* cleavages of modern industrial society on Canadian party politics in the face of economic regionalization and cultural divisions not only simplified the role of the Liberals as the center party exploiting the ambiguities and contradictions of liberal-democracy — rather than becoming a victim of them, as in the case of the British Liberal party — but also gave a very particular cast to the structure of the party. It is no exaggeration to say that the structure of the Liberal party in this era can *only* be understood in the light of the impact of federalism on the inherited political structures of the British parliamentary system.

Party Finance

The relationship between the party and its financial supporters was a complex one, to a degree which rather forbids easy generalizations. The celebrated Beauharnois affair of 1930 was a highly misleading guide to the financial state of the party. The penury into which the party fell following the defeat of that year illustrates two points: first, whatever the motives of corporate donors to political parties, a party which sustained a major defeat was quickly abandoned. This was particularly crucial for the Liberal party, whose traditional links had been more to government contractors than to significant sections of big business whose interests closely related to party policy or ideology. A party which depends heavily on government contractors is in obvious difficulties when faced with a period out of office. The second point to emerge from this period is that the party was clearly unwilling to compromise its policies in return for financial support. In the case of the banks and the mining companies, as well as the railway unification issues and the wheat marketing board, there is evidence that the party — and here the decisive role of the party leader must be emphasized — would not alter policy at the behest of businessmen armed with financial inducements. On the other hand, the party's own ideological bent, while it might distance itself from some capitalist interests, drew it close to certain sectors of the corporate world. Capitalism is not a monolithic set of interests, except in those comparatively rare moments when it is challenged by other classes from below or external enemies from without.

There was always some sectors of the corporate world, even if not the greater part, which were willing to work with the Liberals, particularly where their interests coincided closely with Liberal policy. Even while still in opposition there were those who found such an identity of outlook — particularly the retail chain stores and the meat packing industry. Later, the Liberal party in office was able to greatly widen the scope of its friendly relations with the corporate world, as the identity of interests broadened and deepened with the years of power.

The contract levy system which Norman Lambert enforced in the late 1930s was predicated upon the desire of business to maintain good public relations with government as a major purchaser of goods and services from the private sector. This system not only was maintained after Lambert's departure from active party work, but was extended and deepened. Two developments made this consolidation possible. The enormous growth of government intervention in the private sector, arising out of the demands of the wartime economy and the commitment to interventionist Keynesian fiscal policies following the war, along with the maintenance of relatively high levels of defence expenditure in the Cold War period, had a specific meaning for the financing of the government party. A greatly expanded state sector which involved government in continuous interaction with private corporations as sellers of goods and services to this sector enhanced the scope for party finance — on a contract levy system where tenders were in force, or on a straight patronage basis where public bidding was not the practice. That this growth of state activity was expressed initially through the federal government, and that this centralization was closely associated with the policies of the Liberal party, also meant that the position of the federal party was reinforced in relation to its provincial counterparts. Of course, business generally wishes to retain good relations with government parties, especially when government intervention in the private sector becomes less predictable than in the past. There is also the motive of wishing to purchase access to decision-makers in case of difficulty. Thus, with or without specific connection of government contracts, the federal Liberal party was able to increase its capacity for financing its activities as a partisan organization through the 1940s and into the 1950s. Another sign of this improved financial position was the growing regularization of funding over the inter-election period, reflected in the growing ability of the party in the 1950s to finance its day-to-day operations on a normal business basis — a condition which had certainly not existed in the 1930s.

Party finance was not an isolated factor; party organization was intimately, even inextricably, bound up with the problem of party finance. Adequate financing was the necessary, although not the sufficient, condition for the vitality of the party as an organization. The genesis of the National Liberal Federation in the early 1930s was as much, if not more, a matter of fundraising as it was a matter of creating an extra-parliamentary organization for electoral purposes.

This concentration of the extra-parliamentary party on fundraising may indicate an endemic condition of cadre parties with their aversions to mass membership participation in policy-making or leadership selection and their extreme vulnerability to a small number of corporate donors, but it also illustrates two specific factors of the Canadian political experience in this era. First, the Liberal party, especially under King's leadership, found considerable political utility in a formal separation of the fundraising apparatus from the parliamentary leadership of the party. There is very little evidence of demands for participation by the rank-and-file membership in policy-making or even leadership selection in this era of the Liberal party's history. Nor is there much, if any, evidence of a perception of electoral threat from mass party techniques of campaigning. The move of the Liberal party toward extra-parliamentary organization had much more to do with the demands of party finance.

The second major factor forcing the national party's attention on party finance was the divergence between the concentration of economic power in the private sector — both in the corporate and in the regional sense — in a small handful of influential corporations in Toronto and Montreal and the decentralized nature of the formal political system. As a political organization, the Liberal party was based on the constitutional distribution of elective offices into more than two hundred local constituencies and nine provinces (ten after Newfoundland's entry into Confederation). However much the central regions might dominate the party as a whole, such centralization could in no way match the centralization of private economic power. Indeed, the autonomy of the local units of the party in a political and electoral sense was one of the characteristics of the Liberal party as an organization, and the very structure of the formal institutional arrangements of election under the parliamentary system of single-member constituency voting ensured that this would be so. Consequently, the scope of such political activities as electoral organization and policy-making on the part of an extra-parliamentary national office was necessarily limited; on the other hand, the importance of the small number of party donors in two concentrated geographical locations meant that local units of the party at the provincial and constituency level were generally incapable of generating the necessary contacts for fundraising purposes — but for the crucial exception of the provincial units in these areas. With this exception and its consequent problems aside, it is clear that party finance would necessarily be one area of party activity best left to an extra-parliamentary wing of the national party. Hence the high degree of concentration on this one activity most relevant to the extra-parliamentary national party.

Party Organization

There is no doubt that the Liberal party was a cadre party: parliamentary in origin, small in membership, deriving support from local notables, and so on. Yet I have already suggested that there is little evidence of Duverger's "contagion from the left" as a factor shaping the party's structure. The growth of an extra-parliamentary party alongside the parliamentary party did not come about as the emulation of a successful mass socialist party organization on the left — since such never did develop fully at the national level in Canada — but rather as the consequence of electoral defeat, in 1930, or the fear of defeat during the Second World War. Even when, as in the latter case, it was fear of a leftward trend in public opinion and the possible capitalization of the CCF on this trend that moved the party to change its approach, the specific *organizational* changes introduced in the party were not significant; changes rather took place on the level of policy and party program. There was no democratization of the party organization or any shift of influence from the parliamentary to the extra-parliamentary party; rather the parliamentary leadership skilfully manipulated the extra-parliamentary structure to help initiate desired policy changes. Once the next election was won, the organization reverted to its former state.

The point is that a cadre party operating in a federal system is particularly vulnerable in an organizational sense to the loss of office, not only because the fruits of power are useful resources for party organization but also because the party lacks a firm and loyal *class* basis of support in the electorate. Moreover, the fact that the party's provincial bases are not really bases at all, but rather problematic elements in the overall structure of the national party, with different electorates, different concerns and even different sources of party funding, means that a national cadre party out of office cannot rely on the provincial parties as a second, fall-back position for the national party in its hour of organizational need. Conversely, if it does (as in the case of Ontario in the 1930s), it may be creating organizational and political problems for itself in the long run.

The alternative in this situation is for the defeated cadre party to create an extra-parliamentary structure to undertake some of the functions normally carried out by the cabinet ministers while in office. This in turn reflects the particular cast which federalism gives to cadre parties in office, which can be called a *ministerialist* system of party organization. This system places a premium on the regional representativeness of the executive and encourages the emergence of regional power-brokers as key cabinet ministers, who thus play a double role as administrators and as political leaders of regions. When the administrative powers of patronage are severed from the political role of regional power-broking, ministerialist organization becomes a liability rather than an asset to the party. Hence the attempt to create an extra-parliamentary wing of the party as an electoral alternative, particularly when the party leader, as in the case of King from 1930 to 1935, is unwilling to personally assume the organizational burden.

On the other hand, when the party returns to power the extra-parliamentary party diminishes drastically in importance in the face of the return of ministerialism. In the case of the Liberal party after 1935, however, one can see a new factor entering into the parliamentary versus extra-parliamentary equation. In the absence of strong class bases to national politics, cadre ministerialist party organization rests most comfortably on what can be loosely called a patron-client model. The regional discontinuities of the country lend themselves to a clientist type of politics in which one sees vertical integration of subcultures and horizontal accommodation among the elites generated by these subcultures. So long as politics revolves mainly around questions of patronage and regional bargaining, ministerialism fits in well with the needs of the party as an organization. Even out of office, as with the creation of the National Liberal Federation (NLF) in the early 1930s, the promise of future patronage considerations is a powerful weapon to line up political support. Yet to the extent that the forces of industrialism and urbanism and events such as depressions and world wars intrude on this somewhat petty little political stage (the provincialism and sordidness of which was noted by earlier outside observers such as Lord Bryce and André Siegfried), the attention of governments is drawn inevitably toward wider problems, which demand universalist, bureaucratic solutions rather than the old-fashioned particularistic solutions of patronage political cultures. Under the pressure of these external forces, ministerialist government becomes administrative government, politics turns into bureaucracy and the Liberal party becomes the government party. Paradoxically, ministerialist organization thus becomes an impediment to the political health of the party as a patronage organization, as well as the source of the necessary instruments of that type of politics. In these conditions there is a continued need for some sort of extra-parliamentary wing of the party to maintain the necessary contacts between the party's external supporters and the largesse of the government, to coordinate the patronage side of the party's operations and to remind it constantly of its role as an electoral as well as an administrative organization. Thus the NLF did not disappear entirely after the return to office in 1935, as had happened in 1921. The partisan ceasefire in the war years coupled with the intense and accelerated bureaucratization and centralization of the wartime government led to such a political crisis for the Liberal party that it found it necessary to call the extra-parliamentary party back into existence to help get the electoral machine functioning once again. Ministerialism thus generated its own limitations.

The electoral victory of 1945, in which the party's ability to respond to *class* politics as well as regional politics was tested, and the return of prosperity in the aftermath of war, laid the foundations for an apparent reversal of the relationships just indicated. After the war the extra-parliamentary party was relegated to the status of a mere paper "democratic" legitimatization of ministerialist organization. Even party publicity was in effect "farmed out" to a private advertising agency in return for government business, thus directly linking party publicity with state publicity. The Liberal party's transformation into the government party had reached its logical culmination, with the virtual fusion of party and state. The Liberals won two general elections under this arrangement and convinced most observers that they could continue indefinitely. But they lost the third election, and then suffered a devastating collapse when faced with the necessity of running while out of office, suddenly bereft of ministerialist organization, yet lacking any real extra-parliamentary party organization.

Ministerialist organization thus appears a curiously ambiguous factor in party organization. Partly as a result of this ambiguity, the role of the national leader in the Liberal party was of paramount importance. When the party was out of office in the early 1930s the leader was in a very real sense the sole representative of the national party. In the aftermath of defeat, it is no exaggeration to assert that Mackenzie King had become the sole personal embodiment of the party in any significant way. The parliamentary party remained, but without clear responsibilities, and often without either the inclination or the ability to function as a continuing party organization. Hence King's frantic efforts to set up an extra-parliamentary organization for the purposes of election planning and especially fundraising, since the responsibility for these activities was forcing an intolerable burden on his own shoulders. It should also be noted that when out of office the potential patronage powers of the leader of the opposition in a future government are almost the only inducements available to the party for organizational purposes. This places the leader squarely at the center of the political stage, to a degree which would appear to almost match the domination of the party by an incumbent prime minister. There is no doubt that Mackenzie King returned to office in 1935 in a stronger and more commanding position over his parliamentary party and his ministers than that which he had enjoyed before defeat. The circumstances of that period of opposition may have been exceptional, and no attempt should be made to generalize on the role of the leader of a party on the strength of this example. What is clear, however, is that the crucial role of the leader in the party organization was enhanced by this experience, and that the creation of an extra-parliamentary party was not a detraction from the role of the leader but rather an instrument of the leader's continued influence over all aspects of the party's operations.

The well-known patronage powers of an incumbent prime minister, his direct relationship with the voters, his prerogative of dissolution and his financial control over the fortunes of individual candidates, all demonstrate that the role of the party leader while in power is of enormous importance. Yet ministerialist organization, as well as the concentration of the prime minister on policy and administrative matters, tended to push the Liberal party in power towards a somewhat more diffuse distribution of responsibilities for party organization than had been the case while out of office. This tendency became quite striking when a new leader, Louis St. Laurent, who showed not the slightest interest in matters of party organization, allowed a still greater degree of devolution of responsibility in these matters to his ministers. Paradoxically perhaps, the greater strength of ministerialism in the St. Laurent years is itself an indication of the discretionary role of the leader in shaping the party organization; Liberal leaders had the capacity to leave their personal stamp on the party structure, even if, as in St. Laurent's case, this stamp was delegation of authority to his cabinet colleagues. Under King's direction the party organization, as well as the cabinet, was under tighter control. Yet it must also be pointed out that this greater control was only a matter of degree. It is clear from the historical record that King's ability to dominate his colleagues was limited, the limits being well recognized by King himself. Ministerialism was more than a tactic of a certain kind of prime minister; it was a structural feature of cabinet government in a regionally divided society. The historical circumstances and the accident of personality might allow greater or lesser scope for ministerialism, but the *fact* of ministerialism was not subject to these vicissitudes. National party organization when the Liberal party was in office derived its basic structure from the interplay of the leadership of the prime minister and the ministerialist distribution of responsibilities.

The domination of the extra-parliamentary by the parliamentary leadership was an inevitable feature of a cadre-ministerialist party in a federal political system. This did not make the administrative task of the extra-parliamentary officials an easy one, in the sense of a division of responsibilities and recognition for their work.

That the party leadership expended considerable anxiety and energy at the various advisory council meetings over the question of preventing anything remotely critical of the parliamentary party's policies from being aired is a striking indication of how far parliamentary control over policy went: the extra-parliamentary membership was not only to be powerless in deciding policy, but it had to be *seen* to be powerless as well. The smallest hint of disagreement over policy among Liberals — which is to say, the hint of any dissension from the policies adopted by the parliamentary leadership — was to be avoided at all costs. Democratic legitimation of the internal processes of decision-making in the party was accepted, but only at the most rarefied and abstract level, that of the mandate of the party leader derived from the majority vote of a party convention at one point in time. The autonomy of the parliamentary party in policy-making was justified in rhetorical terms by the invocation of the constitutional supremacy of parliament. Whatever the merits of that argument, it was rendered somewhat problematic by the increasing bureaucratic influence on the policies of the parliamentary leadership, to the extent that by the last years of the St. Laurent period, virtually all Liberal policy was formulated by the permanent civil service. Policy-making was delegated to an institution which was, in the formal sense at least, non-political as well as non-partisan. The exclusion of the extra-parliamentary party membership from policy-making may thus be viewed as a matter of practical expediency rather than as one of constitutional principle. The party membership was not judged competent to formulate policy.

The 1948 national convention which chose Louis St Laurent as King's successor best illustrates these relationships within the Liberal party. The extraordinary lengths to which the party leadership went, in this unique example of a national party meeting throughout the period of this study, to prevent any public manifestation of criticism or disagreement within the membership, extended not only to policy questions but to the matter of leadership itself. The evidence clearly indicates that the convention format was manipulated throughout to ensure that King's chosen successor should receive as little opposition as possible. On the other hand, the necessary democratic legitimation seemed to demand that St Laurent receive some token opposition. Both imperatives were carried out in a remarkable example of stage-management conflict, in which the two genuine opponents of St Laurent were effectively utilized for maximum public effect and minimum internal impacts. Even in the case of the selection of the party leader, then, the "democratic" mandate becomes highly questionable, and the domination of the party by the parliamentary leadership is seen to be decisive.

Conventions at the constituency level during this era would appear to have served equivalent legitimation purposes for the parliamentary elite. Nomination votes by the constituency association membership were often, although not always, called before elections. Rarely were these exercises more than empty formalities. Sitting members were virtually assured of renomination; defeated candidates from the previous election had the inside track; and if neither of these conditions obtained, the local cabinet minister and his organizers would normally anoint the man they wanted for the nomination. The association would then ratify the choice. It did not happen like this in every instance, but it was the general rule. Observers of contemporary Canadian political culture who have noted the "quasi-participative" nature of Canadian democracy might examine the role of the Liberal party, the dominant party in Canadian politics for well over a generation, in the political socialization of its members and supporters. The Liberal party was certainly no training ground for participatory democracy, however loosely that phrase might be defined. If anything, the dominant values which it propagated as a mediating institution between the state and the mass of the citizens were those of deference and unreflective loyalty.

Deference and loyalty are political values appropriate to the clientist web of relationships which formed the basic structure of the party. Clientist relationships, moreover, flourished in the era of one-party dominance, when the Liberals as the government party monopolized the basic medium of exchange in patron-client politics: patronage. But the general condition referred to earlier, the transformation of politics into bureaucracy in the period of one party dominance, had a double effect on the party as an organization. The use of the state as a reward system for party loyalty effectively drained away the human resources of the party as a partisan organization into levels of the bureaucracy and judiciary where they could no longer be of political use to the party. Second, as an inevitable consequence of the first problem, the party had to rely heavily on direct cooperation from the bureaucracy or the private sector to replenish its parliamentary leadership. Thus it merged more and more intimately with the senior civil service, both in terms of policies and personnel, and with the corporate elite outside the state system itself but in regular contact with government. For these organizational reasons, as well as for the more general ones mentioned earlier, the party became less and less distinct as an entity, its separation from the state system and the private sector more and more blurred. The government party was becoming in a curious sense a non-partisan party, so long as its hold on office was not challenged. Some might prefer to argue that it was a case of the bureaucrats being made into Liberals. Yet however one approaches the question, it seems reasonable to conclude that the Liberal party, as a political party, was growing less distinct, that the party was more a vehicle for elite accommodation, involving not only the elites of the two linguistic and cultural groups in Canada but the bureaucratic and corporate elites as well, than a partisan organization. When partisanship got in the way of elite accommodation it was partisanship which was usually discarded. No better example of this can be found than in the examination of federal-provincial relations within the Liberal party in this era.

Federal-Provincial Party Relations

Quebec, as the homeland of French Canada, held a special status within the national Liberal party, based on tradition and a mild form of consociational tolerance. Yet it was Ontario, with its strong and semi-autonomous economic base, which mounted the toughest challenge to the dominance of the national party in this era. In both cases the federal party ran into difficulties with its provincial counterpart, to a moderate degree in Quebec and to an extreme degree in Ontario. In Quebec, electoral defeat for the provincial party in the mid-1930s gave the federal party, which remained ascendant in its own electoral sphere, the opportunity to control the provincial party, even to the extent of guiding it back into office briefly. Eventually, the federal party settled into a pattern of constituency collaboration with its provincial party's enemy, and more or less accommodative intergovernmental relationships with the Union Nationale in terms of federal-provincial affairs, including accommodations which sometimes drastically undercut the political position of its provincial counterpart. In Ontario, a politically (and even financially) stronger provincial party in the mid-1930s waged open war on the federal party, even extending its campaign to Quebec, both on the intergovernmental and political fronts. This vigorous challenge was finally defeated by intelligent mobilization of the federal party's resources, and the intervention of an external event, the coming of the Second World War. Following the provincial defeat, the federal Liberals managed very well in Ontario by allowing a much weakened and discredited provincial party to flounder unaided in the further reaches of opposition, while dealing with the Conservative provincial government in federal-provincial relations with little regard to partisan considerations. Thus, in both cases, the long-run result was the same: the federal party prospered in the two largest provinces without a strong provincial wing. Little was done to aid the provincial parties, and, in the Quebec case, much was done to damage the provincials. This distant relationship was matched by an emphasis on intergovernmental relations with the provincial administrations of the opposite political color. In other words, executive federalism overrode federal-provincial party solidarity. The government party at Ottawa preferred to deal with other governments.

Intra-party relationships with the hinterland regions of Canada were not normally troubled by financial competition between the federal and provincial wings. The financial superiority of the federal party was almost always evident. In the Atlantic provinces this financial strength, in conjunction with competitive two-party systems and patronage political cultures, resulted in highly integrated party organizations and low levels of intra-party strains. Newfoundland was a somewhat exceptional case, representing one-man provincial rule in close cooperation with the federal Liberal party and the federal state, but even here there was a close meshing of the two parties, albeit with rather more provincial direction than in the Maritime provinces. Basically the Atlantic provinces represent a case study of the Liberal party as an integrative device within Confederation, drawing the provincial units into the federal sphere of influence and control, a political reflection of economic and administrative domination of poor and undeveloped provinces by the federal government.

The West presents a striking contrast with the Atlantic region. Although very much in a state of economic inferiority to central Canada, the western provinces resisted a status of political inferiority to the government party at Ottawa, first by giving relatively weak electoral support to the party in federal elections and second by tending to strike out on experimental routes with the party system in provincial politics. Thus the Liberal parties in Manitoba and British Columbia entered coalitions at the provincial level while maintaining their full partisan identities in federal politics. Even in Alberta unsuccessful moves were attempted in this direction. In all cases severe intra-party strains became apparent. Only in Saskatchewan was a consistently high level of federal-provincial party integration maintained, due to tradition, strong partisan leadership and relative provincial political strength. Yet even in Saskatchewan prolonged relegation to provincial opposition bred growing internal party disunity. The Liberal party at Ottawa during its long period of domination grew further apart from its provincial counterparts in the West, which were either cooperating with its federal party competitors or floundering in opposition. Eventually, a pattern of intergovernmental relations with provincial administrations ranging in partisan coloration from quasi-Liberal to social democratic to Social Credit began to predominate over the kind of intra-party integrations which the Saskatchewan Liberal machine had once represented. The Liberal party's experiences in the West were very different from those in central Canada. Yet the same basic result was reached from different routes: executive federalism proved stronger than federal-provincial party solidarity.

This study in effect constitutes a documentation of the growing confederalization of the Liberal party over a period of almost thirty years. It should be emphasized that this process does not necessarily imply the attenuation of federal dominance over provincial wings of the party. Indeed, in most cases examined, the federal party emerged as the most successful. That this took place in the two central provinces, those best situated in economic, political, and even cultural (in the case of Quebec) terms to mount effective challenges to federal domination of the Liberal party, is a striking indication of the ability of the senior level of the party to maintain its superior position.

Confederalization did mean the separation of the two wings in terms of senior personnel, career patterns, party finance and even ideology. This means that by the 1950s, the government party in Ottawa was loosely linked with unsuccessful opposition parties in Quebec City, Toronto and three western provinces — parties whose weakness was more or less enforced by the very success of the federal party. Nor was this distinctly asymmetrical relationship simply an accident; rather it reflected a crucial problem in federal-provincial relations.

The problem revolves around the inevitable conflict in which two wings of the same party in the same province must engage for the available human resources. An increasing separation and insulation of the two wings at the level of parliamentary leadership was never matched by an equivalent separation of the membership at the constituency level. The critical problem faced by all parties of the mobilization of the party rank and file at election time to perform the multiple organizational tasks necessary for successful electioneering, could become itself a cause of contention and competition between two wings of the party in the same area. Only in the extreme — and in the Canadian context, unlikely — eventuality of complete jurisdictional accord between the province and the national government might political conflict at the governmental level not cause conflict at the party level. Another factor capable of overriding intra-party divisions might be a cross-provincial ideological cohesiveness within the party; in the case of a brokerage party like the Liberals, this was never true in practice, and doubtful in theory. Nor could pure patronage politics serve to override divisions.

In Quebec provincial disputes spilled over into federal constituency politics; the federal party reasserted stability by the subordination of the provincial wing, first by directly placing it in office, later by abandoning it to successive terms of opposition while collaborating with its opponent. The capacity of the federal wing to enforce a permanent opposition status on its provincial counterpart derived from its superior political and financial resources accruing from the national office, and its evident unwillingness — except in the very special circumstances of 1939 — to utilize these resources on behalf of the provincial party. Superior political and financial resources combined to ensure superiority in the attraction of human resources. Yet, in the long run, the provincial Liberals were able to rebuild their strength, not through prior solution of their financial problem, but by generating new and separate organizational structures which could serve as alternative sources for the mobilization of human resources. In other words, political resources were developed independently of the federal party.

To a degree in Manitoba and much more so in British Columbia, coalition arrangements in provincial politics put severe strains on constituency organization and the loyalties of local party activists. There is definite evidence for British Columbia that the federal Liberals were in a much stronger position when the provincial party went into opposition in the 1950s than when it had been the dominant provincial coalition partner earlier. Saskatchewan, in the period of joint Liberal rule in both capitals from 1935 to 1944, appears to offer a contrast, inasmuch as party integration was smoother than it was later when the provincial party was out of office. In this case, Saskatchewan is closer to the example of the Atlantic provinces when intra-party unity was bought at the price of clear federal domination, exercised in the Saskatchewan case, however, with some autonomy at the level of the federal cabinet by Jimmy Gardiner as the regional prairie power-broker at Ottawa. In other words, federal Liberal domination within Saskatchewan did not preclude regional representation of some significance within the cabinet, a regional power which was backed precisely by the high level of intra-party integration and the bargaining leverage this placed in Gardiner's hands. Saskatchewan thus represented a model of party politics as a vehicle of regional representation quite different from those adopted elsewhere in the West. The Liberal parties of the Atlantic provinces, on the other hand, did not appear to utilize party integration as a bargaining lever within the federal cabinet to the same extent.

Here party loyalty overrode regional discontent and the same local activists could be mobilized equally for either level of electoral politics with the same well-integrated set of rewards backed by the political financing of Montreal and the coordinated patronage inducements of the federal and provincial states. Only in Newfoundland is there real evidence of this Liberal loyalty being translated into any real provincial influence on the federal party, but here the small size of the province and its state of underdevelopment and poverty severely limited its power. The Maritimes aside, it is clear that in the case of Saskatchewan federal-provincial integration as a vehicle of provincial political representation is not without strain when one party loses office. In the late 1940s and in the 1950s it became apparent that a certain tension between two wings at the leadership level was being reflected in problems at the local level.

There is a sense, then, in which federal and provincial wings of a party are often locked into a rather self-destructive relationship. If, as many observers have argued, political parties act mainly as recruitment agencies for the staffing of elective office — and the weakness of the Liberal party as a channel of demands on the political system through extra-parliamentary policy formation appears to give added weight to the emphasis — then federal and provincial wings of the same party are necessarily locked into competition for the same pool of human resources. Provincial weakness matched by federal strength guarantees the latter wing against too much competition. Dealing with governments of another political color at the provincial level, on the other hand, avoids this problem. The claims of other governments can be treated as a matter of intergovernmental negotiation. The claims of party become a complicating factor, adding new levels of conflict which can be avoided when the problem is simply intergovernmental. The intra-party dimension of federal-provincial relations is thus a matter of *additional* complexity. It is difficult to generalize beyond this from the limited time period which has been examined, but it does seem safe to conclude that a government party will prudently seek to avoid such complications. They may opt, as the federal Liberals did in Ontario and Quebec, for underwriting the position of their provincial wings as permanent opposition parties, thus keeping the party name before the provincial voters while at the same time minimizing their impact on the federal level. Thus the dominant strategy of the federal Liberals in confronting this organizational problem in Ontario and Quebec was to downplay partisanship between levels of government.

In a country as diverse and as decentralized as Canada, and especially in the case of provinces as crucially influential in relationship to the federal government as Ontario and Quebec, a party in power in Ottawa could not afford the intra-party strains involved in attempting to use the party as an integrative device in federal-provincial relations. Instead, the Liberal party reverted to intergovernmental, even interbureaucratic, relations as the major channels of accommodation. This not only helped account for the weak and underdeveloped nature of extra-parliamentary national party organization in this era, but also strongly reinforced the tendency already present in the government party to transform politics into bureaucracy and party into state.

Perhaps this may be the final, paradoxical conclusion to be drawn from this study. The curious lack of definition of Canadian parties, which has troubled so many observers of our politics, is only reinforced as the evidence concerning their structures is marshalled. The Liberal party was an organization seeking not so much to consolidate its distinct partisan identity as to embed itself within the institutional structures of government. Its fulfillment was not so much organizational survival as it was institutionalization as an aspect of government: control over recruitment channels to senior levels of office. The deadening of political controversy, the silence, the greyness which clothed political life at the national level in the 1950s, were reflections of a Liberal ideal of an apolitical public life. In place of politics there was bureaucracy and technology. This in no sense meant that Canada stood still. Profound changes were taking place in the nation's political economy. But these changes tended to take place outside the realm of traditional political debate. Instead, it was between the great bureaucracies, whether public (federal and provincial) or private (Canadian and American), that debate and policy refinement took place. The Liberal party had truly become the government party — an instrument for the depoliticization and bureaucratization of Canadian public life. The vision of Mackenzie King in his almost forgotten *Industry and Humanity* had begun to take shape: "whether political or industrial government will merge into one, or tend to remain separate and distinct" was King's question for the future in 1918. He concluded that "the probabilities are that for years to come they will exist side by side, mostly distinguishable, but, in much, so merged that separateness will be possible in theory only."

14 Power in Trudeau's Liberal Party*

CHRISTINA McCALL-NEWMAN

In order to fufil his aims for Quebec, Trudeau needed to retain power. To retain power he needed the Liberal machine, and to that end he was willing to bend his iron will to the party's needs. To quite a remarkable degree, as the seventies drew to a close these needs were interpreted for Trudeau by a few men who were usually called in Liberal circles "The PMO in-group" or "the Coutts 'n' Davey gang." It was tacitly considered to consist of eight people, two of whom weren't Liberals at all. Besides Coutts and Davey, there were Coutt's assistants, Tom Axworthy and Colin Kenny, plus Davey's closest cronies in Toronto, Jerry Grafstein, the lawyer, who was an expert in communications, and Martin Goldfarb, the pollster, who was officially a non-partisan interpreter of voter behaviour since he had accepted contracts in the past for Conservative provincial parties. Then there was Richard O'Hagan, the Prime Minister's media consultant, whose opinions had been heeded by Coutts and Davey for nearly twenty years...and Michael Pitfield, the Clerk of the Privy Council, who would have been appalled at the very idea of being identified as a Grit but who undoubtedly had more influence on the Leader's thinking about the political process than any other English Canadian....

The small size of the PMO group was all the more remarkable in light of the fact that it was made up of the remnants of two successive waves of political reformers — the Pearsonian New Guard and the Just Society Trudeauites — who had entered politics in order to democratize the Liberal Party, to make it more open for what the Pearsonians had called "the grass roots" and the Trudeauites "the people."

In the previous twenty years, there was no doubt that the Liberal Party had changed from the old King-St. Laurent male club reeking of whisky and cigar smoke, with its hints of electoral skulduggery, campaign funds alloted by party bosses, parachuted candidates, big donations from big

*From *Grits* by Christina McCall-Newman. Copyright © 1982 Christina McCall-Newman
Reprinted by permission of Macmillan of Canada,
A Division of Gage Publishing Limited.

business, and powerful cabinet ministers lording it over their regions, with a party membership held together by patronage and ancestral memories. On paper, it had been democratized. It now had a more open formal structure. A national executive, elected by the party membership rather than appointed by the leader, met regularly. Delegates from the constituencies gathered in convention every two years (in contrast with the King-St. Laurent era when the party met only three times, in 1919, 1948, and 1958, and then only to choose a leader). The party's elected president and appointed national director were invited to take part in the political planning committee, the group of ministers and officials from the Prime Minister's Office who met once a week, and in the deliberations of the national campaign committee whenever it convened.

Despite these changes, and others of their ilk, haggled over in party committees and enshrined in party documents, despite the rhetoric of participation and leader accountability, of membership renewal and policy consultation, despite the open nomination meetings in the constituencies and the reform of fund-raising practices, the party was in essential ways no more powerful than it had been under King and St. Laurent. In fact, some political scientists argued that it was slightly less so, since King had been dependent on the good will of the party's regional elites — if not its grass roots — in order to hold the various factions of his alliance together and had altered his policies to suit their demands, as expressed by regional cabinet ministers, in effect sharing decision-making with them. Now that the party's elites were dependent on the leader's ability to swing the electorate's votes rather than the other way around, and cabinet ministers were engrossed in the management of their departments, the party was often described by both its adherents and its opponents as little more than a leader's machine driven by a small cadre on his behalf, with policy made by government bureaucracy far from the party's sight. To many Canadians, it seemed as though the Liberal Party had gone from oligarchy to oligarchy in one generation.

The most publicized participants in the new oligarchy, Jim Coutts and Keith Davey, were talked of by journalists and other politicians as though they had grabbed power for themselves out of insatiable ambition and unmatchable cunning. But they knew that whatever power they possessed was ephemeral, that it was derived entirely from their relationship to Trudeau and the control over the party and the government that his office bestowed on him.

Grattan O'Leary, who had been a close observer of the Canadian political process for more than sixty years, once remarked, "It would be plainly foolish for anybody trying to fathom how Canada works not to come to grips with the power of the prime minister. It has always been an office of enormous weight in this country. Ministers are servile to him because of his control over their careers and his party caucus even more so. The senior civil servants are dependent on his favour; the judiciary is appointed through him, as is the Senate. Success at the top of the governmental hierarchy depends on catching the prime minister's interest and currying his favour. If the Canadian power structure is a pyramid, there is absolutely no doubt who is on top. And in the Trudeau era, because of the tenor of the times and personality of the man himself, this power has become self-evident to all who have the wits to see."

O'Leary made these statements without real rancour just as the man he had hoped would occupy the top of the pyramid, Robert Stanfield, was preparing to bow out as Conservative Opposition Leader, after losing a third election to Pierre Trudeau in 1974. It was O'Leary's view that the prime minister's importance would have grown inexorably as government had expanded over the previous ten years, no matter who occupied the office. Other observers were less sanguine. It had been repeatedly charged that Trudeau had wilfully "presidentialized" the prime-ministership at the expense of the parliamentary system. No matter how many arguments were raised by Trudeau's defenders about the limits on prime-ministerial power that had been devised or refined during the Trudeau era (the collegial cabinet system, the reformed committee system in the House of Commons, the caucus consultation process, the efforts of participatory decision-making within the Liberal Party) or the limits that the Canadian political system itself had always imposed (Parliament with its emphasis on the Opposition's right to question and obstruct and the even more constraining division of powers between the federal and provincial governments), his opponents' view of Trudeau remained fixed. He was seen as the most powerful political leader of Canadian history, a man whose mastery of the techniques of modern leadership politics — the deployment of an expert staff whose loyalties and energies were devoted to him personally, the use of polls in the reading of public opinion and of television in manipulating it — was the secret of his strength. Reflecting on this phenomenon, O'Leary observed, "I have always wanted to amend Lord Acton's formula. Power doesn't neces-sarily corrupt but in my experience, it almost invariably accrues. If people think you possess it, they endow you with more by acceding to your demands."

• • •

The concept of keeping up your network was essential to the style of the contemporary Liberal Party. "He has a reliable network," one Grit would say admiringly of another, meaning he knows a lot of people and can call in many favours. "I'll get Joe to m.c. my fund-raising dinner. He owes me one," a Liberal would remark. Or, "I'll ask David to speak to Don and Ron about a judgeship for Stephen/to come with me for lunch at Le Mascaron when I have another go at talking Turner into running in Eglinton/to canvass a poll for John to show everybody's behind him."

What the English-Canadian Liberal Party had become in 1979 — other than the "important instrument in the Canadian reality" that its leader so coolly described — was the crucial "network", the one that had Keith Davey and Jim Coutts sitting at the centre with the rest of the leader's cadre, reaching out to a huge circle of friends who comprised the party elite, though that was a word they themselves would never use. They liked to talk about "insiders," "networks," "activists," and "the grass roots," instead of the cadre, the elite, the campaign workers, and the committed supporters the political scientists described. Grits preferred to think that any member of the grass roots could become part of the network and then get to be an insider if only he worked hard enough.

Keith Davey estimated that there were ten thousand Liberal activists. "Twenty-five hundred come to party conventions," he said, "and there are three more like them at home," with about two hundred and fifty of those intensely involved as insiders. Then there were another 240,000 committed Liberals who identified themselves as supporters of the party, the people who had to be mobilized in a campaign, to staff candidates' offices, to stuff the voters' mailboxes with literature, to give coffee parties, to be taken in busloads to large rallies, or to drive voters to the polls. To win a majority of the available parliamentary seats in English Canada, eighty to ninety per cent of these Liberals had to be motivated to vote, or so Colin Kenny, who made a career of studying these matters, believed. Mobilizing all those "gut Grits" was the purpose of the marked voters' lists kept in the ridings in the hands of the experienced poll captains.

The purpose of all the rest of the party's hard-learned professional campaigning techniques — the expensive opinion-polling and the even more expensive television and print advertising, the superlative speeches written by the high-priced help to be delivered by the leader at the huge rallies with the orchestrated crowds, the massive efforts to get the right headlines in the press and the right stories on the television news — the purpose of all that was to win the floating vote. It wasn't the Liberal grass roots that occupied the minds of the insiders as the campaign drew near. They had been given their due: the visits from the leader at nomination meetings, the trips to the policy conventions for their association presidents, the mailings from headquarters cheering them on to the Liberal nirvana in the future. It was the uncommitted voters that the insiders talked about with so much anxiety in the winter of 1979, to the frustration of their law partners, lovers, wives, children, aged parents, or any other dependents they might be harbouring....

The Liberal Party had been the party of the middle in terms of class as well as policy for most of the previous century. Members of the upper class, that thin layer at the top of the heaving Canadian mosaic, the people with the inherited money, the old-family names, and the international connections, had rarely engaged directly in politics and even more rarely in Liberal politics. They preferred to contribute to the campaign funds of the middle-class men who had the time, the techniques, the ability, and the ambition to do the governing....

15 The Liberal Party: Reform Pre-empted (1979-80)*

JOSEPH WEARING

Looking at the history of the Liberal party in perspective, one can see a cyclical pattern of decay and renewal; the decay coming after a number of years in power and the renewal prompted by electoral defeat, either threatened or actual. During the periods of decline, the parliamentary party and the leader have become progressively more isolated from opinion in the party and in the country at large, while the volunteer or extraparliamentary wing have grown disillusioned and uninterested. The sobering reality of electoral losses has then prompted the parliamentary leadership to take the volunteer wing more seriously, as King did after 1930 and 1943, as Pearson did after 1958 and as Trudeau did after 1972. The extraparliamentary wing has subsequently become the source of new ideas and fresh faces; but, with the party safely back in power, the whole cycle starts again within a few years.

The other constant theme in Liberal history is the interplay between two *leitmotivs:* an idealistic one that seeks to make the Liberal party into a democratic reformist broadly based organization, and a cynical one in which the party is controlled autocratically by an ever-diminishing coterie around the leader; the volunteer wing is then used only for whatever it may contribute to the winning of elections....

A number of the party's problems are directly attributable to Trudeau's difficulties in adapting to the role of party leader. More specifically, he has often been insensitive or inconsiderate of the needs of people in the party. Several years after having won the leadership, he admitted that, at first, he had regarded the party as a "mechanical thing," as "a powerful lever." Subsequently, he came to recognize that it was also a very fragile, complex organization of human beings that could not be programmed.[1] But his effectiveness as a party leader has suffered from his inaptitude in managing people. He is naturally solitary, in contrast to the gregarious Pearson. ("Pearson was a groupie, Trudeau is a loner," in the words of one man who knew them both.)...

*Reprinted from *The L Shaped Party: The Liberal Party of Canada*, by Joseph Wearing, by permission of McGraw-Hill Ryerson Ltd., Toronto, 1981.

Trudeau's other major problem as party leader was that of infusing new blood into the party and into the cabinet. Here too, Trudeau has been reluctant to emulate King, who used all his wiles in appealing to a sense of duty in those whom he wished to draft into his service. Both King and Pearson, moreover, often looked to the provincial legislatures, the bureaucracy, and the private sphere for ministerial recruits, whereas Trudeau has mostly restricted himself to a more obvious source, the parliamentary caucus. As the years passed, Trudeau, like Laurier before him, lost his outstanding ministers one by one. While their successors may often have been just as capable in cabinet and in their departments, they were mostly unable to catch the public imagination; nor could they establish political bases in their respective regions or appeal to particular constituencies of opinion within the country or the party. According to one minister, they either spent too much time in Ottawa deciding policy or filled a kind of "royal function" — which they mostly did not know how to exploit politically — at *pro forma* occasions away from Ottawa.

Geographically, the government's base became too narrow. The Atlantic provinces and Quebec were represented in cabinet by effective regional lieutenants, but there were serious gaps in Ontario and the western provinces....

As the Liberals began to face the possibility of an election, in 1978 or 1979, they encountered a number of problems. The first was a direct fallout from the successful campaign against the Conservatives' call for a wage and price freeze in 1974....During the 1974 campaign, the Liberals had claimed to have their own contingency plans if controls ever became necessary, but because Trudeau unwisely had gone too far in ridiculing the Conservative plan as a disaster looking for another place to happen, he found it harder than it need have been to justify his government's own control measures fifteen months later. For the first time Trudeau's credibility was called into question and the problem continued to plague him.

The party's second problem was the public's perception of what its concerns were, as revealed by the surveys. In the wake of the Parti Québécois victory in November 1976, national unity became the electorate's principal concern even in the face of declining disposable incomes in late 1976 and early 1977. The Liberals were seen as the party who could best deal with the Quebec problem and, as a result, its standing in the Gallup poll reached heights comparable only to those it achieved after the October Crisis of 1970. The following year, people became much more concerned about their declining purchasing power, even though disposable incomes actually went up steadily through late 1977/78. The problem was psychological or perceptual and left Liberal strategists in a quandary as to how to deal with it.[2]

The third problem was simply that the electorate had got tired of the Liberals and especially Trudeau. In December 1978, a poll published by the *Toronto Star* revealed that, with John Turner as leader of the party, the

Conservatives' eight-point lead over the Liberals would be turned into a Liberal four-point lead.[3] This news produced a flurry of speculation about the possibilities of a leadership convention before the election, but Turner's alleged disloyalty had aroused strong opposition to him within the parliamentary party and that option was quickly discarded....

When the election finally came in 1979, the familiar Davey-Coutts hallmarks were even more pronounced than in 1974. The campaign was tightly controlled by a handful of men and there was no opportunity for countervailing opinions. In response to surveys showing that there had been a dramatic increase in the percentage of the population who were dissatisfied with the direction in which the country was going, Liberal strategists attempted again to revive the leadership issue, but with the variant theme that tough, experienced leadership was needed to deal with the uncertainties of the future.[4]

Trudeau himself played on the public's general malaise by attempting to revive its flagging interest in Quebec separatism. Thus, Liberal strategy described the election as "the lull before Canada's most intense political storm begins: the fight for the survival of our Canadian confederation."[5] Trudeau's abiding concern about Quebec was genuine, but the national unity issue was perceived by many as a last desperate ploy whose rallying cry had been used once too often. Even Liberals began to suspect that their party thrived more on national *disunity*....

Although the Liberals sustained minimal losses in the Atlantic provinces and actually gained seats in Quebec, the party lost twenty-three seats in the crucial province of Ontario. The West, where the party's standings fell from thirteen to three, was little short of disaster.

With defeat, the party's rebuilding cycle began again, although the national executive, true to form, hesitated to take any initiatives itself. For several months, it even procrastinated about setting the date for the policy convention which was due in 1980, because that would inevitably mean a vote on whether to call a leadership convention. Trudeau finally grasped the nettle himself when, in November, he announced his resignation.

Other initiatives were being taken by others in the party. The caucus, after so many years of having to accede to Liberal cabinets, was moved into a central policy-making role when Trudeau established twenty-one caucus committees to re-examine the party's position in a whole range of policy fields. There were some mutterings from the volunteer wing that caucus ought not to presume that it could establish party policy, but the caucus committees at least filled a void left by the formal structures of the Liberal Party.

The most interesting challenge to the party establishment came as a result of the independent initiative of a group who met in Winnipeg in October, 1979. Apart from the ever-diminishing circle of Trudeau's closest advisers and the John Turner loyalists, the meeting brought together the leading activists from the volunteer wing and a number of the reform-minded members of caucus. The press made much of the implicit challenge to Trudeau's leadership, but the meeting was more interesting for what it revealed about the broader concerns of active Liberals.

For Keith Davey and Jim Coutts, the point of winning is as self-evident as it is for the Montreal Expos or the Toronto Maple Leafs; but the Liberals gathered at Winnipeg greeted defeat almost with relief because of the chance it gave the party to redefine its goals. Concern was expressed about the power of the bureaucracy, the weakness of parliament and the diminishing relevance of political parties. Several participants argued that it was absolutely necessary for the party to decide on new directions *before* ministers again became the captives of their bureaucracies.

Some of the discussion was a hodge-podge of well-informed comments mixed with the ill-informed — the sort of meeting which tended to confirm cabinet ministers' worst fears of such party meetings, admitted one former PMO official — but the conference provided a forum for a variety of viewpoints to be heard. In the Liberal party, it is *only* at such meetings that East and West can engage in a dialogue, which, on this occasion, was described by Nick Taylor, the Alberta Liberal leader, as the best he had seen in the party for fifteen years. As the meeting concluded, one had the sense that the renewal had begun, that an agenda for the future was beginning to take shape in areas such as individual rights, freedom of information, negative income tax, and proportional representation....

Trudeau's astonishing comeback after the party's defeat in 1979 was one of the most extraordinary feats in Canadian political history, even more than Sir John A. Macdonald's return to power in 1878 or Mackenzie King's victory in 1926. But the strategic decision to run negative television attacks on Clark and to bore the electorate in order to avoid anything that might disturb the Liberals' eighteen- to twenty-point lead over the Conservatives in December created a disturbing malaise among many Liberals, the media and the electorate. Liberal strategists, in defence of their campaign, argue that Conservative experience had shown how unwise it was to make specific, highly visible promises that were not part of a comprehensive well-planned program. Accordingly the Liberal platform committee adopted the rule that it would not announce any policies unless it could also give the indication of the financing. Inevitably too, because the government had been defeated on its budget, the Liberal campaign had to dwell on the budget's alleged faults.

The longer term danger, however, is that the lessons of 1979/80 will determine the stance for the future — both eyes glued to the polls and both hands carefully covering the party's backside. But, at the same time, both the electorate and the party rank and file may well become increasingly disillusioned with what they regard as the cynical competition of the political parties....

Canadian parties, however, do face a more subtle challenge which arises out of the realities of contemporary electoral technology. As election campaigns have become more sophisticated, the parties, while attempting to exploit the possibilities offered by television, opinion surveys and jet-age transportation, have become the captives of the very technologies which they seek to control. The accepted wisdom is that the only campaign which sinks into the public consciousness is one that endlessly reiterates a few points, allowing no room for detail or complexity. Television with its thirty-second clips accentuates the need to give a narrow, personalized focus to a campaign and makes the negative, personal attack more effective than the positive, broad program, which simply cannot be dealt with on television. These maxims for campaigners have always had their place in election campaigns, but technology has pushed the parties ever further in that direction. In 1980, for example, the Liberals conducted elaborate market research to test their television ads. The studies showed that the undecided, marginally interested voter liked the hard-hitting attacks on Joe Clark best. When people within the party were shown the same set of advertisements, they preferred the softer, more positive ones. But it was the undecided vote that counted, so the negative ads were run.

The danger is that the battle may be won at the cost of losing the war. Many voters, including many Liberals, were disgusted with the 1980 campaign and that was probably reflected in the lower turnout on election day. The fault lay not only with the Liberals. The early Conservative ads featured unflattering portrayals of Trudeau in an attempt to revive the public's 1978-79 antipathy to him....

ENDNOTES

1. "Interview with Prime Minister Pierre Elliott Trudeau," *Maclean's*, January 10, 1977, p. 4.
2. Interview with Jerry Grafstein, August 24, 1978. Department of Finance, *Economic Review*, (April 1979), p. 135.
3. *Toronto Star*, December 9, 1978.
4. See, for example, the advertisement in the *Globe and Mail*, May 19, 1979.
5. Jerry Grafstein in the *Toronto Star*, April 1, 1979.

16 The Progressive Conservative Party*

GEORGE C. PERLIN

In the first three decades of Confederation the Progressive Conservative party (then called the Liberal-Conservative party) won six out of seven federal elections. Since 1891, however, the party has won only seven out of twenty-six federal elections. This transformation from dominant to minority party status is largely due to the party's failure to compete effectively among the French Catholic community, which constitutes four fifths of the population of Quebec.

The Conservatives' alienation of Quebec has deep historical roots. Conflict between French Catholics in Quebec and English Protestants in Ontario had immobilized government in Canada before Confederation. The federal constitution established by Confederation, of which Sir John A. Macdonald, the Conservative leader, had been a principal architect, attempted to deal with this problem by delegating to the provinces the authority to legislate on matters of language and religion. For a time this mechanism worked and Macdonald was able to build a Conservative majority which cut across the traditional cleavages. But linguistic and religious issues could not be kept out of federal politics. In 1885 Macdonald refused to commute the death sentence imposed on Louis Riel, a French-speaking Métis who had led an armed rebellion against the civil authority in western Canada. Riel's hanging, which was bitterly opposed by French-Canadians, inflamed opinion against the Conservative party in Quebec, with the result that the Conservative majority in Quebec was overturned.

Defeat in Quebec became self-perpetuating. Left in the control of an English Protestant majority, which remained persistently insensitive to French-Canadian opinion, the party continued to make decisions that offended French-Canadian voters and permitted Quebec to become a Liberal Party stronghold. Only once since 1887 has the Conservative party been able to win a majority in Quebec. Its normal share of Quebec's seats has been less than twenty percent. Thus the party has been excluded from

---

*Reprinted from *Canada at the Polls: The General Election of 1974*, by permission of the author and the American Enterprise Institute for Public Policy Research.

significant support in a province which elects more than one quarter of the members of the federal parliament.

At one time the Conservatives could count upon a countervailing majority in Ontario. In the fourteen elections from 1878 to 1930 they won a majority in Ontario twelve times and secured one plurality and one tie. But as Ontario developed a predominantly industrial-urban character, the concerns of its English-speaking Protestants with the issues of language and religion, which had bound them to the Conservative party, gave way to new concerns, and the Conservative majority was broken. In the fifteen federal elections since 1935, the Liberals have won Ontario ten times. Today the Conservatives have no secure base with which to offset the Liberal advantage in Quebec.

The Conservative party has survived as the only serious rival to Liberal power for two reasons. First, provincial Conservative parties have continued to compete at the level of government or official opposition in all but three provinces. Provincial leaders, responding to their own needs and to the pressures of intergovernmental relations in a federal system, have frequently limited their support to the national party, but the existence of competitive provincial parties is of symbolic value to the national party and assures it of access to some minimal level of financial and organizational assistance....

Second, in the Anglophone provinces, the Conservative party, in contrast to the smaller parties — the New Democratic party on the left and Social Credit on the right — has been able to adapt its appeal to the conditions of a country which is divided by cultural and economic characteristics into distinctive regional societies. Regionalism in the form of a strong attachment to regional and provincial political identities has persistently blunted the effect of appeals to interests cutting across regional boundaries. The Conservative party, which seeks to accommodate a broad range of socioeconomic interests and which has adapted itself to this characteristic of the Canadian political culture, has been better able than the smaller parties to mobilize interregional support.

Despite its aggregative strategy, the Conservative party does not draw its support in the same proportion from all groups in Canadian society. Reflecting these patterns, members of the Conservative party's parliamentary caucus are predominantly English-speaking, Protestant and from small towns and communities. Members of the parliamentary elite are much more representative of Canadian society as a whole. This is because the formal structures of the extra-parliamentary party have been organized in a manner which ensures that all regions and all constituencies are fully represented. This has created a special problem for the party because it has meant that on many issues of both public policy and political strategy the extra-parliamentary party and the parliamentary party have had different perspectives.

It has been argued that in ideological temperament and tradition the Progressive Conservative party is quite similar to the Conservative party of Britain. According to this view, the model of a conservative as laissez-faire economic liberal — the image usually evoked to describe American conservatives — does not fit the mainstream of opinion in the Canadian party.

Robert Stanfield, recent leader of the Progressive Conservative party, says the fundamental principle of Canadian conservatism is a belief in the achievement of freedom through the recognition and maintenance of social order. This implies more than just "law and order." It implies a conception of the community as an integrated whole, respect for the mutual responsibility of all members of society toward one another and a belief that the public interest transcends any particular private interest. The history of the party demonstrates that while Canadian Conservatives believe in private enterprise, they have been willing to use the power of the state to intervene in the economy to protect the interests of weaker members of society or to pursue purposes deemed to be in the broader collective interest. As Stanfield puts it, the philosophical tradition to which the Progressive Conservative party belongs holds that "self-reliance and enterprise should be encouraged, but (it) does not place private enterprise in a central position around which everything else revolves."

Extensive interviews with a sample of the current party elite suggest, however, that Canadian Conservatives are less willing to use state power than Canadian Liberals. Members of the sample commonly opposed what they called "Liberal statism," that is, what they believe to be the Liberal party's conception of state action as a sufficient and desirable instrument for dealing with any social problem. This distinction between the two parties is confirmed by data from surveys of delegates to the Conservative and Liberal national leadership conventions of 1967 and 1968. Substantially larger numbers of Conservative delegates agreed that "government interferes too much with business," "too much money is spent on welfare," and "social security benefits, such as old age pensions and family allowances, should only be paid to those who need them."

While the Conservative party as a whole opposes the Liberals on this question, there are invariably disagreements among Conservatives themselves about the scope and need for government action with respect to specific issues. This has given rise to a view, frequently asserted in the press, that the party is deeply divided between "progressive" and "conservative" wings. Analysis of data from the 1967 convention survey from a separate study of delegates to the 1971 biennial meeting of the National Association suggests that this ideological divergence has been exaggerated. Relatively few members of the two samples take consistently opposed views on all issues, or to put it another way, most members of the two samples take positions from issue to issue which diverge in a variety of patterns. The only issues in which there is any significant linking of opinion are those of a regional and cultural nature. For example, substantial minorities among both samples opposed both special language rights for French-speaking Canadians and proposals to grant a special constitutional status to the province of Quebec.

Ultimately, party policy at any given time is what the party leader declares it to be. This authoritative role of the leader is partly inherent in the nature of parliamentary government. The only members of the party who have the capacity to give public effect to party policy are the leader and his colleagues in parliament. They alone have the power to create public policy. In principle this is a shared power, but the leader is recognized to have the continuing and untrammeled right to make overriding pronouncements on behalf of the parliamentary caucus or to designate others to make such pronouncements. This right can be ascribed both to the leader's broadly based legitimacy — he is the only figure in parliament who is chosen by a body representative of all elements of the party (a national convention) — and to the practical consideration that only the leader can embody the collective will of the caucus when the caucus is not assembled. It can also be ascribed to the emphasis placed on leadership in the party's internal system of values — an emphasis incorporated from the British conservative tradition. In addition, because of the party's efforts to embrace the full range of regional interests that comprise Canadian society, the leader has had a special role in giving symbolic expression to the party, of giving it both coherence and cohesion. It is not surprising, therefore, that the party has found a symbol for its failures in its leaders. Since the death of Macdonald in 1891, except during the tenure of Sir Robert Borden from 1901 to 1921, there has been recurring conflict over the party leadership. No leader has long remained unchallenged and no leader since Borden has left office without some conflict, usually ill-concealed.

The Minority Party Syndrome[1]

There is a reciprocal relationship between the Progressive Conservative party's electoral defeats and its vulnerability to internal conflict. This relationship is an aspect of what might be described as the minority party syndrome — characteristics acquired by minority parties which tend to reinforce their weakness. This aspect of the syndrome may be explained as follows. Because of the party's exclusion from office, its members tend to interact in internal party politics on the basis of motives that make conflict difficult to resolve. Because conflicts recur frequently and the party is subject to manifest or latent factionalism, it is unable to achieve optimum organizational effectiveness and it projects an image of internal instability which undermines public confidence in its ability to govern. Thus, electoral defeats contribute to conflict in the party, and conflict in the party contributes to its electoral defeats.

A second aspect of the minority party syndrome relates to the level of ability of the people attracted to activist roles in the party. In general, when two parties pursue the same basic goals, the party which has the greater chance of winning is likely to have greater success in recruiting people of first-rate ability. There has been frequent criticism of the quality of the Conservative party's candidates — both from journalists and from members of the party. The party has usually been able to present a credible front bench, but is has clearly lacked deep resources of parliamentary talent. As John C. Courtney observes, "The Liberals have succeeded in dominating most of the predictable areas from which the Conservatives might attempt to co-opt their parliamentary notables: the civil service, universities, businesses and corporations."[2]

In addition, the Conservative party has had difficulty in getting imaginative and innovative people to assist it in policy development. There appear to be two dimensions to this problem. The first is that such people will be more likely to become involved in a party which offers them a better chance of getting their ideas translated into public policy. The second is that many Conservatives have developed an attitude of mistrust toward intellectuals — an attitude illustrated by the controversy which has attended every "thinkers" conference in the party's history. There is a widespread suspicion that intellectuals will never make a commitment to the Conservative party — that sooner or later they will be beguiled by the Liberal party. This suspicion tends to be self-fulfilling. The party does not make intellectuals welcome, with the result that they turn away.

This reinforces the effect of a third aspect of the minority party syndrome — the existence in a minority party of an "opposition mentality." A party which is habitually in opposition becomes absorbed entirely in the strategy and tactics of criticism. It tends to approach all debate with an attacking, destructive style. Therefore it appears to lack ideas of its own and projects a negative popular image. Edwin R. Black has provided some insight into the "opposition mentality" of the Conservative party in his description of the establishment of the party's parliamentary research office. Black's comments on his efforts — as the first director of the research office — to interest the party in in-depth research on major issues is particularly telling, both in illustrating the effect of this opposition mentality and in demonstrating the lack of cohesion in the caucus:

> Party leader, committee chairmen and backbench MPs all piously agreed on its desirability. Never, however, would the opposition caucus agree on a set of basic priorities. Tory members remained a gaggle of political private enterprisers who selfishly preferred to pursue their separate ways to the electoral gallows rather than hang together and work as a united opposition.[3]

A fourth aspect of the minority party syndrome relates to the experience of the party's leaders. A minority party normally must choose from potential leaders of more limited experience than those available to a dominant party. In the past four decades the Progessive Conservative party has had few leadership candidates with federal ministerial experience. But even when such candidates have been available, the party has passed them over.[4] Instead is has shown a preference for provincial premiers. Premiers have had an advantage in seeking the leadership because of the resources they control, because they have the aura of success and probably, because they have been free of taint from the conflicts in the federal party. Although they have had the experience of governing, provincial premiers are at a disadvantage when they enter federal politics. Their perspective is more parochial, the issues they deal with are different, they work under a different set of constraints and they exercise their leadership in an unfamiliar political milieu.

The interpretation of the Conservative party's weakness presented here may have wider application to the study of political parties and may help to explain the development of single-party dominant systems. The concept of the minority party syndrome deals directly with the weakness of minority parties in such systems. Its concomitant is that the dominant party will be more cohesive, attract members and leaders with more effective personal resources and be more positive in its outlook. Thus this concept also helps to account for the resilience of the dominant party.

Explanations for patterns for single-party dominance commonly focus on the social context in which the party system operates. They relate the electoral strength or weakness of parties to their ability to appeal to certain social groups. The Conservative party's alienation of Quebec was obviously crucial in that it put the party at a permanent disadvantage which precipitated its reduction to minority status. But the party's defeats have reflected a lack of support in other provinces as well as in Quebec. Moreover, analysis of data from survey research shows the party's weakness cuts across most social cleavages — even the historically important cleavages of religion and culture. Thus there is a good reason to infer that the party's minority status must be explained by some more general factor. The concept of the minority party syndrome is proposed for this purpose.

ENDNOTES

1.   Reprinted from George Perlin, *The Tory Syndrome: Leadership Politics in the Progressive Conservative Party* (Montreal: McGill-Queen's University Press, 1980), by permission of the publisher.

2.   John C. Courtney, *The Selection of National Party Leaders in Canada* (Toronto: Macmillan, 1973), p. 159.

3.   Edwin R. Black, "Opposition Research: Some Theories and Practice," *Canadian Public Administration*, Vol. 15, No. 1 (Spring 1972), p. 37.

4.   For data on and discussion of this aspect of Conservative leadership recruitment, see John C. Courtney, *The Selection of National Party Leaders*, pp. 137-60.

17 The Tory Quest for Power*

PATRICK MARTIN, ALLAN GREGG and GEORGE PERLIN

Since March, 1962, with the defeat of the last Diefenbaker Government, the federal Progressive Conservative party has held office for less than seven months. This record is a matter of fact to the general public. But it constitutes part of the very identity of those who gathered in a sweltering Civic Centre in Ottawa to deny a national leader, for the second time in that twenty year period, the opportunity to succeed himself after his power had been wrested from him by his followers.

Many of the delegates who gathered in Ottawa in June, 1983, and conspired against Joe Clark for two years before that, associated him with the division that had disrupted the party over the last twenty years. When Dalton Camp led the first successful attempt to "dump Dief," Joe Clark was there. Since that time, the anti-Diefenbaker wing had been most emphatically "in charge" of the party. Joe Clark was also definitely part of that wing, as were "his" people — those who supported him in his parliamentary caucus, and those who held the key appointments in the party hierarchy.

For many at Ottawa, Joe Clark stood for all that was wrong with the Progressive Conservative party. In him they saw the wishy-washy compromise that blurred the distinction between them and the Liberals, and that had cost them the popularity enjoyed by successful conservative politicians like Margaret Thatcher and Ronald Reagan. Furthermore, his stewardship during the short-lived government of 1979, bespoke an even worse sin...being out-manoeuvered by "the Grits." For many others, the continuing acrimony in the National Executive, between the federal and provincial wings of the Party, and in private meetings wherever Conservatives met, only served as a reminder that the legacy of opposition continued to endure under Clark's leadership.

By June 11, 1983, the issue was not even personal. Joe Clark had become a symbol. And in an attempt to exorcise themselves forever of that symbol,

---

*Excerpted from *Contenders: The Tory Quest for Power*, Prentice-Hall Canada Inc., 1983.

a majority of Tory militants decided that Clark had to go. Having reached that decision, however, the question became "What next?". Not for Joe, but for the party....

Clark had won the leadership [in 1976] as a compromise. On the first ballot he had placed third with the votes of only 12 percent of the delegates. The man who had led, Claude Wagner, the first Francophone to contest the Conservative leadership and a former Liberal minister from Quebec who had not become a Conservative until 1972, was unacceptable to many delegates because he had remained aloof from the party during his brief period as a member and held views that many thought were too rigid. The candidate in second place was Brian Mulroney, a bilingual Anglo-Quebecer with an accomplished record as a labour lawyer who was well-connected with the party. Although he had never been elected to office and had no legislative experience, for a time Mulroney seemed to be the candidate most likely to attract delegates who opposed Wagner. But he had run an expensive campaign that led many delegates to wonder how much substance lay behind the artifice of his public relations expertise. Thus the anti-Wagner delegates turned to Clark, a likeable man with moderate views, also well-connected, who had run an effective, low-key campaign.

In one sense Clark's lack of a public profile was an advantage, because it meant that he was free to create his own image from the position of leader, but it also meant his image would be formed on the basis of his performance in uniting the party, a task that had defied and ultimately destroyed many Conservative leaders before him.

Recurring electoral defeats have deprived Conservative leaders of patronage to back their claims to support, attracted to the party some individuals who are by temperament unwilling to submit to internal party discipline, and created an obsessive concern among party members with their role as losers. All of these things have contributed to instability in the Conservative leadership. The party has been fractious and difficult to manage, which has undermined public confidence in its leaders; and as its leaders have failed to deliver electoral victories, the party has forced them out.

Adding to the strains in the Conservative caucus were the residual effects from Clark's own victory and, even more important, those that persisted from the conflict over John Diefenbaker's leadership in the 1960's. Most of the leaders of the group who had fought with Diefenbaker never forgot their bitter defeat in 1967 and many refused to accept the authority of his successor, Robert Stanfield. By 1976, the number of Conservatives who still thought of themselves as belonging to a Diefenbaker faction was relatively small (only 15 percent of the delegates who attended the 1976 convention), but they remained a vocal and, therefore, potentially disruptive force. For Joe Clark they posed a special problem because he was clearly identified with the old anti-Diefenbaker alliance and his victory at the leadership convention could be seen as a further demonstration of the ascendancy of this faction within the party.

In seeking to master the caucus, Clark was handicapped by the fact that he had no broad base of personal support either within or outside the party. He would be buttressed for a time by the legitimacy of his endorsement from the convention, but legitimacy will not carry a leader for long if he is ineffective. And Clark's effectiveness would be measured by the strength of his popular following. Thus Clark's problem was circular. He needed a broad personal following among the electorate to command the support of potential dissidents within the party, but he needed to demonstrate his ability to master the party if he were to be successful in creating an image that would command a personal following among the electorate.

Using the same technique as Robert Stanfield, Clark tried to build support by distributing his shadow ministerial appointments among every faction within the party. Claude Wagner was made shadow minister for External Affairs and appointed to a new position as chairman of the committee of shadow ministers which was intended to symbolize his status as deputy leader, while Jack Horner, the most vocal of Robert Stanfield's critics from the Diefenbaker faction, was made shadow minister of Transport. Clark also sought to build consensus within the caucus by launching an elaborate process of policy-making in which every member had an opportunity to take part. He hoped through this process not just to provide the party with new policies, but to encourage caucus members to learn to work together and try to find common ground that would bridge their differences.

But these efforts were to no avail. In the summer of 1976, less than four months after his election as leader, he was caught in an embarrassing dispute with a caucus backbencher [who challenged him for the party nomination in the new riding of Bow Valley.]...Clark backed down, fearing that it would be...harmful to have to fight for his constituency nomination. In the eyes of those who had been looking for a sign of the kind of leadership Clark would provide, this was a damaging episode. Clark was the national leader of his party, hut he could not even get its nomination in his home constituency.

This was just the beginning. In the fall, Claude Wagner, who had never reconciled himself to his defeat at Clark's hands, resigned his position as chairman of the shadow ministers committee. Then he and Clark became involved in a battle over the election of a new president for the Quebec provincial association, a battle which Clark won, but which further alienated Wagner.

Events in the country also turned to Clark's disadvantage. In the fall of 1976, the Parti Quebecois had been elected in Quebec, which focussed public attention on the Liberal party's strength — its claim to be the only party that could deal with Quebec. By April, 1977, the lead the Conservatives had enjoyed in public opinion polls since Clark's election had passed to the Liberals and in May the Conservatives lost six by-elections....

By early 1978 the image of Joe Clark as a weak leader was firmly established and the Liberals, although floundering in their efforts to deal with rising unemployment and inflation, looked confidently toward a new general election. The Liberals' expectations for the forthcoming election were shared by many Conservatives....But the country's economic problems continued to worsen and, as they did, the fortunes of the Conservative party began to rise....The Liberals were on the road to defeat.

But Joe Clark's image continued to hurt the party....He did not handle himself well on television and, because of his inexperience and the limited resources available to him for policy research, he was led into policy mistakes in public statements and interviews. In the election campaign that began in April, Clark's image remained a liability to the party. The Conservatives won not because of Joe Clark's image, but in spite of it. They won because outside Quebec a majority of voters had had enough of the Trudeau Liberals. But Clark's image had caused enough concern to voters to prevent the Tories from winning a majority in parliament. Clark became prime minister in a minority government.

The new government was determined to show the country that it was decisive and could provide strong leadership, but it was ill-prepared to govern. For one thing, having been so long in opposition, it took ministers some time to grasp the scope of their departments' activities and to find consensus among the disparate views within the caucus. Lack of adequate research support had produced many policies that were inconsistent or unworkable. This led to conflicting statements from ministers, delays in the declaration of policy, and a backing off from some campaign commitments. Far from appearing decisive and competent, the government seemed ineffectual and uncertain of its sense of direction. There was now a complete symbiosis of the images of the party and its leader.

By the end of the summer, as the economic crisis deepened, this merged image had so undermined public support in the government that it was running 20 percentage points behind the Liberals in the Gallup poll. It was in this context that the government was defeated on its budget in parliament and forced into a new general election.

Although there was considerable truth in the Conservative claim that they had not had a fair chance to effect real change, voters were unresponsive. They were more concerned with economic problems, the tough measures the government had proposed to deal with the economy, and the image of the party and its leader.

Never was a party leader subject to such cruel personal criticism as in the election campaign of 1980. The devastating effect of Liberal television commercials, which played on Clark's physical mannerisms as well as his public record, was added to by the "Joe Clark" jokes that swept the country.

Clark became an object of ridicule. He was not actually disliked, but neither was he seen to have the qualities of a prime minister. And so the Conservative government fell…and Joe Clark began his long, tenacious and doomed struggle to hold onto power….

For two years Clark fought to hold his leadership — assailed virtually without interruption by a disparate group of opponents, some motivated by ideological discontent with his moderate Conservatism, some by personal grievances, and some by the conviction that his image was so bad that, whatever his real personal qualities, he would always be a serious electoral liability to the party. At the biennial meeting of the party in 1981, 33 percent of the delegates voted for a leadership convention. While Clark's leadership had been re-affirmed, the minority against him was large enough to keep the issue open. Subsequently, he promised the caucus that if he did not do better in the vote on leadership at the next biennial meeting, he would ask the party to call a convention. Thus, when 33 percent of the delegates voted for a convention at the biennial meeting of January, 1983, Clark announced his resignation. At the same time, however, he also declared that he would be candidate in the forthcoming leadership convention. At the convention, held in Ottawa in June, Clark led the field of eight candidates on the first ballot and continued to lead for two more ballots as other candidates were forced out. But on the last ballot he was defeated by the one remaining candidate, Brian Mulroney.

Clark's inability to a capture the convention after leading on the first ballot was one story — a story of failed expectations, seven years of acrimony, and the politics of opposition. Mulroney's victory, however, was quite another. After all, other candidates, including Clark, were seen as more likeable, more competent, and tougher than Mulroney, and were considered to have a sounder grasp of policy. The Anyone But Mulroney sentiment was as real and large as the Anyone But Clark feelings. The major difference was that the Anyone But Mulroney camp was housed almost exclusively in the Clark delegation, while the ABC movement was spread throughout the convention.

So it would be easy to conclude that Mulroney was the choice of the majority of delegates, in the end, because he was the *only* candidate in a position to stop Clark, given his placement on the first ballot. The principal reason Brian Mulroney won, despite the fact that he was not seen as the "best candidate", has to do with the overriding concern of Conservatives: their quest for power. When asked how influential various factors were in their choice of a candidate, three-quarters of the delegates said finding a candidate who would best help the party win power was "very influential". No other reason was mentioned as often. In 1983, the Conservatives were looking for a winner. And Brian Mulroney looked like a winner.

One thing that Brian Mulroney understood was that during Joe Clark's leadership there had been a large number of Progressive Conservatives who thought of themselves as "outsiders" in the party: people who felt they had little or no influence in the direction of party affairs, or were cut off from a leader who relied too much on technical advisers. More than half of the delegates interviewed expressed these concerns, saying that they believed there was an establishment in the party and that they were not part of it. And on the last ballot nearly two-thirds of those delegates voted for Brian Mulroney.

There are different reasons why many Conservatives considered themselves to be outsiders in their own party. Some felt this way because of their social situation. Although comfortable financially, they felt insecure because they perceived themselves to be remote socially from the centre of power in Canada, which they saw as dominated by a technocratic elite operating through the bureaucratic structures of big government and big business. These individuals were proprietors of small businesses, farmers, fishermen or members of the lower middle class; they were residents of the smaller communities across the country, and/or they were inhabitants of one of the hinterland provinces. These "social outsiders" were attracted to the Conservative party because it is both the party of opposition and a party that is conservative. The problem for many of them was that they saw the same style of technocratic power entrenching itself within the Conservative Party. They looked with suspicion on the growth of the party's bureaucracy, with its commitment to the uses of the new techniques of political organization, and on the leader's dependence on this bureaucracy and these techniques.

To many outsiders in the party, John Diefenbaker was the symbol of what they stood for...or, rather, what they stood against. Diefenbaker's populism had been directed toward them. Thus, when Brian Mulroney constantly reminded delegates of his affection for, and connections to "The Chief," and when he won the endorsements of such prominent Diefenbaker loyalists as Alvin Hamilton and Robert Coates, he identified himself with those outsiders.

Mulroney had made the mistake in 1976 of looking too much the prisoner of technocracy. His campaign had offended people because of its slickness and sophistication. He did not make the same mistake in 1983. Mulroney was still a showman, but his campaign played in the rec rooms of the nation. He let the delegates reach him personally in homey surroundings.

And even though Brian Mulroney was the president of one large corporation, held directorships on the boards of several others and often lunched with Conrad Black of Argus and Paul Desmarais of Power Corp., he knew enough not to flaunt such connections in the presence of delegates. Instead, he reminded them that he was "one who has worked as a labourer and truck driver and whose father was a unionized electrician." His humble beginnings included not simply a childhood in the North Shore town of

Baie Comeau, but "a father who, during his entire life held down two jobs to provide for the needs of his family with neither complaint nor regret."

Mulroney's description of himself was, of course, unashamedly senti- mental. Yet it appealed not just to the "social outsiders" in the party; it also identified him with the "average" Conservative delegate. Most of the Con- servative delegates are people with family incomes putting them in the top 10 percent of the population. They are high achievers in their careers, yet most of them report they came from families which were "just able to get along" or were "badly off." By portraying himself in this way Brian Mul- roney was displaying his understanding of the party and its politics. And when delegates made the inevitable comparison of his roots to his current status, they saw a man who had arrived — a winner, like the one they were looking for.

There was another thing that Brian Mulroney understood about the Conservative party that was very important in his victory, and that was a change in the ideological disposition within the party. He was able to capi- talize on the mood of conservatism among the Tories. At the convention of 1976 only 43 percent described themselves on the right of the party. By 1983, 57 percent placed themselves on the right. As Mulroney's support grew from ballot to ballot he drew his major strength from these delegates. On the fourth ballot 75 percent of right-wing identifiers voted for Brian Mulroney although 30 percent of the delegates who placed themselves on the left and 38 percent of the "centre" also voted for him.

While delegates may identify themselves as being on the right of the ideological spectrum, the position they take on specific issues may not be consistently right-wing. For instance, while a majority said they would sell all or part of several crown corporations, 60 percent said they believed in government ownership and while a majority called for cuts in government spending, they did not want them across the board: a majority called for *increased* spending on defence and high technology development as well as for education, manpower training and assistance to the disabled.

There is nothing inconsistent in this. The Conservative party in Canada has always embraced two different traditions: the first, of social responsi- bility — a sense of duty towards others in society; the second, of individual enterprise or self-reliance. Historically, within the party, the balance between these two traditions has fluctuated in adapting to social and eco- nomic conditions.

Although strong positions on specific issues did not form an integral part of the Mulroney campaign, he and his organization did take special steps to insure that the candidate would not be tagged as "insubstantive" or "plastic." The book he released during the campaign, *Where I Stand*,[1] was designed precisely with this aim in mind. The remedies were never very complicated: Federalism isn't hard to master because "...(t)here is nothing that Canadians cannot do in a reasonable and thoughtful way once they set their minds to it. We must begin by purging the negativism and the vitriol from our public life and our private manner." In equally succinct terms, Mulroney states that the nation's economic sickness has one "principal cause...the productivity factor."

In another area, however, Mulroney adopts an approach that is diametrically opposed to the policies of his predecessors, Clark and Stanfield. The issue is that of constitutional accommodation. Says Mulroney: "In any discussion of constitutional reform, I start from the premise of an indivisible Canada...I do not believe in a theory of two nations, five nations, or ten nations...Nor do I believe in any concept that would give any one province an advantage over any other."

The heart of the book is found in "A View from Baie Comeau." In this chapter, his personal view of the world and how it can be used for utmost political advantage, Mulroney offers not a reminiscence of his childhood, but an evocation of the...individualist strain in the Tory tradition. According to Mulroney, Baie Comeau was a place where investors, managers and workers took "great risks...in the development of the North Shore." But the risks were worth it: "We have all been, *as it should be*, rewarded for our efforts." The author concludes with a paean to liberty and free enterprise.

• • •

From what started on the first ballot to be an impressive, but narrow, support base made up of Quebec delegates, Ontario youths and a smattering of senior delegates from across the country, Mulroney was able to build an impressive coalition on each successive ballot. He was the only candidate who set out to exhibit more of those qualities a power-starved party *required* of a leader, regardless of what outsiders might deem to be the "best" qualities.

There is nothing paradoxical about all this. There is no conflict between the image of the hard-ball playing politician and the man with the vision from Baie Comeau. Brian Mulroney knew that the first rule for any politician is to know your constituency and secure it. That may require an adaptability that seems cynical in the eyes of those who want politicians not just to be true to principles, but always to be seen to be true to them. Brian Mulroney *did* talk about the things he believed in during the campaign; but what he was most concerned with was winning and Mulroney won because he followed the first rule of politics and shrewdly applied it to the realities of the Progressive Conservative party.

Asked what factors most motivated them to make their leadership choices, the delegates replied: first and foremost, who was the most electable; second, what was the candidate's stand on issues; third, the fact that other candidates were less attractive; fourth, personal attraction to the candidate; and fifth, personal friendship.

Probably no criteria better reflect the kind of campaign Brian Mulroney waged, and the kind of candidate he set out to portray to the PC delegates. Winning was his constant theme. Even the emphasis he constantly placed on his Quebec origins had little to do with accommodation, national unity or federal-provincial relations. It was a way of reminding conservative delegates of their successive electoral defeats and it associated his candidacy directly with these people's first concern — the quest for power. On the issues, he avoided detail, but what he did put forward fully satisfied the right-wing faction of the party without hampering the party's electability. Through his public utterances and campaign publications, Mulroney was able to speak directly, not simply to the delegates' issue concerns, but more importantly to the unique mindset that produced those concerns.

Without ever having been elected to public office, Mulroney was also able not only to be the obvious alternative to Clark but the only alternative, given the choices offered. His business background, his fluency in both official languages, his "image," and even the altered style of campaigning he adopted, were all cultivated *in contrast* to the other candidate's attributes and not simply as desirable characteristics unto themselves. He was the "complete candidate"...who developed his image as a counterpoint to all the deficiencies Conservatives traditionally associated with their leaders. Finally, there is the question of personal friendship. Rarely has a Canadian politician understood the importance or used the influence of personal friendship in party politics more than Brian Mulroney.

• • •

Brian Mulroney is better placed than either of his predecessors to unite the Conservative party....In his victory on the fourth ballot, he put together a broadly-based coalition that won in every province except Prince Edward Island, Nova Scotia, Quebec and Manitoba, and even in these provinces he was supported by substantial minorities. His majority cut across cleavages on virtually every dimension of social identification and interest. But Mulroney's greatest strength lies in the fact that he has provided a focus for uniting groups that have been fundamentally divided for a generation and even longer.

One important opportunity lies in the bridge he has built across the cleavage between the French and English within the party, a cleavage that has caused more disruptive conflict in party history than any other. While on the fourth ballot he did not have a majority of the Quebec French, he had very close to a majority and in the post-convention survey these delegates gave him a strong endorsement. At the same time he had a majority of the delegates who have opposed bilingualism and concessions to Quebec. He is uniquely positioned, therefore, to bring these groups together, particularly if he can provide the party with some success in Quebec. A stronger Francophone presence in the party caucus would alleviate much of the cause of the difficulties of the past because it would leaven the effect of the small minority of anti-French members and make others who have been cut off from discourse with Francophones more sensitive to French-

Canadian concerns. In the interim he can count on the support of the Anglophones because most of them believe that he is going to help the party win seats in Quebec.

A second important opportunity is presented by the fact that he has the support of most of those Conservatives who have felt themselves to be outsiders in the party. Many of these people have been losers in internal party battles for nearly 20 years — since the beginning of the struggle over John Diefenbaker's leadership. It was from the ranks of these outsiders that most of the dissent came during the leadership of Stanfield and Clark. Now they are winners, positions of power and influence are open to them, not as symbolic gestures to conciliate them from leaders whom they did not want, but from a leader who is leader by their choice. And, although a small majority of the *ex officio* delegates at the Convention voted against him on the fourth ballot, Mulroney will also have the loyalty of the party's established elite. While most of the Clark appointees in the key roles around the leader will be replaced by Brian Mulroney's men and women, the elite as a whole will support him because they will continue to hold their power and because they, above all, are committed to the principle of loyalty to the leader.

Thirdly, Mulroney has the opportunity to unite the party ideologically. He understands the vitally important distinction between using right-wing symbols and advocating right-wing policies. Because, in the use of symbols, he captured the "conservative" mood of the party, he carried with him the vast majority of the delegates who *think* of themselves as being on the right, but because he articulated a political view that was pragmatic and emphasized the basic Progressive Conservative sense of social responsibility he appealed to their basis issue positions. Three-quarters of the delegates expect Mulroney to lead the party in a direction which is more to the right than the direction in which Joe Clark tried to lead it. But, given his positions during the campaign and his insight into what the party wants, that probably does not mean much in the way of change on basic issues of social and economic policy. However, the party under Mulroney will be more right-wing on symbolic issues and on issues that are remote from the daily concerns of Canadians such as foreign and defence policy — an area in which the party is substantially united in seeing the world in "we/they" terms.[2]

As important for Mulroney as the breadth of his base in the party is the fact that the party has the will to unite behind him. More than anything else it wants power and its members are deeply conscious of the harm internal division could do to their chances of winning power. In addition, most party members believe that despite their divisions there is a basis for consensus and accommodation within the party. Even most of those who say that there are big ideological differences in the party do not believe these differences are so big that they cannot be reconciled. And, most important, a large majority of Conservatives believe the outcome of the convention was a good thing for the party — good for its chances of uniting and good for its chances of winning. Seventy-one percent (71%) of the delegates believe Mulroney will have greater success than Clark in uniting the caucus, while 68 percent believe he will have greater success in uniting the party as a whole. And 73 percent say Mulroney's election has improved the party's chances of winning the next election.

For all of these favourable circumstances, Brian Mulroney will still have to be adept in the exercise of his leadership. The real test for him will be in the caucus. His majority is not monolithic; it is a coalition of diverse groups and individuals. Moreover, while public dissent is officially disapproved of by most party members, it has become part of the culture of the party, something that is accepted because of the Tories' individualism and because little can be done to prevent it in a party that is out of power. What makes Mulroney's task more difficult is that the party's rivals and journalists will be looking for the slightest sign of discontent because of the party's reputation for divisiveness. Internal conflict is what is expected of Conservatives. The big political question for party watchers then, is whether that expectation will truly be unfulfilled this time.

In approaching this problem Mulroney can choose from three alternative models of leadership. The first is the model of Stanfield and Clark. That is the model of conciliation through the widespread distribution of appointments and consensus-building through an attempt to engage caucus members directly in policy-making. That model didn't work — for three reasons. First, there were members so hostile to Stanfield and Clark that they were not prepared to work with the leader. Second, neither man articulated a clear vision or found a concept to articulate a clear vision around which the party could unite. In pursuing the politics of consensus they allowed the course of the process to determine the direction rather than providing a concept to give coherence to the process. Third, neither man possessed at the beginning, nor was able to develop, a strong independent popular base to sanction his authority in caucus.

The second model is the model of strong one-man leadership provided by John Diefenbaker. Diefenbaker's style worked for a time because he did have a vision and he did have a base in the country, but it ultimately failed because government is too complex for one-man leadership to work and because he included no one in his inner circle who was not completely a Diefenbaker loyalist and, therefore, had no independent channel of advice.

The third model combines elements of both of these and, judged by what the delegates say, it is a model that seems to fit what the party wants. The delegates want to share in party decisions, but they are prepared to follow a strong leader who will provide them with a sense of direction.

For some time, the Conservative party has been a minority not just in Quebec, but in all of Canada — English as well as French. The party's minority status is best represented by the fact that over the past 25 years the number of Canadians who have been committed Conservatives — those who have felt some sense of identification with the party — has always been fewer than the number who have been committed Liberals. The party under Joe Clark spent a considerable amount of its time grappling with the "minority party" problem. Research uncovered the fact that the Progressive Conservatives were viewed by the electorate as old-fashioned, out-of-step with the 1980s and narrow-minded; representative mainly of farmers and businessmen, while providing little room for women, "ethnic" groups and the poor. The research showed further that the perception that the party had a narrow political base prevented it from widening that base.

Canadians gravitate toward broad-based, representative organizations and avoid narrow-based, unrepresentative ones. They value compromise and seek consensus. Political parties which are seen to serve exclusively the interests of one group over another are viewed by the electorate as politically unacceptable. Still another problem for the Conservative party has been the popular belief that it was not as competent as the Liberal party. It has been seen as a party less able to manage its own internal affairs, lacking the level of skills the Liberals possess to provide effective government.

While the Conservatives entered the 1979 election with 10 percent fewer partisans that the Liberals, they were on a sounder political footing at that point than at any time in recent history. But, by the end of the 1980 election, there were 22 percent fewer self-confessed Conservatives in Canada than there were Liberals! By forming the government, the Progressive Conservative party — elected as an agency of change — had shifted the association of problems with the Liberal party to the association of problems with all political parties. Nothing had changed, the problems still existed, and therefore there was nothing to choose between the Liberals and the PCs. In the 1980 election the issues for the average voter once again came down to the question of "which political party is most like me?" and "which one is most for me?" — in other words, "which one do I identify with?". Given the Progressive Conservative party's chronic image problem, it was no contest.

But with the Liberals' return to power, the trend once again began to emerge, and by May 1982, *for the first time ever,* the Progressive Conservatives' national polling showed that there were more Canadians who considered themselves to be Progressive Conservatives in federal politics than there were Liberals.

Now, after the convention, Brian Mulroney has what may be an unprecedented opportunity to transform the Progressive Conservative party of Canada and, in so doing, change the entire complexion of Canadian politics. The electoral position he inherited, the improvement in his party's image and the growing disenchantment with the Liberal party all bode well for the new leader. In addition, the party for once seems prepared to give the "new guy" a chance.

ENDNOTES

1. Brian Mulroney, *Where I Stand* (Toronto, McClelland and Stewart, 1983).
2. The delegates wanted the country to take tough stands in dealing with the Soviet Union and to seek closer political relations with the United States.

SECTION FOUR

Third Parties

Canadian old line parties, although vague in their policies, have generally disciplined parliamentary groups, requiring of their members a high degree of conformity. The leader can have great authority and there is little room for dissidence. Protest, then, must occur outside the old parties, and if it is to be effective, must itself assume the form of a political party. There have been many such parties in Canadian history, but here we refer to only two: the Progressive movement, which has disappeared, and the New Democratic Party. Each achieved its greatest success in the West, where it was built upon the structure of voluntary associations already existing among the farmers. Each also appeared in a time of economic crisis.

The Progressive movement appeared after the First World War, as a farmers' party protesting against eastern capitalist domination of Canadian economic and political life. It attracted wide support from the frontier provinces of Alberta and Saskatchewan, as well as from the farmers of Manitoba and Ontario. Eastern support weakened its militant sectionalism and prompted some of its leaders to move into the Liberal party. The failure to develop effective leadership and organizational structures and reliable financing arrangements doomed the party to an early demise. Its place was taken by other radical movements which attracted the support of its members, notably the Social Credit and Cooperative Commonwealth Federation parties. The latter formed the nucleus of the New Democratic party.

As the major third party at the moment, the New Democratic Party has had its problems assimilitating different streams of radical opinion. This has led it to expel its radical nationalist wing and to form a lasting alliance with the Canadian Labour Congress.

18 The Progressive Tradition in Canadian Politics*

W.L. MORTON

...The Progressive movement was a revolt against a concept of the nature of Canadian economic policy and of Canadian political practice. The concept of Canadian economic policy which the Progressives had formed and on which they acted was that of a metropolitan economy designed, by the control of tariffs, railways and credit, to draw wealth from the hinterlands and the countryside into the commercial and industrial centers of central Canada. The concept of Canadian political practice which the Progressives had formed and on which they acted was that the classic national parties were the instruments used by the commercial, industrial and financial interests of metropolitan Canada to implement the National Policy of tariff protection and railway construction by dividing the vote of the electorate on "political" issues and by the compromises and majority decisions of the legislative caucus.

To what extent did these concepts correspond to actuality, what success had the Progressive revolt against them and what are the consequences of its success or failure in Canadian history?

That the national economic policy of the period was mercantilist in its inspiration and metropolitan in its operation may be affirmed without subscribing to the heated conviction that deliberate greed or malice entered into its formulation, or even that it rested on the blind and selfish inertia of its beneficiaries. Arch Dale's cartoons in the *Grain Grower's Guide* of bloated capitalists siphoning off the hard-earned dollars of the western farmer were effective for their purpose and are amusing comments on an epoch in Canadian history, but they belong to the realm of folklore rather than to that of historical interpretation. The National Policy was designed to make central Canada into a commercial and industrial empire, based on the development of the hinterlands of the West and North by the construction of railways to serve both East and West. During the Laurier boom, conditions were favourable, and great success was enjoyed in exploiting the virgin lands of the continental West. When those conditions passed, an

*Reprinted from *The Progressive Party in Canada*, University of Toronto Press, 1950.

adjustment of the policy was necessary. The metropolitan East was challenged by the Frontier West it had called into being; the old National Policy was confronted by the new. The adjustment could be either a modification of the policy towards freer international trade, as by an agreement for reciprocity with the United States, or by the metropolitan area assuming, as part of the whole country, the costs of increased benefits to the hinterland areas.

It was to force such an adjustment that the farmers took political action in 1919. Unfortunately, as the controversy over the Wheat Board revealed, they at once fell into confusion about which alternative they would pursue. They strove for results as far apart as a tariff for revenue, and a system of open and organized lobbying in group government, which would have been in practice a scramble for economic benefits distributed by the state. The farmers in the movement represented conflicting interests themselves and were also responsive to the forces impelling the swift transition from the free economy of prewar years to the economic nationalism of the 1930s. The seeming unity of purpose of 1919 to 1921 was soon dissolved. In federal politics, the agrarian voters of the West for the most part returned to the Liberal party. In economic matters, the great body of farmers found hope in the new cooperative movement which gave rise to the wheat pools. But resentment of the long Liberal domination, and the vision of a stable farm income ensured by government action through a wheat board, remained to drive Conservative voters to support new, anti-Liberal parties, to maintain the United Farmers of Alberta (UFA) in power in Alberta, and to erode the old economic individualism of the farmer with the hope of state action, which would counter the discrimination of the tariff by underpinning the farm economy.

The Progressives, nevertheless, gained certain material benefits for their constituents, especially in the matter of railway rates and communications. The restoration of the Crow's Nest Pass rates, the completion of the Hudson Bay Railway and the proliferation of branch lines in the 1920s were their work or owed much to their effort. "With a split representation from the West," wrote the *Free Press* in 1930, "the Crow's Nest Pass rates would never have been restored. The 'National Policy' on this question, favored along St. James Street, would have been imposed upon both parties had there not been a parliamentary contingent from the West free from control in caucus by an eastern majority."[1] This was spoken in the authentic accents of Progressivism, and it expressed, no doubt, a partial and limited view. If national politics were a struggle for sectional benefits, however, the Progressives had won a measure of success.

At the same time, the Progressives influenced Liberal fiscal policy to the extent of forcing abstention from increases in the tariff and ultimately of actual reduction. The electoral success of 1921 checked a swing towards economic nationalism evident in most countries after the war, even in free-trade Britain, and notably in the United States. After the disappointments of the Liberal budgets from 1922 to 1929, they seemed at long last to be on the threshold of success in the Dunning budget of 1930. Indeed, the Conservatives were able to use the cry of western domination with effect in Quebec in 1930.[2] Otherwise their successes, as the reimposition of the Crow's Nest Pass rates on east-bound wheat and flour and in the construction of the Hudson Bay Railway, were in the nature of sectional concessions won from the dominant metropolitan area. On the whole, the Progressive movement left the metropolitan economy of central Canada unaltered in substance or spirit.

Against the concept they held of Canadian political practice the Progressives revolted with notable results. Again, of course, they were divided. There were those who revolted against the composite party because in caucus a sectional group might be consistently outvoted. These, the Manitoban or Liberal Progressives, sought to force a realignment of parties along the lines of the liberal and conservative elements in the electorate. They wished not to abolish the practices and conventions of party government but to use them in the interests of the primary producers, as a party of liberal principle. The others were the doctrinaire or Albertan Progressives, who rejected party government as such and proposed to replace it and its accompanying conventions by group government.

Both, however, were in revolt against the traditional parties as the instruments of the beneficiaries of the metropolitan economy. Did this concept correspond with actuality? While the Progressive view, undoubtedly, was a caricature of the relations of the national parties and the beneficiaries of the metropolitan economy, the caricature has that grasp of salient features which makes a caricature recognizable. Both parties from 1896 on were the practically indistinguishable proponents of the National Policy, and they acted through the caucus, the party-managed nominating convention and the distribution of campaign funds.

It was these three focal points of party government at which the Progressives struck. That sovereignty had passed from the legislature to the majority in caucus they recognized, and also that that meant the subordination of the weaker to the more populous sections of the country. Henry Spencer said before the United Farmers of Canada (Saskatchewan Section) in 1931: "Of 240 odd members in the Dominion, the great majority went from Eastern Canada, and so it didn't matter which group was in the majority. The Western vote was so absolutely submerged in the caucuses, that however good a man might be, his vote was lost. That was the reason we took independent action."[3] To restore sovereignty to the legislature, and to make sectional views known, the Progressives refused to be bound by decisions taken in caucus. Nominating conventions they proposed to take away from the parties and restore to the electorate. Campaign funds filled by private donations, they wished to replace by public subscriptions and a levy on party members.

The revolt against caucus, however, could only have succeeded by reversing the development of parliamentary government. No modern cabinet in the parliamentary system could undertake the vast work of the annual financial and legislative program without reasonable assurance of the consistent support of its followers. The independence of the legislatures of an earlier day was no longer possible; parliament had become the critic, not the master, of cabinets. The popular control of nomination and provision of campaign expenses depended, moreover, upon a zeal for public affairs the electorate failed to display for any length of time. The Progressives put a challenge to democracy which only the U.F.A. met successfully.

Did the restoration of the old parties in 1930, then, and the rise of the CCF and Social Credit parties, essentially composite parties like the old, mark a complete defeat of the Progressive revolt against the party system? To a great extent it did. Yet the old order of Macdonald and Laurier, when party affiliation was hereditary and party chieftains were almost deified, was not restored. The two-party system did not return in its former strength. The rules and conventions of parliament made provision for more than two parties. The electorate became more independent, indeed, to the point of political indifference. The authority of the whip became lighter, the bonds of caucus weaker, than in the old days. These were effects of the Progressive movement and constituted its mark on Canadian political life.

The mere modification of political conventions and modes was perhaps a slight result of so much effort. Yet where could the sectional and agrarian revolt have led except to secession or class war, or to an acceptance of the composite party once more chastened, no doubt, but essentially unchanged? A free society is an endless compromise between anarchy and authority, union and secession. To compromise, no doubt, is to corrupt — to corrupt the simplicity of principle, the clarity of policy — but if so, then all politics corrupt and federal politics, the politics of the vast sectional and communal aggregations, especially. To this conclusion all purists, all doctrinaires and all Progressives must ultimately come or abstain from power. The logical alternative is Robespierre guillotining the guillotiner.

Yet the Progressive insurgence was not merely a sectional protest against a metropolitan economy, it was also an agrarian protest against the growing urban domination of the Canadian economy and of national politics. As such, it was closely allied to the sectional protest. As an agrarian protest, the Progressive movement was a response to the industrialization of the economy and the commercialization and mechanization of agriculture. In the years of the Progressive movement Canada was undergoing an industrial and urban revolution. To meet the challenge of the coming order, the old, hard-working farmer with his faith in long hours and sweat was ill-equipped. He had to be made over into a manager, a business man and a skilled technician. The work was largely done in the farm organizations from which the Progressive party sprang. The professional men and especially the lawyers whom the old parties put before the voters to elect were inadequate, not so much to make the legislative adjustments required by the transition from manual to mechanized agriculture, but to express the resentment and discontent the farmer experienced in the throes of the transition and to speed the work of adjustment. This task the Progressive movement performed, particularly in the two agricultural provinces it captured and held, Manitoba and Alberta. Its very success caused its passing, for the farmer came into business in the cooperatives, into politics in the parties, old or new, to stay. He stayed, not to protest further, but to get on with the job of looking after the interests of the new commercialized and mechanized agriculture. In this aspect the Progressive movement was the expression of the late phase of the transformation of the old semi-subsistence agriculture into the business of farming. With the Progressive revolt, farming ceased to be a way of life and became simply another occupation. Countryman and city dweller no longer inhabited separate social orders; the city had prevailed over the country, but in prevailing had learned, not a little because of the Progressive movement, to respect the countryman. No one after 1921 would have thought of writing Gadsby's "Sons of the Soil," in which the farmers of the great anti-conscription delegation of 1918 had been ridiculed by a slick and too clever journalist.[4]

In a larger view, also, the Progressive movement marked a profound transformation. Behind the sectional protest lay not only resentment of the National Policy and of its agents, the political parties. Behind it lay also resentment of the inequality of the provinces of the continental West in Confederation. They had been created with limitations, imposed "for the purposes of the Dominion." They entered Confederation, not as full partners, as sister provinces, but as subordinate communities, subject to the land, fiscal and railway policies of the metropolitan provinces and the special interests of the French Canadian in the French dispersion in the West. They were, in short, colonies under the form of provinces "in a federation denoting equality."[5] The Progressive party was a full-blown expression of the West's resentment of its colonial status. As such, it was one phase of the development of the Canadian nation.

As such, also, it had a great measure of success. Not since the days of the revolt has the West been subjected to the indifference, the neglect and the fumbling administration which provoked the troubles of 1869, the Rebellion of 1885 and the movement itself. The swaggering hopes of the boom days, that the West would dominate Confederation by holding a balance of power in Ottawa, were happily not realized. But the increase in cabinet representation from the one lone minister of Laurier's day to the minimal three of the present, was not merely an exercise in abstract justice, but a response to the political weight of the West in the Union government and to the force of the Progressive movement. The choice of western leaders by political parties from 1920 on was a similar response to the political power and electoral independence of the West. At the same time, it is to be observed that just as the Dunning budget denoted the beginning of Progressive success in fiscal matters so the transfer of the natural resources in 1930, the purposes of the Dominion having been fulfilled, marked the end of the colonial subordination and the achievement of equality of status by the West in Confederation. This, too, was a response to western pressure embodied in the federal Progressive party and the provincial governments the movement threw up. The progressive movement, in short, marked the achievement of political maturity of the West and the symbols of equality could no longer be withheld.

Yet the resolution of the sectional animosities, of the narrow complacency of the East and the equally narrow assertiveness of the West was to be accomplished not by the bitter exchanges of the 1920s or by enforced concessions. The work of reconciliation, a work of time, of patience, of manoeuver, the Progressive party advanced by proving that the West, too much tried, would and could resort to independent political action. The work might have been completed in that way. It was, however, completed by tragedy. No sooner had the West, through the Progressive movement, begun to win a modification of the National Policy and no sooner had it achieved equality of status in Confederation, than depression drove the country into a defensive economic nationalism. Drought ruined the agrarian economy of the West and threatened the great cooperatives and the provincial governments with general bankruptcy. The West was saved by federal action, and from the disaster of the thirties came, in East and West, a deeper sense of interdependence than the past had known. The Rowell-Sirois Commission, the great inquest provoked by the disaster, accepted and elaborated the basic thesis of the Progressive movement, that in a federal union of free citizens and equal communities, there must be such equality of economic opportunity and such equality of political status as human ingenuity may contrive and goodwill advance.[6]

ENDNOTES

1. "The Fruits of the Progressive Movement," *Manitoba Free Press,* August 6, 1930, p. 13.
2. *Ibid.*
3. *Minutes of Annual Convention of United Farmers of Canada* (Saskatchewan Section) (1931), p. 317.
4. H.F. Gadsby, "The Sons of the Soil," *Toronto Saturday Night,* June 1, 1918, p. 4.
5. C.C. Lingard, *Territorial Government in Canada: The Autonomy Question in the Old North-West Territories* (Toronto: University of Toronto Press, 1946), p. 251.
6. See R. McQueen, "Economic Aspects of Federalism," *Canadian Journal of Economics and Political Science,* I (August 1935), pp. 352-67 for a sober analysis of these points.

19 The CCF-NDP: Fifty Years After

ALAN WHITEHORN

The New Democratic Party's roots lie in the Great Depression of the 1930s. In 1932, 131 delegates gathered together in Calgary and decided to form the "Co-operative Commonwealth Federation (Farmer, Labour, Socialist)." A year later, the CCF held its first annual convention in Regina and drafted the Regina Manifesto, a statement of principles and to many the touchstone of Canadian socialism. In the midst of the world-wide recession of the 1980s the New Democratic Party, the successor to the CCF, celebrated the fiftieth anniversary of the Manifesto and 51 years of CCF-NDP history. Inevitably, the half-century milestone has generated a mood of celebration and pride in the party's political accomplishments, combined with serious reflection and critical self-appraisal of its past and some uncertainty concerning its future.

Amongst the questions frequently posed by party members, press and scholars alike are the following:

1. Is the NDP stalled as a distant third party?
2. Has the NDP in the main failed in its efforts to be more successful than its predecessor, the CCF?
3. Why, despite its image repackaging, has the NDP made no breakthrough in Quebec?
4. Is the NDP's provincial base in the West beginning to erode?
5. Has the NDP ceased to provide a clear socialist alternative to the two old-line parties?
6. Is the NDP more of a brokerage party and less of an ideologically-based movement?
7. Why, in the midst of the depression of the 1980's, has the NDP not made greater gains?

These questions will be analyzed to provide an overall evaluation of the CCF-NDP, fifty years later.

Support

The CCF vote reached its peak at 15.6 percent in 1945 and its support dropped consistently in the four subsequent elections to 13.4 percent (1949), 11.3 percent (1953), 10.7 percent (1957) and 9.5 percent (1958). The CCF was clearly on the path to oblivion and might well have gone the way of the Socialist Party of the United States.[1] The birth of the NDP gave new electoral vitality to Canada's socialist movement. In its maiden election in 1962 the NDP polled 13.5 percent of the vote, higher than all but one of the elections contested by the CCF. Electorally, the federal NDP has polled an average 16.5 percent of the votes, versus 11.1 percent for the CCF, a clear gain of 5.4 percent of all votes cast and a 48.6 percent increase in percentage of votes cast for the party. In five of the eight federal elections since 1962 the NDP has gained a higher percentage of votes than the CCF did in its best year — 1945.

While it is quite clear that in terms of the percentage of the federal vote the CCF-NDP has never broken through the threshold of the 20 percent barrier[2] and thus has not become a major party, it would be a mistake to conclude that the NDP has not shown growth in support in recent years. In the 1980 federal election, the NDP vote was above its 17 year average (1962-1979) in every single province or region. Most importantly, the party achieved an all-time CCF-NDP peak in support in Nova Scotia, New Brunswick, Ontario, Manitoba, British Columbia and nationally.[3]

Despite these overall gains, it should not be concluded that NDP electoral support has shown improvement over the CCF in all regions equally. Regionalization between and within parties is a fact of life in Canadian politics. The CCF-NDP is no exception. When data are compared regarding the average federal vote by province for the CCF and for the NDP (see Table I), we find that two provinces saw decreases in party vote. In Alberta the vote dropped from 10.2 percent for the CCF to 9.3 percent for the

TABLE 1   **Average Percent CCF-NDP Federal Vote By Province (1935-1980)**

Province	CCF (1935-1958)	NDP (1962-1980)	Difference
B.C.	28.0%	31.5%	3.5
Alberta	10.2%	9.3%	- .9
Saskatchewan	34.7%	30.2%	-4.5
Manitoba	23.3%	25.2%	1.9
Ontario	10.7%	19.9%	9.2
Quebec	1.5%	7.3%	5.8
N.B.	3.0%*	8.7%	5.7
N.S.	8.1%*	11.8%	3.7
PEI	1.7%*	4.7%	3.0
Newfoundland	.3%*	9.4%	9.1
Yukon/NWT	22.3%*	22.7%*	.4
Canada	11.1%	16.5%	5.4

* did not contest every federal election in the province/territory. Average is based only on elections contested.

NDP. More significantly, the party's Saskatchewan vote declined from 34.7 percent to 30.2 percent. In the main, Saskatchewan support faltered most in the years 1962-1965, when it returned no MPs, the only years in the history of the federal CCF-NDP that this has been so. Several factors offer explanations: (1) the resentment of the transformation of the CCF into the NDP in the only province where the CCF had formed a government, (2) disappointment by Saskatchewan residents at T.C. Douglas' departure from provincial politics and return to federal politics, (3) the growing disenchantment with the provincial CCF as it neared the end of its second decade of uninterrupted power.

The NDP was formed in part with urban and labour oriented Ontario in mind and its greatest increase in support occurred in Ontario, where the vote went from a 10.7 percent average for the CCF to a 19.9 percent average for the NDP. Ontario, a primary NDP target, has seen a virtual doubling of the party's votes, a five-fold increase in its percentage of seats (from 1.6 percent to 8.0 percent), and an equally large increase in the percentage of the party's total seats from that province (from 7.1 percent to 31.0 percent).

The old CCF was an electoral disaster in Quebec. It averaged a mere 3.6 percent of the vote. Problems emerged right from the start. Few Francophones were present at the founding convention. The name Co-operative Commonwealth Federation did not translate well into French. In addition, the party had an image of being atheistic, materialistic and anti-clerical.[4] In policy the CCF stressed the need for a strong federal government and central planning at the expense of provincial powers and jurisdiction. The heavy Anglophone membership of the Quebec CCF reinforced the image of the party being antithetical to French Canadian interests. The NDP was created to a large degree to make a new and better start in Quebec. While a breakthrough has not yet occurred, the NDP, in electoral terms, with an average 7.3 percent of the votes, has fared much better than did the CCF. Quebec has become the province with the party's third largest increase in votes and third highest percent of the party's total votes (11.8 percent).

The NDP has been better able than the CCF to establish a presence in all parts of Canada. This can be seen in terms of the greater percentage of candidates the party has run for office (61.3 percent for the CCF vs 95.0 percent for the NDP)[5] and in gaining votes for all regions of Canada. (See Table 1). For example, the average percentage vote for the NDP in the province in which it has done worst (PEI) is still a vote percentage higher than what the CCF usually received in a number of provinces.

A common portrayal in many writings on the CCF is that of a Western protest movement.[6] Certainly, the leaders of the CCF came from the West as did the vast majority of its MPs (89.3 percent)[7] (See Table 2). However, there is a tendency by many to overestimate Western and 'farmer' input in the CCF vote and to underestimate Eastern and 'labour' support. The CCF

TABLE 2 **Percent of Party's Total Federal Seats By Region (1935-1980)**

Region	CCF (1935-1958)		NDP (1962-1980)	
	N	%	N	%
Maritimes	4	3.6	4	2.2
Nfld.	0	0.0	1	.5
PEI	0	0.0	0	0.0
NS	4	3.6	3	1.6
NB	0	0.0	0	0.0
Quebec	0	0.0	0	0.0
Ontario	8	7.1	57	31.0
Prairies	71	63.4	51	27.7
Manitoba	19	17.0	27	14.8
Sask.	52	46.4	24	13.0
Alta.	0	0.0	0	0.0
B.C.	29	25.9	68	37.0
NWT/Yukon	0	0.0	4	2.2
Total	112	100%	184	100%*
East		10.7		33.2
West		89.3		66.9

Sources: R. Gibbins, *Prairie Politics and Society*, p. 115
   J.M. Beck, *Pendulum of Power*
   Canadian Parliamentary Guide, 1981
* does not total 100% due to rounding

voting base was greater in the West (59.3 percent)[8] but not to the degree often assumed. (See Table 3). On average 40.7 percent of the CCF's votes came from the East. As early as 1949, eleven years before the NDP's founding, Ontario provided more of the CCF votes than did the Prairies.[9]

The NDP has collected 61.2 percent of its votes from the East versus 39.0 percent from the West. In terms of votes, the NDP is very much an Eastern party. Votes, however, are not everything. In terms of seats, the party's representation continues to have a Western orientation with 66.9 percent of the NDP's MPs coming from the West. This is a lower rate than the CCF days but still somewhat at variance with its total votes.[10] The 1980 election continues this pattern of asymmetry between votes and seats, perhaps to the detriment of peace within the party.

In two other very important ways the NDP retains a very strong Western orientation. Data on membership (see Table 4) reveal that 69.5 percent of the party's individual members[11] are found in the West. To a considerable degree this may reflect the strong provincial bases for the NDP in this region since federal party members are also simultaneously provincial party members. The only CCF-NDP governments to date have occurred exclusively in the West, from 1972-75 in British Columbia, from 1944-1964 and

TABLE 3 **Percent of Party's Total Federal Vote By Region (1935-1980)**

Region	CCF (1935-1958) %		NDP (1962-1980) %	
Maritimes		4.3		5.9
Nfld	0.0		1.0	
PEI	0.1		.2	
NS	3.4		3.1	
NB	0.8		1.6	
Quebec		3.6		11.8
Ontario		32.8		43.5
Prairies		38.5		19.8
Manitoba	12.2		7.2	
Sask	20.8		8.6	
Alberta	5.5		4.0	
B.C.		20.8		19.0
NWT/Yukon		0.0		0.2
Total		100%		100%*
East		40.7		61.2
West		59.3		39.0

Sources: A. Cairns, "The Electoral System and the Party System in Canada, 1921-1965",
  CJPS, Vol. 1, #1.
  J.M. Beck, *Pendulum of Power*
  H. Penniman, *Canada At the Polls: The General Election of 1974*
  H. Penniman, *Canada At the Polls, 1979 and 1980*
* does not total 100% due to rounding

from 1971-81 in Saskatchewan, and from 1969-1977 and 1981 to the present in Manitoba. Any decline in the party's provincial fortunes in this region, therefore, is likely to have an effect upon the federal party's position in terms of membership and thereby finances. Thus, no analysis of the federal NDP would be complete without some discussion of the NDP's key provincial bases in British Columbia, Saskatchewan and Manitoba.

In Saskatchewan the defeat of the Blakeney government in 1982 occurred with a forcefulness that is still being felt. The party received only 37.2 percent of the vote, the worst in forty-four years. Its fall in seats from 44 to 8 was the most precipitous drop ever for the provincial Saskatchewan CCF-NDP[12]. It will, of necessity, be a time for renewal, but a considerable NDP base remains.

The failure of the provincial B.C. NDP to tap the discontent amidst the recession and return to power after 8 years as the official opposition was also a severe blow to party hopes. Its percentage of the vote, however, at 44.9 percent in 1983, down slightly from its all time previous high of 45.2 percent in 1979, suggests that the B.C. provincial NDP is still in reasonable health.

TABLE 4 **Membership in the NDP c.1983**

Province	N	%
British Columbia	30 807	25.4
Alberta	14 200	11.7
Saskatchewan	27 754	22.9
Manitoba	17 824	14.7
Ontario	26 962	22.2
Quebec	500	.4
New Brunswick	564	.5
Nova Scotia	1 360	1.1
Prince Edward Island	170	.1
Newfoundland	264	.2
Yukon	760	.6
Northwest Territories	100	.0
Total	121 265	100%*

Source: *Canadian Democrat*, 1983
* does not total 100% due to rounding

The NDP's success story to date in the 1980's is the Manitoba victory in 1981. Not only did the party come back to power with its largest number of seats at 34 but also with its highest ever vote: 47.4 percent.

As far as the federal NDP is concerned there is disappointment in the fate of two of the three NDP provincial parties but overall the Western provincial base still seems significant.

Electoral Bias and Distortion

The impact of distortion in the single member constituency system has been ably analyzed in a pioneering study by Cairns.[13] It is particularly a problem for a third party which endeavours to draw votes from across all regions. It is thus not surprising that both the federal CCF and NDP have suffered by our current electoral system. Whereas the CCF averaged 11.1 percent of the votes, it collected only 6.2 percent of the seats, a difference of 4.9. The NDP, despite increasing its overall vote to 16.5 percent, has collected a mere 8.5 percent of the seats, a difference of 8.0 (See Chart I). If one accepts as a fundamental premise that, in a democratic polity, each vote should count equally, then it seems reasonable to conclude that both the CCF and the NDP should have received a percentage of seats closer to their percentage of vote. As the data suggest, this is not a problem that is likely to diminish in the foreseeable future. In fact, the bias in the electoral system seems to be operating even more strongly against the NDP than it did against the CCF. On average, the CCF should have received 79 percent more seats and the NDP 94 percent more. In 1980 for example,

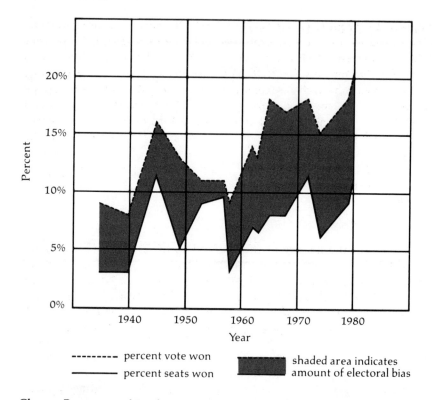

Chart 1 **Percentage of Total Votes and Seats Received by the CCF-NDP (1935-1980)**

instead of winning 32 seats, the NDP should have been closer to receiving about 60 seats. Modification in our electoral system which might bring it closer to proportional representation would clearly help the NDP. Curiously, the federal party has not been a strong proponent of this idea.

A number of scholars have already observed[14] that beyond reducing the representation and importance of a party, electoral distortions can also transform an image of a party. Thus, while 40.7 percent of the CCF's vote come from the East, only 10.7 percent of its seats come from that region. This fostered the impression of the CCF being overwhelmingly a Western rural-based party, an image that did not always help the party in its efforts to represent itself as a truly pan-Canadian party.

Much has been made of the CCF-NDP failure in Quebec. There are a number of reasons for this. One reason frequently overlooked is the bias in the electoral system. The CCF-NDP from its birth contested federal elections in Quebec. In total it received 1,581,912 votes but it has never received a single seat.[15] From 1949 to 1965 the CCF-NDP showed a consistent trend of increasing its vote: 1.1 percent (1949), 1.5 percent (1953), 1.8 percent (1957), 2.3 percent (1956), 4.4. percent (1962), 7.1 percent (1963), 12.0 percent (1965). Yet no CCF-NDP MP was ever elected from any riding. What would have been the outcome if an electoral system had been in place that would have responded to the growing support for the party? Would the NDP have had more articulate voices speaking on behalf of Quebec? Would the NDP have been encouraged to try harder in Quebec? Would the overwhelming Liberal one-party dominance in Quebec have lessened? Would Canadian politics be better served by each party receiving adequate representation in each region of the country?

Leadership

In the history of the CCF-NDP, there have been six party leaders: J.S. Woodsworth, M.J. Coldwell, Hazen Argue,[16] T.C. Douglas, David Lewis and Ed Broadbent, with an average tenure of 8.5 years (vs 12.8 years for the Liberals and 5.7 years for the Conservatives in the same period). All three CCF leaders were from the West, as was the first NDP leader. The two most recent leaders, Lewis and Broadbent, have come from the East.

Perhaps not surprisingly, the NDP acquired a peak of eleven Ontario seats in 1972, its highest ever, under the tutelage of an Eastern leader, David Lewis. Since that time the number of Ontario NDP MPs has declined consistently. Whereas in 1974 half (8 of 16) of the NDP MPs were from Ontario, in 1980 this has dropped to 16 percent (5 of 32). No matter what personalities might have been involved, it seems that a certain amount of tension would be inevitable in a situation in which the leadership was Eastern-based, while 27 of 32 MPSs, 69.5 percent of the party membership, the most successful provincial NDP parties and the only NDP government were Western-based. To some, particularly in the West, it might seem time to see the leadership revert back to a Westerner. Indeed, the rumblings of NDP MP Doug Anguish seem to suggest such a concern. Before a headlong plunge into a possible leadership challenge, it might be appropriate for those same people to recall that 61.2 percent of the party's vote comes from the East and 43.5 percent from Ontario alone. (See Table 3). The case for a Western federal leader, therefore, is not as strong as many seem to assume.

For the moment, Broadbent's tenure seems secure. He was re-elected by acclamation at the 1983 convention, although not without a brief moment of doubt.[17] His re-appointment seems appropriate given that in the last election he led the party to its highest ever vote total and number of seats. Still, the party has not made the long hoped for breakthrough and that alone may be sufficient grounds for discontent.

Ideology and Policy

There has been much written about the CCF-NDP shifts in ideology and policy.[18] More often than not this literature has also raised the interrelated themes of a protest movement becalmed, ideological decay in a third party and the increasing bourgeois appearance of a working class organization.[19] It may, nevertheless, be useful to raise a few queries and provide some data as a stimulus to thought.

In the history of the CCF-NDP four key statements of principles predominate. The Regina Manifesto of 1933 is by far the most enduring, and given its enunciation at the birth of the CCF in the midst of the depression, it will always have special significance to most party members. The Winnipeg Declaration of 1956, drafted in the depths of the Cold War and during world-wide debates about the means to achieve socialism, continued the ideological re-thinking that ultimately led to the creation of the NDP and the issuing of the New Party Declaration in 1961. In 1983, a new Regina Manifesto, fifty years after the first, has been drafted to guide the party in the 1980s. Each document provides a useful insight into the evolution of socialist thought in Canada.

A certain mythology has arisen about the 1933 Regina Manifesto. Because of a few provocative passages, the Manifesto has acquired an image somewhat more radical than the text as a whole conveys. A content analysis of the four texts reveals the frequency of usage of key terms such as socialism, social democracy and class (See Table 5). Underhill and his colleagues certainly did not dwell upon the terms "socialism" or "socialist" as self-description. In fact, the solitary usage suggests the terms were approached "gingerly" and somewhat timidly, not unlike in the 1950s. The LSR drafters in 1933 preferred to choose words such as "socialization" or "social ownership" which appeared less intimidating to potential supporters. While the fairly moderate language of the Regina Manifesto became even more moderate in the 1950s and early 1960s, it seems implausible to argue that the NDP in 1983 has shied away from a fundamental commitment to

TABLE 5 **Frequency of Use of Key Terms in CCF-NDP Manifestoes**

Term	1933 Regina Manifesto	1956 Winnipeg Declaration	1961 New Party Declaration	1983 New Regina Manifesto
Socialism/Socialist	1	4	0	13
Social Democracy	0	1	1	0
Class	3	0	0	2

socialism. Its statement of principles is emphatic in its employment of the term — far more than in any other official party statement of principles.

To observe this is not to suggest that the socialism of the 1980s is identical to that of the 1930s. Canadian socialists have realized that any ideology, to be meaningful, must be an evolving doctrine that endeavours to change the environment, but in turn is also changed by the environment. An ideology which fails to interact with the socio-economic base will ultimately recede into quixotic scholasticism and irrelevance.

When compared to the 1933 Manifesto the 1983 Manifesto is a less centralizing document which stresses "Stronger provincial and local governments capable of realizing important tasks of economic and social development..." and "...the demand by Canadians to decentralize, where feasible..." so that they can "participate more directly in the political decisions...." It acknowledges much more readily a "respect for its [Canada's] regionalism, and for its duality" and "the unique and enduring identity of the French Canadian people...." It also reflects a less technocratic view and belief in central planning by asserting that "planing must...not [be] imposed...from above" and that "social ownership" does "not simply [mean] the transfer of title of large enterprises to the state" but rather involves "decentralized ownership and control" and the "progressive democratization of the workplace." The document also proceeds to recognize the need to set "ecological priorities" and the danger of "annihilation of our species in a nuclear holocaust." The importance of the "women's movement" and "aboriginal peoples" are also stressed.

Beyond the committment to a socialist Canada, the party also shows its distinctiveness from the two major parties by its unequivocal demand for Canada's withdrawal from NATO and NORAD, cessation of all Cruise-testing in Canada and call for Canada to become a nuclear-free zone.

The NDP is now, as was the CCF, a blend of different colours of the political rainbow.[20] It is composed of individuals whose attitudes range from Marxism to reformism.[21] There has always been a "ginger group" striving to push the party further left. Over the years the names of the ginger groups have changed: the Socialist Party of Canada, the B.C. Socialist Fellowship, the Ontario Ginger Group, the Waffle, or more recently the Left-Caucus. The result is inevitably the same: a militant minority sufficiently strong to provoke lengthy and often intense debate, but rarely able to construct a winning majority. For example, at the recent convention, the new Regina Manifesto was approved by a two to one ratio. The Left-Caucus organizational and strategy meetings attracted between 75 and 100 persons; and in the elections to the governing federal council of the party, the Left-Caucus leaders who chose to run averaged about 200 votes (20 percent of the total). This is enough support to be felt, but not enough to achieve any real power within the NDP.

The Future

After fifty years what does the future bode for the party? Curiously, while the CCF was born in the midst of the Great Depression of the 1930s, it was unable to form a federal or provincial government in that decade. It was not until the worst of the unemployment had receded in 1944 that the CCF formed its first pioneering government in the province of Saskatchewan. Similarly, despite the high rates of unemployment in the recession of the 1980s, the NDP's progress seems slower than expected.

Contrary to the assumptions of many socialists, an increase in economic deprivation does not necessarily lead to a corresponding increase in support of a socialist party. This comes as a paradox to most socialists who expect exploitation and poverty to generate immediate demands for political change. Why have the gains been less than anticipated?

While the NDP was born amidst great fanfare concerning trade union financial support, organizational assistance and votes, there is some evidence to suggest that the support may not be as strong or enduring as many might have hoped. Data on rate of union affiliation to the NDP suggests a fairly steady decline from a peak of 14.6 percent of all unions in 1963 to a low of 8.2 percent in 1981.[22]

A perusal of CIPO and Gallup data for the past two decades reveals that Canadians as a whole fear "Big Labour" (33 percent in 1968 and 29 percent in 1982) far more than "Big Business" (17 percent in 1968 and 13 percent in 1982).[23] Further evidence of a class-biased culture can also be seen in data cited by Chi and Perlin[24] showing that more Canadians prefer a right-wing party (28.6 percent) than a left-wing party (9.4 percent).

Perhaps not surprisingly, the CCF's and NDP's social welfare policies have fostered an image of the party encouraging the growth of government spending and employment. In recent years such a perception has become a greater liability as more Canadians are concerned that "Big Government" is the greatest threat (23 percent in 1968 vs 46 percent in 1982).[25] It is somewhat ironic that in the year 1984, "big brother" rather than "being my brother's keeper" has become the pressing concern of many. The NDP's new stress on decentralization is perhaps a recognition of the difficult path it walks — toward the co-operative commonwealth and into its second fifty years.

ENDNOTES

1. The Socialist Party went from an all-time high of 919,799 votes in 1920 to 6,898 votes in 1980. F. Smallwood, *The Other Candidates: Third Parties in Presidential Elections* (Hanover: University Press of New England, 1983).
2. There have, however, been occasions when the CCF-NDP has passed this barrier in Gallup polls. The most famous example occurred in September, 1943 when the CCF polled 29 percent vs 28 percent for the Liberals and 28 percent

for the Conservatives. More recently, in February, 1982 the NDP polled as high as 26 percent vs 36 percent for the Liberals and 35 percent for the Conservatives. *PC Journal,* Vol #2, #4, 1983, p. 6.

3. See "Appendix: Federal Election Results 1878-1984" in H. Thorburn, ed., *Party Politics in Canada,* 5th edition (Scarborough: Prentice-Hall, 1985).

4. The irony here is that a substantial number of the party activists were recruited from church ranks. (e.g., J.S. Woodsworth, T.C. Douglas, Stanley Knowles). See Richard Allen, ed., *The Social Gospel in Canada* (Ottawa, National Museums of Canada, 1975) and R. Allen, *The Social Passion* (Toronto: University of Toronto Press, 1973). See also G. Baum, *Catholics and Canadian Socialism* (Toronto: Lorimer, 1980).

5. J.M. Beck, *The Pendulum of Power* (Scarborough: Prentice-Hall, 1968) and data from the Chief Electoral Officer. Data on NDP support by ethnicity, class, education and sex can be obtained from H. Clarke, et al., *Political Choice in Canada* (Toronto: McGraw-Hill Ryerson, 1979).

6. S.M. Lipset, *Agrarian Socialism* (Berkeley: University of California, 1971, revised and expanded edition) p. 188.

7. Data derived from R. Gibbons, *Prairie Politics and Society* (Toronto: Butterworths, 1980) p. 115.

8. Data derived from Beck, *The Pendulum of Power,* A. Cairns, "The Electoral System and the Party System in Canada, 1921-1965," *Canadian Journal of Political Science,* Vol. 1, #1, H. Penniman, *Canada At the Polls: The General Election of 1974* (Washington: American Enterprise Institute, 1975), H. Penniman, *Canada At the Polls, 1979 and 1980* (Washington: American Enterprise Institute, 1981).

9. Derived from Beck, *The Pendulum of Power.* The League for Social Reconstruction, the CCF's 'brains-trust', was largely an Eastern phenomenon. See M. Horn, *The League for Social Reconstruction* (Toronto: University of Toronto Press, 1980).

10. This is a theme so ably demonstrated by Cairns, *The Electoral System and the Party System in Canada, 1921-1965.*

11. Some care should be taken in the interpretation of the data since members can also belong to the party indirectly through union affiliation. Here, of course, Eastern representation is far more significant.

12. P. Fox, *Politics: Canada,* 5th ed. (Toronto: McGraw-Hill, 1982), pp. 682-4.

13. Cairns, *The Electoral System and the Party System in Canada, 1921-1965.*

14. Cairns, *ibid,* and Gibbins, *Prairie Politics and Society.*

15. In the period 1962-80, 11.8 percent of the NDP's total federal vote has come from Quebec yet it has never won a seat in that province. A similar case can be made with the province of Alberta. Over the years 718,505 Albertans have voted for the CCF-NDP but the party has never elected a federal MP from that province.

16. In party literature and many of the press accounts, one leader's name is consistently omitted. Hazen Argue, the man who defected to the Liberals and later became a Liberal Senator and Cabinet minister, has become a virtual nonperson as far as the NDP is concerned. While such a partisan view is understandable, analysts should focus more attention on this individual since he is a significant example of co-optation and the calculation that it is more desirable to participate in power immediately rather than waiting for an NDP government. Prime Minister Trudeau is perhaps another and more prominent example of this phenomenon.

17. John Bacher, a young member of the Ontario Left-Caucus, initially chose to run as a leadership candidate. Upon reflection and counsel from colleagues and foes alike, he chose to withdraw his nomination.

18. See for example M. Cross, ed., *The Decline and Fall of a Good Idea: CCF-NDP Manifestoes 1932 to 1969* (Toronto: New Hogtown Press, 1974), L. Zakuta, *A Protest Movement Becalmed* (Toronto: University of Toronto Press, 1964), and W. Young, *The Anatomy of a Party: The National CCF* (Toronto: University of Toronto Press, 1969).

19. A. Whitehorn, "An Analysis of the Historiography on the CCF-NDP: Part I The Protest Movement Becalmed Tradition" in B. Brennan ed., *Building the Co-operative Commonwealth* (forthcoming).

20. It should be kept in mind that, as in the case of MPs, convention delegates need not be fully representative of the general party membership.

21. For an elucidation of this theme see R. Hackett, "The Waffle Conflict in the NDP" in Thorburn, *Party Politics in Canada,* 4th edition, R. Hackett "Pie in the Sky: A History of the Ontario Waffle" *Canadian Dimension* Oct-Nov, 1980, special edition, John Bullen, "The Ontario Waffle and the Struggle for an Independent Socialist Canada: Conflict Within the NDP" *Canadian Historical Review* 1983, #2, M.J. Brodie, "From Waffles to Grits: A Decade in the Life of the NDP" in Thorburn, *Party Politics in Canada* 5th edition. Data from Hackett and Brodie are derived from 1971 and 1979 surveys of NDP convention delegates conducted by Perlin and his associates. Preliminary analysis from my own 1983 survey of NDP delegates reveals a breakdown very similar to that found by Perlin and associates. The 1983 distribution is as follows: Marxist 3.4 percent, socialist 33.9 percent, social democrat 49.4 percent, ecologist 1.4 percent, social gospel 4.0 percent, populist 1.1 percent, reformer 5.1 percent, liberal 1.7 percent. Some caution should be taken in the interpretation of the data. For many in the NDP the terms socialist and social democrat are interchangeable. See for example David Lewis, *The Good Fight: Political Memoirs 1909-1958* (Toronto: Macmillan, 1981) p. 301.

22. K. Archer, "The Failure of the Federal NDP: Unions, Unionists and Politics in Canada," a paper presented at the annual Canadian Political Science Association meeting, Vancouver, June, 1983. It should be noted that numbers of members affiliated have continued to increase but at a slower rate than that of unionization.

23. CIPO, *Toronto Star,* Aug 16, 1978 cited in F. Fletcher and R. Drummond, *Canadian Attitude Trends 1960-1978* (Institute for Research on Public Policy, Montreal, 1979) and Gallup, *Toronto Star,* Sept 4, 1982.

24. N. Chi and G. Perlin, "The New Democratic Party: A Party in Transition" in Thorburn, *Party Politics in Canada* 4th edition.

25. CIPO, *Toronto Star,* Aug. 16, 1978, and Gallup, *Toronto Star* Sept. 4, 1982.

20 From Waffles to Grits: A Decade in the Life of the New Democratic Party

M. JANINE BRODIE

More than a decade has passed since the New Democratic Party, torn internally by ideological factionalism and interpersonal animosities, expelled the militantly nationalist left caucus, the Waffle, from its ranks. Such schisms are not uncommon in the history of either the Canadian left or third-party movements. In fact, most political parties at some point or another find themselves embroiled in conflict over questions of political strategy and party policy. The Waffle episode, however, continues to generate both partisan and academic debate.[1] This is perhaps because the wounds have not yet healed, but more important, there remain many unresolved questions about why this opposition developed within the NDP only ten years after its birth and how the dissolution of the party's self-appointed left-wing has affected the orientations of the NDP during the 1970s. This paper examines these unresolved issues with survey research data collected from NDP party activists attending the 1971 federal leadership convention and the 1979 federal policy convention.

The Waffle was primarily a radical nationalist caucus of the NDP which first gained visibility in 1969 with the publication of "For an Independent Socialist Canada" — the so-called "Waffle Manifesto." Its popularity and strength within the party were dramatically illustrated in 1971 when its candidate for the party leadership came much closer to displacing the party's heir apparent, David Lewis, than most had expected. Recent autopsies of the Waffle suggest at least three explanations for its rise within the ranks of the NDP during this period. A familiar theme is that it was a product of the times — the turbulent sixties, when many orthodoxies were called into question, especially among youth, and the United States lost its cold war image as a benevolent super-power.[2] From what is essentially an historical perspective then, the Waffle was a peculiar Canadian variant of the protest decade. Another interpretation is that the Waffle was a predictable manifestation of the internal dynamic of all parties of the left, the inevitable friction between forces of radicalism and moderation. In this view, the Waffle was a radical caucus representing "the constant resurgence of left tendencies within social democratic parties."[3] Finally, and somewhat related to the above, is the view of the Waffle as a reaction to, if not a consequence of, the CCF/NDP's post-war policies and alliance strategies — specifically its electoral moderation and its attempts to form a new coalition between the liberally-minded middle class and organized labour.[4] Each perspective obviously captures a dimension of the Waffle conflict. The following, however, expands upon the last theme.

The New Party Project: Uncertain Foundations

The birth of the NDP institutionalized several tendencies which had increasingly preoccupied the CCF during the post-war years and which, in turn, set the stage for the Waffle conflict that followed.[5]...After a promising spurt of popularity during the war, it appeared to lose its distinctive place in the federal party system and was bleeding to death at the polls.[6] The party's repeated electoral failures in the postwar forties and the fifties were interpreted by many as evidence that the dogmas and visions of the Regina Manifesto were out of step with the times. Thus, similar to so many other social democratic parties of the period, the CCF undertook to reassert itself in the federal party system by restating its aims and principles.

The driving forces behind the movement for redefinition were convinced that the party's future, if not its very survival, depended upon forging new alliances with two distinct and hitherto largely elusive constituencies — organized labour and the "liberally-minded" middle class. An alliance with labour was critical because in many minds Canadian social democracy could not emerge out of the political wilderness unless, and until, the CCF followed the example of the British Labour party and established financial and organizational links with the trade union movement.[7]

The CCF's second objective of gathering the support of the liberally minded middle class also faced significant hurdles. First, while the middle class was growing much more quickly than organized labour in the post-war years, it was an amorphous constituency, lacking obvious organizations and issues to define it. A second and more important obstacle was the party's proposed labour orientation,...which held few appeals for many elements of the middle class. However, this potential friction in the very design of the new party, while underpinning the formation of the NDP in 1961 and its initial policy orientations, was not debated or perhaps even recognized at the time.

Within the context of the 1950's this attempt to revitalize the old CCF implies gradualism and moderation. Indeed very few within the middle class or even, for that matter, organized labour were familiar with socialist analysis of capitalism, let alone committed to socialist goals such as nationalization and collective ownership. Moreover, key strategists within the party no longer believed that these goals were especially appropriate in post-war Canada. For David Lewis, unquestionably a key figure both in the creation of the new party and its subsequent orientations, the programme of the NDP necessarily had to contain elements "that may not have anything particularly to do with socialism as such."[9]

The CCF had always been a diverse coalition but the proposition that the party should actively court yet another two groups was not welcomed by the entire membership. Many "old-time" socialists and the party's left feared that an influx of too many new faces and interests would dilute the party's programmes.[10] There was also reluctance among some Saskatchewan CCF activists who, enjoying the fruits of provincial political power, had little motivation to change. The most pervasive objections to the new party, however, arose over the reformists' overtures toward organized labour. The farmers, a mainstay in the old CCF, feared that their once strategic position in the party organization would be smothered by the numbers and financial resources of the trade union movement and the party's focus shifted from the west to the industrial centre.

Elements of the CCF's left also suspected labour. This faction lamented the increasing moderation of the party, interpreting it as "a bit of expediency to woo labour."[11] In addition, there was suspicion that "power-mad labour bosses" would dominate the party and thereby, dislocate long-time party activists from what they perceived as their rightful place in the party hierarchy.[12] Finally, the "toughest and most down-to-earth" objections, at least in the mind of David Lewis, came from those who doubted whether the new alliance strategy would work, whether the labour leadership could or would actually deliver the funding and votes which seemed so necessary for the party's survival.[13] All of these tensions simmered in the early days of the NDP and caused a few notable desertions from the party. Whatever the intensity of these anti-labour sentiments, however, they largely remained submerged and unorganized. Clearly, they were not sufficient to divert the party from its vision of a new social democratic-labour alliance or its commitment to a course of moderation.

Ten Years Later: Tensions from Within

The major challenge to the NDP's new orientations came from the Waffle Group, which criticized almost every strand of the party's thinking, especially its moderation and gradualism, and indirectly its links with organized labour. It also injected into the party's debates two issues, Canadianization and democratization, which previously had not been particularly controversial themes within either the CCF or the NDP. The Waffle's goals were to build an independent socialist Canada and to make the NDP a truly socialist party. These aims were to be accomplished through a three-fold agenda. First, it argued that socialism was impossible without economic independence from the United States. It was not simply

capital but American capital which constituted the major obstacle to socialism in Canada. Second, Wafflers urged the NDP to pursue and offer the
electorate the option of extensive public ownership. Finally, the Waffle
Manifesto called for extra-parliamentary action. The CCF had some roots
in extra-parliamentary organizations, especially the radical farmers'
movement, but it had from the beginning dedicated itself to the parliamentary or electoral road to socialism. The NDP had also adopted this course
uncritically. The Waffle argued that this was a fundamental weakness, and
urged the party to move outside the electoral realm and participate in
conflicts between labour and capital and community and industry in order
to create and nurture a socialist consciousness.[14]

Obviously, each of the above aims implied both a critique and an alternative to the vision of the NDP as a moderate social democratic-labour alliance
and as such also constituted a challenge to the proponents of this vision,
who for years had been deeply entrenched in the party's hierarchy. For
example, the Waffle's marriage of Canadian nationalism and democratic
socialism questioned the CCF/NDP's post-war alliance strategies. Rather
than pursuing organized labour and the liberally-minded middle class, the
Waffle suggested a new alliance, one between socialists and nationalists.
The Waffle's professed goals of extensive public ownership also challenged
the party's long-standing policies of moderation, which were designed to
ease popular anxieties about its socialist legacy. A similar friction arose over
the question of extra-parliamentary action. For years, the CCF/NDP
endorsed the formula that the party had to capture power before mobilization for socialism could begin. The Waffle, however, argued for the necessity
of creating a mass movement in order to bring a socialist party to power.
Clearly, then, the Waffle challenged the consensus which had directed the
CCF in the post-war years and had given birth to the NDP.

The downfall of the Waffle often is attributed to its radicalism. From this
perspective, the entire Waffle episode was simply a predictable and classic
restatement of the constant friction within parties of the left — between
utopian goals and electoral necessities, ideology and pragmatism, party and
movement. The extent to which the Waffle was too radical and differed
substantially from the party's rank and file on the issues of moderation,
Canadianization and public ownership will be examined below. There is,
however, a related but alternative explanation for the tensions within the
NDP. Notably, the Waffle affair also exposed the NDP's uneasy and tentative relationship with labour.

According to at least one observer, the Waffle's antagonistic relationship
with the labour wing of the NDP was unintentional, yet it was hardly
surprising.[15] Their language alone may have been sufficient to alienate the
traditionally conservative labour movement, but their optimistic nationalism
likewise threatened the immediate economic interests of many of the unions
affiliated with the NDP. It was all very well for the Waffle to argue for the
necessity of economic independence from the United States and extensive

public ownership, but many Canadian unions, particularly the industrial unions of Ontario's manufacturing heartland such as the Steelworkers and the United Auto Workers, were dependent on American capital both for their organizational existence and their members' well-being.[16] To reduce the conflict between the Waffle and labour solely to policy disagreements, however, may distort what was at the heart of the conflict within the NDP during the early 1970's. The Waffle also may be seen as an unsuccessful challenge to the legitimacy and position of labour within the NDP (and to some extent outside it), as well as to elements of the party's establishment which had for so long pursued the single-minded goal of a social democratic-labour alliance in Canada.[17]

Economic nationalism and extra-parliamentary action were the two most prominent policy orientations that encouraged conflict between the Waffle and the labour wing of the NDP. In the case of the former, the Waffle's case against organized labour, especially international unions, was both predictable and self-evident. Wafflers considered labour a potential ally in their goal of achieving socialism via economic nationalism but, as a precondition, they argued that, as with Canadian industry, the international component of the Canadian labour movement had to be repatriated from the United States and freed from the influence of American capital, abandoning its international structure and merging into autonomous national entities.

The Waffle's commitment to extra-parliamentary action, however, proved far more threatening than the issue of full autonomy, principally because it challenged the legitimacy of the existing labour leadership both within the NDP and in the union movement at large. The Waffle argued that rank-and-file unionists should pursue workers' control in the workplace as well as displace the existing leadership structure and take more direct control over union affairs themselves. The Waffle implied or directly indicted the labour establishment for being bureaucratic, conservative and "staff professionals of the internationals," who were remote from, if not unrepresentative of, their constituency.[18]

The labour leadership responded with equal rancour. The Waffle was described as a "haven for social misfits," practising "snobbery for assuming that workers are stupid enough to permit the union leadership to manipulate them."[19] Underlying all of this animosity was one inescapable theme: the party had no business interfering with the trade-union movement.

The intervention of elements of the party into the internal affairs of its labour affiliates was a precedent in the politics of the NDP. In its eagerness to draw labour into a coalition, the NDP had accepted the labour movement as it was and essentially built a new party around it. The Waffle's call for full autonomy drew the party perilously close to sacred ground which if trespassed upon could destroy the fabric and logic of the party. Ultimately then, the Waffle threatened the party's hierarchy, whose entire post-war electoral strategy, indeed, its survival, hung in the balance.

To summarize, there appear to have been at least three sources of division within the NDP underlying the expulsion of the Waffle. The first was the Waffle's radicalism on the questions of moderation and public ownership, which potentially alienated the party's rank and file. The second was the Waffle's position on economic nationalism which threatened the immediate economic well-being of labour and third, was the challenge to the structure and legitimacy of trade unions within the NDP.

What were the relative strengths of these cleavages within the party during the early 1970s and what effect, if any, has the dissolution of the Waffle had on the subsequent policy orientations of the NDP? Survey data collected by mail questionnaire from 776 NDP activists attending the 1971 federal leadership convention and 520 delegates attending the 1979 federal policy convention are employed below to assess these questions.[20] Admittedly, survey measures capture neither the rich complexities of partisan debate nor the intrigues of factional manoeuvring. Nevertheless, they do enable us to assess the division among the party rank and file on many of the dimensions discussed. The delegates were asked to indicate whether they agreed or disagreed with all of the survey questions displayed below.

Concepts	*Survey Measure*
1) Electoral Radicalism	The NDP should emphasize its more left-wing ideas, even if that were to mean losing votes now.
2) Canadianization	We must ensure an independent Canada, even if that were to mean a lower standard of living for Canadians.
3) Nationalization	A) Canada should nationalize key foreign-owned resource industries. B) Canada should nationalize key resource industries, regardless of who owns them.
4) Labour Orientation	A) Canadian affiliates of international unions should have full autonomy. B) Trade unions in the NDP have too much influence.

The 1971 NDP Leadership Convention

The results of the 1971 NDP delegate survey suggest a number of pronounced divisions between the Waffle faction and both the party's rank-and-file constituency delegates and the labour wing.[21] For example, the question of electoral moderation clearly isolated the Waffle from other elements of the party in 1971 (Table 1). Some 88 percent of the Waffle disagreed with a course of moderation and endorsed the view that the NDP should turn further left even if it cost votes. Only 25 percent of

TABLE 1 **Selected Orientations of 1971 NDP Party Activist by Party Sub-group**
(% in Agreement)

	Constituency* N=263	Local Union N=155	Union Leadership N=31	Waffle Supporter N=260
1) Electoral Radicalism	25.1%	31.2%	48.4%	87.7%
2) Canadianization	76.8%	56.7%	58.1%	87.3%
3) Nationalization				
A	72.6%	72.6%	67.7%	96.2%
B	56.8%	62.4%	64.5%	91.9%
4) Labour Orientation				
A	74.5%	77.7%	87.1%	86.9%
B	22.4%	12.1%	3.2%	52.7%

*excluding Waffle supporters

the constituency delegates and 31 percent of delegates for union locals held a similar view. The argument that the Waffle was too radical for the NDP, therefore, finds some support here. Few others in the party shared the Waffle's vision of pushing the NDP any further to the left.

There is far less evidence to support the contention that the Waffle conflict arose over the party's policy orientations concerning economic independence and public ownership. The Waffle was more radical than other elements of the party on these questions but the divisions were not pronounced (see Table 1). Concerning the party's policy on nationalization, for example, almost all of the Waffle supporters and approximately three-quarters of the other party groups agreed that Canada should nationalize all foreign-owned resource industries. This consensus is perhaps not too surprising considering that the party adopted a policy resolution on economic independence in 1969. There was less party consensus concerning the question of whether Canada should nationalize all key resources regardless of ownership, but still the majority of all the groups endorsed this proposition. Labour, however, was much less likely than either the constituency delegates or Waffle supporters to agree that economic independence was a necessary party goal even if that were to mean a lower standard of living. In this case, the percentage difference between the Waffle and other constituency groups was less marked (11 percent) than the difference between the constituency group and labour (20 percent). Since the majority of all groups agreed with the goal of economic nationalism, however, this division probably was inconsequential.

Intra-party consensus appeared to be even more pronounced concerning the question of whether Canadian affiliates of international unions should achieve full autonomy from their American counterparts (Table 1). Three-quarters of the constituency and union local delegates and 87 percent of the union leadership and the Waffle supporters endorsed the goal of full autonomy. However, there may be a problem with interpretation. It is conceivable that union delegates could endorse the goal of full autonomy without discarding international unionism. There is no such ambiguity concerning the question of the proper place of labour within the NDP. Fully 52 percent of the Waffle supporters agreed that trade unions had too much influence within the NDP while 22 percent of the remaining constituency delegates expressed a similar resentment of union power. In contrast, some 12 percent of the union local delegates and only 3 percent of the union leadership agreed that trade unions had inordinate influence within the party. Among all the issues examined here, the question of power most clearly divided the Waffle and labour in 1971. The anti-union sentiments which were evident at the conception of the NDP had not disappeared with time, but rather, as Desmond Morton aptly assessed the conflict, the Waffle "exploited the deep well of anti-union sentiment" with the party.[22]

Parties, especially new parties, frequently find themselves torn by factionalism and sometimes they are forced to make trade-offs to ensure the party's survival. The choices for the NDP hierarchy in the early 1970s, however, were particularly unpleasant. On the one hand, in the face of the Liberal party's success among new voters in 1968, the NDP was keenly aware that it needed young recruits who were nurtured in and aspired to the middle class, as well as intellectuals who could potentially supply agendas and leadership for the party in the future. The Waffle appeared to draw these types into the party. At the 1971 leadership convention, for example, one-half of the Waffle supporters were under 30 years of age, almost one-third were students or academics and one-fifth were teachers or professionals.[23] On the other hand, it was equally apparent that if left unchecked this faction threatened to compromise the party's alliance with labour. The party had an admittedly difficult choice. Should it embrace the popular if radical faction and risk losing labour (along with its considerable financial and organizational resources), thereby giving up any hope of the CCF/NDP's long anticipated electoral "take-off" among Canadian workers? Or, should it force the Waffle to dismantle itself and tow the party line at the risk of losing it and the new elements it appeared to be attracting to the party?

Considering that so many of the party's movers and shakers at the time (not the least of which was David Lewis, the party leader) had for many years been dedicated to the vision of a Canadian variant of the British Labour Party, it is not surprising that the latter option was chosen. The considerable intrigue which forced the Waffle's capitulation need not be recounted here. it is nonetheless informative to recall some of the charges levelled against it. For David Lewis, the Waffle was trying to "build a machine" to push the party around.[24] That the Waffle was not going to be allowed to compromise the NDP's vision of a social democratic-labour alliance was more clearly articulated by Stephen Lewis who issued the party's final ultimatum to the radical group. He charged that:

> The Waffle had poisoned the atmosphere of debate within the party, had maintained the separate structure of a party within a party and had displayed a "sneering, contemptuous attitude towards official trade unionism and the labour leadership."[25]

The Aftermath

What effect, if any, did the Waffle episode have on the direction and policy orientations of the NDP? In the early seventies it was generally agreed that the conflict forced many of the NDP's youngest and most vigorous elements out of the party and indeed, there were some signs of an exodus, although there has been no detailed accounting of its extent. Some prominent Wafflers left the NDP for the "Movement for an Independent Socialist Canada," a movement which basically was oriented toward extraparliamentary activity. The Saskatchewan Waffle maintained its name and organizational structure but also pursued mainly non-electoral, extraparliamentary activity. The explusion of the Ontario Waffle, as Ed Broadbent conceded, had cost the NDP "a number of intellectual recruits."[26] More generally, it is assumed that the dissolution of the Waffle effectively deradicalized the NDP, reaffirming its moderate orientations. What, then has been the legacy of the Waffle within the NDP?

A mail survey of delegates attending the 1979 federal NDP policy convention provides some tentative answers to this question. First, the responses give support to those who claim that the seepage from the party as a result of the Waffle conflict was not all that large. Some 36 percent of the 1979 convention delegates surveyed indicated that they had been Waffle supporters. But, the intervening decade did make its mark on the remnants of the Waffle within the NDP. Only 4 percent of the ex-Wafflers were students, while 60 percent were firmly entrenched in the middle class as professionals, executives, administrators and small proprietors. Indeed, ex-Wafflers were twice as likely to be professionals as non-Waffle supporters (34 percent vs 16 percent).[27]

A comparison of the 1971 and 1979 delegate responses to the questions of electoral moderation, Canadianization and nationalization show that there have been some changes in the policy orientations of the NDP during the 1970s (see Table 2). The 1979 delegates were 7 percent less likely than the 1971 delegates to agree that the party should promote more left-wing ideas, whatever the electoral costs (see Table 2). The ex-Wafflers were the most likely to support radicalism but, again, this group appears to have mellowed. Only 57 percent of the ex-Waffler's pushed for greater radicalism

TABLE 2 **Changes in NDP Party Activists's Orientations 1971-1979 (% in Agreement)**

	1971 *N=776*	*1979* *N=520*	*% Change*
1) Electoral Radicalism	46.3%	39.4%	−6.9
2) Canadianization	76.0%	76.7%	.7
3) Nationalization			
A	79.4%	94.0%	14.6
B	70.2%	77.5%	7.3
4) Labour Orientation			
A	79.0%	88.7%	9.7
B	30.0%	11.0%	−19.0

in 1979 compared to 88 percent in 1971 (see Table 3). The entire party, however, appears to have radicalized on nationalization policy. There was, for example, a 15 percent increase in the proportion of the delegates concurring with the proposition that Canada should nationalize foreign-owned resources. Similarly, there was a 7 percent increase in the party's agreement concerning the nationalization of all resource industries (see Table 2). Moreover, all of the party groups that have been examined here demonstrated increased agreement on these two policy areas (see Table 3). The proportion of the party endorsing the necessity of economic independence, however, remained unchanged at 75 percent in the 1971-1979 period.

Did the Waffle radicalize the party's Canadianization and nationalization

TABLE 3 **Selected Orientations of 1979 NDP Party Activists by Party Sub-group (% in Agreement)**

	*Constituency** *N=132*	*Local Union* *N=73*	*Union Leadership* *N=32*	*Ex-Waffle Supporter* *N=165*
1) Electoral Radicalism	27.0%	28.8%	22.7%	57.6%
2) Canadianization	77.9%	65.8%	72.7%	79.4%
3) Nationalization				
A	93.6%	89.0%	100%	97.0%
B	74.5%	71.2%	86.4%	85.5%
4) Labour Orientation				
A	90.7%	84.2%	85.7%	92.7%
B	12.9%	5.5%	0.0%	10.3%

*excluding ex-Waffle supporters

policies? This question cannot be answered definitively here but it seems doubtful. There was already a broad consensus on these issues in 1971. The events of the intervening years — the oil crisis, American policies, and the general decline of the Canadian economy — probably served to strengthen the party's resolve for economic independence. Clearly, as the Gallup Polls have shown, the mood of the general public has shifted decidedly toward a more nationalistic stance during the 1970s. The proportion of the public agreeing that U.S. investment in Canada is a good thing decreased from 70 percent in 1954 to approximately 40 percent in 1976. Moreover, by 1975 some 70 percent of the public thought that there was too much American capital in Canada, although this percentage had decreased to 65 percent in 1979.[28] The shifts in the NDP policy positions, therefore, appear to parallel those of the general public although it may be that the Waffle episode sensitized the NDP to the Americanization issue.

The most pronounced shift in the orientations of the NDP which have been examined here concerns trade unions. In the years since the dissolution of the Waffle, a consensus appears to have grown around the question of the proper place of trade unions within the NDP. Indeed, the proportion of the party agreeing that trade unions have too much power in the NDP dropped from its 1971 level by 19 percent. Moreover the most marked change occurred among the Waffle (although anti-union sentiment also declined by 10 percent among the constituency delegates). In 1971, 52 percent of the Waffle supporters expressed a resentment of union power within the party compared to 10 percent in 1979 (see Table 3). It cannot be determined from these data whether the anti-union component of the Waffle left the party or whether there was an attitude change among those who remained. It is clear, however, that the party's moderation on the question of union power is the most marked transition among all of the orientations and policies examined here. The goal of creating a social democrat-labour alliance appears to have been reaffirmed within the NDP in the late 1970s.

Discussion

The rise of the Waffle induced a deep and troublesome cleavage within the NDP and, as with all party factionalism, it was not resolved without costs. The NDP did lose some of its activists and an air of disenchantment, if not bitterness, clung to the party for some time. The survey results presented here, however, show that the wounds are healing. The disappearance of the Waffle corresponded to a reaffirmation of the NDP as a moderate, labour-oriented, social democratic party. Our findings suggest that the NDP leadership has been successful in rebuilding a consensus among its activists around its particular vision of Canada's social democratic option.

Despite the NDP's apparent commitment to a course of moderation, a commitment which the Waffle bitterly denounced, it has not reaped significant electoral victories. Neither has the NDP established a solid electoral constituency among unionized workers, even though the same labour leadership that the Waffle openly challenged made decided efforts in 1979 and 1980 to draw its membership into a voting coalition behind the NDP. In other words, while the Waffle's positions may have "scared the hell" out of the electorate, as one unionist at the time suggested they would, the strategy of moderation has not attracted many voters either.[29] If anything, the NDP's continuing course of moderation and its ongoing efforts to broaden its appeal to encompass all disgruntled voters may have only further diminished its distinctiveness in the federal party system.

If the NDP has contributed anything to the economic debate of the past decade, it would appear to be the option of economic independence and Canadian control of the resource sector. Obviously, too, the Waffle played an important role in raising this option. Considering the Liberal party's recent flirtations with economic nationalism, however, it appears that the NDP, once again, may have lost what little unique space it had carved out for itself in the federal party system.

ENDNOTES

1. For a discussion of the Waffle see: Gary Teeple, "Liberals in a hurry: socialism and the CCF-NDP" in G. Teeple, ed., *Capitalism and the National Question in Canada* (Toronto: University of Toronto Press, 1972); Desmond Morton, *Social Democracy in Canada*, 2nd ed. (Toronto: Samuel Stevens, Hakkert and Company, 1977), Chapter 5; Ivan Avakumovic, *Socialism in Canada* (Toronto: McClelland and Stewart, 1978); Dan Heap, "The Waffle — the recipe?" *Canadian Dimension* (December 1981); Jim Harding, "or the griddle," *Canadian Dimension* (December 1981); Jo Surich, "Purists and Pragmatists: Canadian Democratic Socialism at the Crossroads," in H. Penniman, ed., *Canada at the Polls: The General Election of 1974* (Washington, D.C.: American Enterprise Institute for Public Policy, 1975); and especially Robert Hackett, "Pie in the Sky: a History of the Ontario Waffle," *Canadian Dimension* (November 1980); Robert Hackett, "The Waffle Conflict in the NDP," in H. G. Thorburn, ed. *Party Politics in Canada*, 4th ed. (Scarborough: Prentice-Hall, 1979).
2. See for example, Hackett, "Pie in the Sky," Much of this paper draws on Hackett's thorough analysis of the Waffle episode. For the historical explanation see Heap, "The Waffle — the recipe?"
3. Harding, "or the griddle," p. 45.
4. M. Janine Brodie and Jane Jenson, *Crisis, Challenge and Change: Party and Class in Canada* (Toronto: Methuen, 1980), Chapter 8; Morton, *Social Democracy in Canada*, Chapter 5; Avakumovic, *Socialism in Canada*, pp. 199-203, 236-240.
5. For material on the transformation from the CCF to the NDP see Gad Horowitz, *Canadian Labour in Politics* (Toronto: University of Toronto Press, 1968); Walter Young, *The Anatomy of a Party* (Toronto: University of Toronto Press, 1969); L. Zakuta, *A Protest Movement Becalmed* (Toronto: University of Toronto Press, 1964).

6. See Brodie and Jenson, *Crisis, Challenge and Change*, ch. 8.

7. Horowitz, *Canadian Labour in Politics*, p. 203.

8. *Ibid*, p. 202.

9. David Lewis, *The Good Fight* (Toronto: Macmillan of Canada, 1981) p. 294.

10. For discussion of these frictions see: Horowitz, *Canadian Labour in Politics*, pp. 136-146; Lewis, *The Good Fight*, pp. 488-491.

11. Horowitz, *Canadian Labour in Politics*, p. 203.

12. *Ibid*.

13. Lewis, *The Good Fight*, p. 489.

14. Hackett, "The Waffle Conflict in the NDP."

15. Heap, "The Waffle — the recipe?"

16. Brodie and Jenson, *Crisis, Challenge and Change*, pp. 285-288.

17. Morton, *Social Democracy in Canada*, p. 132.

18. Hackett, "Pie in the Sky," p. 41.

19. Dennis McDermott, then leader of the UAW, as quoted in Hackett, "Pie in the Sky," pp. 33-34.

20. I express my appreciation to Professors George Perlin and Stephen Clarkson for allowing me access to these data.

21. The Waffle group is defined as all those indicating that they supported Waffle policies. The other groups are defined by how they became delegates to the convention, i.e. delegate of an affiliated local union, delegate of a central labour body, federal or provincial, and delegate of a constituency association. In the latter case, only those not supporting Waffle policies are categorized as constituency delegates.

22. Morton, *Social Democracy in Canada*, p. 97.

23. See Hackett, "Pie in the Sky."

24. Hackett, "Pie in the Sky," p. 25.

25. Morton, *Social Democracy in Canada*, p. 132.

26. Hackett, "Pie in the Sky," p. 63.

27. Not shown in tabular form.

28. Malcolm Brown, "Public Opinion and Economic Nationalism in Canada," Honours B.A. Thesis, Dept. of Political Studies, Queen's University, Kingston, May 1982.

29. Hackett, "Pie in the Sky," p. 25.

SECTION FIVE

Regional Politics

Canadian regionalism is largely a reaction against the domination of Canadian economic and political life by the English-speaking elite of Central Canada centered in Toronto and, to a rapidly declining extent, Montreal. To assuage regional discontent, the federal government has granted the outlying areas increased subsidies for their provincial governments, improvements in transportation and communication and support for specific industries. Reactions to this situation of domination vary. The Atlantic provinces have maintained their cautious conservatism by continuing to support the old parties, hoping for "better terms" in exchange. They have preferred to be on the winning side in national elections and to exploit their advantages within the old party structures.

In Quebec there has been a rapid radicalization since 1960, culminating in the election in 1976 of a Parti Québécois government committed to winning independence for Quebec with economic association with the rest of Canada. At the same time, the Liberals have continued to sweep federal elections in the province. The impact of the current economic crisis on this radicalization has tended to blunt its impact and to turn the province in the direction of accommodation with the federal power.

In the west, wealth from natural resources created an optimism that led to "province-building" and a taste for the wielding of power by provincial governments. The recent economic crisis has blunted this thrust as well. This section includes essays on all five regions of Canada and examines how they have coped with recent and rapid changes in fortune.

21 The Parti Québécois in Power: Institutionalization, Crisis Management and Decline

RAYMOND HUDON

When I wrote for the fourth edition of *Party Politics in Canada*[1], the Parti Québécois (PQ) had just been elected in Quebec. Although the 1976 Quebec election did not reveal any unsuspected feelings among the voters, it meant a great reversal for the Liberals who had won 102 seats out of 110 in 1973. A few days following November 15, 1976, the Liberal leader, Robert Bourassa, resigned. The PQ's promise of a better government appealed to many Québécois. The party insisted on differentiating itself from the "old parties," the Union Nationale (UN) and the Liberals. Clearly, Quebec voters did not elect the PQ to support its independence option. However, the victory of the PQ was related to the steady shift which has been occurring in Quebec nationalism since the beginning of the sixties.

Seven years later, after a second PQ electoral victory in 1981, a look at Quebec politics reveals some changes. First, according to opinion surveys, the Liberals would have received the support of more than two-thirds of Quebec voters if a provincial election had been called in September 1982.[2] Second, referring to the Liberal leadership campaign to choose Claude Ryans' successor, more than two Québécois out of three seemed to prefer Robert Bourassa as a "new" leader of the Liberals over the two other candidates, Daniel Johnson and Pierre Paradis.[3] Another survey showed that Johnson, whose father had been a UN Premier between 1966 and 1968, had probably more popular support than Bourassa.[4] However, the support for the Liberals was again shown to be substantial: over 60 percent.[5]

This picture of the relative strength of Quebec political parties in the autumn of 1983 is practically the reverse of the situation in 1976. Moreover, the survey data showed that Bourassa was preferred as a leader by a larger number of Quebec people than Lévesque.[6] In fact, at their leadership convention held on October 15, 1983, the Liberals gave Bourassa 75 percent on the first ballot.

The opponents of the PQ were relieved to contemplate its coming defeat. Nevertheless the next election will not be a mere formality because, as Maurice Pinard noted in interpreting the public opinion surveys,[7] the opposition trend against the Lévesque government also applied against the Trudeau government. This point is especially important in the context of Quebec politics.

This article suggests that the decline of both the PQ and the federal Liberals relates to their management of the economic and social crisis of the last few years. The disillusionment of Quebec voters is possibly more pronounced since they had good reason, only a short time ago, to believe that a PQ government would be a different kind of government. It can be argued that the PQ has changed as it experienced, like any government party, a process of institutionalization, the effects of which were made more visible because it was elected only seven years after its founding. An analysis of these two questions — crisis management and political institutionalization — should permit us to draw some conclusions about the future evolution of Quebec politics, although we must be cautious in speculating about the future.

Crisis Management

Statements about the economic crisis have proliferated over the last few years. Many of these statements refer to the effects of "the worst economic crisis" since the Great Depression. The more analytical of them point out the differences between this crisis and that of the thirties: unemployment rose to comparable levels, but inflation, although reduced, did not turn to deflation.[8]

It is crucial to consider this point because it helps interpret the fierce attacks currently being conducted against labour organizations in Quebec. In fact, while the crisis of the thirties partly resulted in new patterns of relationships and in some accommodation with labour organizations, one can observe, fifty years later, as Vincent Dagenais says, "a tremendous redeployment of capital domination over labour."[9] This crisis however is not limited to industrial relations, although the tension both between labour and capital and between the state and its employees is most obvious.

To speak of the domination of capital over labour does not mean that capital has been unaffected by the crisis. Indeed, a capitalist crisis could be typically presented as a period during which capital is in the process of restructuring itself. Concentration, bankruptcies, the decline of specific sectors and the relocation of production illustrate the extent to which this process has gone over the last fifteen or so years.

Comparable phenomena have occurred in most national economies of the western industrialized world. On the other hand, considering the specific features of the Canadian structure of production, it is understandable why Canadians have scarcely been able to cope with some aspects of the crisis. Nevertheless, some problems created by the crisis were not resolved because they were not really policy priorities to be dealt with. For instance, despite almost unprecedented levels of unemployment, inflation was the first preoccupation of policy-makers because of the nature of the crisis.

As capitalism is a worldwide system, national economies cannot be analyzed as closed systems. And it is the transformations that have occurred in that worldwide system that explain the decline or at least the difficulties that have recently marked national economies. The penetration of the markets of the West by producers of the East, and vice-versa, the increasing competition between western countries themselves, particularly following the creation of the European Economic Community (EEC) and the remarkable strengthening of the Japanese economy, and the development of some Third World economies, the so-called new industrialized countries (NICs), are factors that have challenged the national economies of the industrialized world to which Canada belongs. The United States was at the centre of the restructuring process, not to say its principal "victim," and the well-known dependency of the Canadian economy on the American might have been expected to deepen the effects of these changes on Canada. The continental character of the Canadian economy could no longer guarantee economic growth at previous rates, since American leaders had become greatly concerned with their own decline within the world economy, and with its political effects. Canada had to become more competitive by relying more on its own means.

Post-war economic policies for growth and prosperity had therefore to be revised. Here is not an appropriate place to define all the reorientations that have marked Canadian economic policies over the last decade. Many have argued that one important dimension, the Third Option, was a failure. The problem with evaluations of this sort is that this policy is then narrowly seen as a policy designed to diversify Canada's international trade.[10] Thus, one may forget that possibly the most important element of Canadian economic policy of the recent period was, beyond diversification, the awareness of the need for restructuring the Canadian economy and industry in order to make them more competitive on world markets.

Practically, that called for a further concentration of Canadian industry and capital and, more politically sensitive, industrial adjustments. As long as this policy only means modernization and technological changes to industrial sectors that are least capable of facing international competition (e.g. textiles, clothing, etc.), it can be afforded politically and justified easily. But since it also means decreased protection for these same sectors in order to allow larger support for those which are more productive and where there are conspicuous technological advancements, and where more competitive results can be expected, one must be especially careful. This has been especially true in the Canadian context, since different industries and types of industry are unevenly distributed over the national territory. It is in this broad context that the recent evolution of Quebec politics can be best understood.[11]

First, the implementation of a policy of restructuring the Canadian economy required, it was believed, increased federal powers over the economy. The federal and provincial stands were made quite clear in the summer of 1980 during the constitutional negotiations that took place following the Quebec referendum. No province but Ontario wold agree to give Ottawa increased or preponderant power over the economy, since they believed that a federal policy of industrial development in the context of a changing world economy would benefit Canadian regions and provinces unevenly. Considering that a good part of Quebec manufacturing consists of threatened sectors, it is understandable that the Quebec provincial government strongly opposed federal plans. This opposition was quite visible before the referendum of May 20, 1980, and was explicitly articulated in the government paper on economic policy published in 1979, *Bâtir le Québec*.[12]

Second, plans for the reorganizations of the Canadian economy required that labour also be reorganized in order that these plans be implemented. The PQ government was slow to condemn the federal government action. To some extent, its reaction, although it had declared its sympathies for the workers immediately on its election in November 1976, resembled that of the Trudeau government. As collaboration and "tripartism" were not totally successful, the federal Liberal government decided in 1975 to implement wage and price controls. Three years of controls did not make collaboration an attractive option for the labour organizations. After failing again to make voluntary compromises acceptable to labour, Ottawa decided on its "six and five" program.

In very few words, the federal government action did work.[13] Thus, as compared to the situation in other industrialized countries, the wages of Canadian workers in the manufacturing sector declined significantly between 1970 and 1980. But as the Economic Council of Canada (ECC) commented: this "improvement" does not resolve the competitive disadvantages of Canada in relation to the NICs,[14] so it is likely that considerable pressures on the labour movement still lie ahead. It is particularly relevant to emphasize that the actions of the PQ government did not differ from those of the Liberal government in Ottawa.

To be sure, during its first mandate, the Lévesque government seemed more committed to the interests of workers than the former Bourassa government had been. Did this Liberal government not come to believe, before the 1976 election, that one of its priorities was to defend business against the unions?[15] As a result, the PQ found itself in a position to win over the support of many union activists who, from inside the party, had made it shift closer to the unions' positions. Although many activists already strongly believed that a PQ government was not an ideal solution for the labour movement, they could not ignore some of this government's decisions: the increase in the minimum wage; the abolition of the Quebec Anti-Inflation Board; the cancellation of more than 7,000 strikers' fines imposed following the common front of 1975-1976; the important revision of personal income taxes presented in Finance Minister Parizeau's second budget; the adoption of an anti-scab law; the adoption of a law imposing minimum conditions of work that every employer would have to recognize for all workers, unionized or not; the enactment of a new consumers' protection code; etc.

Other decisions of the PQ government, however, led the leaders of organized labour to believe that the government had chosen rather to placate investors. In the next section, additional reasons will be presented why the government's commitment to "establish an economic system which would eliminate every form of exploitation of workers, and which would respond to the real needs of all Québécois, rather than to the demands of a privileged minority,"[16] was not really implemented. At this point, it is nevertheless appropriate to suggest that the most immediate reasons had been the depth of the economic crisis. In the name of the fiscal crisis of the Quebec state, the PQ government intervened strongly against public service employees, and it then became apparent that the meaning of "privilege" had shifted from reference to capitalists to supposedly better-paid workers.

Strong attacks against public service employees were undertaken in a series of laws adopted in 1982 and 1983 by the PQ government. First, in June 1982, Bill 68[17] was passed to reduce the pension fund benefits of those employed in the public sector. Second, in the same month, Bill 70[18] unilaterally determined the salaries to be paid to these same people if an agreement was not reached between their union and the government (it was to be understood that such an agreement would have to be true to the "guidelines" originally defined by the government). Understandably, the unions were reluctant to negotiate, although Bill 70 did not settle conditions of work apart from salaries. When it appeared that the December 1982 deadline for agreement, established by the political authorities, would not be met, the government passed Bill 105.[19] Once again, it unilaterally defined conditions of work for public sector employees until the end of 1985. Moreover, it imposed 20 percent cutbacks on public sector employees' salaries for a period of three months at the beginning of 1983, so that increases agreed to for the second half of 1982 were mostly taken back. Finally, to end the protest strike of teachers in public schools and CEGEPs, the government voted Bill 111[20] sixteen years to the day after the passing of Bill 25[21] by a UN government. Bill 111 was unprecedented in imposing fines and determining the status of unions in the case of the continuation of strikes. Many, inaccurately though appropriately, referred back to the Duplessis era.

It is true that these actions of the PQ government, like those of Duplessis, pleased the financial markets. However, the fiscal situation of the two Quebec governments was substantially different. Furthermore, their attacks against labour did not have exactly the same meaning. It is certainly correct to assume that, for both the Duplessis and Lévesque governments, the intention was to reduce labour costs in order to favour new investments. In addition, the PQ government' more or less acknowledged objective was to force a restructuring of wages linked to the restructuring of production referred to above. Indeed, in order to make it easier to reorganize production, both by specialization and rationalization, it had been decided to facilitate labour mobility, both geographical and sectoral. One of the conditions considered necessary was increasing the disparity between lower and higher wage levels. And the ECC made it quite clear that one of the main limitations in that direction was union action.[22] It was assumed that workers would accept relocations more easily provided they got sufficient gains following retraining.[23] But the advantages gained by workers in the public services worked against efforts to reorganize wage structures and relocate the labour force efficiently in a changing production structure.[24] This is particularly important in the context of a program aimed to reorganize Canadian production, a program that the ECC[25] and now governments[26] consider unavoidable.

It is only by understanding this background that it is possible to explain the attacks by the PQ government (and others)[27] on the public service employees who represent the core support that made possible the election of the PQ in 1976 and 1981. To complete the picture we must consider at least one other central dimension in the dynamics of the party's politics, especially when it forms the government.

The Process of Institutionalization

Despite some awareness of what labour might expect from a PQ government, many union activists were disappointed with the actions taken by the government in managing the economic crisis. Some of them have been confused by what actually happened. For instance, most union leaders assumed that the government's initially declared position relating to the 1982-1983 public sector contract negotiations was simply tactical; they believed that the position put forward at the "national conference" of March 1982 (translated in Bill 68 and Bill 70) aimed simply to provide the government with a positive bargaining advantage in the coming negotiations.[28]

These assumptions by some members of the labour movement were rooted, it might be suggested, in their dual analysis of the Quebec state of the previous fifteen or twenty years. On the one hand, the state was presented as being at the service of capital and the dominant interests; this "real" state had to be converted into an apparatus to serve the masses of the Quebec people. It was assumed, before 1976, that this "imaginary" state could possibly *begin* to emerge with a PQ government, despite the limits of its program for political and social change. This ambivalent vision of the Quebec state under a PQ government led union leaders to misinterpret the real determination of the government to reduce the gap between workers of the private and of the public sector and, above all, to bring to an end the pressure and "leadership" exerted by unionized public sector employees regarding salary increases. The PQ government found it easier to strengthen its position by pointing to the financial situation of the government, something a large portion of the population saw as disastrous.

It is not easy to explain the disenchantment of unionists since, from the beginning of the PQ's first mandate, they sought to avoid the mistakes made in 1960 after the defeat of another anti-union government, that of Duplessis, and the coming to power of the Lesage reformist government. After the 1975 election, the leadership of the *Confédérations des Syndicates Nationaux* (CSN) interpreted the victory of the PQ as a "union victory," "the victory of the Quebec people," probably because it coincided with the defeat of the anti-union Bourassa government. Nevertheless unionists were reluctant to support the PQ government unconditionally. In fact, the "favourable bias" towards workers declared by Lévesque in his first press conference after the 1976 election paralleled his invitation in 1960, when he was a minister in the Liberal cabinet: "I urgently ask you to remember that the government is, more than ever, sympathetic to labour...."[29]

At the beginning of the sixties, the labour movement collaborated enthusiastically with the new government. The revision of the Labour Code in 1964 appeared as a positive move for organized workers. But the first round of negotiations with the government as an employer after the reform of the code caused disappointment among union members: the government was like any other employer, not wanting to concede a more evenly balanced relationship between workers and employers. The labour leadership, after further analysis and reflection, demanded changes in the system as a whole. Mere changes in the governing elites seemed less and less adequate. The problem was no longer confined to which men (and women) occupy which positions in government, but the discussion was enlarged to consider the role of the state in the capitalist system.

This reorientation, however, did not prevent high hopes from remaining. After all, had the Minister of Labour and Immigration not promised after the 1976 election to enact a new "social contract" by which employers would no longer think *only* of making money? To some extent, workers' spokesmen were trapped or, more accurately, misled in their interpretations of the evolution of the political situation in Quebec — a situation that was itself linked to a process of institutionalization that almost inevitably accompanied the election of the PQ.

Before 1976, Quebec society was experiencing a process of social polarization[30] that produced significant effects on party politics. With the radicalization of the labour movement, corporations and business in general had decided to develop closer links with the state, to organize a better defence against the growing claims of the workers. The Bourassa government's devotion to free enterprise and economic growth was revealing. It was encouraging to investors and businessmen but did not initiate any special relationships. However, once under way the complacent attitude of the government towards business was then pushed to an ultimate point.

After the election of the PQ, the reorientation of the special relationship that used to exist with the Bourassa government was most disquieting for business. For instance, the President of the Montreal Board of Trade (MBT) affirmed that, for the first time in its history, this organization had to fight openly and publicly: "With previous governments more discrete negotiations were the rule. Never before did the President of the Board of Trade have to make public declarations."[31] Business dissatisfaction was profound; so labour organizations took advantage of the election of a "pro-union" government, without developing great expectations. In short, while the style of the newly elected PQ government shocked businessmen, it was clear that the workers had not come to power.

The mere presence of new governing elites is not enough to end the tensions within a society, or to end the domination of specific interests. Profound transformations of a society *may* bring about reorientations of the state. On the other hand, a program of profound social transformations, under the leadership of state authorities, requires significant reappraisal of the nature of the state itself, and calls for actions that go beyond declarations of intent. It seems clear that the business community's distrust of the PQ government was not due to any real radical questioning of Quebec's economic and social structure by the party.

From its foundation in 1969 until 1972, the PQ simply espoused a reorientation of capitalist development which would benefit the Québécois people. With the publications of its manifesto of 1972 and the following national conventions, it undertook a critique of North American capitalism. Although the dominant group in the government adhered to the earlier position, businessmen remained concerned about the presence in the party of activists favouring significant economic, social and political change. This incited some businessmen to make theatrical declarations overemphasizing the "socialist" orientations of the PQ. Such behaviour was felt necessary to press the government, so that it would not pay too much attention to its radical wing. Capital felt uncomfortable about a party which, though not really determined to transform the bourgeois order of capitalist society, did not stick firmly to the bourgeoisie's interests. This ambivalence also led to disillusionment within the labour movement.

Beyond its central objective of making Quebec "independent," the PQ openly sought to restore "social" peace in Quebec. Its major immediate problem was that both capital and labour were suspicious of its intent and actions. Consequently, it was hardly able to realize the role that all states must play, that of guardian of social cohesion. In its attempts to perform this proper function of the state (in Pierre Birnbaum's sense)[32] by making peace with business and employers, the PQ government, perhaps inadvertently, reduced the polarity that had characterized party politics in Quebec. It modified its stand on state intervention in the economy by pointing out its concern with "creating and maintaining conditions favourable for the development and the dynamism of private enterprise," and by affirming its belief "that the market economy should generally be preserved as the system most able to ensure the efficient allocation of resources."[33] Thus, to state that it did not intend "to call into question the principle of direct state intervention"[34] could be interpreted as simple rhetoric.

All this suggested that the PQ had moved closer to the position of the Liberals. Six months after the 1976 election, the Liberals published a manifesto which proclaimed a total commitment to free enterprise. While Claude Ryan was the party leader, there was some disagreement on this point. However, the election of Robert Bourassa as leader in October 1983 shows how experience with power can teach a party not to take dogmatic stands. Bourassa actually adopted a position close to that presently held by the Lévesque government. In any case, it had become less and less easy for the Liberals to stress the PQ's "socialism," as it was for the PQ to denounce the Liberals' clear commitment to capitalism. The only course for the Liberals was to relate the economic problems of Quebec to a lack of business confidence in a PQ government determined in its attachment to an independent Quebec.

These changes in the relative position of the PQ and of the Liberals show how fragile is any strict political conception of the state as an instrument either for domination or for liberation.[35] They serve to illustrate that a government party neither dedicated to ending capitalism nor totally capitalist-oriented may be compelled finally to follow the dictates of capitalism, unless it adopts the objective of radically changing the existing order. In this sense we understand why party pronouncements are mostly statements derived from other statements, as Jean-Pierre Beaud suggests in his account of the Quebec parties' statements on the economic crisis.[36] This process of depolarization at the level of political parties has been possible because of an evident "de-radicalization" of the labour movement, especially in the private sector, since the late 1970s.

This transformation is related to one major factor, the economic crisis. Inevitably, unions have become preoccupied by the unprecedented increase in unemployment. As a consequence, long-term political change appeared less and less appealing as a solution to immediate economic problems. To be sure, "reformism" did not become the official program of the unions; they still state that the improvement of the workers' situation calls for important political changes. Practices, however, have been adjusted. Invitations to *collaboration* sound better than they did some years ago. Some compromises are felt to be urgently needed to prevent a further deterioration of working conditions. The former President of the *Confederation des Syndicate Nationaux* (CSN) made this quite clear in April 1983.[37]

However, public sector employees were less ready to accept such compromises. First, they assumed that the state as an employer did not have to behave like a private entrepreneur. Their leaders argued that, especially in a time of economic crisis, the state had an obligation not to exacerbate the social problems created by that crisis. Of course, such statements were "unpopular," since most people thought that public sector employees were much better off, in terms of job security and working conditions, than their counterparts in the private sector. The actions taken by the PQ government against those employees were generally and strongly denounced by union leaders. But, at the same time, these leaders (except for the President of the *Centrale de l'enseignement du Québec* (CEQ) whose members are almost exclusively employed in public services) were participating in secret meetings with representatives of business and government.[38] One possible interpretation is that the PQ was realizing its objective of instituting dialogue, at least as far as organized private sector workers were concerned.

Thus, just as the Liberals, when they formed the Quebec government from 1970 to 1976, became more nationalistic than they officially had been in 1969-1970, so the PQ has come to resemble the Liberals since becoming a government party. Such a shift can be partly explained by the fact that the PQ has had to manage government affairs in the context of a serious crisis. But, more fundamentally, it has had to take account of its new responsibility of assuring the general cohesion of Quebec society. Consequently, it has had to be more aware of the many political forces active in this society, and the various opinions that these forces express. It is understandable that those who expected the most, felt the most betrayed; "Instability and transformation led the state and the bureaucracy to look for solutions;"[39] so it is not surprising that the Lévesque government has been behaving as if it sought to accomplish a better distribution of wealth in society without fundamentally changing the society.

To be sure, both capital and labour reproached the PQ for having chosen to favour one side against the other. Superficially it seems that the PQ has been more open to labour's demands in its first mandate, while it has become evidently more sensitive to capital's critics since the beginning of its second mandate in 1981. On the whole, we may say that the government has tried to reduce tensions between most of the main social and economic actors in Quebec society, giving consideration to the degree of exasperation felt by them at specific times. In such conditions, power represents a disappointment since, as Sylvia Biarez said, "organization circulates a commitment whose realization is constantly postponed."[40] Since the state represents the ultimate level of organization (and institutionalization) of political life in a society, it has been argued (or hoped) that the independence option in Quebec would die a natural death. Such a conclusion remains fragile since, contrary to what Dominque Clift seems to suggest,[41] a crisis of *péquisme* does not naturally mean that the Quebec national question has been satisfactorily resolved.

Conclusion

As the figures reported at the beginning of this paper clearly show, the PQ in 1983 is not in a very enviable position, electorally. However, to predict the defeat of the PQ in the next election is premature, although this is, for the moment, a foreseeable outcome.

One may conclude that the intense attack by the PQ government on the labour movement inevitably will lead to a rupture of the relationship between workers' organizations and the party. As has been pointed out above, this is not so clearly the case as far as private sector workers are concerned. Moreover, it can also be suggested that the PQ will not necessary lose heavily, since the other political parties seem to be benefitting temporarily more than fundamentally from the disappointment created by the PQ's actions. The question remains: are workers' organizations going to support the Liberals against the PQ, since, between 1970 and 1976, they had so strongly opposed the government led by Robert Bourassa, the same man who was (re-)elected the "new" leader of the party in October 1983? Furthermore, alternative options on the left appear to have little chance of attracting significant support in the near future, precisely because their leadership is seen as either belonging to the "old" political elites who have influenced Quebec politics since the "Quiet Revolution" or emerging from social organizations which are no longer (or are not yet) attracting substantial support. In these conditions, the *péquiste* hegemony over the labour movement is not automatically condemned, although it could possibly be recast.

The Liberals' chances in the next election depend upon whether the magic of job creation will work (as it did in 1970). They are well aware of the limited area available for manoeuvre and are certainly the last ones to want a campaign revolving around the national question. This is not to say that independence is presently very "popular" on the Quebec political market. On the other hand, it is still premature, as Pierre Fournier writes, "to bury the national question in Quebec irrespective of the electoral fortunes of the Parti Québécois," since "the problems and questions which prompted the development of a pro-independence movement in Quebec remain unresolved." Also the action of the federal government following the referendum of May 1980 "may have created the conditions for an even more serious challenge to the federal system."[42]

It is difficult to imagine that Quebec nationalism has been discarded once and for all. Further realignments of political parties, and of their support, is not excluded in the future development of Quebec politics. This could possibly take the form of a return to the PQ of support which has eroded in the recent past. We should avoid any deterministic view of the future in politics; after all, the re-election of the PQ in 1981 followed a period when its defeat seemed very likely.

In the final analysis, the state and the parties are political entities that contribute to the process of institutionalization of politics — that is, to the reduction of conflict. We must bear in mind that organizations like unions, employers' associations and others are also, despite appearances, institutions that participate in the same process. And their involvement may, at any time, work in favour of *either* the PQ *or* the Liberals.

ENDNOTES

1. Raymond Hudon, "Political Parties and the Polarization of Quebec Politics", in Hugh G. Thorburn (ed.), *Party Politics in Canada,* 4th ed. (Scarborough: Prentice-Hall of Canada, 1979), pp. 228-242.
2. See Pierre O'Neill, *Le Devoir,* October 6, 1983, pp. 1, 8.
3. Pierre O'Neill, *Le Devoir,* October 4, 1983, pp. 1, 14.
4. J.-Jacques Samson and Michel David, *Le Soleil,* October 14, 1983, pp. A1, A2.
5. See *Le Soleil,* October 15, 1983, p. A1.
6. J.-Jacques Samson and Michel David, *Le Soleil,* October 15, 1983, p. A6.
7. Maurice Pinard, *Le Soleil,* October 15, 1983, p. B3.
8. On that point, see Paul M. Sweezy, "La crise économique aux Etats-Unis," in Gilles Dostaler, ed., *La crise économique et sa gestion* (Montreal: Les Editions du Boréal Express, 1982), p. 36.
9. Vincent Dagenais, "Crise économique et stratégie syndicale," in *Ibid.,* p. 159.
10. For a critical appraisal of these views, see Gérard Hervouet, Raymond Hudon and Gordon Mace, "La politique canadienne de Troisième option et la nouvelle division internationale du travail: la politique commerciale et au-delà," a paper presented at the conference *Canada and the New International Division of Labor* held in Ottawa, January 28-30, 1983.
11. The main elements that are summarily presented here have been developed in Raymond Hudon, "Quebec, the Economy and the Constitution," in Keith Banting and Richard Simeon, ed., *And No One Cheered: Federalism, Democracy and the Constitution Act* (Toronto: Methuen Publications, 1983), pp. 133-153.
12. Quebec. Ministère d'Etat au Développement économique, *Bâtir le Québec. Enoncé de politique économique* (Quebec: Editeur officiel du Québec, 1979).
13. For more developments, one can refer to Raymond Hudon, "La construction de solidarités nationales contre le mouvement ouvrier," in Gérald Bernier and Gérard Boismenu, ed., *Crise économique, transformations politiques et changements idéologiques* (Montreal: Association canadienne-française pour l'avancement des sciences, Cahiers de l'ACFAS, no 16, 1983), pp. 399-428.
14. Economic Council of Canada, *Les temps difficiles. Politiques et contraintes* (Ottawa: Supply and Services Canada, 1982), p. 62.
15. See, for instance, the declaration of Guy Saint-Pierre, Industry and Commerce Minister, as quoted in *Le Jour,* April 10, 1975, p. 10.

16. Parti québécois, *Un gouvernement du Parti québécois s'engage...* (Montreal: Les Editions du Parti québécois, 1973), p. 38.

17. *Loi modifiant diverses dispositions législatives concernant les régimes de retraite*, Quebec National Assembly, 32nd Legislature, 3rd session, assented to June 23, 1982.

18. *Loi concernant la rémunération dans le sector public*, Quebec National Assembly, 32nd Legislature, 3rd session, assented to June 23, 1982.

19. *Loi concernant les conditions de travail dans le secteur public*, Quebec National Assembly, 32nd Legislature, 3rd session, assented to December 11, 1982.

20. *Loi assurant la reprise des services dans les collèges et les écoles du secteur public*, Quebec National Assembly, 32nd Legislature, 3rd session, assented to February 17, 1983.

21. *Loi assurant le droit de l'enfant à l'éducation et instituant un nouveau régime de convention collective dans le secteur scolaire*, Quebec Legislative Assembly, 28th Legislature, 1st session, assented to February 17, 1967.

22. Economic Council of Canada, *Pénuries et carences. Travailleurs qualifiés et emplois durant les années 80* (Ottawa: Supply and Services Canada, 1982), p. 77.

23. On that point, see Economic Council of Canada, *Pénuries et carences*, p. 75.

24. This is strongly suggested by a remark of the Economic Council of Canada on the measures taken by the Reagan administration against American air traffic controllers. See *Les temps difficiles*, p. 107.

25. Economic Council of Canada, *Pour un commun avenir. Une étude des relations entre le Canada et les pays en développement* (Hull: Supply and Services Canada, 1978).

26. As far as the Quebec government is concerned, this orientation has been made clear. See Quebec. Ministère d'Etat au Développement économique, *Le virage technologique. Bâtir le Québec — Phase 2. Programme d'action économique 1982-1986* (Quebec: Government of Quebec, 1982).

27. Is it necessary to recall the Bennett government's action in British Columbia after its re-election in May 1983.

28. Some of the elements presented here are also presented in Raymond Hudon, "Polarization and De-Polarization of Quebec Political Parties," in Alain G. Gagnon, ed., *Quebec State and Society in Crisis* (Toronto: Methuen Publications, 1984).

29. The convention of the Quebec Federation of Labour (QFL) in December 1960.

30. This process of social polarization has been described in a more detailed form in Raymond Hudon, "Les groupes et l'Etat," in Gérard Bergeron and Réjean Pelletier, ed., *L'Etat du Québec en devenir* (Montreal: Les Editions du Boréal Express, 1980), pp. 263-284.

31. As quoted in *Le Devoir*, May 19, 1977, p. 23.

32. Pierre Birnbaum, *La logique de l'Etat* (Paris: Librairie Arthème Fayard, 1982).

33. Quebec. Ministère d'Etat au Développement économique, *Le virage technologique*, p. 21.

34. *Ibid.*, p. 22.

35. This statement is formulated precisely by Pierre Birnbaum, *La logique de l'Etat*, p. 7.

36. Jean-Pierre Beaud, "Discours des partis sur la crise et crise des discours partisans au Québec," in Gérald Bernier and Gérard Boismenu, ed., *Crise économique, transformations politiques et changements idéologiques*, p. 430.

37. See Pierre Pelchat, *Le Soleil*, April 16, 1983, p. 3.

38. See *Le Devoir*, April 6, 1983, p. 3.

39. Sylvie Biarez, *Institutions et groupes sociaux. Hypothèses et problématique* (Paris: Centre d'étude et de recherche sur l'administration et l'aménagement du territorie, 1976), p. 44.

40. *Ibid.*, p. 26.

41. Dominique Clift, *Quebec Nationalism in Crisis* (Montreal: McGill-Queen's University Press, 1982).

42. Pierre Fournier, "The Future of Quebec Nationalism," in Keith Banting and Richard Simeon, ed., *And No One Cheered*, pp. 171-172.

22 The Parti Québécois from René Lévesque to René Lévesque*

JEAN-PIERRE BEAUD

The Parti Québécois (PQ)[1] was founded in October 1968 as a result of the merger of the *Mouvement Souveraineté-Association* and the *Ralliement national*. It became the second largest provincial party in Quebec as early as 1970, based on the number of votes cast in the general election. Then in 1973, it became the official opposition. In the November 1976 general election, just over eight years after it was founded, it came to power. Therefore its political and social perspectives were bound to create interest, uncertainty and hope both within Quebec and elsewhere in Canada.

Many intellectuals cannot discuss the political, economic, social and cultural scene in Quebec without taking into account the "national question" and, by extension, the organization which tries to deal with this question in a concrete fashion. They defined the PQ, but for various reasons (the defeat of the Yes forces in the May 1980 referendum, the reality of the present crisis, etc.), their attention has since been focussed since the early 1980s on other subjects, e.g. the recent policies of the PQ government. However, the PQ, *as an organization theoretically separate from the government formed by it,* hardly participated in the debate over the consequences of those policies. This situation revealed how formal, even illusory, the autonomy of the PQ organization was in relation to the government: in this regard, the PQ has perhaps become a party "like the others."

The subject of the national question and its relationship to the PQ has been replaced in the media and political speeches by the constitutional debate and socio-economic issues. Nevertheless, it is impossible to analyze the PQ without also analyzing what has been written and said about it, since this has, up to a point, contributed to making the PQ what it is today. It is important to realize how critical writing, particularly from the left, has made the PQ appear to be a centrist, moderate organization, both in terms of its social and political perspectives and its strategies.

---

*Alix d'Anglejan-Chatillon and Jeanne Dancette assisted in the translation of this essay.

The Party has been in power for seven of the fifteen years that it has been in existence. By the time of the next general election in 1985 or 1986, the PQ will have been in power longer than in opposition, and it will have been led by a man who sat in a Liberal cabinet twenty-five years earlier. Should we therefore conclude that the PQ has become a governmental party led by a career politician? This is in direct contradiction to the perception of the party as a young organization with a young membership, led by a new generation of politicized men and women. What is the true image of the PQ?

In his history of Quebec political parties,[2] Robert Boily defines the PQ as a party of mixed origins — parliamentary and extraparliamentary. The PQ is the product of both political structures which are well-entrenched in the parliamentary scene, (mainly the Liberal party), and the expression of extra-parliamentary groups and movements.

It is undoubtedly of parliamentary origin. In part, it is the result of the October 1967 defection of a group of Liberals following René Lévesque and his Independence-Association option.[3] The Liberal defeat in the June 1966 general election was an ideological liberation for René Lévesque. As early as September 1967, he began to discuss his sovereignty theory in public — the result of many years' reflection about "the basic conditions of the economic, social and cultural progress, as well as the political future, of the Québécois people."[4] He first presented his arguments to the Liberals in his riding, then in a series of articles in *Le Devoir*,[5] and, shortly before the October 1967 Liberal convention, he spoke to other Liberals. Finding no following in the Liberal party, which did not want to hear about his option, Lévesque left the party and founded the *Mouvement Souveraineté-Association*. This provisional structure, intended to regroup all those who agreed with the former minister, succeeded in expanding from the November 1967 group of approximately 400 members of the MSA to encompass several thousand Québécois who joined the PQ the following year.

In the early days of the PQ, the former Liberals made up a minority of the members in the organization, and it seemed that their role would continue to decrease with time (especially when the former members of the *Rassemblement pour l'Indépendance Nationale* (RIN) joined the PQ in 1969-70); nevertheless they made a lasting impression on the organization. To a large extent the message conveyed by the PQ in 1983 is the same as that proposed sixteen years ago by the most prestigious of the ex-Liberals, René Lévesque. The other parties in Quebec also contributed to the new independentist Party. Former members of the *Union nationale,* former *Créditistes,* along with ex-Liberals, while a minority, lent the new organization a credibility which certainly contributed to its victory in November 1976.

The PQ is also of extra-parliamentary origin. The Mouvement Souveraineté-Association joined with the Ralliement National, itself a product of the merger of a right-wing splinter group of the RIN and the Ralliement des Créditistes — or Social Crediters. The *RIN,* led by Pierre

Bourgault, had been the most powerful voice in the independentist mouvement. Founded in 1960, it became a party in 1963, and received 5.6 percent of the votes in the June 1966 general election as compared to 3.2 percent for the *Ralliement National*. In 1968 many of its members left to join the MSA, so the organization decided to disband in October 26, 1968, thereby leaving the field open for the newly-founded PQ. Thus the PQ became the only political voice of the independentist movement in Quebec, and in theory brought together all of the forces subscribing to the sovereignty option. However the RIN did not accept the MSA's terms for a merger, and we do not know if all Pierre Bourgault's followers joined the PQ. A small minority, not satisfied with the new party's social and political perspectives, participated in other independentist groups, especially after 1976.

Thus, as early as November 1968, the PQ was the only substantial independentist political organization in Quebec, and it had an almost complete monopoly at least until 1976. Of course, other groups (unions, community groups, nationalists, etc.), sometimes incorporated independentist principles into their social perspectives.

René Lévesque, the only president of the party since its inception, sat as an independentist member of the National Assembly after leaving the Liberals, but the PQ was not a parliamentary party in its early days. At least until 1970, the Executive[6] and the ruling circle were mainly non-parliamentary. Then the PQ members of the National Assembly (seven from 1970 to 1973 and six from 1973 to 1976) began to play an increasingly important role, although they were prohibited from holding certain positions in the party Executive. After the PQ came to power in 1976, their role was to grow. The Executive became extremely dependent on the parliamentary wing, which in 1976 became the government. The changes in the elected members of the Executive since November 1976 reflect this shift in power towards the members of the government. The election of a woman as Vice-President of the party at the Seventh National Convention (June 1979) seems less significant than if it had occurred while the party was still in opposition. Furthermore, while a greater number of women have become members of the Executive, that body has itself been losing influence.[7]

Since November 1976, the PQ has changed from an opposition to a government party. Therefore a new power structure, favouring the members of the National Assembly over the grass root members of the party, has arisen. These changes, which were becoming apparent before the party came to power, caused the internal tensions that generally occur when a mass organization comes into power. This can be seen in the results of the Eighth National Convention in December 1981 (one and half years after the defeat of the Yes option[8] and a few months after the reelection of the PQ[9]). The delegates voted for a radical change to the party platform: the concept of "association" was almost completely eliminated from the sovereignty-association option. A resolution was also adopted to set in motion the process of attaining independence as soon as the party gains a majority of the seats. As René Lévesque was opposed to these resolutions he chose to go directly to the party members through an internal quasi-plebiscite. Almost all of the votes were in favour of reexamining the resolutions passed in December dealing with the independence process. Shortly thereafter, the convention resumed its work. The delegates adopted a new resolution providing for the independence process to be set in motion only when the Party received a majority of the *votes* (as opposed to seats) in future elections, which would deal with sovereignty. Economic association was to be proposed to Canada without necessarily being a condition for sovereignty.[10]

Certainly, this was not the first time that René Lévesque and his team (a good part of the Executive and of the members of the legislative assembly) differed "radically" from the majority of delegates. The history of the party could be read, as several observers have shown, as one of struggles and tensions between ideological groups, between "technocrats" and "participationists,"[11] between those favouring electoral victory and those devoted to the cause, between "nationalists" and "social democrats," between right and left, between different tendencies (of class, of class factions, of professional groups,...).[12] Throughout its short but volatile history the party has endured confrontations over such issues as language, party organization, and the question of abortion.

However René Lévesque, his team and the groups he represents never before went so far in facing up to the problem of intra party divisions. Up until 1981 the threats of the leader to to resign had been enough to turn the delegates back "onto the right road." Since the PQ formed the government it was enough for René Lévesque to remind the party that the government was not bound by the decisions of the convention in order to remove all practical significance from resolutions passed over his objection. In 1981-82, he challenged the legitimacy of certain decisions taken by the convention. In the name of its own conception of democracy, René Lévesque appealed against the decisions taken by the "democratic" machinery which the party had created for itself by sending the decisions back for the consideration of the rank and file.[13] The president of the party invoked direct plebiscitary democracy over indirect representative democracy.

What lessons are to be drawn from this struggle and its result? First of all it is clear that the "victory" of René Lévesque and his team, rendered more important after it was recognized as legitimate by the losers themselves (since they had agreed in the second part of the convention to reconsider their previous positions), had the effect, for a time, of shutting up the internal opposition to the policy pursued by the party leadership and/or the government. This was one important stage in the process of post-referendum "normalization." Some months later, when the government had bills 68, 70, 105 and 111 passed, and when it encountered trade union opposition, particularly from those representing the public service employees, the party, which still counted a large number of trade unionists, union activists, and public service workers in its ranks,[14] remained almost silent, not reacting at all.

This event also unveiled the tensions which parties of militants almost inevitably experience, especially when, once elected, they tend to become catchall parties. Committed, at least theoretically, to the defence and propagation of a cause, these "ideological" parties have a more difficult time than the others when in power, as the possibility of disillusionment is likely to be as great as the hopes which the organization's founding declaration instilled. Paradoxically, these organizations, because they are usually well organized and well led, are able despite everything to adapt their declarations to circumstances; and are perhaps the ones which cope best with the difficulties of being in power.

For the Parti Québécois, this was precisely its problem. To begin with, if one believes the result of the referendum and almost all of the polls dealing with the political objective of the party, we have to notice that the party has never succeeded in instilling the core of its message into the majority of the Quebec electorate. Worse, the economic crisis which Quebec is going through at present, far from making the voters more favourable to the PQ's message, seems to have weakened its appeal. The party points out, however, that the crisis is indicative of the dramatic effects for Quebec of its situation of political dependency.[15]

Moreover, the party is experiencing many difficulties in mobilizing its traditional electorate. The last by-elections have revealed the party's weakness; the latest fund-raising campaign scarcely aroused enthusiasm; party membership has been in decline; "generational" problems have appeared. For a long time the Parti Québécois had been considered the party of the young; now young people are joining it less than before, and those who do often find themselves feeling ill at ease.

Under these conditions, it is not surprising that some people have proposed to "revive the militant spirit" by proclaiming a new objective (the creation of the Parti Nationaliste to carry the "souverainiste" message onto the federal scene), or by commencing a reconsideration of the party program, which might, as Sylvain Simard (the vice president of the party) said, go as far as questioning that program.[16]

The PQ has been, for North America, a most original party creation. As Daniel-Louis Seiler commented, "it is...the only mass party existing in North America and, on the other hand, it is the only North American party, along with the little NDP, to declare itself social democratic on the German and Swedish model."[17] Is the Parti Québécois a mass party? It would appear to be one, according to the usual definitions. Consider first of all the complex organizational structure which it has erected, and which provides for considerable member participation. These organizational structures (on three levels: national (i.e., province-wide regional and local), were built up only with difficulty, and there was a "considerable gap between the letter of the constitution of the PQ and its practical application."[18] At election time in particular, the more traditional type of organization reappears within the party, which tends to draw the party closer to the North American model. On the other hand we note the mass character of the party, the method of popular financing which it has created, and once it was in power, which it imposed on all the other Quebec parties.[19]

Is the Parti Québécois a social democratic party? It seems more difficult to make this label stick. The party organization, its leaders, the members of the government itself and no doubt most of the militants define themselves as social democratic. Moreover, numerous points in the party program reproduce typical social democratic positions. However, the program is far from being social democratic in its general inspiration. Actually, as several analysts have demonstrated, one must look at the program of the PQ as the result of struggles between the different tendencies within the organization, which are not all social democratic in orientation. We should be even more cautious when we analyse not only the statements but also the policies of the party, not to say the government. Observers' judgements in this regard are generally full of subtle distinctions. Alongside legislation inspired by social democractic ideals, they perceive some which could not be so considered. For this question and the related one of the class nature of the party, both of which require lengthy discussion, we should look to the studies which several observers, mostly on the left of the party, have prepared since 1968 and, most particularly, since 1976.[20] On other points the PQ is (or perhaps was) an original party. Consider the place occupied by youth, the type of political personnel it has recruited and produced...[21]

This picture of novelty, of originality, of youth which has attached to the PQ, but which really no longer corresponds to reality, is one of the tools the party relies upon most in its present political struggles. But for the new voters who have not known any other government party than the Parti Québécois, is it not inevitably "the old party?"

ENDNOTES

1. In current expression, the designation "PQ" has just about replaced the original designation "Parti québécois". From it is derived the adjective "péquiste" (one often speaks of the Péquiste government), and the noun "péquiste" (for a supporter of the Parti Québécois). These abbreviations had at first a somewhat pejorative connotation.
2. "Les partis politiques québécois-perspectives historiques", in V. Lemieux, *Personnel et partis politiques au Québec* (Montreal, Boréal Express), 1982, pp. 43-44.
3. René Lévesque uses the terms "independence" and "sovereignty" interchangably. For him the two mean the same thing.

4. "L'option de René Lévesque: indépendence ou (sic) association" *Le Devoir*, mardi 19 septembre 1967, p. 5.

5. See *Le Devoir*, 19, 20 and 21 September 1967.

6. According to the official constitution of the Parti Québécois, "the National Executive Council directs the party and administers its business in general conformity with the general lines of action, the program, the directives and decisions adopted by the convention and the national council." Theoretically then the National Executive Council (or Executive) is only a hierarchical agency subordinate to the National Convention ("the supreme organ of the party"), and at the National Council. ("...the highest authority of the party between the conventions"). All of the operating rules and especially the practice show that such a hierarchy is largely a formality. In fact the Executive was undoubtedly, at least until 1976, the most important part.

7. For an analysis of the different national executives of the Parti Québécois, see my doctoral dissertation, *Structures et élites: analyse diachronique du Parti québécois,* Université Laval, October 1979, Chapter II.

8. In the referendum of May 20, 1980, the Nos won with 59.6 percent of the votes cast (against 40.4 percent for the yeses).

9. In the general election of May 13 1981, the Parti Québécois won power with 80 seats (out of 122) and 49.2 percent of the votes cast. (In November 1976, the PQ had 72 of its candidates elected out of 110 constituencies).

10. For a description of these events, see Lucille Beaudry et al., *Le Souverainisme politique au Québec, Le Parti québécois et les courants indépendantistes 1960-1980, recueil bibliographique,* research note no. 22, Department of Political Science, Université du Québec à Montréal, April 1982, and in particular the chronological summary. See also the *Gazette* of December 7, 1981, which carried the comments of the president after the first part of the convention: "To reinstate an excellent English proverb (...), I believe, alas, that we have thrown the baby out with the bath water...", p. 2.

11. See Vera Murray, *Le Parti québécois: de la fondation à la prise du pouvoir,* Montreal, Hurtubise HMH, 1976, as well as her text, with Don Murray, in the 4th edition of *Party Politics in Canada.*

12. See, Centre de formation populaire, *Au-delà du Parti québécois; lutte nationale et classes populaires,* Montreal, Nouvelle optiue, 1982.

13. "...there is something there — in the party program — which strikes at the very heart of the democratic process." *The Gazette,* December 7, 1981, p. 2.

14. For a sociological analysis of the MNA's, leaders, militants, members and voters of the Parti Québécois, see my "Hiérarchie partisane et sélection sociale: l'exemple du Parti québécois, (1968-1978)", in V. Lemieux, *Personnel et partis politiques au Québec* (Montreal, Boreal Express, 1982), pp. 229-252.

15. *La souveraineté: outil de développement économique,* a document distributed by the National Secretariat of the Parti Québécois, undated.

16. The preceding analysis is drawn from my "Discours des partis sur la crise et crise des discours partisans au Québec", in Gérald Bernier and Gérard Boismenu, *Crise économique, transformations politiques et changements idéologieques,* Montreal, ACFAS, 1983, (cahiers de l'ACFAS no. 16).

17. *Partis et familles politiques,* Paris, PUF, 1980, p. 387.

18. Vera Murray, *Le parti québécois*, p. 169.
19. On this subject see Harold M. Angell, "Le financement des partis provinciaux du Québec", in V. Lemieux, *Personnel et partis politiques au Québec*, pp. 69-89.
20. There is a very complete bibliography in Lucille Beaudry *et al.*, *Le souverainisme politique au Québec...*,
21. See my, *"hiérarchie partisane et..."*

23 The Pattern of Prairie Politics*

NELSON WISEMAN

Canadian historians and social scientists have usually thought of the prairies as a more or less homogeneous unit whose politics have been essentially a response, a reaction, to externally imposed conditions: the tariff, the withholding of authority over natural resources by the federal government, discriminatory transportation policies, etc. This approach tells us substantially about east-west Canadian relations. By itself, however, it tells us little about diversity of political traditions *on* the prairies. What is needed is an interpretive analysis which comes to terms with intra-regional differences. Why, until quite recently, has Manitoba politics been so dominated by Liberal and Conservative regimes? Why has Saskatchewan been so receptive to the CCF-NDP? Why did Alberta spawn such a durable and unorthodox farmers' government (the UFA) and then, overnight, become the bastion of an equally unorthodox Social Credit regime?

Answers to these questions do not lie (although some clues do) in an analysis of the east-west relationship. Nor do the answers lie in analyses which focus strictly on party systems or economic conditions. An economic analysis may be used to explain why, in the landmark federal election of 1911, Saskatchewan and Alberta endorsed the Liberals and freer trade, but it will not explain why Manitoba endorsed the Conservatives and protection. An analysis of party systems may be used to explain why, at the provincial level, Saskatchewan and Alberta rejected the two older parties in favour of third parties. It will not explain, however, why those two third parties are at opposite poles of the Canadian political spectrum. Identifying and accounting for the differences among the three prairie provinces, therefore, is essential. But this too is insufficient because striking diversities are to be located not only among but also *within* the provinces. By the 1890s, for example, Manitoba had been remade in the image of western Ontario. Yet in 1919, Winnipeg exhibited a level of class consciousness and class conflict that was decidedly more reminiscent of the European than the

---

*Reprinted from Queen's Quarterly, Volume 88 Number 2, Summer 1981.

North American scheme of things. In Saskatchewan, until 1945, the federal Liberal party was consistently stronger than in any other English Canadian province. But it was this same province that returned North America's first social democratic government, a CCF government whose ideology was rooted in the British Labour party. Inconsistent political patterns seem no less profound in Alberta where governing parties that are defeated at the polls have faded almost immediately.

The analysis employed here utilizes the concepts of ideology and ethnicity. Elements of Canadian toryism, liberalism, and socialism[1] have been present in varying positions in each province. Political representatives of these ideological tendencies on the prairies include men as diverse as Rodmond Roblin, John Diefenbaker, Charles Dunning, J. W. Dafoe, J. S. Woodsworth, Tommy Douglas, Henry Wise Wood, and William Aberhart, none of whom were born on the prairies. Because the prairie provinces and their societies were moulded in the late nineteenth and early twentieth centuries this is not surprising. Ideas and ideologies first appeared on the prairies as importations.

It is very unlikely that a Rodmond Roblin or a Tommy Douglas, preaching what they did, could have become premiers of Alberta. William Aberhart would not likely have succeeded in Manitoba or Saskatchewan. Politicians are reflectors of their society, their environment, their times. They may be examined in terms which transcend quirks of personality. Their ideas and actions may be seen as reflections of the popular and ideological-cultural basis of their support.

The key to prairie politics is in the unravelling of the dynamic relationship between ideological-cultural heritage and party. In Manitoba, the imported nineteenth-century Ontario liberal party tradition (with "a tory touch") maintained political hegemony until 1969. In Saskatchewan, the dominant tone of politics has reflected a struggle between Ontario liberal and British socialist influences. In Alberta, Americans populist-liberal ideas gained widespread currency beginning in the very first decade of that province's existence. In all three provinces minorities of non-Anglo-American origins have, in their voting, helped make and break governments. These minorities, however, have not determined the ideological coloration of any major party.

Prairie political culture is best seen as the product of the interaction of four distinct waves of pioneering settlers. The first wave was a Canadian one. More precisely, it was largely rural Ontarian. This wave was a westward extension of English Canada's dominant charter group. Ontarians were a charter group in each prairie province but their impact was greatest in Manitoba. It seemed both fitting and telling, that one of Manitoba's premiers (Hugh John Macdonald) was the son of Canada's first prime minister. Tory-touched Canadian liberalism was the ideological core of nineteenth-century Ontario and its prairie offshoot.

(2) British urban working class
 – settled in Winnipeg
 – rural Sask → N.D.P.

A second distinct wave in prairie settlement was a new, modern, British group. Coming near the turn of this century, it was largely urban and working class. Transformed and battered by nineteenth-century industrialism, Britain's working class had begun to turn to socialism. Despite the cultural and ideological differences between the Ontario and new-British waves, their social status in the west was roughly equal, both groups being British subjects and Anglo-Saxon pioneers in British North American. The new-British wave had its greatest impact in the cities, most powerfully in the largest prairie city, Winnipeg. In Saskatchewan relatively large numbers of new British (and European-born) immigrants settled in rural areas and they produced Canada's most successful provincial social democratic party. It seemed both fitting and telling that Saskatchewan's premier in this labour-socialist tradition (Tommy Douglas) was British-born and grew up and was politically socialized in Winnipeg's new British labour-socialist environment. ③ AMERICAN – RURAL – liberal – individual

Alberta
 – Soc
 Credit

The third wave in prairie settlement was American. More specifically it was midwest, great plains American. Like the Ontario wave, but unlike the new-British wave, it came out of an agrarian setting with deeply rooted agrarian values and settled, in overwhelming numbers, in rural areas. Because of their values and racial origin American Anglo-Saxons became the only non-Canadian, non-British charter group on the prairies. The dominant ideological strain carried by the American wave was similar but not identical to that carried by the Ontarians. It was, to be sure, liberal, but its liberalism was devoid of toryism. It was a radical "populist" liberalism that stressed the individual rather than the community or the state as a tory or socialist would. This wave's greatest impact was in rural Alberta, the continent's last agricultural frontier. Populist liberalism expressed itself in an unconventional farmers' movement/government known as the United Farmers of Alberta (UFA) and in the long tenure of Social Credit. It seemed both fitting and telling, that this wave's leading representative figure was a veteran Missouri populist (Henry Wise Wood).

①

– tolerated
② deference
③ influence
CCF, NDP

The fourth and last wave of prairie settlement consisted of continental Europeans. Because of their numerous national origins, their roots and traditions were the most diverse of the four waves. They were, however, neither a charter group nor did they have a significant ideological impact (the eastern European and Finnish influences in the Communist Party being a minor exception). The non-Anglo-Saxons were "alien" and suspect in the eyes of the other three groups. At times their very presence was attacked and challenged; at best they were tolerated. The ideological and political role of the continental wave became largely one of deference. The continental wave had its greatest urban impact in Winnipeg and its greatest rural impact in Saskatchewan. These areas were also those in which the new-British wave had its greatest impact. The combined voting strength of these two waves was to lead to CCF-NDP victories in Manitoba and Saskatchewan in later years. The Old World ideological attributes of the continentals were dismissed as illegitimate on the prairies. Because of this, continentals deferred to to the parties based on the other three groups; but the continentals represented the largest swing factor in voting of the four waves. They helped elect and defeat parties anchored by the other waves; they neither anchored nor led a major party.

The foregoing description of the four distinct waves of prairie settlers is not intended to imply that all Ontarians were tory-touched liberals, that all new Britons were labour-socialists, that all Americans were populist-liberals, and that all continentals deferred ideologically and politically. Furthermore, it should be understood that not all Ontarians voted for the Liberals and Conservatives, not all new Britons voted CCF, and not all Americans voted UFA-Social Credit. The contention here, simply, is that without the new-British impact the CCF would never had attained the stature it did (indeed, it might not have been created at all); similarly, without the American impact the UFA-Social Credit phenomenon in Alberta would not have been anything like what it was; and without the Ontarians, prairie Liberal and Conservative parties would not have gained early hegemony.

The evidence for the interpretation presented here is to be found in prairie historiography, but this evidence is generally disregarded. The notion that Ontario, British, American, and continental European people and influences have helped shape prairie politics is not a new idea. But it might as well be, because it is an idea that has never been developed. There are ten excellent books in a series entitled "Social Credit in Alberta: Its Background and Development." Not one of these books, however, devotes one paragraph to the American impact on Alberta, an impact unparalleled in Canada.

The impact of transplanted ideas was greater in Canada's west than in the United States because the physical impact of immigrants was greater. In 1914, for example, the year of greatest immigration to the US in the decade, one immigrant arrived for eighty in the population. In Canada, in contrast, one immigrant arrived for every thirteen in the population in 1913. The bulk of them, whether from Britain, continental Europe or the United States, went west.

Initially, Ontarian settlement prevailed on the prairies. Ontarians occupied the best agricultural lands and secured homesteads along the new Canadian Pacific Railway. Their power was most profound in Manitoba which, having entered Confederation in 1870, offered the first and most accessible frontier for westward migration. The Ontarians were soon followed by waves of Britons, Americans and continentals. The British came from the most urbanized industrial society in the world, but one that offered no rise in real wages between 1895 and 1913. More than a century of slowly developing working-class consciousness was represented by this new-British group. The American settlers, in contrast, came largely from the rural midwest. The Jeffersonian physiocratic notion that the soil was the sole source of wealth guided their policies. Their interest in the Canadian frontier was fueled by Canadian government propaganda which employed the agrarian ideal, the Horatio Alger tradition and the log cabin stereotype, all prominent features of American liberal mythology. The continental immigrants were largely from eastern and central Europe, where land tenancy systems were in some cases only a half-century removed from feudalism. Of these three groups the Americans were the most likely and the British the least likely to homestead. Many Britons and continentals were to find their way into the new and growing prairie cities: Winnipeg, Regina, Calgary and Edmonton.

In addition to differences in immigrant distribution among the provinces there were differences within each province. Although there were equal numbers of Americans and Britons in Alberta, for example, in the 1920s Americans outnumbered Britons in all fifteen of Alberta's rural census divisions, by a ratio of about two to one. In a province where the rural MLAs prevailed this meant an extraordinary American political influence. In twelve of the fifteen rural census divisions in Alberta Americans also outnumbered continental-born settlers. All three exceptions were in the northeast — that part of the province that provided the strongest rural opposition that both the American-influenced United Farmers of Alberta and Social Credit encountered.

In Saskatchewan, in the 1920s, Britons only slightly outnumbered Americans. The relative rural homogeneity of Saskatchewan, however, produced a dramatically different equation than in Alberta: the overwhelming majority of Britons settled in rural areas. Paradoxically, Saskatchewan had fewer Britons than either Alberta or Manitoba, but the Britons it did have penetrated rural Saskatchewan in a way that the Britons in neighboring provinces did not. Furthermore, in Alberta the majority of American settlers were Anglo-Saxons; in Saskatchewan Anglo-Saxons were in a minority among Americans. This was important because a condition for political success was an Anglo-Saxon background. The largest number of Britons who entered Manitoba and Alberta generally headed for the cities; in Winnipeg population quadrupled between 1901 and 1915.

The four distinct waves of immigrants differed in religion as well as political ideology. Methodists and other social gospellers had their greatest impact in places in Winnipeg where the British-born labourist wave was particularly strong. Catholicism, brought over by many continental Europeans, was strongest in Saskatchewan and contributed to the Liberals' long hold on power there. Anglicans, with roots in both Ontario and Britain, reinforced Conservative tendencies in all three provinces. Many fundamentalists, and they represented an exceptionally high twenty percent of Alberta Protestants, came to that province as American Bible Belt populists.

Ethnic voting studies have not been able to provide a coherent interpretation of prairie politics because studying "ethnic" voting by listing "Anglo-

Saxons" as against Germans, Ukrainians, French, etc., fails to appreciate that some "Anglo-Saxons" were from the "Red" Clyde of Glasgow, others from Perth County, Ontario, and still others from the populist state of Kansas. Different types of divisions of course existed within other ethnic groups. Between the 1920s and 1950s the key distinguishing features in Anglo-Saxon voting in Winnipeg were class status and birthplace. For example, in one part of Winnipeg represented almost continuously since 1921 by MPs J. S. Woodsworth and Stanley Knowles, large numbers of British-born, low-income residents voted overwhelmingly CCF. The city's highest income Anglo-Saxon area with relatively fewer British-born, in contrast, voted overwhelmingly Liberal and Conservative. In both areas Canadian-born Anglo-Saxons far outnumbered other Anglo-Saxons. This revealed that second and third generations reflected inherited ideological-cultural traditions which continued to be expressed in party voting.

Although their demographic impact was great, continental immigrants did not play a leading role in early political developments. Rather, they yielded to the politics of the charter groups. Large numbers of them were isolated in rural ethnic colonies; many were in marginal farming areas where federal agents had directed them. In response to their new opportunity, and in their related effort to prove their loyalty to their new country, these minorities voted Liberal in Alberta from 1905 to 1921, and Liberal in Saskatchewan from 1905 to 1944. In Manitoba too the Liberals were the main beneficiaries of this vote although occasionally, as in 1914, proof of loyalty expressed itself in a Conservative vote. Winnipeg was an exception to the rest of the prairies only in that its working-class continentals were sufficiently numerous, concentrated and class-conscious to form a vibrant community party after 1920. The politics of deference, however, did little to raise the status of the European minorities. Racist prejudice against the continentals was widespread.

Ontarian influence seemed dominant in all three provinces until at least 1921. During World War I, for example, all three provincial premiers, their ministers of agriculture, and a majority of MLAs were Ontarians. In Manitoba the grit agrarianism of Ontario express itself in the selection of every premier from the 1880s until Ed Schreyer in 1969. Its distinct mark was reflected in the transplantation of the Ontario municipal system and in the School Question. In Saskatchewan this same, essentially Protestant and English grit outlook dominated the Saskatchewan Grain Growers Association (SGGA), the province's federal and provincial Progressives, and the Liberal party. But in Saskatchewan, unlike Ontario and Manitoba, the dominance of this liberal grit tradition was dependent on support from other elements in the population, specifically non-Anglo-Saxons, of which Saskatchewan had English Canada's highest percentage. Moreover, Saskatchewan's version of grit agrarianism was to encounter a powerful ideological competitor in the form of British-style socialism. The votes of the continentals helped elect a prairie version of the British Labour party in 1944.

American populist influences were greater in Saskatchewan than in Manitoba but they were secondary and not nearly as significant as in Alberta. In Alberta the American-style populist farmers association (the UFA) determined the complexion of successive provincial governments for years. Alberta populism, like American populism, attracted some socialists, but it rejected socialist ideology. CCF socialism, embraced in Saskatchewan, was rejected by Alberta farmers on the peculiarly American grounds that it represented a repudiation of their "rugged individualism."

Manitoba was the province most true to the values of rural Ontario. In the language rights debates it was more Orange than Ontario. Manitoba imported its early American-inspired farm organizations — the Grange and the Patrons of Industry — only after they had become established in Ontario. Manitoba's Tory farmers rejected any suggestion of possible seccession from Confederation and American annexation in the 1880s.

A good representative of Manitoba's tory-touched liberalism was Rodmond Roblin, premier from 1900 to 1915. His toryism was reflected in the debate over direct legislation, an idea brought to the prairies from the United States. Every political party on the prairies supported the proposal except Roblin's Conservatives in Manitoba. Roblin attacked direct legislation on the basis that it was "A Socialistic and Un-British Plan." This permitted him to appeal to a fundamentally liberal but tory-touched rural Manitoba. According to Sir Rodmond, direct legislation represented a form of "degenerate republicanism," much too strong a phrase to use successfully in Alberta, but not in Manitoba.

T. A. Crerar was a typical Ontarian in rural Manitoba. As a member of the dominant charter group on the prairies, Crerar became a spokesman for the west but remained a product of the east. Between 1919 and 1922 he was offered the premierships of both Ontario and Manitoba. Crerar's liberalism was expressed in his leadership of the Progressive party and in his role as the architect of federal Liberal-Progressive rapprochement. He insisted that his party was not appealing to any specific class in society. Alberta's Henry Wise Wood, in contrast, insisted that it must make a class appeal to farmers by demanding occupational representation or what became known as "group government." Wood's approach was typical of the American left, wholly within the confines of monolithic American liberalism, defining class in liberal (equality of opportunity) rather than socialist (equality of condition) terms. Crerar's liberalism, closer to British liberalism, denied any connection with class politics. Crerar represented the tory-touched rural liberalism of Manitoba; Wood reflected the radical populist liberalism of Alberta.

Although Manitoba Liberal and Conservative governments relied on rural support from continental-born immigrants, few Europeans, of either British or continental origins, were to be found in the higher echelons of either of these parties. Nor were many to be found in the United Farmers of Manitoba (UFM). "Canadian Ukrainians do not have any influence," declared one Ukrainian paper in 1932 the year of the CCF's birth. "We are poor and need political help. Ukrainian farmers and workers depend for their livelihood on the more powerful. This forces us to support a politically influential party. Affiliation with small radical parties brings us Ukrainians only discredit, and ruin." Such deference, however, did little for continental immigrants in the city. In the 1930s none of Winnipeg's banks, trust companies, or insurance firms would knowingly hire a Jew or anyone with a Ukrainian or Polish name. Nor would Anglo-Saxon premiers pick them for their cabinets.

Labour-socialist politics in Manitoba were as much determined by newly arrived Britons and Europeans as agrarian politics were determined by Ontarians. Winnipeg became the home of Canada's first independent Labour party (ILP), and by 1899, twenty-seven separate unions appeared at the May Day parade. A year later, the editor of Winnipeg's labour newspaper *The Voice* was elected to the House of Commons.

Within a decade the labour-socialist sectarianism of Europe was reproduced in Winnipeg. Two groups working outside of the dominant ILP influence were the Social Democratic party and the Socialist Party of Canada. By 1920-21 the two permanent parties that emerged were the British-led labourist ILP and the continental-based Communist party. Every imprisoned 1919 strike leader, except one, came from Britain to Winnipeg between 1896 and 1912. So too did most of the ILP leadership. The Communists, on the other hand, drew their inspiration from the Russian Revolution and scientific socialism. A small and insignificant British minority, including One Big Unionist and strike leader, R. B. Russell, stayed out of both camps. In Manitoba, as in Britain, labourism won over Marxism and syndicalism. By 1923, when the Ontario ILP was falling apart, the Manitoba ILP could boast that it held more than two dozen municipal and school board seats, the mayorality of Winnipeg and representation in both federal and provincial parliaments. This modern, turn of the century British labourist tradition had its greatest Canadian urban impact in Winnipeg and Vancouver and, thus, the strength of the CCF-NDP in these cities.

Until at least 1945 much of the politics of the large Ukrainian community in North Winnipeg were still tied to the Russian Revolution and its aftermath. Those against the Revolution supported the Liberals. The CCF, for many virulent anti-communists, was a socialist step in a hated communist direction. Those supporting the Revolution embraced the Communist Party. The CCF, for many communist sympathizers, was a naive, liberal, social democratic, reformist gang. Since World War II, however, ethnic assimilation has contributed to strengthening the CCF-NDP position within both the former Liberal and Communist Ukrainian groups. The CP withered because the older continental-born generation died and the party lost its base. The ideology of British labourism, in contrast, in the form of the

ILP-CCF, survived and took root. Other socialist traditions among British and continental immigrants either accommodated themselves to this dominant influence on the left or they generally faded as did the SPC and CP.

Liberal, Conservative and Farmer governments dominated provincial politics. Winnipeg counted for little in the government's considerations and center and north Winnipeg, where the British and European-born had settled, counted for less. It was unpenalized neglect because a rurally biased electoral map ensured agrarian dominance. Between 1920 and 1949, for example, Winnipeg had only ten seats in a fifty-five seat legislature. In the 1922 election labour votes equalled those for twenty-seven non-labour MLAs, but Labour won only six seats. In 1945 the CCF received as many votes as the Liberal-Progressive and almost double the Conservative total, but the CCF won only ten seats to the Liberals' twenty-four and the Conservatives' thirteen.

Successive Manitoba governments reflected an alliance of Anglo-Saxons in the southwestern wheat belt and in south Winnipeg. This alliance went under various labels at different times: Liberal, Conservative, United Farmers of Manitoba, Progressive, Liberal-Progressive, Brackenite, Coalition, and even Non-Partisan. What distinguished it from its main ideological opponent was class and heritage, not ethnicity. In 1919 the warring Strike Committee and Citizens Committee had one feature in common: Anglo-Saxon backgrounds. In working-class Winnipeg the European minorities lined up behind the British-born Strike Committee because the Citizens Committee gave them little choice, identifying them as alien radicals. In rural Manitoba these minorities deferred to the established Canadian-born anti-strike forces.

These divisions were reflected in voting patterns. There seemed little basis for farmer-labour cooperation in Manitoba. They shared little in common. Labour issues, such as the eight-hour day, were ridiculed in the countryside, and every rural newspaper in Manitoba condemned the 1919 strike. Labour's attitude to Manitoba's farmers was also suspicion and until 1927, UFM members were ineligible to join the ILP.

Manitoba's farm leaders went the way of Ontario's. Alberta's UFA, Saskatchewan's UFC (SS) and even Ontario's UFO affiliated with the federal CCF in 1932 (although the latter disaffiliated in 1934). The UFM, like its forerunners a half-century before, was true to the values of rural Ontario and remained aloof. In the late 1940s agrarian politics in Manitoba began to shift somewhat with the rise of the Manitoba Farmers Union (MFU). The MFU's membership came largely from more northerly, less prosperous, continental-born, and second generation Canadian farmers. By the 1950s, ethnic interaction over the course of forty years made possible the viability of such an organization. To the MFU leadership the Manitoba Fenderation of Agriculture, like its UFM predecessor, represented the wealthier, established, Anglo-Saxon Liberal farmers. After John Diefenbaker and provincial

Conservative premier Duff Roblin left their respective leadership posts in 1967, the provincial NDP capitalized on gaining informal MFU support in certain rural areas. It was a breakthrough that helped the NDP win enough rural seats to form a government in 1969. For a combination of reasons, including the fact that he was the son-in-law of the first president of the MFU, Ed Schreyer was the only figure in the Manitoba NDP who could attract such support.

Manitoba was ripe for an NDP victory in 1969 in a way that Ontario was not. In Ontario the impact of Anglo-Saxon voters, most of them long established in Canada, was more powerful than in Manitoba. This is another way of pointing out that Ontario is ideologically older than Manitoba in its conservatism, particularly in the rural areas, but in the cities too. There was a significant new British labourist impact in Ontario (e.g. Toronto mayor Jimmie Simpson in the 1930s) but, because of Ontario's relative oldness, it was not as profound as it was further west.

Manitoba had enough of Ontario in it to have sustained the only provincial Conservative party west of Ontario that has never collapsed. But is also had enough of modern Britain and continental Europe to provide CCFer J. S. Woodsworth and provincial Communist leader Bill Kardash with parliamentary seats between the 1920s and 1950s. Manitoba also had enough of the prairies in it to produce national and provincial Progressive parties in the 1920s. Their Ontario-born liberal leadership however, led both of them back to the Liberal party. SASKATCHEWAN

As in Manitoba, provincial politics in Saskatchewan initially meant transplanting Ontarian politics. The provincial Liberal government operated at the pleasure of the Saskatchewan Grain Growers Association, the dominant political and economic organization in the province. Both the Liberals and the SGGA were led by the same figures and most of them had Ontario roots. The Progressive debacle in Ottawa, however, and the inability of the SGGA to break with the Liberals fuelled the formation of a rival agrarian organization: the Farmers Union of Canada. It was founded and first led by L. B. McNamee, a former British railway worker and trade unionist. This difference between the SGGA's Ontarian leadership and the Farmers Union British leadership broadly represented the difference between Ontario liberal and British socialist influences. The division became a central feature of Saskatchewan politics.

The success of the Farmers Union led to the formation of the United Farmers of Canada (Saskatchewan Section) and that, in turn, led directly to the Farmer-Labour party, led by British socialists and Canadians sympathetic to socialism. It then took three elections and ten years, from 1934 to 1944, to catapult this party to power under a CCF label. This became possible because enough continential-origin voters transferred their preferences from the Liberals to the CCF.

Liberalism at first seemed unbeatable in Saskatchewan. Although it came later than in Manitoba, the Ontarian impact was the first in Saskatchewan and it was, as in Manitoba, generally Liberal. While the national, Manitoba, and Alberta Liberal parties were rejected in the early 1920s, the Saskatchewan Liberals carried on. All six of Saskatchewan's daily newspapers supported them. A key factor for the Liberals in Saskatchewan was the province's large numbers of Catholics and eastern and central Europeans. In eastern and central European rural districts the provincial Liberals reaped the rewards of the federal government's immigration program.

In Saskatchewan, however, unlike Manitoba and Alberta, there was a significant new-British *rural* presence. Although Saskatchewan attracted fewer Britons than either Manitoba or Alberta, it had almost as many British-born farm operators as the other two provinces combined. This British influence, coming later than the Ontario influx, took a longer time to assert itself. The farmer-labour connection in the Farmer's Union was unique among prairie farm organizations of any significant size. Much of its support came from farmers in continental-based areas, areas that switched from the Liberals to the CCF between 1934 and 1944. The SGGA, like the neighboring UFM and UFA, had largely ignored the non-Anglo-Saxon farmers and had almost no following in areas settled by Europeans. All three organizations were rooted in the oldest and most established areas.

The United Farmers of Canada (Saskatchewan Section), a product of a merger of the growing Farmers Union and the declining SGGA in the mid-1920s, was socialist in a way that no other Canadian farm organization had ever been. That socialism, like Saskatchewan's early made-in-Ontario liberalism, was imported. The two most important permanent officials of the new UFS (SS) were former members of the British Labour party and the Socialist Party of the United States. The UFC (SS)'s socialist, British, labourist, and agrarian heritages could be summed up by isolating two planks in its 1930 platform: "Abolition of the competitive system and substitution of a cooperative system of manufacturing, transportation, and distribution," and "Free trade with the mother country." The UFC (SS) also endorsed a land nationalization scheme, one patterned on the British Labour Party's rural program. The UFC (SS) also forged a political alliance with the Saskatchewan Independent Labour Party. Formed in the late 1920s, the ILP was largely composed of teachers, some unionists and British socialists. It was patterned on the successful Manitoba ILP. When the UFC (SS) and the ILP came together in 1932 they formed the Farmer-Labour party and elected a British-born Fabian, M. J. Coldwell, as their leader.

A contributing factor to the rise of socialism in Saskatchewan was that the cooperative movement was stronger there than any other province. Moreover, Saskatchewan's cooperators were more socialist than their provincial neighbors. The cooperative movement became an integral part of the CCF's constituency in Saskatchewan and all the movement's growth in the province was aided by a provincial government branch headed by a British immigrant experienced in the British cooperative movement. This "British" link reappears often in Saskatchewan history.

The story of the CCF's success in Saskatchewan need not involve, as most sources do, a discussion of the Depression. When the Farmer-Labour (CCF) party ran in 1934 it was largely an unknown entity in politically cautious and deferential continential-origin areas. It had to contend, moreover, with the Catholic Church. Official Church opposition to the CCF was important to the party in Saskatchewan because it was the most Catholic of the prairie provinces. A papal encyclical and a 1934 statement by the Archbishop of Regina attacking socialism as contrary to the Catholic faith aided the Liberals. The Liberals swept both the Ontario-anchored regions and the continental, particularly Catholic areas. Voting among Anglo-Saxons divided, however, between areas that were largely Ontarian in origin and areas that contained large numbers of British-born. In both the 1934 and 1938 elections cultural rather than strictly economic factors provided the clues to unravelling the voting patterns.

The CCF succeeded because it was British-led and ideologically British-based. The CCF's Britishness, its cultural acceptability, made it difficult to attack as alien. Its cultural legitimacy made it politically acceptable. It could therefore become an alternative to the Liberals for Saskatchewan's continental-origin citizens. Even more than in Manitoba, continental-origin citizens represented a large potential swing factor in voting. This helps explain why the CCF-NDP's success in Saskatchewan came twenty-five years before it did in Manitoba and why it was more profound in terms of votes and seats. The large rural British presence, combined with a large rural continental presence relative to Manitoba and Alberta, made it easier for continental-origin citizens in Saskatchewan to attach themselves to the CCF. This was exhibited in 1943 when another barrier to CCF aspirations was lowered: the Catholic Church declared its support for the cooperative movement, expressed concern respecting social welfare, and told its members they were free to vote for any party that was not communist. The CCF victory in 1944, therefore, was no surprise.

The surge in CCF support in 1944 was most dramatic in the previously Liberal, continental-origin areas. Many CCF rural leaders were of non-Anglo-Saxon origins, a dramatic contrast to the overwhelming Anglo-Saxon character of the Liberal and Conservative leaders. The swing among continentals from the Liberals to the CCF was no less pronounced in urban areas. Between 1934 and 1944, for example, support for the CCF rose 218 percent in the most European part of Regina.

American influences in Saskatchewan were secondary to the Ontario and British influences. In contrast to Alberta, however, the Americans in Saskatchewan tended to help the fortunes of British-led anti-liberal organizations such as the Farmers Union and the CCF. In Saskatchewan, unlike

Alberta, the majority of Americans were non-Anglo-Saxons. Moreover, few of them in Saskatchewan had English as a mother tongue. Among these European-Americans in Saskatchewan were large numbers — larger than in Alberta — of Scandinavians, European and American Scandinavians in Saskatchewan were much more receptive to socialism than Anglo-Saxon Americans — the majority American group in Alberta. Therefore, European-Americans, such as Scandinavians, encountered a powerful, legitimate and culturally acceptable ideological ally in Saskatchewan in the form of the British-influenced CCF. In Alberta, in contrast to Saskatchewan, there were both fewer British farmers and fewer European-Americans. British labour-socialism, moreover, was not a leading ideological force in rural Alberta as it was in Saskatchewan. In Alberta European-Americans represented a minority among Americans in rural areas. Moreover, they had no corresponding powerful rural British labour-socialist strain to attach themselves to. Thus, in Alberta, there never arose a socialist agrarian rival to the UFA as there was to the SGGA in the form of the Farmers Union.

The connection between British birth and labour-socialist politics has been demonstrated in Manitoba. It was also reflected, as late as 1942, in Alberta where four of five CCF provincial executive members were British-born, and in British Columbia where nine of the fourteen CCF MLAS were British-born. In Saskatchewan, in slight contrast, there were four Americans yet only three Britons among the eleven-member British-led CCF caucus at this date. Some of the Americans elected as CCF MLAs in 1944 had voted for Socialist Eugene Debs in the United States. In the United States, as the Socialist Party withered, socialist supporters of European origins on the American great plains returned to the established American parties. In Saskatchewan, in contrast, as the socialist-farmer-labour movement grew, American socialist sympathizers of European ancestry, not overwhelmed by American liberalism as they were in the US, had alternatives not restricted to the established parties.

In the late 1950s Saskatchewan produced another political phenomenon, John Diefenbaker, who made it possible for the Conservatives to become a national party for the first time since 1935. In the 1940s, Manitoba preferred the Liberals, Saskatchewan the CCF, and Alberta Social Credit. Diefenbaker, unlike other national leaders, was neither Anglo-Saxon nor was he identified with Central Canadian financiers. This made it possible for European-origin farmers to flock, for the first time, to the Conservative banner. Ethnic interaction and the passing of earlier prejudices no longer crippled the Conservatives in Saskatchewan's European-origin areas. At the same time, Diefenbaker's toryism and commitment to agricultural interest made him equally acceptable to rural, Anglo-Saxon, prairie farmers. They recognized him as an established, Ontario-born Canadian not as a European, naturalized one. Diefenbaker's populist image, another side of this phenomenon, helped him in Alberta where agrarian populism, as in the

United States, eased its way into agribusiness. The prairies could therefore embrace the federal Conservative party after the 1950s because it was a qualitatively different party under Diefenbaker than it had been under Arthur Meighen, R. B. Bennett, John Bracken, and George Drew.

Seymour Lipset's *Agrarian Socialism* is something of a misnomer in reference to Saskatchewan. The Saskatchewan CCF-NDP consistently fared better in cities than in the countryside. More precisely, it had been a case of British-style socialism succeeding in an unexpected agricultural setting. M. J. Coldwell, Tommy Douglas, Woodrow Lloyd, and Allan Blakeney were never farmers. Nor was British-born and longtime Toronto MP Andrew Brewin who drafted Saskatchewan's "showpiece" labour legislation in the 1940s. Saskatchewan did produce one British-born non-socialist premier: Charles Dunning. But he represented an older part of Canada's British heritage. Dunning succeeded as easily in Prince Edward Island, which he went on to represent as finance minister in Mackenzie King's cabinet. The only part of the Maritimes that would have sent a Tommy Douglas to Ottawa was Cape Breton because it had been subject to the same type of new British influx as Saskatchewan. This connection between British-birth and socialist inclinations was revealed in the 1970s when Douglas represented Nanaimo (British Columbia) as an MP. In the 1920s, Nanaimo was the most British city in Canada, almost half its residents having been born in the British Isles. The British labourist-socialist connection became, paradoxically, most successful in Canada's most agrarian province.

The politics of rural Alberta was as much influenced by the values of the American great plains as the politics of rural Manitoba by the standards of rural Ontario. In Alberta the various cultural waves, from Ontario, Britain, continental Europe, and the United States, came closest to arriving simultaneously. Early Ontario settlers in rural Alberta, as in Saskatchewan, encountered another ideological strain. It was not, however, a socialist challenge as it had been in Saskatchewan. It was, rather, a more militant, more radical, less tory form of petit-bourgeois liberalism, than was the Canadian norm. It was not so much a challenge as a reinforcement, a radicalization, of the natural liberalism of transplanted Ontarians. There seemed little need, as there had been in Saskatchewan, for two rival agrarian organizations or for an ideologically distinct opposition party. The older parties simply re-oriented themselves. The Liberals and Conservatives became competitors vying for support from the American-influenced UFA. An MP remarked in the House of Commons that Alberta, "from the border northward to Edmonton, might be regarded as a typical American state."

American populism pervaded Alberta politics. Many Canadian-and British-born settlers, to be sure, were to be found in the vanguard of the agrarian movement. But Americans and American ideas played an influential role in Alberta that was unparalleled in Canada. An early example of this in the UFA was that both sides in the debate over whether or not to enter electoral politics argued their cases with references to experiences south of the border, one side referring to the sad end of the People's party and the other side pointing to the Non-Partisan League's success in North Dakota.

When Social Credit came to power in 1935 there was no significant shift of ideological allegiance in rural Alberta. UFAers had been nutured on inflationary monetary theories in the United States and at UFA conventions throughout the 1920s. The overwhelming majority of UFAers found socialism alien and voted for a technocratic, "pragmatic" remedy in Social Credit. It was a response with American (Free Silver, Greenbackism), not Canadian, antecedents.

The American influence in rural Alberta expressed itself in many ways. In sheer numbers, more than one in five Alberta residents at one point was American-born while the national ratio was less than one in twenty-five. Canadian branches of the American Society of Equity, containing large numbers of transplanted Nebraskans and Dakotas, were the core of the UFA when it was formed in 1909, and about one-half of the directors on the UFA's board were American-born, outnumbering both British-and Canadian-born.

In sharp contrast to T. A. Crerar and Manitoba's farmers, Henry Wise Wood and the UFA's break with the Liberals was to be final and complete. The division between the UFA brand of third-party populism and the Manitoba brand of third-party parliamentarism, one longing for a reconciliation with the Liberals, came at the very founding convention of the national Progressives in 1920. Wood intended that the UFA govern Alberta with no reference to the other parties. This never happened in Ontario-anchored Manitoba. This difference meant that the federal and provincial Liberal party was doomed in Alberta. In Ontario, Manitoba and Saskatchewan, in contrast to Alberta, most of the federal Progressives who had been elected to replace Liberals became Liberals.

American-style populism prevailed in Alberta because a heavily rurally oriented electoral map, like Manitoba's, meant agrarian dominance. The new British labour-socialist impact in Calgary and Edmonton was insufficient to offset American populist-liberal dominance in the rural areas. Although one-third of Calgary was British-born and it served as the site of the founding conventions of both the OBU and the CCF, as well as being the constituency of Labour MP William Irvine, Calgary was in the largely rural province of Alberta and was also subject to an American impact: it became the headquarters of the Society of Equity, the Non-Partisan League, the UFA, prairie evangelism, and Social Credit, all of which had American roots.

Alberta's preoccupation with monetary theories was a result of the American influence. Low agricultural prices in the United States led American farmers to fight for the free coinage of silver and an inflation in the money supply. When J. W. Leedy, the former populist governor of Kansas, and US credit expert George Bevington and many other Americans emigrated to Alberta, they brought along their monetary theories. Throughout the 1920s and 1930s UFA conventions became debating forums for the monetary theorists. The monetary issue was second to none. In Manitoba and Saskatchewan, in contrast, it was rarely debated. When C. H. Douglas's Social Credit theories appeared they had much in common with notions already present in the UFA. The UFA had contributed to this link by distributing Douglas's books throughout the 1920s. Social Credit, therefore, could be regarded as a supplement rather than as an alternative to UFA thinking.

Wood's retirement from the UFA presidency led to a crystallization of the majority and minority positions in the UFA. The American-influenced majority was occupied with monetary reform; a British-influenced minority was more interested in socialist efforts at the national level. Both positions gained recognition at the 1931 UFA convention: Bevington's annual inflationary money resolutions were endorsed and British-born, socialist leaning Robert Gardiner became the new UFA president. Gardiner led his federal Ginger Group caucus into an even closer working arrangement with J. S. Woodsworth's Labour group. When the UFA's federal leadership in 1932 took the UFA into the CCF, Gardiner's caucus in Ottawa became isolated from majority sentiment in rural Alberta. Neither Wood, nor UFA Premier Brownlee, nor his cabinet ever endorsed the "farmer-labour-socialist" alliances as the CCF described itself.

Social Credit was the political heir of the American-influenced monetary reform wing of the UFA. William Aberhart succeeded only because the monetary reformers in the UFA had tilled the soil so well for him. It was the UFA, he continually reminded his audiences, that had introduced Social Credit thinking into Alberta. By 1935 UFA locals throughout the province were clamoring for some form of Social Credit. During the election campaign Social Credit was really not a partisan issue: few dared attack it. It became, rather, an assumption. Even the Liberals promised Social Credit and the Alberta Federation of Labour indicated enthusiasm as well. Aberhart's Social Credit message was consistent with Alberta's populist history. The American monetary reformers had done their work well. Social Credit's sweeping victory in 1935 was therefore no surprise. Had Social Credit not appeared, another party would have arisen preaching much the same gospel.

American analogies are logical in Alberta. There is something to the argument that Aberhart comes closest among Canada's premiers to looking and sounding like a radical, populist, American governor. Many of his supporters referred to him as Alberta's Abraham Lincoln. But no one could compare prairie CCF leaders such as Douglas, Coldwell, Woodsworth, Queen, or even Irvine to American populists. One could identify them with a Norman Thomas but, to be more accurate, one would have to look to a Briton like Ramsay MacDonald, Labour's first prime minister.

An examination of Alberta's voting patterns reveal that they may be related directly to the patterns of settlement and to the ideological-cultural heritages of the settlers. Initial Ontario settlers in the south, particularly those who came before 1896 and settled along the CPR line, voted for the party of the railroad, the federal Conservatives. The early twentieth-century American influx altered this. The American impact was most pronounced in southern and eastern Alberta, an area representing the key to political power in the province just as the southwest represented that key in Manitoba. The southern, American-settled parts of Alberta which were most favourable to prohibition in 1915 became the most favourable to the UFA from 1921 to 1935 and to Social Credit from 1935 to the early 1970s. Those areas in northern Alberta that tended toward the UFA were those whose population most closely resembled the American-anchored south.

Continental-origin and French Canadian voters in northern Alberta represented a Liberal electoral base for the same reasons as in Saskatchewan and Manitoba: the Liberals were the party of immigrants and Catholics. The UFA, in contrast, was overwhelmingly Anglo-Saxon, composed of Canadian-, American- and a sprinkling of British-born farmers. I argue UFA and Social Credit majorities were produced by the electoral map which ensured that the party that swept the south was the party that won elections. UFA and Social Credit vote totals were never as high in the continental and French Canadian north as in the Ontarian and American south. These patterns reflected how much the UFA and Social Credit had in common with each other and how little either had in common with the CCF.

The new British labour-socialist element in Alberta was largely isolated in the urban centres. Consequently, the CCF floundered. The British-anchored provincial CCF never managed to win more than two seats in Alberta. Significantly, both CCF MLAs in the 1950s were from the north and were second generation Ukrainians, as were large numbers of their constituents. These northeastern areas were among the very few where, in the 1920s, continental-born farmers outnumbered American-born ones. The CCF success here confirmed the shift, in a much less dramatic fashion than in Saskatchewan, from the Liberals to the CCF among non-Anglo-Saxons of continental, particularly eastern European, origin. In Saskatchewan, large numbers of rural continentals had swung their votes to support the party of large numbers of rural Britons, the CCF. In Alberta, however, there were both fewer continentals and fewer rural Britons. Thus, the CCF was a relatively minor force in Alberta's rural areas.

Manifestations of the American influence in Alberta abound. One example of a republican liberal tendency was the Alberta government's refusal to appear in 1938 before the Royal Commission on Dominion-Provincial Relations, addressing its comments instead to "the Sovereign People of Canada." Parliamentary government was described as a form of state dictatorship. Another example was the complaint of a Nebraska-born

MLA who called the caucus form of government undemocratic and criticized the speech from the throne for making more of the 1937 coronation festivities than of Social Credit. Could such a sentiment respecting the coronation have been expressed at Queen's Park or in any other English Canadian provincial legislature?

In the 1970s prairie politics continued to be tied to prairie history. The hegemony of Ontario-anchored politics in Manitoba had succumbed temporarily to an alliance of an urbanized multi-ethnic working class and poorer non-Anglo-Saxon farmers led by the NDP. This alliance was unlike Saskatchewan's because it had little rural Anglo-Saxon support. In Saskatchewan, the CCF "formula" of 1944 has repeated itself with some consistency. Urbanization and ethnic assimilation in both provinces have generally aided the CCF-NDP, although this pattern may yet reverse itself as intermarriage and acceptance of ethnic leaders in the older parties increases. In Alberta, Social Credit gave way to the Conservatives; both are right-wing liberal parties which have, for half a century, offered politics that are either American in origin or in benefit. In part, Social Credit led to the Conservatives in the evolutionary, not radical, ways that the UFA led to Social Credit. Although the conditions of the 1980s are different from those of the 1930s, Alberta Social Credit may yet disappear, just as the UFA did. The Conservatives have captured the ideological and popular base of Social Credit support just as Social Credit captured the ideological and popular base of UFA support.

ENDNOTES

1. For Canadian definitions of these terms as used here see Gad Horowitz, "Conservatism, Liberalism, and Socialism in Canada: An Interpretation," *Canadian Journal of Economics and Political Science,* **32,** 2 (May 1966). A short version of this essay appears as chapter 4 of this volume.

24 Grits and Tories on the Prairies*

DAVID E. SMITH

In her book *Survival,* Margaret Atwood describes the motif of early prairie fiction, where man kills nature in his attempt to control it, as "straight line wins over curve."[1] It is an evocative theme for westerners, whose vulnerability to external forces has driven them to seek protection through political and social experiments. In this region too, line has another meaning, quite a different context, for here the development of Canada is seen as moving over two centuries from Atlantic to Pacific with the Prairies locked in direct relationship to central Canada: "Not western development," wrote Vernon Fowke, "but western development exclusively integrated with the St. Lawrence economy, was the national policy of the Fathers of Canadian Confederation."[2]

Thus, in fiction and in history, as in geography, the prairie perspective is linear. Yet that plane has distinct physical boundaries — east of Winnipeg, west of Calgary and north of the Saskatchewan River basin. (Prairie residents have never fully adjusted to the fact that more than half of the region is neither plain nor parkland, but pine.) Only to the south is there no break in topography, yet the eight hundred mile border with some of the least populated of the American states has acted quite as effectively as a regional boundary. Nowhere else in Canada is the United States more accessible yet less pervasive.

Except for the brief but dizzy optimism reflected in the boom before World War I, the mood of the Prairies has alternated between latent and overt resentment of its position in Confederation. Its natural resource economy (which includes the most famous staple of all — wheat), reliant on external capital and cooperative federal legislation, created a dependence the West has found difficult to accept or to break.

The federal government's retention, until 1930, of the Prairies' natural resources indicated that provincial autonomy for Manitoba, Saskatchewan

---

*This is a revised and updated version of the paper that appeared in the Fourth Edition of this book.

and Alberta was to be different from that enjoyed elsewhere. The resources were judged too important to the national interest for equality of treatment. Thus the center dominated and the frontier, which in the United States became a vital influence in that nation's development, was never "allowed free expression" in Canada.[3] Limited freedom transformed rare concessions into inalienable rights, as the modern history of the grain industry bears witness.

Natural gas, oil and potash are glamorous newcomers whose future is inextricably linked to the region's, but whose combined impact can never approach that of grain. Because grain came first, its roots are the Prairies' roots, for it determined the settlement pattern and transportation network and on these bases all else rested. But wheat is hauled over rails laid three quarters of a century ago, at statutory rates more than half a century old and under direction of the Canadian Wheat Board, now in its fifth decade. Economic dependence has forced the Prairies to rely upon shibboleths like freedom of choice, orderly marketing and, of course, the family farm to guard its major industry against external attack, traditionally depicted as coming from central Canada but more recently from multinational corporations as well. Advocates of change pose a threat to the western farmer, who can marshall evidence to support his view that the change initiated from outside the region has been detrimental to his interests.

Since Sir Clifford Sifton's time, a distinctive characteristic of prairie society has been its ethnic heterogeneity. Along with Quebec, the prairie provinces have a large minority population, but unlike elsewhere that minority is neither English nor French. There is a French population but nowhere on the Prairies is it the second or even third largest of the ethnic groups. Whether or not the existence of minorities "contributes to a sense of self-conscious identity for all groups,"[4] prairie leaders from the beginning of this century were keenly aware of the "non-English." For some, ethnic diversity was a problem to be solved through "Canadianization;" for others cultural assimilation was less important than the immigrant's vote. Either directly or subsumed under the provincial versus minority rights debate, the ethnic question provided a cleavage around which parties formed, and in the heated exchanges that followed some participants forgot to distinguish between the French and the other non-English.

This insensitivity to Canada's dual ethnic origins can be traced in the main to the region's English-speaking settlers: especially those from Ontario, who viewed the West as a preserve, and those from the British Isles, who sought to save Canada for the Empire. Both expected British institutions to prevail. Nonetheless, parliament had provided for denominational education rights in the three provinces and, then as now, religion and language became confused. By 1900, the battle for publicly supported Roman Catholic schools had been lost in Manitoba but it flared up in Saskatchewan and Alberta in 1905 and was revived once more in Saskatchewan in the twenties by the Ku Klux Klan. The bicultural cleavage, which had originated in central Canada, persisted in prairie politics as long as these denominational disputes lingered. When the ethnic debate subsided, another cleavage, economic in character, replaced it and "has dominated politics in western Canada since."[5] The succession did not occur at the same time in each of the three provinces. Because of the Klan's racism, it came last in Saskatchewan where the Liberal party, with its bicultural reputation strengthened after World War I, continued to function as a partisan force long after its counterparts in Alberta and Manitoba had all but disappeared.

The Trudeau government's language policies...resurrected an issue that was thought to have been laid to rest. The emphasis upon French as an official language does not conform to the view those of British origin have of their history, while it is interpreted by the descendants of the non-English as devaluing their status as well as their contribution to Canada. Whether one argues that the West is a mosaic, with a variety of cultures of which French is only one, or a melting pot, where there are no "hyphenated Canadians," the indisputable fact remains that the frame or mold of prairie culture today is of English Canadian design. The Canadianization of the non-English did succeed: line was imposed on curve. If this explanation is correct, then it is not difficult to understand hostility toward an official policy that promotes linguistic distinctiveness. This recognition of French is a daily reminder of the price paid by others to be English.[6]

Of course western grievances did not begin with bilingualism and biculturalism. In fact, they predate the first shipment of wheat from the region in 1876. The seed of discontent was sown early by the federal government's practice of ignoring local opinion and experience in almost all matters affecting the region.[7] Acquiescence in western demands, such as the Macdonald government's granting of provincial status to a diminutive Manitoba, was a rare event and, in this particular case, one which encouraged later generations of exasperated westerners to translate Louis Riel from rebel to regional hero.

The character of the Prairies is defined not only be grievances but by innovation. The settlement pattern fostered a recognition of societal dependence rather than a spirit of rugged individualism. Westerners were never loathe to experiment together, for example in the provision of health care or the establishment of farmers' cooperatives or in sparking the creation of the United Church. Equally distinctive was their pragmatic politics. No party on the current scene has failed to tap a significant portion of the region's electoral support at some time or other. In fact, kaleidoscopic partisanship holds out hope to those parties now out of favor, as well as to those who would begin anew with yet another party, movement or league.

It is beyond the scope of this paper to recount in detail the party history of the Prairies. That the region was fertile ground for the founding of third parties is well known and documented. Less frequently remembered, however, is the continuing claim of the two old parties on the loyalties of westerners. In this century, except for 1921, when the Progressives cap-

tured 38 of the Prairies' 43 seats, the Liberals and Conservatives have won
a majority of Manitoba's seats at every federal election except 1980, and a
majority of Saskatchewan's in all but four (1945, 1953, 1957, and 1980).
Their record in Alberta was poor, however, failing to capture a majority of
that province's seats from 1921 through 1957. In terms of a popular vote,
though, the Liberals and Conservatives have always won a majority in
Manitoba, 50 percent or better in Saskatchewan, and failed to garner at
least 50 percent in Alberta only in the federal elections of 1935 and 1945.

In the last 20 years some of the most intriguing questions about party
politics on the Prairies center on the fluctuating fortunes of the Liberal and
Progressive Conservative parties. The liaison with the Progressive Conservatives has matured into what appears to be a lasting union, while the
rejection of the Liberals appears equally emphatic. Between these extremes
the other parties have fared poorly in federal politics, although the ill
effects have not been transmitted so clearly into the provincial sphere,
where partisan fortunes have become compartmentalized, as has the federal
system itself.

Liberal Dominance and Decline

Between the elections of 1958 and 1980 there were 425 constituency contests of which the Tories won 337 and the Liberals 29. Liberal
unpopularity became legend but it was not always so — in the decades
before the Diefenbaker sweep, the Grits in Saskatchewan and Manitoba
(but neither of the old parties in Alberta) were almost as unassailable as the
Tories today. The switch in voter allegiance, which continued even after
the Liberals returned to power nationally in 1963, meant the region was
virtually excluded from the councils of the governing party. That the cost
has not proved intolerable for either the West or the Liberals indicates the
gap that now exists between regional interests and influence on the one
hand, and Liberal interests and power on the other.

At one time the Liberal party's claim on the West was indisputable.
Identified with prosperity before the First World War and racial tolerance
during it, the Liberals' new leader after 1919 healed the inter-party schism,
inherited from the fight over Union government, and reined in the agrarian
revolt after its first success. One characteristic of Mackenzie King's leadership, evident from his first administration when he sought to reduce the
Progressives' threat, was his ability to co-opt into his cabinet powerful
regional spokesmen like Thomas Crerar from Manitoba, Charles Dunning
and James G. Gardiner from Saskatchewan and Charles Stewart from
Alberta. Indeed King became the most skilful practitioner of this Canadian
variant of consociational democracy. But his accommodation went beyond
mere obeisance to the traditional federalized cabinet. It extended to sub-
groups of the executive like the Wheat Committee of cabinet and to individual ministers like Gardiner to whom King frequently deferred in western

matters: "Gardiner…seemed to feel that he was right in his own judgment. He is not only Minister of Agriculture but a former Premier in a Western province, and I think he knows the West as well as anyone. I feel, in such a situation, there is nothing left to do but to accept this advice and let him proceed."[8]

Accommodation was neither the sole reason for Liberal supremacy nor was it equally successful in each prairie province. It worked best where there was a strong, stable party organization on which a minister could depend. In Saskatchewan, problems were few, but in Manitoba, where the Liberal battalion was divided into federal and provincial companies, much time was taken with intra-party negotiation, while in Alberta, guerrilla skirmishes over patronage made accommodation impossible and truces temporary. Accommodation was important for what it symbolized — a provincial spokesman among the mighty — but also for what it presumably caused to happen — policies favourable or at least not detrimental to the region. Cause without effect would give the lie to accommodation as a political technique and for this reason King had to acquiesce occasionally in a minister's desires even when, as in the case of Gardiner, they might strike him, a number of other ministers and a significant section of caucus as profligate, political rather than principled, and in conflict with the party's national interest.[9]

The touchstone of Liberal fortunes on the Prairies during the King period was the government's wheat policy. Described succinctly, the policy was one of reluctant intervention. Except in response to wartime disruptions, the Canadian federal government had largely stayed clear of involvement in the industry other than to set the ground rules early in the century. Significantly, the Liberal party had not been in power at any time that departures from the open-market system were deemed necessary, and when in office during the twenties the King government had had the good fortune of coexisting with the Pools, whose determination to remain independent of government was welcomed by all elected officials. Thus it was only in the chaotic economic conditions of 1935 that the Liberals were forced to determine their government's position towards the country's chief export.

Their immediate dilemma arose from the Bennett government's creation, during its last weeks in office, of the Canadian Wheat Board, which the Liberals had supported once compulsion was removed (although even then they found the principle of state intervention repugnant to their laissez-faire sensibilities). Liberal history and ideology ranged from the progressivism of Dunning's Saskatchewan to the conservatism of Gouin's Quebec, but it did not countenance interference that smacked of "socialism." While there were strong opponents in the party who wanted to scrap the Wheat Board, others accepted the need on emergency grounds and in preference to increased relief payments to destitute western farmers.

Before the end of the decade, the Liberals discovered that they could not backtrack even when they were united and economic conditions had improved. Western grain farmers had fought unsuccessfully in the twenties for the reinstitution of a board like that of 1919-20, which was given credit for the record high prices that year. Constitutional barriers and the King government's philosophical reluctance had pushed farmers into cooperative Pools, which had prospered until the market collapsed in 1930. Later in the decade, Gardiner proposed that the Pools resume their marketing responsibilities but the farmers were not convinced and, as a result, the Pools' energies to the present day have been devoted solely to the elevator business. The Board's lure was that it replaced the peaks and troughs of the futures market with the assurance of an advance initial payment based on projected sales of wheat, and a final payment calculated on the pooling of returns from actual sales. Orderly marketing in fact meant the removal of domestic competition and thereby the realization of the western farmer's dream of first-line protection in the tumult of the international market. The Board was truly a "steward of producers' interests" and the fervor with which the vast majority of farmers has defended it reveals how great was the need it satisfied.

The Board created by Bennett was voluntary and thus the open market, in the form of the Winnipeg Wheat Exchange, continued to function. But in 1943 the press of war demands on limited wheat supplies threatened the government's price control policy and, "to arrest an advance rather than a decline in the price of wheat," the Board was given monopoly control.[10] This action, earnestly sought by generations of western farmers, signalled both the end of Exchange trade in wheat and further entanglement of government.

The ardent attachement to the Board among farmers, and the government's treatment of it as an affair of convenience was part of the explanation for the Liberal's spectacular losses on the Prairies in the general election of 1945. In Saskatchewan, the citadel of wheat and Liberal strength, the party's popular vote fell ten percentage points to the lowest level since 1921, and its seats were reduced from 12 to two. Mackenzie King lost Prince Albert, which he had held since 1926, and Gardiner squeaked through in Melville with a majority of 28 out of 20, 162 votes cast. These results gave added urgency to the government's, and especially Gardiner's, search for markets in the postwar period in the hope, thereby, of protecting the farmer from a repetition of the disastrous drop in price experienced after World War I.

As with everything else associated with the Board's history, this initiative was viewed in the West as a precedent which bound successor governments. And this presumption of government responsibility determined the course of later events: for those in power it meant they should try to sell wheat, while for the producer it meant government should be concerned about his welfare. Conflict over the meaning of responsibility ultimately defeated the Liberals in the fifties and firmly joined farmer to Tory in the sixties.

The Wheat Board originated in a concern about scarcity of income and crops. But the intractable problem of the postwar period has been recurring surpluses which, according to some observers, so distorted the grain-handling system 25 years ago that the effects still remain.[11] When the Liberals were defeated in 1957, a record volume of unsold wheat (640 million bushels) was piled on the Prairies, although the average annual marketing of all grain between 1945 and 1950 was only 458 million bushels. As a consequence, the huge carryover was the principal cause of the St Laurent government's unpopularity on the Prairies. The *Western Producer* commented:

> We do not say that the manner of financing pipelines is not important nor do we suggest that all the sound and fury has been inspired by political motives. But we do state that at the time when the failure of agriculture may be at stake it is sheer madness — a modern version of fiddling while Rome burns — to devote the time of the government and Parliament to what in comparison are minor matters.[12]

But it was less the government's inability than its apparent disinclination to move wheat that angered the farmers. Economic orthodoxy on the part of the Liberals once again proved the stumbling block. This time the lightning rod for discontent was C. D. Howe, Minister of Trade and Commerce since 1948, whose formidable talents and energy in different portfolios had piloted Canada's expansion for two decades (coincidentally up to the pipeline legislation itself) but whose knowledge of the grain trade, as engineer of most of the country's terminal elevators, was even older. Anxious to increase sales, western farmers and farm organizations pressed the government to grant easy credit and accept cheap money. Howe would do neither, arguing instead that sales on credit or for foreign currency would discriminate against and lose old customers. He did think the price of wheat might have to be reduced, as long as a "fetish" were not made of holding the line, but the farmers were unwilling to carry the cost despite the government's claim that they were better off than at any time in the last 25 years.[13] Cynics among them noted that the last quarter century began in the early thirties.

A related issue, which harmed Liberals most, was the debate over advance payments. Since farmers got paid only for wheat delivered to elevators, and since this was regulated by quotas which, because of the glut, were low or non-existent, they argued for some payment in advance of delivery. The suggestion was not new. It had been made at the beginning of the war, before there were quotas on deliveries and where congestion had occurred. After investigating the initial proposal the Liberals had decided the scheme could not be administered efficiently or fairly, since it did not get to the root of the problem of income disparity between rich and poor farmer. It would also impose on the Wheat Board, the only feasible administrative agent, a relief function that would conflict with its primary job of selling wheat. Thus, in the mid-fifties, the Liberals rejected the resurrected proposal with a finality that implied they knew better and, perhaps more inflammatory to westerners, that the problem was not as serious as claimed. Both Howe and St Laurent reminded prairie audiences that they should be thankful, not critical of "Providence's bounty."[14]

Eventually the government did respond with a scheme for low-interest bank loans, but farmers everywhere rejected this alternative, claiming that it meant they had to "pay" for their own money. The episode of the advance payments had serious repercussions for the Liberals beyond contributing to their defeat at the next election. First, it exacerbated relations between federal and provincial Liberals across the Prairies. In Alberta, already, the feeling was abroad among local Grits that the St Laurent government, especially Howe and the Alberta member, George Prudham, Minister of Mines and Technical Surveys, were too friendly with the Socred government in Edmonton and the oil industry in Calgary while they let the provincial group languish.[15] In Saskatchewan, where dissension was widespread, the provincial leader "Hammy" McDonald described the loan plan as "less effective than a stirrup pump at a forest fire."[16] The Manitoba Liberals, led by Douglas Campbell and still disguised as Liberal-Progressives, were the most conservative of the provincial parties. They criticized the loan scheme, the Liberals' wheat sales record (which the Manitoba Minister of Agriculture said he would improve by selling "to the devil himself" on easy credit) and the St Laurent government's health and welfare programs, which the premier described as "socialistic."[17]

But the loan scheme was equally significant for its effect upon Liberal relations with organized farm groups, particularly the three prairie Pools. They were held in the highest esteem by leading Liberal politicians and by senior public servants who looked upon these organizations as indispensable to the grain trade and as allies. Relations with the United Grain Growers were similarly close, stretching back to Crerar's agrarian leadership days. For the other farm organizations, especially the Farmer's Union, there was not such sentiment, although the Liberals sought not to antagonize even these groups, who they saw as CCF-inspired.

The debate over cash advances created a division between the Pools and the Liberal party which never disappeared. Ultimately they found themselves aligned with the CCF and the Farmers' Union in support of cash advances. Unlike these organizations the Pools did not condemn the bank loans, but they persisted in arguing that the scheme was insufficient. They had disagreed with federal legislation before but always there had been compromise leading to a reconciliation of positions. In alienating this traditionally friendly behemoth the government convinced many westerners, in the clearest possible way, that it was inept and remote, frailties not previously associated with the Liberal party.

The Diefenbaker Revolt

The Progressive Conservatives formed their government in June 1957 mainly as a result of a large shift in voter support in the Atlantic provinces and Ontario; Quebec and the Prairies followed suit nine months later. Time was needed to shatter Grit bedrock in those parts of the country used to seeing Progressive Conservatives as enemies, if they saw them at all. In the West the adjustment was helped by the new government's quick action on two pressing matters: early passage of the *Prairie Grain Advance Payments Act,* assented to less than a month after parliament opened in October 1957 and, the following January, the appointment of John Bracken, former Liberal-Progressive premier of Manitoba and later Progressive Conservative national leader, as a one-man royal commission to inquire into the distribution of boxcars.

The latter initiative signalled federal sympathy for a grievance that had aroused farmers but not Liberals for four years. Boxcars, like "crow rates," are one of those incandescent subjects which kindle western wrath with remarkable regularity. In the battle with the CPR and the elevator companies early in this century the farmers fought all the way to the Supreme Court, and won, the Sintaluta case, which upheld the individual producer's right to equality of treatment by the railroads in the distribution of cars needed to transport grain to lakehead terminals. The first-come, first-served principle in allocating box cars was a vital part of the farmer's much-vaunted freedom of choice. But 50 years later when the cooperatives owned the majority of elevators, a large percentage of which were filled with wheat, that freedom seemed illusory. Equality of boxcar distribution did not help clear a system whose member companies were unequal nor did it guarantee individual producers the right to patronize their own companies. Complaints which accompanied congestion increased in the wake of the Liberals' ineffectual responses.

Under Diefenbaker the Tories responded to western grievances in a manner different from their predecessors. It was not that they were initially more successful at dealing with the old problems — they were not — but their publicized open-door to farmers, leading directly to the prime minister, who was himself a westerner, assuaged the prairies' desire for attention, which in the fifties the Liberals seemed more often to withhold than to give.

Regional demands were often rejected by Liberals because they *were* regional: "[Howe] raised the question as to whether we could expect special treatment in Western Canada. Did we know that the fishermen at the Eastern Coast may be worse off than the wheat growers of the West?"[18]

The invocation of other interests to deflect prairie demands was not unique to C. D. Howe: Mackenzie King had done it years before and Pierre Trudeau, during another unmanageable wheat surplus, was to remind farmers of the same fishermen.[19] Liberal rejection of narrow regionalism was belied, westerners thought, by the friendly reception given to demands from the business interest of central Canada. As a result, Liberal pleas for economic flexibility and regional balance were interpreted more and more by westerners as a cavalier rejection of their interests.

The Diefenbaker government's disagreement with western demands which, after 1958 and in response to the ever-bulging granaries, took the form of petitions and delegations in support of deficiency payments, was never viewed in the same light. Deficiency payments were subject to wide interpretation but their irreducible minimum was a commodity support price which gave some surety of income. The familiar argument against the proposal, which the government employed, was that it favoured the large and prosperous over the small and marginal farmer. Although the Tories' alternative, acreage payments of up to $200 per farm, did not meet demands for income security, it was welcomed as an income supplement scheme but most of all as an indication of government responsiveness.

The claim of the Progressive Conservatives on the loyalties of the West was nurtured by the change in government attitudes, but it took root and flourished because of two events that occurred early in the sixties. One was the sale of massive quantities of wheat to Communist China. The sale meant a dramatic rise in income for prairie farmers and the onset of the greatest wave of prosperity in memory. But equally important was the buoyancy of spirit which followed. For the first time in ten years delivery quotas were removed and Alvin Hamilton, the Minister of Agriculture and minister responsible for the Wheat Board, called on farmers to grow all the wheat they could. While the Diefenbaker government had not been responsible for the Chinese crop disasters that led to the demand, they did claim credit for Canada's being chosen supplier of the needed wheat. The purchase had been promoted through the introduction of new credit arrangements that later become acceptable practice but at the time, because they were seen as unorthodox, earned the Tories lasting gratitude in the West.

The other event was really not a single happening but a series of governmental moves which together indicated confidence in the region's traditional institutions and way of life. Among these was the decision to go ahead with the South Saskatchewan River Dam, a project which had been promoted for a quarter century by Saskatchewan politicians of all stripes including M. J. Coldwell and T. C. Douglas, John Diefenbaker and J. G. Gardiner, the last of whom however had to acquiesce in a royal commission recommendation and a governmental decision in 1956 not to proceed with construction. Although the plan's irrigation scheme made diversification of agriculture a possibility, the project was seen, by supporters and detractors alike, as a rehabilitation undertaking which would increase grain productivity. Thus, for those who wanted to see wheat farmers more secure in their livelihood, the dam was a vote of confidence in prairie life.

So too was ARDA (*Agriculture and Rural Development Act*, 1961), which was intended to bolster the bases of rural society. The Act was associated with Alvin Hamilton and it reflected that minister's "rural fundamentalist faith in the rejuvenation of the farmer."[20] Any politician determined to protect the region against hostile economic forces, of international or domestic origin, was bound to win strong support. But Hamilton's "grass roots" appeal struck another responsive chord when he defended the farmer against government bureaucrats as well. Always wary of planners, he was especially scornful of politicians who listened to them or, as he later said, who "sold their soul to the mandarins."[21]

Indeed, the emergence since 1963 of far-flung plans and planners destined to renovate the wheat industry has multiplied the fears and complaints about anonymous advisers first articulated by the Tories nearly 20 years ago. The "big magician in the east" is synonymous with "the back-room boys drafting policy" since both are viewed as being engaged in "an academic exercise" unrelated and often in defiance of the realities of grain farming.[22] Because the New Democrats give free rein to boards and planners in the provinces where they exercise power, they too are held culpable by Tory critics.

The most remarkable feature of the Tory revolt on the Prairies has been its entrenchment since the party moved into opposition. If anything, that hold has grown as the Progressive Conservatives ring the changes on their past accomplishments. During the Pearson years, when there was no western minister of long standing in cabinet, the Liberals were ridiculed as ignorant about wheat and this ineptness (which over-shadowed a very creditable sales record) was used to counteract tales of Tory debacles in Ottawa. During the Trudeau period when one minister, Otto Lang, was identified for nearly a decade with the industry and attempts to modernize it, the Tories criticized Liberals not for ignorance but for being insensible to the region's way of life based on the traditional institutions of the wheat economy.

Western Tories, at least some of them, have also challenged the government's policy on bilingualism and biculturalism. That policy has never been popular and in 1969 when the *Official Languages Act* was before parliament, the prairie premiers of the Time (Harry Strom, Social Credit, of Alberta; W. Ross Thatcher, Liberal, of Saskatchewan; and Walter Weir, Progressive Conservative, of Manitoba) talked but did nothing to challenge its constitutionality. Whatever the philosophical base for this dissent, of which "unhyphenated Canadianism" is certainly an important element, it has been transmitted effectively through Progressive Conservative ranks. But that issue has cost the Progressive Conservatives dearly. The breaking of party ranks by Mr. Diefenbaker and 16 other Tories, all but one westerners, on the passage of the *Official Languages Act* thwarted Robert Stanfield in his attempt to open wider the party's doors to Quebec, intra-party opposition harassed Joe Clark in his attempt to appeal to Quebec, and Tory division over institutionalizing bilingualism in Manitoba was among Brian Mulroney's first challenges as leader. The defection of a Diefenbaker loyalist like Jack Horner to the Liberals, in 1977, and the nomination fights among Progressive Conservatives of different hues in the federal constituencies of Alberta are indicative in the continuing strength of those regional emotions first associated with the Diefenbaker revolt.[23]

Return of the Liberals

If Liberal success in the old days could be attributed to those provincial chieftains who sat in the federal cabinet but held sway over local tribes, so too could Liberal failure in 1957 and 1958. In the aftermath of defeat the Liberals set about constructing a new organization centred in Ottawa which assumed as its primary task the promotion and, it was hoped, eventual return of a federal Liberal government. Pursuit of this objective required that power over nominations and patronage, traditionally exercised in and for the Liberals of each province, be transferred to federally designated officials. Not only the conduct of campaigns but their focus was altered as well, first as part of a grand design "to win over to the Liberal party" CCF supporters in central Canada and, second, "to enforc[e] our strength in what might be described as the middle class group of people, particularly in Ontario."[24]

These changes in direction and strategy guaranteed conflict with areas like the Prairies, whose interests and political complexion were not those of the center. Compounding these problems, if not resulting from them, was the inability of prairie Liberals to get elected and stay elected. Relations between Ottawa and the region deteriorated after victory in 1963 secured for the foreseeable future the new organization's permanence. Each of the prairie provinces presented special problems, but it was in Saskatchewan where the flame of dissent burned brightest. There the provincial Liberals defeated the CCF in spite of tepid federal support and for the next seven years the fire of intra-party controversy was stoked by a series of policy disagreements as well as by the constant irritant of organizational strife. Across the Prairies the refusal of the federal Liberals to treat with their established provincial numbers was interpreted as bad faith and poor politics which would ultimately hurt all Liberals, even the strong Saskatchewan Grits who found themselves being held responsible for federal Liberal actions and policies they stoutly opposed.

The federal organization scheme introduced in the early sixties was scrapped later in the decade when it failed for a third time, in 1965, to give the Liberals the majority they wanted. After 1968 the party entered on yet another organizational venture, this time in response to the then popular principle of participatory democracy. The call for democratization of party structures and the abandonment of elite control from the center as well as the periphery, required a bridging of the organizational gap that had antagonized prairie Liberals for nearly ten years. The problem remained, however, that any structure, especially one claiming to be democratic, required cooperation to make it work. This was difficult to achieve when provincial Liberals were fighting for their lives and losing. In Alberta, for example, their share of the vote collapsed from 11 to one percent between 1967 and 1971 and in Manitoba it fell from 33 to 19 percent between 1966 and 1973. In Saskatchewan, the party had not yet begun as precipitous a decline in popular affection, but in 1971, it lost 20 of the 35 seats won in 1967 and its vote declined from 46 to 43 percent.

One symptom of an organization in decline is preoccupation with the subject of organization. The Alberta Liberals, whose demise has been frequently predicted, have made more fresh starts with charts, zones and chains of command than any party in power. The same was true of the Saskatchewan Liberals in the fifties when they alternated between blaming "Jimmy" Gardiner for their plight and reorganizing themselves. For federal Liberals on the Prairies the debate over organization, once it progresses beyond patronage matters, assumes an air of unreality; they think they have little influence on the outcome which, in any case, they consider relatively unimportant. Policies and personalities win elections, they argue, as they look to Tory precedent and the Diefenbaker organization which defied description.[25]

Despite the efforts of the party hierarchy, the breakthrough was not to be the result of personality. A legion of unsuccessful Liberal candidates whose personal attractiveness seemed hard to improve on and a succession of local notables, enticed by the prospect of a cabinet portfolio, proved no match for the Tories. If candidates who were eminently regional failed, then policies made in Ottawa for consumption in the St. Lawrence valley were unlikely to succeed. The reception given the federal government's language legislation has been discussed; in the sixties there was also the Carter Commission's recommendations and the subsequent white paper whose contents the West considered inflammatory. Changes in estate tax, introduction of capital gains tax, as well as the inclusion of all increases in economic gain as taxable income were interpreted as threats to the family farm, which passed from generation to generation as a gift or through inheritance. Proposed changes in tax exemptions on mineral exploration raised the cry of regional discrimination; for Ottawa seemed ready to close the door to investors in western Canada now that Quebec and Ontario had their mining industries. That at least was the view of a number of prairie politicians, especially Liberals, who had spent a good part of the decade fighting Walter Gordon's nationalist economic policies.

In the seventies the natural resources of Saskatchewan and Alberta became the subject of another dispute with Ottawa, this time over pricing. As the international price of oil soared the two provinces were urged to think of the national interest, have compassion for their less fortunate partners in Confederation (including Manitoba) and accept a negotiated increase. Exhortation proved fruitless however, and a tortuous series of events ensued before an energy accord could be reached in 1981. The defeat of the Liberals at the polls in 1979, their defeat of the Progressive Conservatives in parliament and the Liberal win in the subsequent general election were only part of the story. The debate over the retention of Petro-Canada as a public corporation had a differential impact on Canadian attitudes not least between Saskatchewan and Alberta with their NDP and PC governments. But intra-regional differences were papered over when the federal government announced its National Energy Policy. For here again appeared the familiar devil of federal intrusion: more than a century had passed since parliament had created Manitoba but retained her natural resources, yet in spite of the transfer of 1930 the avarice of federal authorities seemed never to wane.

In fact the provinces were already primed to react negatively by two Supreme Court of Canada decisions in 1978 and 1979. In the first (*Canadian Industrial Gas and Oil Ltd. v Government of Saskatchewan, et al.*) a provincial royalty tax to limit windfall gains accruing to petroleum producers was declared to be an indirect tax and therefore *ultra vires* the provincial legislature. In the second (*Central Canada Potash Co., Ltd., et al. v Government of Saskatchewan, et al.*), in which the federal government had entered as a co-plaintiff, the provincial government's attempt, begun by the Thatcher Liberals and continued by the NDP, to control potash production experienced the same fate, for it was seen as an interference with interprovincial and international trade.

Wheat, as usual, received great attention. The Pearson years had been prosperous for the Prairies but the Trudeau administration opened with a market slump that caused a drastic fall in farm income and an unmanageable surplus to clog the system. The federal government's remedy was LIFT (Lower Inventories for Tomorrow), a scheme that paid farmers not to grow wheat. Historically, acreage reduction had never been popular on the Prairies because, in effect, it put farmers on the dole. In the Canadian system the farmer produces all he can, the Wheat Board sells it and any restriction placed on the activities of either is blamed on the federal government. At its most popular, the LIFT program had a mixed reception but it was later roundly criticized as evidence of the Liberal government's lack of confidence in the farmers and in its own ability to get the system moving again.

The emotion triggered by the program was a measure of its impact. LIFT was an unprecedented break with traditional government wheat policy. In the face of surpluses the St Laurent government had waited and then provided low interest loans to help pay storage costs; the Diefenbaker government had also waited after giving cash advances on farm stored wheat, but the Trudeau government did not wait — it legislated the surplus out of existency by curtailing production. For an industry whose structure and function were imperceptibly different from a half century before, LIFT was a portent that roused concern and even alarm.

In the swift and sweeping program that followed the temporary acreage reduction, the government had two broad goals: to provide security of income for the region and to make the grain industry more efficient. Major legislation to achieve the first objective was a grain income stabilization plan based on contributory payments by producers and government from which western farmers as a group would benefit when income on the Prairies declined. The original legislation, introduced in 1970, had to be withdrawn because of prolonged opposition; it was eventually passed in amended form early in 1976. Significantly, the plan did not insure individual incomes — that would have conflicted with the government's belief that the grain industry had to become more, not less, responsive to change. In their desire for efficiency the Liberals thus opened themselves to the old charge that they would sacrifice the "family farm" and in turn those community institutions that depend on it.

The government's reply was to note that an industry so vital to Canada and in a competitive international market could be preserved in its original state but must be modernized if it was to be profitable. As a major wheat exporter Canada is in a unique situation — its grain is grown over a vast area and collected at thousands of delivery points, hauled a thousand miles or more to only three seaports (Vancouver, Thunder Bay and Churchill), the last two of which are ice-locked for more than half the year. The Crow Rates, the ancient roadbeds and the hundreds of antiquated elevators were seen in Ottawa as serious liabilities to achieving efficiency.

The government appointed commissions of inquiry to study the first two (the last depended on action by the elevator companies). During the past 15 years federal research and policy advisers had demonstrated why changes should be made, but their exhaustive findings still were not convincing to the large body of western opinion, which feared change, especially when it was recommended by outside experts.... Therefore, with the federal government (for so long synonymous with the Liberal party) depicted as insensitive and the federal bureaucracy unresponsive, the possibility of popular reform to this major industry seemed dim.

After the Liberals came back into power in 1980, with only two seats of 77 in the four western provinces, they appeared committed to changing the ground rules of the grain industry. During the campaign Mr. Trudeau had talked of doubling prairie trackage and thereby speeding grain haulage. Later, after concerted consultation with farm groups, it was announced that the Crow Rates would be abolished. Notwithstanding differences in cabinet over how this should be done, or opposition from the Saskatchewan and Manitoba governments over the principle of change, or alarm from Quebec meat producers about the effect of change on their livelihood, or obstruction of parliamentary debate by the NDP and PC parties to highlight the significance of the changes, the Crow Rates seem destined to disappear by the early 1990s. Whether a more efficient industry will follow in the wake of higher freight rates and a modernized grain handling system remains to be seen.

Epilogue

The NDP has hardly figured in the foregoing discussion. The reason for this omission is that, in federal politics, the Liberals had always been involved in reciprocal combat with the Progressive Conservatives. This is a strategy that prairie Liberals have often disputed, for instance in Saskatchewan where they look to PC voters to help them dislodge the NDP, but one which federal Liberals have pursued as recently as the constitutional and energy-pricing debates. An NDP premier like Allan Blakeney, despite his impressive national reputation, ultimately had only marginal public influence on the resolution of the constitutional impasse, although it needs to be acknowledged that the addition of the resource amendment (s92A) to the Constitution Act, 1867, goes some distance in breaking that part of the impasse occasioned by conflict over natural resources.[26] There was indeed irony here, for *inter alia,* Blakeney's cautious strategy on behalf of constituitonal change retorted against him and his government in the provincial election of 1982, when the NDP lost 70 percent of the seats it formerly held in the legislature.

Nothing could demonstrate more clearly the hegemony of the Liberals in national politics than this fact: they remain in power despite the repeated electoral failure of their candidates on the prairies. Nor could there be stronger evidence of the prairie region's exclusion from national political influence. That no third party has emerged in this long period of regional political eclipse is impressive testimony as well to the hold the old parties have on national politics. To date western separatist groups have failed to secure a place in provincial or federal elections, while the NDP, as friction between its federal and provincial wings over the constitutional resolution demonstrated, remains an uncertain voice of western interests. The sudden rise in 1982 of a PC government in Saskatchewan for the first time ever introduces a truly unknown quantity into provincial politics on the Prairies. For despite the name, its antecedents and subsequent policies in power suggest a movement more populist than conservative and thus an effect on federal politics that well remained minimal. The two old parties will continue to dominate federal politics in the region and as long as the Liberals continue to rule, the region will find satisfaction in aligning itself with the principal opposition party.

ENDNOTES

1. Margaret Atwood, *Survival: A Thematic Guide to Canadian Literature* (Toronto: Anansi, 1972), p. 123.
2. Vernon C.Fowke, "National Policy and Western Development," *Journal of Economic History,* XVI, No. 4 (December 1956), p. 476.
3. W. T. Easterbrook, "Recent Contributions to Economic History: Canada," *Journal of Economic History,* XIX, No. 1 (March 1959), p. 99.
4. Mildred A. Schwartz, *Politics and Territory: The Sociology of Regional Persistence in Canada* (Montreal: McGill-Queen's University Press, 1974), p. 102.
5. Jane Jenson, "Aspects of Partisan Change: Class Relations and the Canadian Party System," (Unpublished paper prepared for the Conference on Political Change, Saskatoon, March 1977), p. 17.
6. See J. E. Rea, "The Roots of Prairie Society," in David P. Gagan, ed., *Prairie Perspectives* (Toronto: Holt, Rinehart and Winston, 1970) pp. 46-55, and "My mainline is the kiddies...make them good Christians and good Canadians, which is the same thing," in W. Isajiw, ed., *Identities: The Impact of Ethnicity on Canadian Society* (Toronto: Peter Martin Associates, 1977), pp. 3-11. See, as well, "Separate Statement," by J. B. Rudnyckyj in Canada, *Report of the Royal Commission on Bilingualism and Biculturalism.* Book I (Ottawa: Queen's Printer, 1967), pp. 155-69.
7. Lewis Herbert Thomas, *The Struggle for Responsible Government in North-West Territories, 1870-97* (Toronto: University of Toronto Press, 1956), ch. 2.
8. King Diary, March 21, 1939, quoted in C. F. Wilson, *A Century of Canadian Grain: Government Policy to 1951,* (Saskatoon, Sask.: Western Producer Prairie Books, 1978), 596.
9. King Diary, April 20, 1939, and March 5-7, 1941, in Wilson, p. 680.
10. Vernon C. Fowke, *The National Policy and the Wheat Economy* (Toronto: University of Toronto Press, 1957), p. 276.
11. United Grain Growers Limited, "Submission to the Grain Handling and Transportation Commission (Hall Commission)," October 24, 1975.
12. *Western Producer* (editorial), May 24, 1956, p. 6.
13. *Ibid.* June 17, 1954, p. 4.
14. *Ibid.* (editorial), May 15, 1957, p. 6.
15. Interview with Nick Taylor, leader and past president of the Alberta Liberal Association, December 1976; taped interview with J. C. Gardiner by Una Maclean Evans, December 29, 1961 — January 5, 1962, tape No. 6. These tapes are deposited in the Glenbow Alberta Institute. For a general discussion of the period, see John Richards and Larry Pratt, *Prairie Capitalism: Power and Influence in the New West,* (Toronto: McClelland and Stewart, 1979), chs. 3 and 4.
16. *Western Producer,* October 27, 1955, p. 1.
17. *Ibid.,* November 15, 1955, p. 1. and Winnipeg *Free Press,* June 26, 1957, p. 1.
18. *Ibid.,* December 3, 1953, p. 1 (magazine).
19. King Diary, April 24, 1939 quoted in Wilson, pp. 600-01 and *Western Producer,* July 31, 1969, p. 5.
20. Anthony G. S. Careless, *Initiative and Response: The Adaptation of Canadian Federalism to Regional Economic Development* (Montreal: McGill-Queen's University Press, 1977), pp. 75-6.
21. Canada, *House of Commons Debates,* May 3, 1977, p. 5257.

22. *Western Producer*, January 14, 1971, p. 8 and November 11, 1971, p. 13.

23. This bizarre behavior is confined almost exclusively to that province, where the hold of Progressive Conservatives could hardly, in a democratic system, be more total. But as V.O. Key pointed out more than thirty years ago, such behavior is not unusual where one party dominates. *Southern Politics*, (New York: Vintage Books, 1949) pp. 310-11.

24. National Liberal Federation Papers, Public Archives of Canada, W. Ross Thatcher to Lester Pearson, February 24, 1960 and D. K. McTavish (N.L.F. President) to J.J. Connolly, February 27, 1958.

25. Interviews with A.R. O'Brien (National Director of the Liberal Party, 1966-69), January 1977 and Senator H. W. Hays (Minister of Agriculture, 1963-65) February 1977.

26. For an interesting application of the new Section's provisions to the Supreme Court decisions of 1978 and 1979, see William D. Moull, "Section 92A of the Constitution Act, 1867," *Canadian Bar Review*, 61(Dec. 1983), 715-34. See, too, John Bishop Ballem, "Oil and Gas Under the New Constitution," *Canadian Bar Review*, 61(Sept. 1983), 547-58.

25 Quasi-democracy in Alberta*

GARTH STEVENSON

The re-election of Peter Lougheed's Progressive Conservatives with an increased majority in November 1982 suggests the need for a renewed examination of Alberta politics, and of the underlying forces that contribute to their distinctiveness. The duration of Lougheed's rule is still far from unusual, but the overwhelming character of his electoral success has few if any parallels. In three consecutive elections the Alberta Progressive Conservatives have won approximately three-fifths of the popular vote and more than 90 per cent of the seats in the legislature. No party openly calling itself conservative has ever achieved such success under conditions of universal suffrage in the entire history of the world, let along of Canada.

The success of the governing party, formidable as it is, has been matched by a fragmentation of the opposition. In 1982, as in 1979, the principal opposition party was able to attract only half of all the votes cast against the government party. Support for the NDP in 1982, like that for Social Credit in 1979, was concentrated in a few regions of the province while Progressive Conservative support was quite evenly distributed. Most ridings had at least three opposition candidates running in 1982, but, in a sense, that hardly affected the outcome, since the Progressive Conservative candidate won an absolute majority in all but seven ridings.

Lougheed's overwhelming victory in 1982 was the more surprising since there were reasons to anticipate that his majority might be substantially reduced. In fact, conditions seemed almost ideal for the opposition, suggesting that if they could not make a breakthrough in 1982, they could not do so at all.

The economy was in recession, with unemployment close to 10 per cent. Although to some extent this reflected national conditions, as well as the soft state of the oil market throughout the world, it drew attention to

---

*Reprinted from The Canadian Forum, February, 1983, by permission of the author and the editor.

Lougheed's failure to diversify and strengthen the province's economic base, as he had promised to do when the Heritage Savings Trust Fund was established in 1976.

Federal-provincial conflict had subsided since the settlement of the Constitutional issue, largely on Alberta's terms, a year before the election. It seemed improbable that Lougheed could base his campaign on the need for a united front against "Ottawa," as he had done in two previous elections.

As John Diefenbaker used to say, the only poll that counts is the one on election day and half an hour after the polls closed, it was obvious that the new legislature would be little different from the old. However, the distribution of popular votes was interesting. The NDP increased its vote substantially in Edmonton, where it won 32.3 per cent of the votes cast, but the party made no progress anywhere else. WCC support was quite evenly spread across the rural areas where the two opposition parties proved to be about equal in strength, but the separatists made no inroads in the cities. The Progressive Conservatives won more than 70 per cent of the vote in the southern cities of Calgary, Lethbridge and Medicine Hat, more than 60 per cent in the province's agricultural heartland, and more than 50 percent in Edmonton and the north. Although there were more than a hundred candidates bearing a variety of other labels, including Liberal and Social Credit, they collectively managed to win less than seven per cent of the votes cast.

In short, the dissatisfied and the dispossessed divided their votes between two very different opposition parties, neither of which is likely to make a major breakthrough in the foreseeable future. The separatist Western Canadian Concept represents a substantial current of rural populism, but its support is too scattered to have much impact under the current electoral system, and the increasing urbanization of the province will work against it in the long run. It may not disappear immediately, but is seems fated to repeat the decline and fall of the Creditiste party in rural Quebec, which in many ways it closely resembles.

The NDP is clearly more vigorous than the WCC, and it does have a strong base in one of the two major cities, but its prospects outside of Edmonton do not look promising. Even in Edmonton much of the NDP strength may be more apparent than real. The distribution of NDP votes across the city did not correlate very strongly with class or level of income. This suggests both that the party has failed to secure a really strong working class base and also that its apparent support includes many middle class voters who could easily drift back to the Tories. Many of these middle class Edmontonians voted NDP because of local issues such as the absence of a children's hospital and the inequitable sharing of long-distance telephone revenues between the provincial and municipal utilities. The ability of an astute government, backed by the Heritage Savings Trust Fund, to deal with this kind of discontent should not be underestimated.

"...Once a quasi-party state has been established in a quasi-colonial and predominantly *petit-bourgeois* society it may persist indefinitely if the economy of which it is part shows (even intermittently) sufficient expansiveness to contain the aspirations of the electorate; yet no expansiveness can be expected to bring about a reversion to the orthodox party system. It is this which makes it probable that the quasi-party system is the new permanent system in Alberta."

There are more than twice as many people in Alberta today as there were when C. B. Macpherson wrote the words quoted above, and the province's economy has been transformed almost beyond recognition . Yet the more things change, the more they remain the same. Three decades after the publication of *Democracy in Alberta*, the province's politics, as Macpherson predicted, still deviate as conspicuously from the norm as they did when television was a novelty, milk was delivered in glass bottles, and the railways ran on solid fuel. How can one explain this continuity when everything else has changed?

Macpherson's analysis of Alberta politics emphasized the *petit-bourgeois* character of the province and its "quasi-colonial" relationship with Central Canada as explanations for the absence of a normal party system. It is sometimes assumed that the first part of the explanation has been made obsolete by the relative decline of agriculture and the expansion of the petroleum industry. In addition, the size of the Heritage Savings Trust Fund and the ability of Alberta to impose a bizarre constitutional amending formula on the rest of the nation, as it did in 1981, hardly suggest that the province is a helpless dependency of Ottawa and Toronto.

All of this is true, but to suppose that these changes must produce equally dramatic changes in the politics of Alberta is to fall victim to a rather primitive kind of economic determinism. Ideologically, and therefore politically, Alberta remains the prisoner of its past. The persistence of *petit-bourgeois* attitudes and values is revealed most clearly in the universal obsession with real estate. Even young unattached people seem to buy a house at the first opportunity, and apartment dwellers are openly regarded with contempt by Tory politicians, and indeed by most of the population. Duddy Kravitz's grandfather, who believed that "a man without land is nothing," would have found many kindred spirits in Alberta.

A similar ideological backwardness is apparent in the perception of federal-provincial relations. While Alberta is not in fact a dependency of central Canada, and while it is neither oppressed nor exploited in any meaningful sense, most people still talk as though it were. Even NDP supporters sometimes argue in all seriousness that Prime Minister Trudeau is a dictator, that the concentration of secondary manufacturing in Ontario is the result of some mysterious conspiracy, or that representation by population in the House of Commons is unfair to "the west." While Lougheed did not exploit such sentiments as blatantly in 1982 as in previous election campaigns, he benefited from them nonetheless. The Tory election slogan "for Alberta," which appeared on every leaflet and lawn sign, clearly implied that the province needed to maintain a united front against external enemies, and the premier said so explicitly in the last days of the campaign when he warned that Prime Minister Trudeau would be happy if too many opposition candidates were elected to the legislature.

Both the *petit-bourgeois* and the quasi-colonial aspects of Albertan ideology originated in an agrarian setting, but both are equally compatible with the interests of the established order in a province that has made the transition to a petroleum-based economy. Petroleum supports a multitude of small entrepreneurs both directly and indirectly in the service sector of the economy. With its *nouveau riche* mentality, and its congenital suspicion of interventionist central governments, petroleum fits uneasily into the mainstream culture of mature corporate capitalism. It has accentuated, rather than reduced, Alberta's economic distinctiveness in relation to the rest of Canada. Anti-federal rhetoric and the cult of "free enterprise" help to stir up mass resentment against the enemies of the petroleum industry and also divert attention from the uncomfortable fact that Alberta has a higher percentage of American ownership in its economy than any other province. *Petit-bourgeois* ideology remains plausible, also, because every Albertan does in a sense have a direct stake in commodity production through the Heritage Fund and the ability of oil revenues to substitute for tax revenues.

Despite the fact that it bears the same label as conventional parties in other provinces, Lougheed's Progressive Conservative Party is actually a quasi-party in Macpherson's sense of the term. To its convinced supporters the conventional notion that a functioning legislature requires both a government and a loyal opposition is simply unintelligible, or at least inappropriate to Albertan circumstances. Not only would viable opposition parties weaken Alberta in relation to the external enemy, according to Alberta Tories, but opposition parties are unnecessary because there are no significant conflicts of interest within the province, or at least none that the Progressive Conservative Party cannot accommodate.

An interesting extension of this argument, often used by Progressive Conservative candidates in the 1983 election, is the assertion that the actual democratic process takes place not between parties, but within the governing party. On the one hand Alberta Tories boast about the free expression of opinion and the democratic decision-making that allegedly occur within their legislative caucus. Unfortunately such claims cannot be verified, since the caucus meets in secret, and the experience of former MLA Tom Sindlinger, who was expelled from the caucus as a penalty for ideological deviation in 1980, hardly adds to their credibility. Yet they seem to be widely accepted.

The second half of the argument is that the so-called "open conventions" at which Progressive Conservative candidates are chosen provide a more

meaningful form of democratic choice than the election itself. Competition
for nominations is of course keen since acceptance as the party's candidate
means almost certain election to the legislature. The wholesale distribution
of "memberships" by contenders for nomination is cited as evidence that
the party represents the entire population, with the possible exception of
those misguided enough not to believe in "free enterprise" and the compact
theory of Confederation. The same assumption is implicit in the question
that Tory canvassers are instructed to ask during election campaigns: "Can
we count on your vote?" The question is uncomfortably suggestive of the
totalitarian syndrome in which voting is viewed as a ritualistic expression
of support for the regime, rather than an act of meaningful choice.

Yet, as Macpherson argued, a quasi-party system is not the same as a
one-party system, despite superficial similarities. If there is a precedent for
Lougheed's Alberta, it is not to be found among the single-party dictator-
ships of either the left or the right. The analogy that fits best, and one that
has never been referred to in the literature on Alberta politics, is the
American South between the end of reconstruction and the second reconstruction of the 1960's.

Southern politics in those years were distinguished by the absence of
any effective alternative to the Democratic party in national as well as in
state and local elections. The hegemony of the southern Democrats, like
that of the Tories in present-day Alberta, was founded on an ideology that
glorified the region's allegedly distinctive "way of life" and denounced the
threat to it supposedly posed by outsiders, including the federal government. Memories of the Civil War and reconstruction were manipulated by
politicians much as memories of the depression and Alberta's quasi-colonial
past are manipulated in present day Alberta.

The consequences of this in the South were similar to those now becoming visible in Lougheed's Alberta. Both state and national elections became
mere perfunctory rituals, while the Democratic primaries — the precise
equivalent of Alberta's "open conventions" — became the effective mechanism for the selection of political officeholders. As political competition
degenerated into mere struggles between personalities and factions, serious
political issues were ignored. The wealth and power of the dominant class,
and of large corporations, were accepted without question, since the
resentment of the masses was diverted to external scapegoats. The illusion
that there were no internal conflicts of any consequence contributed to a
situation in which inequality and injustice grew steadily worse. The health,
education, and welfare of the people degenerated, at least in relation to the
rest of the nation, along with the standards of political propriety and
morality.

At this point the analogy must end, with a question mark. The South
was eventually rescued from itself by the combined pressure of the black
masses from within and the federal administration from without. Unfortunately, it is not clear who, if anyone, will rescue Alberta.

26 Socialism, Federalism and the B.C. Party Systems 1933-1983*

ALAN C. CAIRNS AND DANIEL WONG

During the past forty years, British Columbia's federal and provincial party systems have moved increasingly apart. Since World War II the federal arena has displayed an evolving mix of voter support and representation for the Liberals, Conservatives and NDP — supplemented by a brief Social Credit appearance of strength in the 1950s — while provincially the two old parties have faded badly and today have been all but completely displaced by Social Credit and the NDP. Thus of the four parties which compete for the favour of the electorate, only one — the NDP — now operates with reasonable strength at both levels. The old parties, which jointly accounted for almost two-thirds of the B.C. federal vote in 1980, received only 5.5 percent of the vote in the provincial election of the previous year, and only 3.9 percent in 1983. Conversely, Social Credit, which has held provincial office for all but three years in the past three decades, has ceased to exist as a federal contender.

The divergence of British Columbia's party systems is part of a more general tendency toward federal-provincial party system asymmetry. The federal system itself is obviously open to distinctive party system complexes in the federal and provincial arenas of each province. However, the divergence of the two party systems does not always happen. When it does the primary explanation is found in the interaction of the structural features of federalism and parliamentary government with political phenomena operating in the province.

At the onset of the depression of the 1930s, Liberals and Conservatives dominated B.C. politics both federally and provincially. However, their control was effectively challenged by the arrival of a new socialist party, the Co-operative Commonwealth Federation (later the NDP) in 1933. Suddenly both party systems had to accommodate themselves to a strong new con-

*This article is a shortened version of a paper written for the University of Victoria, B.C. Project funded by the Social Sciences and Humanities Research Council of Canada.

TABLE 1   **Liberal and Conservative Strength in B.C. Federal Elections 1896-1930**
(percent of vote)

Year	Liberal	Conservative	Total
1896	49.1	45.0	94.1
1900	45.9	40.9	86.8
1904	49.5	38.8	88.3
1908	35.9	46.8	82.7
1911	37.5	58.8	96.3
1917	25.6 (a)	68.4 (b)	94.0
1921	29.8	47.9	77.7
1925	34.7	49.3	84.0
1926	37.0	54.2	91.2
1930	40.9	49.3	90.2

(a) Opposition
(b) Government

tender dedicated to the eventual downfall of the free enterprise system, support for which had long been a hallmark of both Liberals and Conservatives. Moreover, the CCF's attempts to construct a mass party, stressing membership control over policy and leaders, contrasted sharply with the cadre structure and basic political style of the old parties.

The two party systems ultimately reacted to this challenge differently. Although both were affected by the CCF's presence, they were prompted down separate evolutionary paths. The provincial system was transformed radically, with the CCF and its chief adversary, Social Credit, almost completely supplanting the old parties. In contrast, the B.C. federal party system adjusted much more easily, quietly incorporating the CCF into a competitive multiparty system.

We argue that the divergence of the party systems can be traced to the different response of the party elites in the two arenas to the presence of a viable left-wing movement in the province. While voters have the final say in the development of party systems, the catalytic function is located elsewhere. In this study we argue that the voters' choice can only be understood in the context of the prior structuring of electoral choices by party elites.

The practical problem of containing an electorally formidable left-wing party has been a dominant concern in B.C. provincial politics since World War II. It has not been a significant problem in the B.C. federal arena. The different significance of the left in the two arenas of B.C. politics drove the province's party systems along divergent paths.

The polarized politics of the provincial party system has often been explained in terms of class divisions inherent in B.C. society. Yet the B.C. federal party system, which is presumably influenced by that same class divided society, has not been similarly polarized. Since the same society, therefore, is capable of simultaneously supporting two very different party systems, the explanation of either party system or of the differences between them cannot be found exclusively in the provincial society and economy.

The explanation lies in Canadian federalism, which requires the electorate as well as the party elites to respond consciously to different sets of issues, processes, and events at each level.

Provincial politics in B.C. became polarized as a result of complex interactions involving the parliamentary system of government, with its bias toward executive stability based on secure legislative majorities, the strength of the provincial left, and the political manoeuvres of a succession of party leaders from John Hart and R.L. Maitland to Bill Bennett. No similar polarization occurred in B.C. federal politics, not because the left was weaker, which until recently was not the case, but because the potential consequences attributed to left wing provincial strength were not attributed to similar left wing federal strength in the province.

Background: The British Columbia Party Systems to 1933

In order to fully appreciate the CCF's impact upon party politics in British Columbia, it is worth noting that from 1903 to 1933 the federal and provincial party systems of the province were both dominated by Liberals and Conservatives. They monopolized the party systems at both levels, rarely capturing less than eighty percent of the popular vote between them.

From 1896 to the depression of the 1930s there was a consistent, but fluctuating, left wing presence in the B.C. federal party system in the form of Socialist, Labour, Progressive, Communist, and Independent candidates,

TABLE 2 **Liberal and Conservative Strength in B.C. Provincial Elections 1903-1928 (percent of vote)**

Year	Liberal	Conservative	Total
1903	38.5	46.4	84.9
1907	38.0	47.0	85.0
1909	33.8	53.3	87.1
1912	19.4	64.6	84.0
1916	50.9	41.3	92.2
1920	36.9	32.8	69.7
1924	32.5	31.6	64.1
1928	40.9	52.4	93.3

TABLE 3 **Three Partyism in Federal and Provincial Elections, British Columbia, 1933-41 (percent of vote)**

Year	Liberal	Conservative	C.C.F.	Other
1933 (Provincial)	41.7%	—	31.5	26.7
1935 (Federal)	31.8	24.6	33.6	11.1
1937 (Provincial)	37.3	28.6	28.6	5.5
1940 (Federal)	37.4	30.5	28.4	3.7
1941 (Provincial)	32.9	30.9	33.4	2.8

but they were typically more of an irritant than a threat to Liberal and Conservative supremacy.

Throughout this period provincial politics housed a vigorous but small left wing presence. However, the left did not constitute a serious challenge to the Liberal-Conservative party system. It was wracked by internal divisions, and torn by the staple controversy of all democratic socialist movements; the relative significance to be accorded electoral competition as opposed to socialist education. Further, the left often found itself undercut by the governments' generally progressive welfare and labour policies. While both the Liberals and the Conservatives were basically sympathetic to state-aided capitalist expansion, they were also successful in courting the labour vote, and by the late twenties had put B.C. in the vanguard of welfare state development in Canada.

Peaceful Accommodation of the Left in the Thirties

The emergence of the CCF in 1933 did not immediately result in a divergence of party systems in British Columbia. The new party was incorporated with a minimum of difficulty, and by 1940, three-partyism was established at both the federal and provincial levels. There was little evidence, even in the provincial arena, of the intensely polarized politics that were to appear in the next decade.

The CCF was not the central issue in either federal or provincial politics in the province throughout the 1930s. Provincially it could not have been so as long as a three-party system survived; federally it was unlikely to be the central issue as long as it was a weak contender in the country as a whole.

The weakness of the CCF in the thirties further minimized the incentives for old-party collaboration against the left. Throughout this period the CCF was hindered by its own disunity as it struggled to bring together the divergent factions huddling uneasily beneath its banner. In addition, the party's representation in the Legislative Assembly and in the House of Commons was proportionately much less than its share of the popular vote.

However, with three strong contenders, provincial party politics in British Columbia were potentially unstable. The CCF had outdistanced both its major competitors in votes in the province in the 1935 federal election, a performance which, if duplicated in a provincial contest, was unlikely to be treated casually.

Coalition: The Simplification of Provincial Politics and the Ascendancy of the Anti-Socialist Issue

The era of Liberal dominance under Duff Pattullo crumbled when the 1941 provincial election, a quiet election fought in the shadow of World War II, produced only a shaky Liberal minority government. The CCF, with the largest share of the vote at 33.4 percent, received 14 seats; the Liberals won 21 seats with 32.9 percent of the vote, and the Conservatives 12 seats with 31 percent.

In the 1941 election, the CCF was clearly a factor, but not the major campaign issue. The election was generally low key. In the context of the second World War — at a time when France had fallen, Europe had been overrun, Nazi forces were advancing rapidly on the Russian front, and the position of the Allies provided few grounds for optimism — purely provincial issues paled in importance. The chief election issue was Pattullo's leadership following his much criticized provincialist hard-line stand against federal proposals at the 1941 Dominion-Provincial Conference on the Rowell-Sirois Report. While the CCF was clearly not viewed as just another party at this time, it had not yet become the catalyst to unite the non-left and to make socialism and its containment the overriding issue in B.C. electoral politics.

Pressures for coalition were generated by the failure of the 1941 election to produce a single party majority at a time when strong and stable leadership in government seemed to be required by the wartime situation. The possibility of all three parties joining together foundered on the unwillingness of the CCF to participate. Consequently, after a complicated series of negotiations a Liberal-Conservative coalition was put together with former Liberal finance minister John Hart as Premier and Conservative leader R.L. Maitland as Attorney-General.

The uniting of Liberals and Conservatives launched B.C. provincial politics on a distinctive evolutionary path and disrupted the symmetry of the two party systems operating in the province. Coalition at the provincial level was not duplicated in federal politics at the national level. When the coalition broke up in 1952, both parties found themselves in weak positions vis-à-vis the CCF, whose provincial electoral strength had improved as a consequence of coalition, and Social Credit, which was to be the main beneficiary of old-party decline.

Coalition made a major contribution to the ideological polarization of provincial politics. While the elementary left-right struggle, which was to become the animating theme in subsequent provincial elections, dates partially from the inception of the CCF in the province, and has roots in earlier rhetoric, its full-blown expression dates from the coalition period.

The transformation of coalition into an engine of anti-socialism had several causes. First, the CCF's independent stance on the war issue provided ammunition for a Liberal-Conservative coalition regime charged with seeing the province through a national emergency as a loyal member of the Dominion and as an agent of the Allied effort.

Second, a wartime increase in CCF support both within and without British Columbia fed coalition fears that neither the Liberals nor the Conservatives could win the next provincial election alone.

Third, various international factors contributed to ideological polarization in B.C. during the coalition era. The victories of social democratic parties in the United Kingdom, New Zealand and Australia helped to structure the B.C. debate by providing external models in which similar confrontations were taking place. Such external events also muted any suggestions that the forces of democratic socialism were either ephemeral or idiosyncratically confined to the west coast environment. The emergence of the Cold War carried this polarizing trend one step further, for the pro-Soviet sympathies of a handful of CCF officials accentuated the ideological rift in B.C. politics.

Finally, the coalition's strident postwar response to the growing strength of the left was spurred on by the changes of leadership within both of its constituent parties. When Maitland died in 1946 his place as Conservative leader and as number two man in the cabinet was taken by Herbert Anscomb, a staunch defender of the right, who viewed the CCF as a cancerous growth and who, from his position as Finance Minister, launched polemical attacks on the left. In the election campaign of 1949 Anscomb vowed, in collaboration with the new Liberal leader and Premier Byron Johnson, to "carry on the coalition for the duration of the emergency, the emergency caused by the spread of the evil of communism, and its brother, socialism."[1]

As the war moved to its conclusion, British Columbia found itself with a de facto two-party system in which the contestants had come to define themselves in terms of a grand competition between the free enterprise of the coalition and the democratic socialism of the CCF.

For the coalition, socialism was a compelling and useful election issue. Both the 1945 and 1949 elections were fought as principled crusades between the rising tide of socialism and the hallowed forces of capitalism, and in both contests the left was convincingly defeated. With some 55.8 percent of the popular vote in 1945 and 61.4 percent in 1949, the coalition partners came to believe that the CCF, powerful as it may have been, might be contained by methods other than coalition.

Yet despite its apparent success, the coalition proved to be more damaging to its Liberal and Conservative components than to the CCF. Although the

CCF would not win a provincial election in B.C. until 1972, long after its transformation into the New Democratic Party, from the middle of the coalition era onward its role as one of the driving forces in west coast provincial party politics was firmly established. It survived as the second party in the system, while the Liberals and Conservatives never recovered from the breakup of the coalition.

As a result of their resounding victories in 1945 and 1949, the Liberal and the Conservative coalitionists felt able to relax their anti-socialist stance and turn their political attentions elsewhere. In the absence of additional unifying factors, the magnitude of the coalition victories, especially in 1949, eroded the two parties' willingness to sacrifice their separate political identities. Differences of opinion over the perquisites of office and personal acrimony between Anscomb and Johnson were symptoms of a growing coalition malaise. The incompleteness of the merger, with both parties keeping separate organizations, holding separate conventions, and even meeting in separate caucuses, meant that at any time either partner could terminate the arrangement. The continuing submergence of Liberal-Conservative tensions had depended on the widely held perception of a left-wing threat incapable of containment as long as the coalition partners acted alone. The 1949 election results deeply demoralized the CCF, and its apparent foundering fed beliefs that the sacrifices coalition imposed upon the Liberals and Conservatives might no longer be necessary.

Moreover, at the federal level there was no pressure for anti-socialist unity between Liberals and Conservatives, for the CCF's weakness did not require it. Further, the federal wings of both parties were dismayed by the B.C. coalition, which they saw as damaging both old party machinery and voter loyalties. By the decade's end, both coalition partners were under heavy pressure from their federal wings to end the alliance, and in 1952 the arrangement was terminated with Johnson's firing of Anscomb.

The Search for Alternative Strategies to Contain the Left

Two new approaches surfaced to combat the CCF in the wake of Liberal-Conservative disengagement. The first was an ingenious new electoral system employing the single transferable ballot. The second was a new, or effectively new, third party in the form of Social Credit, which was to become the bastion of anti-socialist politics in British Columbia for the next two decades.

The single transferable ballot (STB) was explicitly designed to prevent a minority socialist victory. It was an electoral experiment intended to provide the traditional parties with the opportunity to vie for increased shares of the non-socialist vote, without paying the price of having the CCF win office with only minority voter support.

Behind the experiment was the implicit belief that a minority socialist victory was not only undesirable on practical grounds, but was unacceptable on democratic grounds. The former raised the exaggerated spectre of a root and branch socialism destroying the B.C. way of life. The latter was based on the assumption that an anti-socialist, or at least a non-socialist, majority clearly existed in the province and that it was a denial of democracy to allow secondary divisions within that majority to frustrate its rightful claim to power. Electoral reform was thus an idiosyncratic reversal of the old "divide and conquer" strategy wherein parties and governments keep the opposition weak by playing on its internal divisions. In this case, the proponents of electoral reform sought not to divide their opponents but to prevent their own divisions from allowing the left to rule.

The electoral experiment presupposed a three-party contest in which Liberals and Conservatives would trade second place votes with each other and thus forestall minority socialist victories by aggregating old party voters behind the strongest old party contender in each constituency. Assuming that the voters shared, or could be induced to share, the old party strategists' perceptions of the party spectrum, the CCF could win only where it had majority support on the first count.

However, the STB was not, and could not have been, more than a partial and short-term response to the dilemmas implicit in the various competing purposes of the major non-left actors in the party system. It was inherently unlikely to produce a stable, practical reconciliation, lasting over several elections, of the simultaneous desire to return to a multiparty system and to generate the electoral outcomes of an enduring non-left government, which presupposed one single overriding division in the electorate. Although the STB facilitated electoral competition on the non-left, it could not guarantee a single party majority. It could not therefore guarantee against the recurrence of post-election coalitions as a means of ensuring government stability and keeping the left out, nor therefore against future federal-provincial intraparty tensions such as those which had hurt the Johnson-Anscomb regime. Further, if it had produced a majority Liberal or Conservative government, such a government might return to the first-past-the-post system in an attempt to consolidate its hold on power, thus potentially reinstating those instabilities of a multi-party system which had required coalition in the first place. Finally, the successful operation of such an electoral system required a high degree of political skill and discipline by Liberal and Conservative politicians, for it was necessary, simultaneously, to attack one's former coalition partner while pursuing the even more fundamental consideration of blocking the left by strategic second place voting. The danger clearly existed that the secondary battles between Liberals and Conservatives might deflect attention away from the primary task.

An alternative strategy for containing the left had slowly crystallized in the mind of W.A.C. Bennett, a coalition backbencher since 1941. From

Bennett's perspective, the wartime alliance of Liberals and Conservatives had provided B.C. with its best government ever, but it had major structural weaknesses which made it an imperfect vehicle for the long run: first, the alliance was only temporary and partial — neither the Liberals nor the Conservatives had intended to be united indefinitely, and neither wished to sacrifice its party identity for the sake of a more complete merger. Coalition was not a step in the direction of a new party, but a marriage premised on the ever present possibility of a quick and easy divorce. Second, both parties were insufficiently divorced from their federal counterparts to devote themselves exclusively to the needs of the province. Bennett wished to have a purely provincial party controlling the government, unhindered by the ties of federal party labels and wholly dedicated to the related tasks of containing the left and developing the provincial economy. He became convinced that the Hart and Maitland coalition, in spite of its virtues, was not the best vehicle to perform this task. His tenure as a Conservative coalition MLA was marked by repeated efforts to create a lasting, tighter coalition Party devoid of old line party differences. In 1946 he set up a coalition organization in his home constituency of South Okanagan. In addition, in pursuing his personal political career, he twice ran unsuccessfully for the leadership of the Provincial Conservative Party, unsuccessfully made a bid in federal politics in a 1948 by-election, and returned to the provincial legislature as a coalition MLA in 1949. By this time he was convinced that it would be impossible to weld the Liberals and the Conservatives into a permanent coalition, and in March 1951, in the midst of heated controversy over the hospital insurance issue, he crossed the floor of the Legislature and proceeded to consider the possibilities of forming a new party.

Implausibly, the appropriate candidate turned out to be Social Credit, which had wielded only a sectarian influence in B.C. provincial politics since 1937, never capturing more than 1.4 percent of the vote, and was still heavily dependent on Alberta sponsorship. Yet Social Credit was to prove an ideal vehicle for W.A.C. Bennett. From its roots in Alberta, the party was clearly anti-socialist in principle. Moreover, it had a weak federal existence, and as the Alberta experience had indicated, was capable of rapid growth and was favourably disposed to a decentralized federal system with strong provincial rights and powers. To Bennett, it had the additional advantage that, although growing, it was devoid of experienced politicians; hence a takeover might not be too difficult.

The Social Credit Era Under WAC Bennett

The unexpected 1952 victory of Social Credit under the new electoral rules has been analyzed elsewhere. The electoral system proved to be incapable of reinvigorating the Liberals and Conservatives as separate provincial parties and producing a stable traditional party government. If the Liberals and Conservatives were to exploit the new electoral system to their separate partisan advantage and still keep the left out of office their rivalry with each other had to be muted. They had to compete with each other while keeping alive the larger issue of containing the left. They had to operate a multiparty system and stress a single cleavage appropriate to a two party system.

The degree of mutual animosity engendered by their acrimonious separation made this difficult. Their bitterness toward one another undoubtedly repelled many voters, deflected attention away from the left, and thus minimized the incentives for voters to view them as a team that was split for electoral competition, but was otherwise united behind the goal of an efficient non-socialist government.

The transitional election of 1952, like that of 1941, was not fought on ideological grounds. The Social Credit party, which unexpectedly surfaced as a strong contender, did not single out the left as the enemy as it would in future campaigns. The Liberals and the Conservatives committed extensive resources to battling one another. More generally, the multiparty context in which the election took place, as in the previous multiparty contests of 1937 and 1941, was hostile to a polarized rhetoric of free enterprise vs. democratic socialists.

Social Credit won a minority government in 1952 and consolidated its position with a majority victory in a general election the following year. The 1952 and 1953 provincial elections were not only contests between parties, but also contests between alternative ways to structure the future party system of the province. The STB was a device to combine multipartyism in elections with non-left legislative majorities. The major alternative was a new two-party polarization, structured around competing "isms," and sustained by the traditional British single member electoral system.

With the minority Social Credit victory in 1952 and its majority in 1953 the latter vision triumphed. From Bennett's perspective, multipartyism simply meant an undesirable fragmentation of the non-left, and worked against the consolidation of the non-socialist vote under the Social Credit banner. Further, the consolidation he sought was better designed to transform the non-left into the anti-left than was multipartyism.

By the 1953 election Bennett had realized the kind of party system he deemed appropriate for British Columbia. He had become leader of Social Credit and Premier of the province, and with great political skill had parlayed an inexperienced minority government — only one of whose nineteen members besides himself had ever sat in the Legislative Assembly before — into a clear majority with twenty-seven seats. The process of undermining the traditional parties was well under way. The Premier had cut the party ties with Alberta Social Credit and thus ended the curious position of semi-tutelage under which the B.C. party had been held for almost two decades. He eliminated the STB electoral system and returned to the first-past-the-post system which was more likely to consolidate Social Credit in power. He was now ready to embark on a program of massive development projects unmatched by any other government in B.C. history.

The rhetorical contest between free enterprise and socialism dominated elections for the two decades of Bennett's rule. As early as 1952, Henry Angus, a keen student of B.C. politics, noted that "In addition to its other sources of strength, Social Credit has shown itself a more effective anti-socialist machine than either of the other two non-socialist parties."[2] By 1972 the party's strategy was virtually unchanged, with provincial elections still depicted as struggles between the virtues of capitalism and the evils of socialism.

Bennett's continuous success in exploiting the free enterprise/socialism cleavage sustained Social Credit in a variety of ways. By encouraging the polarization of B.C. politics, he managed to keep both the provincial Liberals and the provincial Conservatives very weak, especially the latter. From 1952 up to the election of 1972 the old parties' share of the popular vote steadily decreased.

Throughout this era, British Columbia's economic elites had little choice but to support Social Credit. In a province where labour was highly organized and extremely militant and where strikes could easily cripple key sectors of the economy, Bennett's policy of provincial economic development, coupled with his unabashed use of government power to control industrial conflict, was obviously attractive to managers, entrepreneurs and investors. By engaging in a symbolic war with the unions, the Premier was able to mobilize the business community and the vast pools of capital it controlled behind his government and thus make it extremely difficult for his opponents not to appear to be pro-union and hence anti-development.

Social Credit lost the 1972 provincial election because the issue of combatting socialism temporarily lost its salience as other issues surfaced. While Bennett continued to insist on the dangers of splitting the free enterprise vote, fewer of the electorate listened as disillusionment with the Social Credit government grew. By 1972 the highways had been paved and the dams had been built. The positive province building component of Social Credit's appeal seemed to be more of an achievement of yesterday than a future goal still to be struggled for, with a resultant decline in the voter appeal of the anti-socialist syndrome with which it had been inextricably linked.

Equally important, the NDP downplayed the socialist issue. This low-profile strategy, which might be called a reverse band-wagon campaign, was used to deny the incumbent party an election issue upon which to mobilize support, rather than to mobilize the NDP's own supporters behind the prospect of a party victory. As a campaign strategy, it proved to be less durable than the anti-socialism issue which resurfaced in 1975, but in 1972, when age and party decay had finally caught up with Bennett and his party, it was sufficiently effective to place the NDP in power for the first time in British Columbia.

The election of 1972 demonstrated that although skillful exploitation of the anti-socialist issue and an unflagging commitment to provincial economic development were effective strategies for keeping the left out of power for many years, they could not succeed indefinitely. Social Credit had benefitted from the histrionics of a polarized politics and the ubiquitous fear of splitting the non-socialist vote. Yet the Social Credit solution to containing the left, like the earlier coalition solution, had its limitations.

In the first place, the leader grew old, the party organization became decrepit, and the government's capacity for policy innovation declined. Unless they constantly renew themselves, government parties fall prey to scandals, to organizational malaise, and to electoral disenchantment. They are always, potentially, their own worst enemy.

In the second place, the continuous replaying of the socialist/free enterprise game required the cooperation of the left. Should the left catch on and refuse to play the game the capacity of the government to polarize the electorate by exploiting fears of a left wing victory would be reduced. Although the NDP had adopted this approach without success in previous elections, in 1972 it worked.

Further, in the long run polarization strengthened the left by increasing its share of what had become a veritable two-party vote. Thus the more successful Social Credit was in polarizing the electorate, the more it ensured that its eventual defeat would be at the hands of the NDP. These developments invited the left to moderate its socialist rhetoric and become a competitor for the centre vote in traditional omnibus fashion. Thus the polarization designed to keep the left out had the paradoxical effect of strengthening the left, moderating its radicalism — thus partly denying the necessity of further polarization against it — and virtually ensuring that it would become the government should the incumbent administration founder. In the 1972 election, Social Credit lost part of its middle of the road support to the NDP and was further weakened by a fragmented vote shared with the Liberals and Conservatives.

The NDP Interregnum and the Return of Polarization

The 1972 NDP victory created an opportunity for British Columbia's federal and provincial party systems to re-converge. If the Social Credit decline continued, as most experts predicted it would, then the Liberals and the Conservatives were likely to recover and the trend toward party system differentiation would be reversed.

This did not happen. Instead, provincial politics became polarized once again, thus reinforcing differences between the federal and provincial party systems. The performance of Dave Barrett's NDP government created a sense of urgency and fear on the non-left. At the same time, under the

TABLE 4 **CCF/NDP Federal-Provincial Vote 1952-83 (Percent of the Vote)**

	Federal		*Provincial*
1953	26.6	1952	30.8
1957	22.3	1953	30.9
1958	24.5	1956	28.3
1962	30.9	1960	32.7
1963	30.3	1963	27.8
1965	32.9	1966	33.6
1968	32.7	1969	33.9
1972	35.0	1972	39.6
1974	23.0	1975	39.2
1979	31.9	1979	46.0
1980	35.3	1983	44.9

leadership of Bill Bennett, the remarkable ability of Social Credit in consolidating the non-left through co-optation meant that two-partyism would continue to be a hallmark of B.C. provincial politics. The Liberals and the Conservatives, who still held 29 percent and 33 percent of the B.C. federal vote respectively, were unable to assert themselves as leaders of the non-socialist camp provincially, and thus found themselves drifting even further off of the provincial political scene.

The NDP government under Dave Barrett was characterized by the populist oratory of the Premier and a blizzard of legislation which, regardless of its individual merits, did little to support the traditional claim that the left was wedded to and capable of coherent planning. The B.C. NDP was far removed from the cool, technical competence of the Blakeney regime in Saskatchewan, or the restrained, cautious administration of the

TABLE 5 **Social Credit Federal Provincial Vote 1952-83 (Percent of the Vote)**

	Federal		*Provincial*
1953	26.6	1952	30.2
1957	24.2	1953	45.5
1958	9.6	1956	45.8
1962	14.2	1960	38.8
1963	13.3	1963	40.8
1965	17.4	1966	45.6
1968	5.8	1969	46.8
1972	2.7	1972	31.2
1974	1.2	1975	49.2
1979	0.2	1979	48.2
1980	0.1	1983	49.8

Schreyer regime in Manitoba. Neither did it combine populist appeals with technical competence, as had the Douglas/Lloyd governments in Saskatchewan from 1944 to 1964. Barrett's skills were electoral rather than managerial, a fact that made his decision to assume the Finance portfolio along with the position of Premier little short of disastrous. The government's public image was tarnished, particularly by the press, which depicted the Premier and his cabinet as a group of inexperienced left wing bunglers whose goodwill far outran their capacity to govern.

Like the Conservatives in federal politics, the NDP suffered from a "minority party syndrome" when it assumed provincial office in 1972. A lengthy and frustrating period of almost forty years in opposition constituted poor preparation for the task of wielding government power. The new government lacked a unifying vision of the goals it hoped to attain. The long history of socialist movements and parties in British Columbia, extending back to the nineteenth century, had contributed very little in the way of theoretical applications of democratic socialism to the very specific circumstances of the B.C. polity and economy. Paradoxically, the party of planning had a much less developed vision of the future, and a much weaker conception of the socioeconomic transformations it sought for the province, than had the Social Credit government which it replaced.

Against this backdrop, three years of NDP rule widened the rift between left and right in British Columbia as never before, and precipitated a crucial competition between the three provincial opposition parties to determine who would emerge as the strongest anti-socialist spokesman. The outcome of the contest was not predetermined. In fact, there was a strong possibility that no one would succeed, and the NDP, aided by a revived multiparty system, would be re-elected. What was clear was that the situation was fluid, and that any one of a number of possibilities for combatting the NDP government might be employed in the next election. There was vague talk of a unity movement; there were proposals that opposition forces unite behind the strongest non-left candidate in each riding after joint nominating meetings; there were suggestions that the old single transferable ballot be reintroduced.

Ultimately, however, the response to the challenge of restructuring the party system was left to a Darwinian competition between the three opposition parties, which competed against one another for the privilege of championing the free enterprise vote. Partly because it was unhampered by ties with a Social Credit federal party, Social Credit emerged as the clear frontrunner in this competition, thus engineering one of the greatest comebacks in the history of Canadian politics. Having successfully erased the tired image of W.A.C. Bennett and his aging government, the party embarked on a massive membership drive and media campaign for its new leader, the son of the former premier who, to the surprise of many, became a formidable politician. Also significant in both symbolic and functional terms was the party's successful recruitment of three of the five provincial Liberal caucus members, and one Conservative member.

Subsequently, in the provincial election of December 11, 1975, the "new" Social Credit received 49.2 percent of the popular vote, its highest figure ever, and obtained a decisive majority of 35 seats. Much of this renewed support came at the expense of the Liberals and Conservatives, who received their smallest ever share of the vote, a combined total of only 11 percent, and won only one seat apiece. Widespread reaction to the left on the part of the right, and even among some who had supported the left in 1972, evoked a right wing Social Credit populism with which the more traditional Liberals and Conservatives could not compete. The possibility of escaping from polarization opened up by the 1972 election was lost.

The polarization pattern continued in the elections of 1979 and 1983. In both campaigns a frequently-heard claim in the Social Credit camp was that NDP victory would simply return to power the same group of inexperienced socialists who had allegedly wreaked havoc upon the province's balance sheets from 1972 to 1975. Social Credit mobilized the vote in its favour — 48.2 percent in 1979 and 49.8 percent in 1983 by painting the NDP as a group of idealists who would mortgage the province's economic future for questionable short-term social benefits. Given the Social Credit government's own less than enviable record, this strategy testified to the government's capacity to mould the electorate's perceptions of political choice.

Socialism, Federalism, and the National Party System in British Columbia

The federal party system in British Columbia underwent a different evolution. The B.C. federal party system is part of a country-wide party system and is therefore constantly influenced, directly or indirectly, by external party developments. Foremost among these extraprovincial factors is the relative weakness of the CCF/NDP in national politics. The left has never threatened to form the national government. Notwithstanding occasional surges of support, the CCF/NDP has never captured more than 20 percent of the vote in a general election, nor held more than 11.7 percent of the seats in the House of Commons.

In B.C. provincial politics, manipulation of the free enterprise vs. socialism issue proved an effective device for mobilizing the non-left vote. The CCF/NDP was strong enough to challenge the parliamentary ideal of having a stable governing executive as long as its opponents were divided among two or more evenly matched parties. By raising the spectre of socialism, the non-left could be united to produce a majority government, whether in the form of a Liberal-Conservative coalition or a new third party such as Social Credit.

A similar strategy was not seriously considered at the federal level. It would have made little sense for either of the traditional parties to turn their strategic efforts away from one another in order to combat a socialist phantom. A more effective strategy was simply to deflate the left by co-opting its most popular policies, not in the name of socialism, but rather in the name of progressive, Keynesian reform.

The Effect of the CCF/NDP on National Political Parties in British Columbia in the 30s and 40s

The CCF's entry into national politics spelled the end of the old party monopoly in British Columbia, but did not lead to a dramatic change of the federal party system in the province as it had with the provincial party system. Instead, it produced a highly competitive three-party arrangement that preserved the Liberals and the Conservatives. In the four federal elections held between 1933 and 1951, for example, none of the major contenders — Liberal, Conservative, or CCF collected less than 25 percent of the B.C. vote; none collected more than 34 percent, and not once did the difference between first and third place finishers surpass 9 percent. The CCF's performance in these elections roughly approximated its performance in the five provincial elections held during the same period.

Yet despite its internal competitiveness, the federal party system in British Columbia did not witness the kinds of strategic manoeuvres that were taking place in the provincial arena. Coalition against the left was unnecessary at the national level and meaningless with respect to federal party competition in the province. Countrywide electoral reform to combat the left in the several provinces where it had federal strength was unnecessary. More generally, polarization to keep the left out was irrelevant at the national level, with the possible exception of the 1945 federal election, and pointless at the B.C. federal level where the strength of the left could not be translated into the possession of a government. Thus, the issue of socialism in B.C. federal politics did not attain the significance it had in the provincial arena. In short, British Columbia's party systems moved apart in this period because the powerful inducements which led to the simplification of the provincial party system had no counterpart either at the national level, or within the B.C. component of the national party system.

British Columbia's Federal Party System in the Social Credit Era

Twenty years of Social Credit populist democracy transformed British Columbia's provincial party system. But the Social Credit impact on federal politics in the province was much weaker and shorter lived. When W.A.C. Bennett's provincial Socreds were defeated in 1972, their federal counterparts, who had temporarily challenged the three major contenders for ascendancy in B.C. during the mid-fifties, had long since been reduced to insignificance.

Like the CCF, Social Credit's entry into B.C. politics was not restricted to the provincial arena. The party made an auspicious debut in B.C. federal competition in the general election of 1953 by collecting 26.1 percent of the vote and sending four representatives to the House of Commons. In 1957, it took 24.2 percent of the vote, won 6 of the province's 22 seats, and ran ahead of the Liberals in both categories. Unlike the CCF, however, Social Credit proved to have limited staying power in federal politics. It was hurt badly by the Diefenbaker landslide in 1958, and after making a partial comeback in the 1960's, it virtually disappeared from the political scene. In 1980 the party captured only .1 percent of the B.C. federal vote, while the provincial party was stronger than ever with 48.2 percent of the vote in 1979, and 49.8 percent in 1983.

Although W.A.C. Bennett launched several "on-to-Ottawa" campaigns in the hope of influencing federal politics through his influence on Social Credit MPs in Ottawa, and for a time was a strong supporter of Réal Caouette, the British Columbia Social Credit party was essentially a provincial creature. Unlike its Alberta counterpart, the B.C. party was not a protest movement against a distant, exploiting federal government. It had negligible interest in being part of a broad national movement to acquire national power. Indeed, a strong national party would have produced those same intraparty complications between federal and provincial party wings which Bennett felt had prevented the provincial Liberal and Conservative parties from devoting their undivided attention to provincial development. Unlike the CCF/NDP, the B.C. Social Credit vision of social change did not extend beyond the provincial scene, and after Bennett assumed the leadership in 1952, Social Credit monetary policy was cast aside as an irrelevancy, inapplicable to the provincial scene to which the party's efforts were directed. Finally, the anti-socialist role which Social Credit performed so effectively in provincial politics did not have to be carried out at the B.C. federal level, where the strength of the left, while deplorable to free enterprise believers, was not threatening.

Recent Developments in the B.C. Federal Party System: The Decline of the Liberals

From the birth of the CCF in national politics to the Trudeau landslide in 1968, British Columbia's federal party system was marked by close competition between three evenly-matched contenders — the Liberals, the Conservatives, and the CCF/NDP, with a brief four party interlude before Social Credit faded from the federal scene. Only recently has this pattern begun to change, with the new order manifest most clearly in the decline of the Liberals and the accompanying strengthening of the Progressive Conservatives. Since the election of 1968, when the B.C. Liberal vote reached 42 percent, its highest level since 1904, the party's support has fallen off precipitously. It has constantly lagged behind the Tories in both votes and seats and in the 1980 federal election it ran a distant third at the polls, sending no representatives to the House of Commons for the first time since 1958.

Conclusion

The divergence of federal and provincial party systems in British Columbia was neither accidental nor inevitable. It results primarily from the differential consequences attached to left wing strength in the federal and provincial arenas, and from the different party strategies those consequences elicit. These strategies have never been responses to the brute fact of CCF/NDP strength *per se*; rather, they derive from the interaction between the institutional incentives which parliamentary government holds out for majority government, and the real and manipulated fears in a divided society over the prospect of a left-wing government.

The parliamentary system of government, which stresses executive stability preferably based on single party majorities, created severe pressures to simplify the provincial party system. As long as that system housed three or more reasonably close competitors, the likelihood of a majority government situation arising was significantly reduced. The same pressures for simplification did not, however, operate in British Columbia's federal party system. The fact that the province's federal party system was a multiparty system which more often than not failed to produce a majority of B.C. seats for any one party was only an interesting oddity. Multipartyism at the B.C. federal level, even when election results produced no single party majority of federal seats from the province, was tolerable. Similar results at the provincial level, as in 1941 and 1952, had convulsive effects. These differential consequences attached to multipartyism, quite independently of the socialist issue, tended to drive the two party systems apart.

Further, it was possible for the CCF/NDP to be a powerful actor in British Columbia's federal party system without disturbing the sleep of economic elites. The very concept of socialist victory, which at the provincial level had a galvanizing effect on the non-left, had no meaning for that segment of the national party system which functioned in B.C. In the B.C. federal arena, the sudden appearance of the CCF had the effect of reducing the Liberal and Conservative vote, but it did not drive the old parties together, nor did it set in motion any tendencies for their elimination, whether jointly or separately. The left was too weak nationally to have been perceived as sufficiently threatening to justify extraordinary strategies for its defeat or containment in those parts of the country where it had federal strength.

At the provincial level, the pressures to overcome multipartyism came not only from the parliamentary system, but also from the existence of a powerful left wing party. The CCF/NDP's consistent capacity to deliver one-third of the vote posed a serious challenge to political and economic elites on the old party side, and thus generated powerful pressures to simplify and consolidate the non-left. In contrast to the B.C. federal arena, where the concern aroused by actual or possible CCF/NDP victories was negligible, similar possibilities in provincial politics produced deep alarm. This differential response was not attributable to differences in left wing strength, but to differences in the expected consequences of left wing strength when control of a government was at stake.

Since the early years of the provincial coalition there has been constant pressure for political actors outside the left to counter the possibility of a CCF/NDP government. In these circumstances anti-socialism is the obvious rhetorical tool for overcoming fragmentary tendencies on the non-left. Anti-socialist mobilization at the provincial level, whether in the form of coalition or of Social Credit, inevitably drives the B.C. federal and provincial party systems apart, and produces serious intraparty tensions between the federal and provincial wings of the same party.

The enduring strength of the provincial left contributed to the continuation of the coalition, and to the ideological polarization so successfully manipulated by subsequent Social Credit governments. The free enterprise versus socialism dichotomy brandished by W.A.C. Bennett was explicitly hostile to any multiparty tendencies which might have allowed the left to slip into office with less than 50 percent of the votes. Social Credit's success was built on the failure of Liberals and Conservatives to establish themselves as credible anti-socialist alternatives, and on its ability to structure the terms of debate so that the business and non-left vote generally would have no real choice but to follow Bennett's anti-socialist forces. The reception and success of the same strategy by the new Social Credit party of Bill Bennett is testament to powerful strains in the political culture, in the context of provincial politics, to which the responses of successive B.C. governments have both been an acknowledgement and a powerful reinforcement.

The coexistence of federal and provincial party systems in British Columbia constitutes a kind of natural experiment which allows the student to isolate the effects of institutional context on party system evolution. Explanations of the provincial party system focussing on class, economy and society are clearly inadequate since B.C. federal politics interacts with the same class system, economy, and society but with very different consequences.

Differences of party system context exerted an institutional bias in favour of party system asymmetry. The playing out of these differences over half a century has destroyed the provincial multiparty system, allowed the federal multiparty system to survive, and thus has driven the two party systems progressively apart. Institutional factors, then, ought not to be ignored by students seeking to understand party systems. The interaction of one common B.C. society with two separate and distinct institutional contexts has resulted in two very different party systems.

ENDNOTES

1. The Vancouver *Sun*, June 1, 1949.
2. H.F. Angus, "The British Columbia Election," *Canadian Journal of Economics and Political Science*, 18 (June 1952), p. 525.

27 Ontario's Party Systems: Federal and Provincial

ROBERT J. WILLIAMS

In August, 1983, the Ontario Progressive Conservative Party quietly marked the fortieth consecutive year of its control over the provincial administration. Ontario appears to enjoy long term stability in its political alignments, since the Liberals had once governed the province for some thirty-three consecutive years and only one government has ever failed to get re-elected after its initial victory. The journalist Eric Dowd has described the modern Ontario PCs as "the Harris tweed of political parties," a phrase which accurately reflects their durability and the mixed coloration of the "threads" which are so skilfully woven together. A young cabinet minister with leadership aspirations observes that "good government is good politics" and the equation causes not a ripple of surprise. In the 1980s, as has been the case for some years now, provincial politics in Ontario is apparently more about management than about partisanship.[1]

The managerial style of the provincial PCs has dominated the way Canadians perceive Ontario's political style. This apparent depoliticization of Ontario, carefully promoted by an avowedly pragmatic government, actually masks real differences among the three dominant parties, those parties which have monopolized parliamentary offices in both the Legislative Assembly at Queen's Park and the House of Commons in Ottawa since the 1950s. It also obscures the real disposition of electoral support among the three Ontario parties for, in contrast to the monopoly over provincial political office exercised by the Tories, only in the elections of 1951, 1955 and 1963 did they come close to capturing one half of the popular vote.[2] The consistent success of the PCs in retaining power is, thus, really only part of that political style.

In federal politics, the Liberal Party has been "the government party" for most of this century.[3] Yet in Ontario, its electoral dominance is not so clear-cut, having only won a majority of the province's federal votes for the first time in 1935. Since then, federal voting records show fluctuating support for the two largest parties, with neither party capturing a majority of the votes cast in Ontario in any election except the 1958 Tory landslide. The CCF and later the NDP also secured a significant component of the vote for itself throughout this period. Ontario has been a major battle ground in recent federal elections, partly because it contains the largest number of seats of any province, but, more significantly, because of the real possibility that many of those seats will change hands in any given election.

Another obvious characteristic of the two Ontario party systems, both provincial and federal, has been the maintenance in each one of a three-party configuration since the 1940s. On the face of it, Ontario appears to have two symmetrical party systems, both of which have persisted for a very long time. The rough similarity of the two party systems has been the cause of some confusion in popular perceptions of party politics in Ontario. It is not clear that there actually is a distinctive Ontario political tradition, one which, ironically, many Ontarians fail to perceive as being "regional" — not to say unique — in the national context.[4]

This brief essay will examine the two party systems operating in Ontario, focussing largely upon recent electoral records and upon the "human image" of the three main parties as reflected in their candidates and caucuses. Three basic themes emerge from the evidence, which together paint a basic picture of contemporary party politics in Ontario. The hypothesis advanced here is that the apparent similarity of federal and provincial parties in Ontario is not the reality.

Regionalism within Ontario

A close examination of the results of the three federal elections and three provincial elections between 1974 and 1981 reveals two basic points about the character of recent party politics in Ontario.

First, Ontario has a highly regionalized party system. The competitive strength of the three parties is significantly different in various corners of the province in both electoral arenas. If we divide the Ontario constituencies into five geographic regions, the aggregate picture of party strength — which is usually taken as the measure of party success (See Table I) — is seen to mask patterns of perceptible strengths and weaknesses in the three parties.

For this purpose, Metropolitan Toronto (20 federal seats in 1974 and 23 later; 29 provincial seats) can be considered one region. Northern Ontario, the area roughly north of the French River (12 federal seats, then 11; 15 provincial seats) will be treated as another region. Eastern Ontario — the entire area from east of Oshawa north through the Kawarthas, Haliburton and Parry Sound and east to the Quebec border — contained 18 federal seats, five of which were based in the Ottawa area. Provincially, there were 24 seats, with 7 of them in the Ottawa area. The so-called Golden Horseshoe region will cover the urbanized belt from Oshawa, north of Metro Toronto, around the end of Lake Ontario and down the Niagara River; it contained 14 federal seats in 1974 and 17 seats later, and 23 provincial

TABLE 1 Aggregate Electoral Results in the Province of Ontario 1974 to 1981

Year	Party	Popular Vote	Seats
Provincial Elections			
1975	Liberal	34.3%	36
	New Democ	28.9%	38
	Prog Cons	36.1%	51
	Total Seats		125
1977	Liberal	31.5%	34
	New Democ	28.0%	33
	Prog Cons	39.7%	58
	Total Seats		125
1981	Liberal	33.7%	34
	New Democ	21.1%	21
	Prog Cons	44.4%	70
	Total Seats		125
Federal Elections			
1974	Liberal	44.9%	55
	New Democ	18.9%	8
	Prog Cons	34.9%	25
	Total Seats		88
1979	Liberal	36.3%	32
	New Democ	20.9%	6
	Prog Cons	41.6%	57
	Total Seats		95
1980	Liberal	41.7%	52
	New Democ	21.8%	5
	Prog Cons	35.4%	38
	Total Seats		95

constituencies. Finally, Western Ontario will be considered to be the entire area from Lake Simcoe down to Windsor which is not covered by the other regions. It could easily be broken down further into smaller regions, but the patterns would not be substantially altered. There were 24 ridings at stake in 1974 and 26 in the two subsequent federal elections and 34 provincial seats in this region.

Tables 2 and 3 provide the results of this re-examination of the fortunes of the various parties. They provide clear evidence of a regional variation in electoral support for the three major parties.

For example, the federal PCs turned in a rather unremarkable performance in Northern Ontario in the three general elections of 1974, 1979 and 1980. There were two Liberal national majorities generated in those contests, yet even in the PC minority victory of 1979, the best that could be managed was one second place finish in the eleven seats in the north. In

TABLE 2 **Ranking of Parties by Region in Federal Elections in Ontario**
            1974-1979-1980

Region	Year (Seats)	Party	First	Second	Third
Eastern	1974 (18)	Liberal	8	10	0
		New Democ	0	0	18
		Prog Cons	10	8	0
	1979 (18)	Liberal	6	12	0
		New Democ	0	0	18
		Prog Cons	12	6	0
	1980 (18)	Liberal	7	11	0
		New Democ	0	0	18
		Prog Cons	11	7	0
Northern	1974 (12)	Liberal	9	3	0
		New Democ	3	7	2
		Prog Cons	0	2	10
	1979 (11)	Liberal	8	3	0
		New Democ	3	7	1
		Prog Cons	0	1	10
	1980 (11)	Liberal	11	0	0
		New Democ	0	10	1
		Prog Cons	0	1	10
Western	1974 (24)	Liberal	12	12	0
		New Democ	1	5	20
		Prog Cons	10	9	5
	1979 (26)	Liberal	6	17	3
		New Democ	1	5	20
		Prog Cons	19	4	3
	1980 (26)	Liberal	12	12	2
		New Democ	1	4	21
		Prog Cons	13	10	3
Horseshoe	1974 (14)	Liberal	10	4	0
		New Democ	1	1	12
		Prog Cons	3	9	2
	1979 (17)	Liberal	2	9	2
		New Democ	1	1	15
		Prog Cons	14	9	2
	1980 (17)	Liberal	5	10	2
		New Democ	2	2	13
		Prog Cons	10	5	2
Metro	1974 (20)	Liberal	16	14	10
		New Democ	2	3	15
		Prog Cons	2	13	5
	1979 (23)	Liberal	10	11	2
		New Democ	1	5	17
		Prog Cons	12	7	4
	1980 (23)	Liberal	17	5	1
		New Democ	2	7	14
		Prog Cons	4	10	9

TABLE 3 **Ranking of Parties by Region in Ontario Provincial Elections in Ontario 1975-1977-1981**

Region	Year (Seats)	Party	First	Second	Third
Eastern	1975	Liberal	5	12	7
	(24)	New Democ	4	4	16
		Prog Cons	15	8	1
	1977	Liberal	5	12	7
	(24)	New Democ	3	4	17
		Prog Cons	16	8	0
	1981	Liberal	6	16	2
	(24)	New Democ	2	0	22
		Prog Cons	16	8	0
Northern	1975	Liberal	2	3	10
	(15)	New Democ	9	4	2
		Prog Cons	4	8	3
	1977	Liberal	2	0	13
	(15)	New Democ	6	7	2
		Prog Cons	7	8	0
	1981	Liberal	1	6	8
	(15)	New Democ	5	4	6
		Prog Cons	9	5	1
Western	1975	Liberal	20	12	2
	(34)	New Democ	4	6	24
		Prog Cons	10	16	8
	1977	Liberal	19	10	5
	(34)	New Democ	4	5	25
		Prog Cons	11	19	4
	1981	Liberal	19	11	4
	(34)	New Democ	1	7	26
		Prog Cons	14	16	4
Horseshoe	1975	Liberal	6	10	7
	(23)	New Democ	7	4	12
		Prog Cons	10	9	4
	1977	Liberal	7	7	9
	(23)	New Democ	6	5	12
		Prog Cons	10	11	2
	1981	Liberal	6	13	4
	(23)	New Democ	4	3	16
		Prog Cons	13	7	3
Metro	1975	Liberal	3	15	11
	(29)	New Democ	14	4	11
		Prog Cons	12	10	7
	1977	Liberal	1	10	18
	(29)	New Democ	14	7	8
		Prog Cons	14	12	3
	1981	Liberal	2	17	10
	(29)	New Democ	9	7	13
		Prog Cons	18	5	6

those two Liberal victories in 1974 and 1980, PC candidates also ran rather poorly in Metropolitan Toronto, winning only 2 of 20 seats in the first instance and only 4 of 23 in the latter. Conversely, in Eastern Ontario (barring four Ottawa-area seats) the PCs were the dominant force and in Western Ontario (barring the three Windsor-based seats) were very much the strongest party. In 1979 and 1980, the federal PC candidates also fared very well in the urbanized belt around the western end of Lake Ontario.

The federal Liberal party is, on the other hand, strong in four of the five regions identified here: in Northern Ontario it is by far the most successful party and in Metropolitan Toronto, its record is quite enviable, having finished as low as third in only 2 of 23 seats in 1979 and in only 1 seat in 1980. While it has been far less successful in Eastern Ontario than the Tories, its record would have been much worse without the strong hold its candidates have had over Ottawa-area and Francophone seats. This suggests that not only does Ontario have regions, it has sub-regions. For instance, in Western Ontario, Liberal candidates tend to be more successful in urbanized seats in areas like Windsor, London and Kitchener while the PCs tend to be relatively more successful in smaller communities and the rural areas.

Finally, New Democrats have little to be happy about in federal elections in Ontario, capturing no more than 8 seats overall in their most successful of the three campaigns examined here. Using second place finishes as a measure of relative strength, the regionalized nature of Ontario politics re-emerges, with good NDP showings in Northern Ontario and more modest successes in industrialized corners of Western Ontario (particularly around Windsor) and Metro Toronto. Evidently Eastern Ontario is a scene of desolation to federal NDP candidates: not one in these three elections managed to finish better than third.

In federal politics in Ontario, the Liberals and PCs are the major protagonists in most of the province, although Liberal-NDP contests are frequently found in the North. The overall picture of Ontario as a three-party system federally is, then, an artifact of these more regionalized patterns of competition.

In provincial politics, the relative strengths of the parties are different. For the provincial Liberals, Western Ontario has been the main building block of its caucus at Queen's Park: not less than 55 percent of its MPPs were drawn from these 34 seats in the elections considered here. Eastern Ontario and the Golden Horseshoe have provided another 30-35 percent of the caucus in the same period. Northern Ontario and Metro Toronto constituencies have been, in contrast, unresponsive to most provincial Liberal candidates.

The provincial New Democrats have some areas of relative strength, in particular Metro Toronto in 1975 and 1977 (the two minority elections) and Northern Ontario where in 1960, despite their general collapse elsewhere,

New Democrats retained one-third of the seats in the region. Like their federal counterparts, the Eastern part of Ontario has been rather unreceptive to NDP candidates, except in certain Ottawa-area seats and in Cornwall.

For the provincial PCs, none of the regions identified here could be considered barren territory, although some pockets of relatively low support can be identified (for example, in the Windsor area). In contrast, third place finishes in Eastern and Northern Ontario are extremely rare.

Provincial aggregate figures, then, also mask an element of regionalism, particularly for the two opposition parties. The more traditional PC-Liberal contests in the East and much of Western Ontario co-exist with PC-NDP battles in the North and Metro Toronto, and all three parties seem to have made good showings in the Golden Horseshoe. There has even been a small set of seats where the main protagonists are Liberals and New Democrats.

Ontario is not electorally homogenous, but is large and complex enough to house various combinations of two-party (and occasional three-party) contests. The aggregate results might determine the composition of the party caucuses at Queen's Park and in the House of Commons but in recent years the regional results provide a more insightful picture of the nature of the Ontario party system.

Symmetry and Asymmetry in the Ontario Party System

The second point to emerge from an examination of the regional support for Ontario's parties is implicit in the first one. As far as the two larger parties are concerned, the regional support patterns noted above are not identical in the federal and provincial arenas. In other words, areas of strength in federal politics are not necessarily areas of strength in provincial politics, and vice versa. This suggests that, although the same three parties are successfully electing MPs and MPPs in Ontario, the relationship of the parties to each other and to the electorate is different in the federal and provincial systems.

At the constituency level, variations are frequently observed. The provincial constituency of Perth, for example, stood among the three 'safest' Liberal seats in 1975, 1977 and 1981, giving the incumbent a minimum of 62.5 percent of the popular vote. the Federal constituency of Perth-Wilmot (later Perth), returned a PC candidate with a comfortable plurality in 1974, 1979 and 1980. In contrast, in the area west of Yonge Street in the City of North York (part of Metropolitan Toronto) there are three federal and three provincial constituencies which cover very much the same territory. The provincial PCs have held all three seats through the three elections considered here while their federal counterparts won one of the seats from the Liberals in the 1979 election, but lost it in 1980. In the east end of Hamilton, the provincial constituency has been a safe CCF-NDP seat since 1959, while Liberal John Munro has represented much the same area in the House of Commons continuously since 1962.

On the regional level, Northern Ontario and Metropolitan Toronto were areas dominated by the federal Liberal party in the election results reported in Table II but they were fairly poor areas for the provincial Liberal party as reported in Table III. Western Ontario showed a marked tendency to favour provincial Liberal candidates over PCs, but in federal politics the relationship was much less one of dominance by one over the other.

On the broadest level, there is a significant difference in the types of constituencies from which the parties draw their electoral support. The NDP, in both arenas, has been most successful in urban and/or heavily unionized constituencies. In the mid-1970s, its fortunes rose dramatically in provincial politics as it garnered extensive support in Metro Toronto, Northern Ontario and the Golden Horseshoe. In this same period, the federal party was most successful in Northern Ontario and Metro Toronto. The New Democratic Party has carved out for itself a place on the left of the political spectrum as the spokesman for the economically underprivileged, as a critic of independent governmental agencies, and as a proponent of a more stabilizing role for the state against social upheaval. It has struggled hard, with intermittent success, to expand its appeal to the rural and more middle-class constituencies, but has been thwarted by the strength of the ties of the two traditional parties to those sections of the community.

To understand the contemporary relationship between the Liberals and the Progressive Conservatives in the two electoral arenas, it is necessary to understand how longevity in office for one wing of each has affected the political dynamics of Ontario. As the "government party" for so long, the federal Liberals have exercised electoral dominance over the PCs through the judicious application of governmental programmes, the momentum of power and the promise of reward. This has forced the federal PCs to play the politics of reaction and frustration in Ontario, leaving it with a caucus composed largely of rurally-based MPs from Eastern and Southwestern Ontario. In the year of its minority victory, the swing to the PCs took place in areas which had not supported the party since the 1958 Diefenbaker sweep, namely in Metro Toronto and the urbanized belt surrounding it (see Table II); many of these seats returned quickly to the Liberal column in 1980.

In provincial politics, these roles have been effectively reversed since the initial PC victory over a divided and directionless Liberal Party in 1943. The provincial PCs have honed the strategic application of the powers of government for electoral purposes from a blunt weapon to a precision instrument. They have, moreover, had a strong urban core of voter support throughout this century[5] and have combined this with effective links to the rural community. Thus, the provincial Progressive Conservatives are not a party of the margins, but a party which draws continued support from throughout the province. The provincial Liberal Party, in contrast, has been unable to achieve consistent support outside of its rural southwestern base, despite the optimistic forecasts which appear after its occasional electoral upswings. In the early part of the century it crusaded against drink, in the 1930s and early 1940s it suffered under questionable leadership and since 1943 it has simply been outperformed by the PCs.[6]

The net result of these developments is that the two arenas are characterized by an entrenched, pragmatic (but not overwhelmingly popular) "government party" which persists through the inability of its opponents to combine effectively against it. The significant point is that the place of the Liberals in federal politics and the place of the PCs in the provincial field are actually very much alike and that it is this configuration of a dominant party (or "power party"[7]) facing two smaller opposition parties gives a measure of similarity to the two Ontario party systems. In conclusion, the federal and provincial wings of each party do not necessarily win seats in the same areas; more importantly, the Liberals and PCs actually play different roles in the two arenas.

The Distinctiveness of Federal and Provincial Politics

The previous observations point towards another major feature of political life in Ontario: the distinctiveness of federal and provincial politics.

The continued success of the Liberal Party in federal politics has given it a dominant place over its provincial counterpart. From the mid-1940s, when the provincial party lost control of Queen's Park, the major organizational and individual focus of most Ontario Liberals has been the House of Commons. The good news in that situation is that some of that success has rubbed off on the provincial party and its continued existence has been assured by the needs of the federal party.[8] The bad news is that federal politics has tended to attract most of the energy, resources and talents of Ontarians who regard themselves as Liberals[9], leaving the provincial party with far less support than has been necessary to win a provincial election.

The Ontario Progressive Conservative Party is one of the preeminent electoral organizations in Canadian politics. The vaunted "Big Blue Machine" which maintained the Tory winning streak intact in the early 1970s stalled in the middle of the decade, but roared back to life in 1981 to convert a modest increase in the popular vote into a decisive victory.[10] During that same time, the federal party has been a pale shadow of the provincial Tories, with fluctuating voter support and ambiguous relationships with both the party membership and the Davis Government.[11]

The NDP has long prided itself on a strong organizational base, one which has served both federal and provincial causes without prejudice. In practice, however, the provincial field has been a more attractive and successful target and the party's provincial office has devoted most of its resources to that cause except during federal elections, when it operates as part of the national campaign structure.

In structural terms, the NDP's integrated federal-provincial party structure is actually the anomaly in Ontario. The PC party office in Toronto serves the provincial party alone, while the Liberals have actually operated two parallel structures in Toronto since 1976 — one for the federal party and the other for the provincial party.[12] These variations in practices reflect both competitive and operational priorities among the three parties, but also demonstrate that two of the Ontario parties have chosen to develop overt signs of independence between their federal and provincial wings. As Wearing has suggested, a close relationship between federal and provincial parties may not necessarily be an advantage when it comes to attracting voters who are disaffected by one level of government or the other.[13]

Another dimension of the distance which exists between federal and provincial politics in Ontario is evident in the experiences of party candidates. Surveys of major party candidates in the federal election of 1974 and the provincial election of 1975[14] reveal that there is very little movement between the two electoral arenas (See Table 4).

Only about 10 percent of all federal respondents had ever sought a seat at Queen's Park and only about 3 percent had ever succeeded. Substantially more provincial respondents had sought a seat in the House of Commons, but three quarters of them were New Democrats, none of whom had

TABLE 4 **Previous Electoral Experiences Ontario Federal and Provincial Candidates 1974 and 1975**

Federal Respondents
Previously a candidate in a provincial election

Liberal	New Democrat	Prog Cons
0.1 (6)	10.0 (7)	9.7 (7)

Previously elected to Ontario Legislative Assembly

1.5 (1)	2.9 (2)	5.5 (4)

Provincial Respondents
Previously a candidate in a federal election

Liberal	New Democrat	Prog Cons
4.3 (4)	22.6 (24)	4.9 (4)

Previously elected to the House of Commons

1.1 (1)	0.0 (0)	2.4 (2)

actually ever been elected an M.P. These findings conform to those presented elsewhere in support of the view that Canadian parties in general "have almost ceased to be instruments of federal provincial integration"[15] and suggest that most of the candidates nominated by at least two Ontario political parties consider federal and provincial politics different enough to channel their political ambitions into one field or the other, but not both. The NDP pattern of movement between the two electoral arenas, which parallels the structural arrangements noted above, is consistent with other findings about that party.[16]

There has been considerable debate over whether Ontario voters distinguish between federal and provincial issues when casting their ballot[17], but it appears that many party activists and the party organizations themselves base their actions upon a recognition of the independence of the two areas, and work towards sustaining the separateness of federal and provincial politics in Ontario.

This lack of movement between contests for the two parliaments assumes a prior decision on the part of potential candidates. That is, it assumes that potential candidates have somehow channelled themselves into one electoral arena or the other, sometimes on the basis of their electoral prospects and sometimes on the basis of greater personal interests in one field than the other. Furthermore, there are systematic biases in the federal system which have worked to make, say, provincial politics more attractive to municipal office holders and federal politics more interesting to individuals with concerns about Canada's role in international development issues.

An examination of some of the characteristics of candidates nominated by the three major parties in Ontario supports these notions of self-selection and bias. The data also reveal something else about the three parties: that certain socio-economic groups of people have aligned themselves differently in the two arenas. To put it another way, the parties — especially the Liberals and PC — have distinctive candidate profiles in federal and provincial politics.

This observation does not necessarily refer to patterns of support among the electorate, although it may be said that the pool of talent from which candidates are drawn may be a reasonable indicator of the way various socio-economic groups line up in the party system. It is an established fact that parliamentary candidates are not a microcosm of society, since they are usually drawn from a minority group in Canadian society — active members of political parties. As such they have much more partisan views of the political process than most Canadians, they have probably been very active in their community, and have an ability and inclination to be a "public person." Parliamentary candidates are also extremely unrepresentative of the rest of the population in many other respects; for example, the age distribution, ethnic backgrounds and the ratio of males to females are all quite unlike the patterns found in society at large.

The data collected from Ontario candidates in 1974 and 1975 reveal, however, two specific dimensions in which there are interesting variations in the human images of the parties which, in turn, speak clearly about the way potential parliamentarians perceive the parties themselves.

The grouping of the federal party respondents by occupational types shows significant differences between NDP candidates, on the one hand, and Liberal and Progressive Conservative candidates on the other. It is also important to observe, however, the very broad similarities in occupational groupings among Liberals and PCs: roughly the same proportion of the samples are drawn from business-related occupations, and both have over forty per cent of the sample drawn from professional occupations (although admittedly the component is larger among the Liberals). The grouping of provincial respondents on the same basis also shows significant differences between NDP candidates and those of the other two parties. More important, though, is the divergence between Liberal and PC provincial candidates in terms of the proportions of business people and professionals in the sample. The provincial PCs, according to this finding, draw a disproportionately large share of candidates with business backgrounds while the provincial Liberals nominate more professionals.

The same sort of pattern can be observed in the data presented in Table 6. First of all, in the aggregate, a greater proportion of federal candidates than provincial candidates have earned a university degree of some sort, and this pattern holds for each of the three parties. Secondly, as above, the profiles of federal Liberals and PCs are significantly different. In certain

TABLE 5 **Selected Occupational Groupings Ontario Federal and Provincial Candidates 1974 and 1975**

Federal Candidates

Occupation	Liberal	Prog Cons	New Democ
Professional	48.5% (32)	41.7% (30)	58.6% (41)
Teachers	15.2% (10)	12.5% (9)	42.9% (30)
Business	24.2% (16)	26.4% (19)	8.6% (6)
Farmers	3.0% (2)	5.6% (4)	0.0% (0)
Manual	4.5% (3)	2.8% (2)	12.9% (9)

Provincial Candidates

Occupation	Liberal	Prog Cons	New Democ
Professional	46.8% (44)	30.6% (22)	47.2% (50)
Teachers	20.2% (19)	9.7% (7)	32.1% (34)
Business	26.6% (25)	61.1% (44)	5.7% (6)
Farmers	3.2% (3)	5.6% (4)	0.9% (1)
Manual	2.1% (2)	0.0% (0)	11.3% (12)

NOTE: 1. "Teachers" are a subset of the category "Professionals"
       2. Percentages do not add up to 100% because not all occupations are reported.

TABLE 6 **University Degrees Ontario Federal and Provincial Candidates 1974 and 1975**

Federal Candidates

	Liberal	Prog Cons	New Democ
Degree	66.6% (44)	60.0% (43)	66.6% (46)
No Degree	33.3% (22)	40.0% (29)	33.3% (24)

Provincial Candidates

	Liberal	Prog Cons	New Democ
Degree	56.4% (53)	37.8% (31)	63.5% (66)
No Degree	43.6% (41)	62.2% (51)	36.5% (38)

respects, these two indicators are opposite sides of the same coin. Nevertheless, they do reflect a consistent pattern of affiliation among federal and provincial candidates.

Why are these two profiles important? First of all, they show that the human image presented to the public by the New Democratic Party is quite similar in both federal and provincial politics in Ontario. Secondly, they seem to indicate that the lines between the two larger parties in provincial politics are much more firm than in federal politics. There are notable variations in the "human image" which the provincial Tories and Liberals present at election time; there are clear preferences for the PC party among politically active business people. In the federal arena, the images of the Liberals and PCs are blurred; in terms of the candidates they nominate, there is very little apparent preference for one party over the other among business and professional people. This suggests that the relationship between the electorate (symbolized by the parliamentary candidates) and the parties is more ambiguous in federal politics than in provincial politics in Ontario. The stability of support for the provincial PCs and the volatility of support towards the two larger parties in federal politics are simply larger manifestations of the same phenomenon.

Conclusions

Ontario is the only Canadian province in which the three major national parties are also the major competitors in provincial politics. This symmetry between the two party systems has given rise to three related misconceptions about party politics in Ontario. First of all it has led to the tendency to treat Ontario as a homogenous political community in which each party is viewed as a significant force across the entire province. It has been argued here that the aggregate support figures are less revealing of the nature of the province's political preferences than are the regional patterns where quite different patterns prevail. Secondly, there is the conception that, because the same three parties are competing for and winning seats, the two arenas are essentially the same. It has been argued here that, at least for the PCs and the Liberals, the patterns of success and even the overall roles played by the parties in the electoral arenas are different. Thirdly, there is a tendency to want to talk of "the Liberals" and "the Progressive Conservatives" as integrated competitive entities in Ontario. Yet, party organizations and practices, and the affiliation of some groups in Ontario society suggest that the people who group themselves together as, say, Liberals for federal elections may not be the same people who do so for provincial elections. The two Ontario party systems are not, then, symmetrical.

The Canadian national party system is not a large-scale version of the provincial party system in Ontario. Nor is the provincial party system to be understood as simply a miniature version of the national party system. Ontarians have long assumed that the prevailing experiences of their own province — whether social, economic, cultural or political — are actually the same as those found throughout Canada.[18] This discussion has attempted to demonstrate, among other things, that Ontario is merely one of the regions of Canada and that, moreover, its two party systems are not typical of those found in the rest of Canada.

As participants in a provincial political system, Ontario voters seem to be inclined to prefer a managerial style instead of ideological posturing. The dominance of the Ontario Tories has been ensured by a mix of shrewd electoral strategy and a pragmatic approach to policy-making which isolates the two opposition parties on the margins of the political spectrum. Ontario's place in federal politics is coloured by a measure of uncertainty about which party is most capable of looking after Ontario's interests. Part of this dilemma emerges because of the very uncertainty over what Ontario's interests really are. From the very beginning, Ontario governments have fought with Ottawa in the cause of provincial rights, to keep the provincial administration independent of control through fiscal transfers and narrowly defined constitutional powers. Yet at the same time, many Ontarians have identified themselves first with Canada and have seen the federal government as primarily their own. This ambiguity has coloured the way Ontarians have participated in federal politics.

In most federal systems, and particularly in Canada, there are clear differences in the responsibilities of national and subnational governments. This means that, to be competitive, political parties which wish to control those governments must be prepared to develop policies, attract candidates and win over voters in two different electoral arenas at the same time. This challenge has never been easy, and the evidence discussed here suggests that none of the Ontario parties has been consistently successful in responding to it in both fields. The two Ontario party systems are unique components of a complex relationship between voters and governments in Canada.

ENDNOTES

1. This theme is explored in John Wilson, "The Red Tory Province; Reflections on the Character of the Ontario Political Culture," in Donald C. MacDonald, editor, *The Government and Politics of Ontario*, second edition (Toronto: Van Nostrand Reinhold Ltd., 1980), pp. 208-226.
2. See the figures presented by Robert J. Drummond in "Voting Behaviour: Casting the Play", in MacDonald, p.275 and in John Wilson and David Hoffman, "Ontario: A Three-Party System in Transition,' in Martin Robin, ed., *Canadian Provincial Politics: The Party Systems of the Ten Provinces*, first edition (Scarborough: Prentice-Hall Canada, 1972), pp. 204-205.
3. This terminology is used by Reginald Whitaker, *The Government Party: Organizing and Financing the Liberal Party of Canada, 1930-1958*. (Toronto: University of Toronto Press, 1977).
4. For brief reviews of the evolution of the contemporary party system, see the Wilson and Drummond essays in MacDonald; Wilson and Hoffman in the first edition of Robin; and Norman Penner, "Ontario: The Dominant Province" in the second edition of Robin.
5. The best discussion of the emergence of the contemporary pattern of party support is found in Charles W. Humphries, "Sources of Ontario 'Progressive' Conservatism, 1900-1914," *Canadian Historical Association Annual Report*, 1967, pp. 118-129. Other discussions of party support in later periods are found in Dennis H. Wrong, "Ontario Provincial Elections, 1934-1955: A Preliminary Survey of Voting", *Canadian Journal of Economics and Political Science*, XXIII, no. 3 (1957), 395-403 and in the Wilson and Hoffman essay in Robin and Drummond in MacDonald.
6. The (mis)fortunes on the Ontario Liberals from the 1920s to the 1970s can be traced, in part, in Peter Oliver, "The Ontario Liberal Party in the 1920s: A Study in Political Collapse" in his *Public and Private Persons: The Ontario Political Culture, 1914-1934* (Toronto: Clarke-Irwin, 1975), pp. 127-154; in Neil McKenty, *Mitch Hepburn* (Toronto: McClelland and Stewart, 1967); and in Jonathan Manthorpe, *The Power and the Tories* (Toronto: Macmillan, 1974); pp. 273-283. See also the references to Wearing and Whitaker in note 9.
7. The term is used in John McMenemy, "Party Organization" in David J. Bellamy, *et. al., The Provincial Political Systems: Comparative Essays* (Toronto: Methuen, 1976), p. 114.
8. See Wilson and Hoffman in Robin, p. 203.
9. Observations on this pattern can be found in such diverse sources as Joseph Wearing, *The L-Shaped Party: The Liberal Party of Canada, 1958-1980* (Toronto: McGraw-Hill Ryerson, 1981), pp. 108-119; Henry Jacek, *et. al.,* "The Congruence of Federal-Provincial Campaign Activity in Party Organizations: The Influence of Recruitment Patterns in Three Hamilton Ridings," *Canadian Journal of Political Science* V, no. 2 (June 1972), 190-205; Manthorpe, p. 282 and Whitaker, pp. 340-342.
10. Note that PC support as a percentage of the registered electorate was actually the same in 1977 and 1981: 26 percent. The different figures in the two elections are accounted for by an increase in the abstention rate from 34 percent to 43 percent.

11. These relationships are discussed in George Perlin, "The Progressive Conservative Party in the Election of 1974" in Howard R. Penniman, ed., *Canada at the Polls: The General Election of 1974* (Washington: American Enterprise Institute for Public Policy Research, 1975), pp. 115-119 and in William P. Irvine, "Epilogue: The 1980 Election" in Penniman, ed., *Canada at the Polls, 1979 and 1980: A Study of the General Elections* (Washington: American Enterprise Institute for Public Policy Research, 1981), p. 359.

12. Joseph Wearing, "Political Parties: Fish or Fowl?", in MacDonald, second edition, pp. 294-296.

13. *Ibid.*, p. 295.

14. These results are derived from a mail survey of candidates in the 1974 Canadian federal election and the 1975 Ontario provincial general election conducted by the author. A total of 208 of the 264 major party candidates in the federal election (78.8 percent of the total) are included in the federal data set and 272 of the 375 major party candidates (72.5 percent of the total) are included in the provincial data set. In the survey, candidates were asked questions about their personal background, political experiences and partisan activities.

15. Donald V. Smiley, *Canada in Question: Federalism in the Eighties* (Toronto: McGraw-Hill Ryerson, 1980), third edition, p. 143. Much the same point is made by R. Whitaker in a short discussion of the careers of Liberal MPs and cabinet ministers in the 1930-1958 period at pp. 343-344.

16. Smiley's evidence confirms this view, as does Jacek's.

17. One discussion of the so-called 'balance theory' and variations in federal and provincial voting in Ontario is found in John Wilson and David Hoffman, "The Liberal Party in Contemporary Ontario Politics," *Canadian Journal of Political Science* III, no. 2 (June 1970), pp. 177-204.

18. Some of these themes are discussed in Peter Oliver, "Introduction: On Being an Ontarian," in his *Public and Private Persons*, pp. 2-14.

28 Party Politics in the Mysterious East

AGAR ADAMSON AND IAN STEWART

Dalton Camp, in his book *Gentlemen, Players and Politicians*, made the following observation:

> Politics is largely made up of irrelevancies. Politicians, when they have nothing else to do, immobilize themselves and everyone near them, obsessed, like Spanish border guards, with the continuous assertion of their authority. It is a mechanism for self-preservation.[1]

Camp, who is no stranger to Atlantic Canada, has perhaps in this one passage aptly summarized the region's politics. In other sections of the country, politics is a part of life to be endured, but in Atlantic Canada, it might be called the bread of life. Nowhere else in Canada are politics followed literally from the cradle to the grave as they are in these four provinces.

If it is true that federal structures are largely the result of regional differences, it is equally true that, once established, these same federal institutions tend to engender further regional diversity. It seems apparent, for example, that there was little sociological justification in 1905 for dividing the new provinces of Alberta and Saskatchewan along a line of longitude (110 West); nevertheless, the pattern of party politics in these two artificially separated political communities quickly diverged. After two centuries of institutional distinctiveness, therefore, one might expect to find many significant political differences within Atlantic Canada. Surprisingly, the reverse is true; as the remainder of this article will demonstrate, the party politics of Nova Scotia, New Brunswick, Prince Edward Island, and even Newfoundland continue to be strikingly similar. Underlying this partisan similarity is a manifestly regional political culture. Because many residents have been tied to a subsistence economy of renewable staples, because both federal and provincial governments have been consistently unable to alleviate the extensive poverty, because the sea to the east and more developed economies to the west and south have served as channels for dissatisfaction,[2] and because immigration was essentially completed by the middle of

319

the nineteenth century, the dominant political orientations of all four Atlantic provinces have historically revolved around the twin elements of traditionalism and cynicism.

There is, of course, disagreement as to whether or not Newfoundland's political culture should be grouped with that of the three Maritime provinces.[3] Every Newfoundland government since Confederation, and particularly those which have succeeded the Smallwood regime, has on every possible occasion made it clear that Newfoundland is not one of the Maritime provinces and that there remains a considerable difference between Newfoundland and the other three provinces. Witness, for instance, the behaviour of the Peckford government with respect to the cod fishery, the various stands taken at federal-provincial conferences, and Newfoundland's 1983 decision to withdraw from the Atlantic Provinces Economic Council. Nevertheless, the gradual demise of the outports has eroded many of the distinctive aspects of the Newfoundland political culture, while integration into the Canadian political community has simultaneously reinforced the pervasive traditionalism and cynicism of Newfoundlanders. In short, and contrary to the Hartzian model, Newfoundland's political culture has recently been converging with that of the three Maritime provinces. It should also be stressed that the relative importance of the United Empire Loyalists to the region's political culture has probably been exaggerated. Unless the Loyalists' impact on Atlantic Canada was akin to that of a fastspreading inkblot on a pool of water, the fact that the bulk of the region's Loyalists settled in New Brunswick and Nova Scotia does not seem to have made traditionalism any more potent in these provinces than in Newfoundland or Prince Edward Island. Of course, there will always be room for some debate over both the precise composition and the extent of homogeneity of the Atlantic political culture. By definition, "political culture" is an abstract concept. Political values and orientations cannot be directly observed; instead, they must be inferred from the presence of more tangible phenomena. In this respect, the position of the contemporary political scientist is not too dissimilar from that of the sixteenth century marine biologist who was forced to deduce from such indirect evidence as air bubbles and wave patterns that something portentous was lurking unseen under the water's surface.

Fortunately, the "air bubbles and wave patterns" in Atlantic Canada unambiguously point to a traditionalistic and cynical political culture. The former attribute can be readily inferred. Dale Poel, for example, discovered that the region's provincial governments have not been major policy innovators,[4] and others have noted that, despite equalization payments and conditional grants from the federal government, the Atlantic provinces have historically been welfare state laggards.[5] Nor have these elite activities been inconsistent with mass desires, for Simeon and Blake observed that, in comparison to other Canadians, residents of the Atlantic provinces have been the least supportive of an expanded role for government, the least supportive of progressive social policy, the least permissive on moral issues, and the most interested in maintaining ties with Great Britain and the monarchy.[6] Finally, that Newfoundland kept the Union Jack as its provincial flag until 1980, that the last two dual-member federal constituencies were in Atlantic Canada, that Prince Edward Island retained alcoholic prohibition until 1948, and that the retention of the monarchy was an issue in the 1978 Nova Scotia provincial election all bespeak a traditionalistic political culture.[7]

The evidence is similarly voluminous with respect to cynicism. Admittedly, residents of the Atlantic provinces are typically more politically informed than are other Canadians; indeed, even at a relatively young age, this phenomenon is apparent.[8] Moreover, with the exception of Newfoundland, Atlantic Canadians have far higher political participation rates than the national average and voting turnouts for both provincial and federal elections are consistently the highest in the country.[9]

Yet notwithstanding these apparent indicators of a "civic culture," Atlantic Canadians can be easily distinguished from their cohorts in the rest of the country by their relative lack of both political efficacy and political trust.[10] In other words, there are curious contradictions in the Atlantic provinces' political culture. Despite the fact that they both distrust politics and politicians and feel incapable of effecting political change, Atlantic Canadians continue to invest politics with high amounts of physical, intellectual, and, as we shall subsequently see, emotional resources. The result of these tensions is a political culture which is characterized, in the words of New Brunswick Premier Richard Hatfield, by an "unhealthy cynicism."[11]

What, then, is the impact of this political culture on the party politics of the region? Not surprisingly, the traditionalistic orientations of Atlantic Canadians have served to maintain a traditional party system. Perhaps the most obvious manifestation of this phenomenon is the stability and intensity of party attachments. Data from one study revealed that whereas 59 percent of Atlantic Canadians claim always to vote for the same party at federal elections, the comparable figure for other Canadians is only 45 percent.[12] In fact, party loyalties can seemingly become matters of heredity in the Atlantic provinces as entire families can remain either Liberal or Conservative for generations. Typifying this phenomenon is the Maritimer who said:

> Yes, we have been Liberals since before Confederation....Well, it was something like your religion. It was emotion really....We would feel that we would be disloyal if we thought of....It was a certain loyalty. I would feel that I was disloyal to Father if I...[13]

A respondent to a questionnaire sent to delegates to the 1971 Nova Scotia Progressive Conservative Leadership Convention aptly answered the question, "When did you become a member of the Progressive Conservative

Party?" with, "At conception."[14] Small wonder, therefore, that with the possible exception of Newfoundland, Atlantic Canadian party politics of the late twentieth century are not too dissimilar from those of the late nineteenth century.

It is clear that the region's traditionalist predispositions have undercut those parties which have periodically challenged the "Grits" and the "Tories." Unlike that in many other parts of Canada, third parties have found the political soil in Atlantic Canada to be extremely barren and strewn with rocks. P.E.I. affords probably the most dramatic instance of this phenomenon. In this century, the only non-Liberal, non-Conservative elected to either federal or provincial office was Jim Dewar, an independent M.L.A. between 1919 and 1923. The New Democratic Party and its predecessor, the C.C.F., has never received more than 8 percent of the vote on the Island and in the 1982 provincial campaign garnered a microscopic 0.5 percent share of the popular vote. As the departing provincial party leader, David Burke, understated, "I'm not filled with joy at what happened."[15]

Third parties have been only slightly more successful in New Brunswick and Nova Scotia. In 1920, a temporary coalition of radical workers and reformist farmers managed to elect eleven M.L.A.s in each province, but dissension stemming from the perceived incompatability of the component wings caused these movements quickly to disintegrate. Since that time, both Social Credit and the Parti Acadien in New Brunswick have made ineffective electoral forays. In 1978 the Parti Acadien captured 4.8 percent of the popular vote; however, as so often happens with third parties, the major parties (and in this case, particularly Richard Hatfield's Conservatives) moved quickly to answer the discontent which had given rise to the Parti Acadien. Hatfield's unprecedented victory, particularly in the Acadien constituencies in 1982, attests to the success of his attack on the root causes of Parti Acadien support. It is now difficult to state categorically that the Parti Acadien is dead, but it is safe to say that after receiving less than one percent of the popular vote in the 1982 election, the party is seriously wounded.

Only the New Democratic Party and its predecessor, the Co-operative Commonwealth Federation, have made perceptible inroads into the support of the two traditional parties. In both New Brunswick and Nova Scotia, the C.C.F.-N.D.P.'s share of the popular vote peaked initially at the end of World War II,[16] retreated through the 1950s and 1960s, and then rose to new highs in the late 1970s and early 1980s. Yet, although the Party did manage to win 16.2 percent of the popular vote in New Brunswick and 20.9 percent in Nova Scotia in the 1980 federal election, they won no seats in either province. The bastion of the C.C.F.-N.D.P. support in Nova Scotia has always been in industrial Cape Breton and they have elected federal and provincial members periodically since 1939. In New Brunswick, on the other hand, the Party has never elected a federal member and did not elect a provincial member until the 1982 success of Robert Hall in Tantramar. In any event, Hall's election can perhaps be credited more to his own personality and popularity than to any perceived attributes of his party.

In Nova Scotia, the party has always been split between Cape Breton and the mainland. As David Lewis has written:

> One thing I learned from my many visits to Nova Scotia during the years following 1938 and 1939 was the difficulty of persuading the Cape Bretoner to accept a person from the Nova Scotia mainland as his spokesman....The attitude of Cape Bretoners led to considerable difficulty in setting up a provincial headquarters, in appointing the occasional organizer,..., and in electing officers for the provincial party.[17]

This enmity between the two major geographic regions of Nova Scotia continues to the present day. In the 1981 general election, the N.D.P. was for the first time able to elect a member on the mainland (though here again the circumstances were similar to those of New Brunswick with the victory more attributable to the calibre of the candidate, provincial party leader Alexa McDonough, than to the party's programme). In the same election, however, the N.D.P. lost its two seats in industrial Cape Breton. At the present time, the Nova Scotia N.D.P. is split. Paul McEwan, the M.L.A. for Cape Breton since 1970, was expelled from the party in 1980 after charging that the N.D.P. was being infiltrated by Trotskyists. McEwan has subsequently formed the Cape Breton Labour Party. The rise of what is a fourth party in industrial Cape Breton does not bode well for the future success of the N.D.P. McEwan may only win his own seat in the next provincial election, but his candidates in the surrounding Cape Breton constituencies may pull enough votes to make certain that the N.D.P. candidates are not successful.[18] At one point it appeared that Nova Scotia, thanks to the presence of the New Democratic Party, was adopting the Ontario party system.[19] In Ontario, there is a solid three-party system, but in many parts of the province, the competition is between two parties (for example, the Conservatives and the N.D.P. in northern Ontario and the Liberals and Conservatives in south-western Ontario). The internal problems within the Nova Scotia N.D.P. have, at least temporarily, inhibited the growth of such a party system in Nova Scotia.

Finally, despite their relatively recent integration into the Canadian political community and despite being without party politics during the fifteen years of Commission government, Newfoundlanders have also rarely deserted the two traditional parties. At first, the basis of support for the two major parties revolved around the issue of Confederation. Those who supported Confederation joined J.R. Smallwood in the Liberal Party and those who were opposed became members of the Progressive Conservative Party. When the union with Canada proved to be an economic blessing, the Tories' initial anti-Confederation stance became a profound electoral hindrance. Over the years, those third parties which have challenged the dominance of the Liberals and Conservatives have been "fragment" parties,[20] originating not out of social protest, but rather out of conflict within the political elite. Hence, the United Newfoundland Party, which won two seats in the 1959 provincial election, reflected a split in the Conservative caucus over the relative generosity to Newfoundland of the Diefenbaker administration in Ottawa and the Diefenbaker handling of a woodworkers' strike, while both the New Labrador Party, which won a single seat in the 1971 provincial election, and the Liberal Reform Party, which won four seats in the 1975 provincial election, largely reflected splits over leadership within the Liberal caucus. The C.C.F.-N.D.P. has never been a potent force in provincial politics (gaining only 3.7 percent of the popular vote in the 1982 provincial election), but the Party did manage to win a federal by-election in Newfoundland in 1978 before losing it in the 1980 general election. In short, the distribution of party strength in Newfoundland bears a strong resemblance to that already observed in Nova Scotia, New Brunswick, and Prince Edward Island; in all four provinces, the Liberals and Progressive Conservatives have been and continue to be the only serious contestants for political office.

It is naturally tempting to ascribe the marked preference of Atlantic Canadians for the two traditional parties entirely to the traditionalist orientations which have already been shown to exist in the region's political culture. A brief, pan-Canadian scrutiny of third parties suggests, however, that the aforementioned cynicism of Atlantic Canadians is also of significance. To understand the nature of Canadian third parties, two premises must be accepted: first, that national integration (in both its territorial and ethnic manifestations) constitutes the dominant socio-political cleavage of this country; and, second, that the Liberals and Conservatives have not completely fulfilled the role of "brokerage parties" assigned to them in the popular mythology. At times, the types of policy compromises required of brokerage politics have been logically impossible; how, one wonders, could all recognised interests have been successfully accommodated on such matters as the hanging of Louis Riel or the imposition of conscription? At other times, certain structural constraints (both economic and electoral) have strongly encouraged policy-makers to discard the role of "honest broker." What is significant in the present context is that, when faced with such situations, both Liberal and Conservative administrations in Ottawa have generally favoured the interests of the heartland over the peripheries (in, for example, tariff, tax, transportation, and resource matters) and of Anglophone Canada — at least until the 1970s — over Francophone Canada (in, for example, the Riel Rebellion), a variety of educational disputes, two conscription crises and, most recently, the patriation of the Constitution). The result of these systematic biases has been latent resentment — in the peripheries against the heartland, and in Francophone Canada, against Anglophone Canada. Such latent resentment constitutes one of the preconditions of successful third party gestation in Canada.

One should not necessarily fault the national parties for their lack of interest in Atlantic Canada. When one looks at the number of seats available in the four Atlantic provinces (currently 32) and compares this with the number of seats available in the Golden Horseshoe around Lake Ontario and, furthermore, if one compares the traditional voting patterns of the residents of Atlantic Canada with those of the industrial heartland of Ontario, one can see why policies have not been developed to obtain electoral support in Atlantic Canada. To put it another way, representation by population in the House of Commons and the lack of an effective regional voice in the upper chamber have worked to the disadvantage of the region.

In any event, this latent resentment against the heartland does exist in Atlantic Canada. Irrespective of Confederation, the region's golden era of "wind, wood, and water" would obviously not have outlasted the nineteenth century. Nevertheless, the union with Upper Canada has been blamed (and not always accurately) for much of the Atlantic region's subsequent economic ills. Nova Scotia, for example, was considered by many to be a "have" province in 1867. Today, of course, it is labelled along with the rest of the region as a "have not" province. It is also true that Atlantic Canada has suffered from the lending policies of central Canadian banks, that the region has received only a minimal return on its share of the investment to open up the West, that its industries have often been unable to bear the high costs engendered by tariffs designed to protect central Canadian enterprise, that it was not compensated for the alienation of Dominion lands to Quebec, Ontario and Manitoba, that it has been relatively disadvantaged in the disbursement of federal monies, and so on.[21] With the accumulation of these grievances has come a "huge reservoir of anti-Upper Canadian feeling which rests near the surface of the collective psyche of Nova Scotia" (and, one might add, of New Brunswick, Prince Edward Island, and Newfoundland).[22]

But if Atlantic Canada has one of the two preconditions to successful third party activity, it clearly lacks the other. In order to galvanize this "huge reservoir" of latent resentment into political action, people must have a high sense of either individual or regional efficacy. Yet, as was pointed out earlier, Atlantic Canadians are notoriously nonefficacious; they believe that neither individually nor collectively can they be politically influential at the national level. As a result, the region's latent resentment is not tapped by protest parties; Atlantic Canada remains a dispirited hinterland.

In any case, even where the two preconditions exist, there must be a precipitant to the formation of a successful third party. That is to say, there must be some crisis, strain, or dislocation (however elastically defined)[23] to catalyze the latent resentment and the high efficacy into third party activity. In Atlantic Canada, there have been remarkably few such dislocations. The contrast between, on the one hand, the wild fluctuations in the economic health of Western Canada and, on the other hand, the relative stagnation of the Atlantic Canadian economy is particularly instructive. Uncertainty, rising expectations, and relative deprivation are all far more likely to engender some form of "strain" than a grinding, but omnipresent, poverty. In short, not only does Atlantic Canada lack one of the two preconditions for successful third party activity, it may also lack that seemingly most common of political phenomena — a precipitant.[24]

Yet even if the Liberals and Conservatives continue to dominate Atlantic Canadian politics, the relative strength of these two parties has changed over time. Residents of the Atlantic region have shown an historic preference for the Liberal Party; an inspection of twentieth century provincial election results across the region reveals that the Liberals have held office for over sixty per cent of the time. Nevertheless, since the mid-1950s, there has been a resurgence in the strength of the Progressive Conservative Party to the point that Conservative administrations are now firmly ensconced in all four provincial capitals. The result of this perceptible shift in voter allegiance has been to transform the region from one which might have been categorized as one-party dominant to one in which there are now two.equally prepared competing political parties. Whether this growth in Conservative support can be attributed to the recruitment of persons such as Robert Stanfield, G.I. Smith, Richard Hatfield, James Lee, David MacDonald, Frank Moores, Brian Peckford, and John Crosbie, who have been able to build strong provincial party machines, or whether the reason lies with the region's antagonism towards the national Liberal Party is a debatable point upon which some people have speculated' but not arrived at a definitive answer.

Because the level of party system symmetry is so high in Atlantic Canada (that is to say, because the Liberals and Conservatives are still dominant at both levels), the region's political parties are far more integrated than are those found in the remainder of the country. For both the provincial and national wings of the two major parties, the same organization is responsible for raising funds, recruiting candidates, fighting elections, and so on. As a result, provincial administrations pay close heed to the results of federal campaigns and it is instructive that many observers regard the 1968 setback of the *federal* Liberals in Newfoundland as the beginning of the end for J. R. Smallwood's *provincial* Liberal government.[25] As both a cause and a consequence of this relatively high degree of party integration across levels of government, voters in Atlantic Canada are far more likely than their counterparts in the rest of Canada to support the same party in both federal and provincial politics. One recent study of Canadian partisanship revealed that while 86 percent of Atlantic Canadians are consistent identifiers across the two levels, the corresponding figure for the other six provinces is only 65 percent.[26]

Even if it may be losing some of its importance as an electoral determinant, the region's traditionalism is also apparent in the lingering impact of religion. It is not a coincidence, for example, that the Halifax-Cornwallis constituency has elected only one Protestant (1970-1978) in its entire existence. In fact, the Smallwood government kept sectarianism alive with elaborate religious gerrymanders and with promises to maintain Protestant denominational schools.[27] The religious cleavage was also institutionalized in Prince Edward Island, where for many decades, the two parties would run one Roman Catholic and one Protestant candidate in nine of the fifteen dual-member ridings and two Protestants in each of the other six constituencies. The result, of course, was that, irrespective of its partisan composition, the provincial legislature would contain twenty-one Protestants and nine Roman Catholics. Whether such norms served to perpetuate or defuse the religious cleavage is unclear, but concern over sectarian tensions was sufficient to ensure that clergymen were banned from elected office in the province until 1967.[28]

Finally, Atlantic Canada's traditionalism is manifested in the overwhelming preponderance of white males in the party elites. The region has been particularly slow to accept women in politics. For example, Nova Scotia has only elected three women members and has yet to have a woman Cabinet Minister, while Prince Edward Island waited until 1970 to elect its first female to the legislature. Politics remains such a male bastion in the region that one prominent Nova Scotia Conservative spoke out strongly within party circles against running women in the 1981 provincial election. Similarly, the black and native populations have not been successful in having members of these groups elected to the provincial legislatures. It is true that there have been black and native candidates, but they have usually run for the New Democratic Party and thus have suffered the same fate as has the party generally.

As to the other major element in Atlantic Canada's political culture, cynicism is also readily apparent in the region's party system. In particular, despite their aforementioned lack of political trust, the low efficacy of Atlantic Canadians permits the many oligarchical features of the region's party politics to go unchallenged. The role and function of the party leader has always been of great importance in all four provinces. Writing of Nova Scotia and Robert Stanfield, Dalton Camp stated:

> In Nova Scotia, politicians are either looked up to or looked down upon, and it was clear that most Nova Scotians looked up to Robert Stanfield. They admired his calm, and they respected him for his presumed financial independence — for they felt that a man's honesty was assured if he was rich in the first place, and thus more likely beyond temptation. And they liked Stanfield's plain, unostentatious manner. The quality of the chieftain matters a good deal to Nova Scotians.[29]

Such successful politicians as Angus L. MacDonald, Louis Robichaud, J. B. McNair, Alex Campbell, and J.R. Smallwood all exhibited these qualities and were consequently able to exercise lengthy political coattails. Nova Scotians in particular have a tendency to loathe an opposition leader until he becomes premier, when of course he is lionized as having chieftain qualities. Once again, Stanfield is an example, as is the current premier, John Buchanan.

Certainly, the position of the party leader and other senior members of the party is more pronounced in Atlantic Canada than is the case in other areas of the country. It has been alleged, for example, that nominating conventions in New Brunswick are of only ritualistic import, with the victorious candidate having already been ordained by the party leader.[30] Moreover, the Nova Scotia Conservatives did not even have a party constitution until 1975, while the Newfoundland Liberals lacked even the most rudimentary elements of a formal party organization until the late 1960s.[31] In fact, with the partial exception of Prince Edward Island, where delegates to the Conservative and Liberal conventions each number in excess of fifteen hundred, surveys conducted at leadership contests in the region have revealed that the party rank and file have exceptionally little opportunity to participate in meaningful party dialogue.[32] Finally, it has proven to be very difficult for political newcomers to rise quickly in these cadre parties; rather, they are expected to go through the normal channels and climb the ladder as did their elders.

Their approach to the electoral process also reveals the cynical orientations of Atlantic Canadians. Elections are not designed to provide the voter with a choice between competing world views; on the contrary, provincial party platforms are "remarkable more for their similarities than their differences,"[33] and voters in Atlantic Canada are, not surprisingly, much less likely than their counterparts in the rest of the country to have an "issue" basis for their selection.[34] Why, therefore, do Atlantic Canadians still continue to invest such heavy resources in the political game? Why do they continue to participate in politics more extensively than other Canadians? Part of the answer lies in the age-old practice of patronage.

Two types of patronage are apparent. The first concerns jobs for the friends of the party, while the second is the use of money and rum on election day. With respect to the first, it is perhaps no worse than that which exists in other provinces except that in Atlantic Canada, it is taken not only as a way of life, but as a part of the democratic process. Because of the relative smallness of the population of the four provinces, patronage is much more noticeable than it would be in a larger province. Also, at least in the recent past, governments tend to change in these four provinces and when they do, the friends of one party are replaced by the friends of the other. Hence, at the 1978 Prince Edward Island Liberal leadership convention Premier Bennett Campbell's floor demonstration was led by two patronage-appointed provincial employees: one drove a school bus and the second operated a snow-plough. In fact, in the 1981 provincial election, the Conservative member for Hants East, Nova Scotia, was defeated by members of his own party because he had refused to fire the Liberal-appointed highway workers. Voters in this constituency had to witness the ludicrous situation of a former Conservative member working to defeat an incumbent Conservative. In other words, party members expect to receive the spoils of office.

There has been little attempt by any of the political parties to come to grips with patronage. In part, this reflects the region's poverty; it has been persuasively argued that in an expanding economy, governments are more likely to concentrate on production, while in a stagnant economy, they turn to "parasitism."[35] Nevertheless, one cannot ignore the reciprocal relationship that exists between cynicism in the political culture and corruption in the party system; as a *Toronto Daily Star* reporter noted in 1967:

> It does not matter much whether the stories of election bribery, corruption, and patronage that one hears everywhere are true or not, the fact is the people believe them and there is this universal cynicism about all things political in this area of Atlantic Canada.[36]

As for election day "treating" as it is described, an effort was made, particularly in the late 1960s and early 1970s, to stamp out these practices. The catalyst for this move was another article in the *Toronto Daily Star* which was titled, "Dollars and Rum Still Buy Votes in Nova Scotia." In that article, the reporter quoted Findlay MacDonald:

> It is a practice...which will be followed by all three political parties. It is also a practice that should of course be stopped and one that Stanfield is doing his best to end. But it's a part of the political scene here and we have to do it because the others will even if we don't. And it probably works out pretty even in the end anyway.[37]

The upshot of these two articles — and it is important to note that the paper which raised the issue was not one in the region, for the local media are exceptionally quiescent on political matters and refuse to take a stand on any matter — was the appointment of a Royal Commission and subsequent legislation to reform the Nova Scotia political system. Yet such legislation, both in Nova Scotia and elsewhere in Atlantic Canada, has had relatively little impact on the region's political practices. Certainly, it is instructive, first, that Richard Hatfield felt compelled in 1974 to reverse his government's initial hostility to patronage and, second, that he was able to declare during an election campaign that patronage was a fact of political life in New Brunswick, without incurring the criticism of his Liberal opponents.[38] In short, elections in Atlantic Canada have changed surprisingly little since the premier of Prince Edward Island, Donald Farquharson, observed in 1900 that "it is simply a matter now of who will buy the most votes and the man who works hardest and is prepared to use means fair or foul will get in."[39]

Those who decry these practices (and most of them are in academia) are criticised for not understanding this system and for being naive about the political process.[40] Furthermore, Atlantic Canadians wonder whether it is any worse to buy votes with rum and money than it is to promise new highways, bridges, school cafetarias, oil sands plants, hockey rinks, and so on. They, of course, have a point; bribery at election time exists in one form or another throughout the country, but it is only in Atlantic Canada, and particularly in the Maritimes, that the blatant use of money and alcohol persists on election day. Presumably the only way it will ultimately be curtailed is not by internal reform or demands from the media, but rather by inflation and rising prices.

What, then, can one conclude about politics in Atlantic Canada? One can see the importance of politics in the lives of most individuals. Politics in Atlantic Canada has a greater social significance than is found in the rest of the country; indeed, one might refer to politics as "the national sport" of Atlantic Canadians. Furthermore, as befits a dependent hinterland, parties are more closely aligned to their federal counterparts than is the case in other regions of the country. One also notes that only the two old-line cadre parties have been successful in Atlantic Canada. Finally, one can detect not only extensive patronage and corruption, but also a lack of desire to reform and cleanse the political process. In short, Atlantic Canada's traditionalistic and cynical political culture (the existence of which was earlier inferred from indicators not directly related to the operation of political parties) is clearly reflected in the region's party system.

Possibly the best way to conclude is once again to quote Dalton Camp:

> There is a coarse, cruel strain in the politics of Canada which one discovers soon enough after becoming involved in its processes. It is necessary, it seems, to foment the passions of fear and suspicion, so that popular leaders may rise to power on their tides.[41]

Nowhere is this statement as true as in Atlantic Canada. On the other hand, to be positive, a viable two-party system now exists and there are legitimate alternatives to the existing parties in power in all four provinces. Can one say this about all other regions of the country?

ENDNOTES

1. Dalton M. Camp, *Gentlemen, Players and Politicians*, (Ottawa: Deneau, 1979), p. 284.
2. It has been demonstrated that, at least for Nova Scotia, outmigrants come disproportionately from the more educated sector of the community. See J. R.

Winter, *Net Migration Rates by County for the Maritime Provinces*, (Wolfville: Acadia University 1970), p. 78.

3. David Bellamy, "The Atlantic Provinces", in David J. Bellamy, Jon H. Pammett, and Donald C. Rowat, eds., *The Provincial Political Systems: Comparative Essays* (Toronto: Methuen, 1976), p. 3.

4. Dale H. Poel, "The Diffusion of Legislation Among the Canadian Provinces: A Statistical Analysis", *Canadian Journal of Political Science*, Vol. 9 (1976), pp. 605-626.

5. See, for example, Marsha A. Chandler and William M. Chandler, *Public Policy and Provincial Politics*, (Toronto: McGraw-Hill Ryerson, 1979), p. 193.

6. Richard Simeon and Donald E. Blake, "Regional Preferences: Citizens' Views of Public Policy", in David J. Elkins and Richard Simeon, eds., *Small Worlds: Provinces and Parties in Canadian Political Life* (Toronto: Methuen, 1960), pp. 84-103.

7. Prince Edward Island even banned automobiles in 1908; eventually, they were permitted on the Island, but those in operation had to be preceded by an individual on foot carrying a red flag! See Marlene-Russell Clark, "Island Politics", in Francis W.P. Bolger, ed., *Canada's Smallest Province: A History of P.E.I.* (Charlottetown: The Prince Edward Island 1973 Centennial Commission, 1973), p. 319.

8. Alan Gregg and Michael Whittington, "Regional Variation in Children's Political Attitudes", in Bellamy, Pammett, and Rowat, eds., *The Provincial Political Systems*, pp. 76-85.

9. See, for example, Allan Kornberg, William Mishler, and Harold D.Clarke, *Representative Democracy in the Canadian Provinces* (Scarborough: Prentice Hall Canada, 1982), pp. 99-103.

10. See Kornberg, Mishler, and Clarke, p. 80, and especially, Richard Simeon and David J. Elkins, "Provincial Political Culture in Canada" in Elkins and Simeon, eds., *Small Worlds*, pp. 346. It may be, of course, that the extent of interregional variations on these dimensions is diminishing over time.

11. J. Murray Beck, "Elections in the Maritimes: The Votes Against Have It", *Commentator*, Vol. 17 (Dec. 1970), p. 7.

12. Mildred A. Schwartz, *Politics and Territory: The Sociology of Regional Persistence in Canada* (Montreal: McGill-Queen's University Press, 1974), p. 148.

13. D. Campbell and R.A. MacLean, *Beyond the Atlantic Roar: A Study of the Nova Scotia Scots* (Toronto: MacMillan, 1974), p. 236.

14. Agar Adamson, "The Nova Scotia Progressive Conservative Leadership Convention: How Representative?", paper presented to the annual meeting of the Canadian Political Science Association, 1972.

15. *The Toronto Globe and Mail*, September, 1982, p. 2.

16. Despite electing only two M.L.A.s, the C.C.F. even constituted Nova Scotia's Official Opposition after the 1945 provincial election.

17. David Lewis, *The Good Fight* (Toronto: Macmillan of Canada, 1981), p. 160.

18. For details on this rift in the Nova Scotia N.D.P., see Agar Adamson, "The 1981 Nova Scotia Provincial Election: Observations and Comments on the Parties", paper presented to the annual meeting of the Canadian Political Science Association, 1982.

19. See John Wilson and David Hoffman, "Ontario: A Three-Party System in Transition", in Martin Robin, ed., *Canadian Provincial Politics* (Scarborough: Prentice-Hall Canada, 1972), pp. 198-239.

20. See John McMenemy, "Fragment and Movement Parties", in Conrad Winn and John McMenemy (eds.), *Political Parties in Canada* (Toronto: McGraw-Hill Ryerson, 1976), pp. 29-48.

21. See Bruce Archibald, "Atlantic Regional Underdevelopment and Socialism", in Laurier LaPierre, Jack McLeod, Charles Taylor, and Walter Young, eds., *Essays on the Left* (Toronto: McClelland and Stewart, 1971), pp. 109-111 and David Alexander, "New Notions of Happiness: Nationalism, Regionalism, and Atlantic Canada", *Journal of Canadian Studies*, Vol. 15 (1980), No. 2, p. 36.

22. G.A. Rawlyk, "The Farm-Labour Movement and the Failure of Socialism in Nova Scotia", in LaPierre, McLeod, Taylor and Young, p. 37.

23. For a marvellous example of employing "strain" as an explanatory variable without first defining its meaning, see Maurice Pinard, *The Rise of a Third Party: A Study in Crisis Politics* (Englewood Cliffs: Prentice-Hall, 1975).

24. Because the preconditions to successful third party gestation exist only in Quebec and the West, these two regions have historically been the most politically turbulent in Canada. From the former have come the Nationalistes, the Union Nationale, and the Parti Quebecois; from the latter have emerged the Progressives, the C.C.F.-N.D.P., and Social Credit. In all cases, it is an easy, but relatively unrewarding, task to discover the dislocation which precipitated their emergence.

25. See, for example, Peter Neary, "Politics in Newfoundland: The End of the Smallwood Era", *Journal of Canadian Studies*, Vol. 7, No. 1 (1972), pp. 9-16.

26. Harold D. Clarke, Jane Jenson, Lawrence Leduc, and Jon. H. Pammett, *Political Choice in Canada* (Toronto: McGraw-Hill Ryerson, 1980), p. 97. See also Schwartz, pp. 154-155.

27. See Peter Neary, "Democracy in Newfoundland: A Comment", *Journal of Canadian Studies*, Vol. 4, No. 1 (1969), pp. 37-45. Smallwood's open support for Protestant groups, in conjunction with the St. John's-Outport cleavage at the time of Confederation, has meant that the Progressive Conservative Party of Newfoundland, like that in P.E.I., but unlike those in the other eight provinces, has historically received the support of Roman Catholics.

28. See Clarke, pp. 299-301. It is also interesting to note that denominational schools were the catalyst for Prince Edward Island's only coalition administration (1876-1879) in which Protestants from both parties formed the government with the Roman Catholics from both parties in opposition.

29. Camp, p. 213.

30. P.J. Fitzpatrick, "New Brunswick: The Politics of Pragmatism", in Martin Robin, ed., *Canadian Provincial Politics*, second edition, (Scarborough: Prentice-Hall Canada, 1978), p. 124.

31. See S.J.R. Noel, *Politics in Newfoundland* (Toronto: University of Toronto Press, 1971), pp. 283-285 and George Perlin, "Patronage and Paternalism: Politics in Newfoundland", in D.I. Davies and Kathleen Herman, eds., *Social Space: Canadian Perspectives* (Toronto: New Press, 1971), pp. 192-194.

32. Agar Adamson and Marshall W. Conley, data from unpublished leadership delegate surveys.

33. Hugh G. Thorburn, *Politics in New Brunswick* (Toronto: University of Toronto Press, 1961), p. 114. Nevertheless, one should note the existence of the Red Tory phenomenon. Such people as Robert Stanfield, Gordon Fairweather, and David MacDonald have ensured that the Conservative Party in the Atlantic provinces has remained to the left of its counterparts in the rest of the country. Flora MacDonald once summarized her belief in Red Toryism when she stated: "I could bring myself to vote for an N.D.P. candidate, but I could never vote for a Liberal." (In an address to students at Acadia University, 1976).

34. Kornberg, Mishler, and Clarke, p. 124.

35. Ralph Matthews, "Perspectives on Recent Newfoundland Politics", *Journal of Canadian Studies*, Vol. 9 (1974), pp. 20-35.

36. *The Toronto Star*, May 29, 1967.

37. *The Toronto Star*, May 26, 1967.

38. John McMenemy, "Party Organization", in Bellamy, Pammett, and Rowat, eds., p. 103.

39. Wayne E. MacKinnon, *The Life of the Party*, Summerside, Prince Edward Island Liberal Party, 1973, p. 73.

40. This conforms with Kenneth Gibbons' speculation that the dominant orientation of Atlantic Canadians towards political corruption is one of "blamelessness." See Kenneth M. Gibbons, "The Political Culture of Corruption in Canada", in Kenneth M. Gibbons and Donald C. Rowat, eds., *Political Corruption in Canada: Cases, Causes, and Cures* (Toronto: Macmillan, 1976), pp. 231-250.

41. Camp, pp. 147-148.

29 Addendum: The 1984 Federal Election

HUGH G. THORBURN

This book went to press immediately after the September 4, 1984 election. It was an election like none other in Canadian history; therefore it deserves some special notice beyond the recording of the results in the accompanying tables. It has all the characteristics of an "election of national realignment," or of a "critical election." That is to say, the old relationships between political parties appear to have been blown away, and new ones put in their place. However nobody can yet say for certain how long these new ones will last. It seems fitting, if hazardous, therefore to offer some comment or interpretation.

What happened? The Liberal Party, generally perceived to be Canada's "government party", which has won eighteen of the past twenty-four elections, and which has never polled less than forty per cent of the total votes in the country, except for the two Diefenbaker elections of 1958 and 1962, (34 and 37 percent respectively), has suddenly been reduced to 28 per cent of the vote and forty MPs, or one-seventh of the House of Commons. The other side of the coin is the Progressive Conservative success: polling half of the votes cast across the country, and winning three quarters of the parliamentary seats. The NDP remains constant at around 20 per cent of the votes and 11 per cent of the seats.

These gross figures are surprising, but what occurred in Quebec is almost unbelievable. In the past seven elections the Conservative MPs elected in Quebec were counted in one figure. Now there are fifty-eight (out of seventy-five). From getting about one vote in five to one vote in six, they now have over half of the votes cast in the province.

In the rest of Canada the Conservatives' success is substantial, but not the kind of *volte-face* that Quebec experienced (an increase from 13 to 50 percent — or 37 percentage points). In the Atlantic provinces the party vote advanced from 6 to 22 percentage points, in Ontario 11 points, in the west from 2 to 11 points.

These results suggest a parallel with the Diefenbaker sweep of 1958 (208 out of 265 seats, with 54 percent of the votes cast) — and everyone recalls what a flash-in-the-pan that was! The Tories were out in five years with their vote down to one in three, where it remained for over twenty years. What is different about 1984? The big difference is in the Quebec vote, which in 1958 was presented to the Conservatives by the *Union Nationale*, which mobilized its provincial machine and invaded federal politics to defeat the Liberals. But the *Union Nationale* is dead — the Tories made it on their own, by becoming a legitimate francophone party. Internal Conservative polls in Quebec reveal that Brian Mulroney is perceived by half of the Quebec francophone voters to be francophone, and by 70 percent of Quebec anglophones as English. Conservative MPs elected in Quebec this time count past supporters of sovereignty-association among them, as well as ex-Liberals and many well placed and highly educated people. In short, the party has mobilized a Quebec caucus behind Brian Mulroney which is just as representative as the Liberals once were. Therefore one should expect the party to have more staying power in Quebec in the future. But on the other hand, if the demands of Quebec are not respected, there could be serious problems in keeping the caucus united.

Another difference from the Diefenbaker sweep is the fact that in 1958 it was a populist revolt based on the messianism of the man. This time the Mulroney victory is a case of "out-Liberaling" the Liberals, of occupying the broad centre of the political spectrum, emphasizing unity, confidence, moderation and fairness, and reminding the voters of the past excesses of their opponents. It will be much harder to dislodge the Conservatives from this position, which has traditionally been occupied by the winner in Canadian politics.

If this picture accurately represents the macro-political situation, what does it mean for the individual parties? The Conservatives appear to have displaced the Liberals as the government party, drawing their strength from Quebec and English Canada, just as they did in the days of Sir John A. Macdonald. This is the formula for success in Canadian politics. But it is a difficult position to occupy over time. It is one thing to mobilize the resentment of the nation against a government too long in power, arrogant and prone to abuse its patronage powers. It is another to win again after a term of office during hard economic times, when the regional interests in the country have had time to play their divisive role, the provincial premiers to make their demands, and the Americans to continue their heedless game of hard-ball as played by the super-powers. In short, the test for the Conservatives is to prolong the fleeting consensus that put them in power, and build up a politics of national solidarity which has escaped this country over the Trudeau years. If they succeed in maintaining the essentials of national unity, they should be ale to maintain themselves in power in the future.

The situation for the Liberals is, in a sense, the obverse of this. They have been repudiated, humiliated and threatened with long-term ineffectiveness. The Conservatives have taken their formula from them and improved upon it, just as Wilfred Laurier took the Conservative formula in 1896, adapted it and won with it. It is centrist, consensual politics — the only formula with lasting winning power in this country. But how do you get the formula back, once you have lost hold of it? You can pray for deliverance through the gross errors of the government. After all this happened before, when the Diefenbaker government fell apart for all to see. This time however such an event seems highly improbable. The other way is to re-fashion the formula and try to make it more attractive than the government version. That is what Mr. Mulroney did, and at the right time.

The Liberals find themselves in a most threatened situation. Not only are they weaker in parliament than they have ever been in our history, but they have only ten seats more than the New Democratic Party. Moreover the NDP caucus is make up of seasoned parliamentary veterans, buoyed up by the relative success (i.e. survival) of the party in the election which cost the Liberals over two thirds of their seats. The first challenge for the Liberals therefore is to mount a credible parliamentary opposition. If they fail they could be by-passed by the NDP.

Canadian politics is essentially two-party politics, divided as it is by the British distinction: government-opposition, with parliament ranged on two sides of a table, government versus opposition. And the electoral law has always left the third parties in a weak position with a much smaller proportion of seats compared to their share of votes cast. For Liberals, the prospect of such a fate is surely appalling.

What are the chances? To begin, Canadians have grown used to the Liberals as a major party — so one would expect traditional affinities to count for something in the end. Also, Canadian politics has long centred on the game of the "ins versus the outs" without a class or ideological cleavage between the major parties. This will not easily be abandoned. And the business interests can be expected to know their advantage and succour the Liberals back to health, to keep the Canadian political debate out of the capitalist versus socialist cleavage around which politics generally revolves in European democracies. On the other hand, the Conservatives may see the advantage in having such a political debate, confident that they could always win over an avowedly socialist party.

What then should the Liberals do? If they veer left (as they usually do when in opposition) they risk losing business support, and being outbidded by the NDP anyway. Since they cannot realistically move to the right of the Conservatives, they could try (as the Conservatives themselves have done under Stanfield and Clark) to be another middle-of-the-road party. This is the thankless role of the traditional opposition party in Canadian politics. This time it will call for staying power, patience and hard work. More important, it will require insight and vision to adapt the formula so as to be more attractive to the voters than the Conservatives. They have an ally in the chronically depressed economy — a burden no government can avoid bearing to some degree.

So there is now a new question on the agenda: will the Canadian party system revert to the two-and-a-half party system of yore, with the NDP constituting the marginal half-party; or will the Liberal party crumble like its British counterpart sixty years ago, and be supplemented by a socialist party? Such a fate for the "government party" sounds far-fetched. But then so did such a fate for Lloyd George's and H.H. Asquith's party. The Liberals face their greatest challenge since Laurier.

The pressures on the new government are bound to be substantial, however. Regional divergences are greater than in the past, and the state of the national economy is very precarious. The question is posed: shall Canada enter into a free trade relationship with the United States, or should it continue to try to make its way alone, facing the United States, the European Community and Japan in international trade? This question of relations with the U.S.A. has divided Canadians and upset political balances before. It prompted Confederation in the 1860s when the Americans abrogated the reciprocity treaty, and it brought the Laurier government down in 1911. It has the potential of dividing the country again. And it may also divide the Conservative caucus, the provinces, or federal-provincial relations. We are condemned to live in interesting times.

But one thing is certain. The vision of a bilingual Canada, in which the French fact is recognized from coast to coast, is now accomplished. It is no longer just Liberal policy; it is personified in the Conservative leader and Prime Minister, Brian Mulroney. Pierre Trudeau must be pleased, because his vision is now supported by all three federal parliamentary parties.

30 Federal Election Results 1878-1984

APPENDIX

I am indebted to Professor Howard A. Scarrow who provided most of the data that follow[1]. The results after and including 1962 are taken from the preliminary results issued by the Chief Electoral Officer and published in the daily press. The information relating to the distribution of seats is taken from the Canadian Press summary. The papers from which the results are cited are the Toronto Daily *Star* and the Kingston *Whig-Standard*.

NEWFOUNDLAND

Election Year	Party Forming Federal Government	Total Seats	Conservative Seats	Conservative Votes (%)	Liberal Seats	Liveral Votes (%)	Other Seats	Other Votes (%)
1949	Lib.	7	2	28	5	72		
1953	Lib.	7	0	28	7	67		5[1]
1957	Con.	7	2	38	5	62		
1958	Con.	7	2	45	5	54		1
1962	Con.	7	1	36	6	59		5[2]
1963	Lib.	7	0	30	7	65		5[3]
1965	Lib.	7	0	32	7	64		4[4]
1968	Lib.	7	6	53	1	42		4[5]
1972	Lib.	7	4	49	3	45		5[6]
1974	Lib.	7	3	44	4	47		10[7]
1979	Con.	7	2	31	4	38	1	31[8]
1980	Lib.	7	2	36	5	47	0	17[9]
1984	Con.	7	4	57	3	36	0	6[10]

1. Including 4 percent CCF.
2. Including 5 percent NDP.
3. Including 4 percent NDP.
4. Including 1 percent NDP and 2 percent Social Credit.
5. Including 4 percent NDP.
6. Including 5 percent NDP.
7. Including 10 percent NDP.
8. Including 31 percent NDP.
9. Including 17 percent NDP.
10. Including 6 percent NDP.

ENDNOTES

1. Complete details can be found in his book *Canada Votes: A Handbook of Federal and Provincial Election Data* (New Orleans: Hauser Press, 1962).

NOVA SCOTIA

Election Year	Party Forming Federal Government	Total Seats	Conservative Seats	Conservative Votes (%)	Liberal Seats	Liberal Votes (%)	CCF — NDP Seats	CCF — NDP (Votes %)	Other Seats	Other Votes (%)
1878	Con.	21	14	52	6	44			1	4
1882	Con.	21	14	55	7	45				
1887	Con.	21	14	50	7	47				3
1891	Con.	21	16	54	5	45				1
1896	Lib.	20	10	50	10	49				1
1900	Lib.	20	5	48	15	52				
1904	Lib.	18	0	44	18	55				1
1908	Lib.	18	6	49	12	51				
1911	Con.	18	9	49	9	51				
1917	Con.[1]	16	12[2]	48	4	46				6
1921	Lib.	16	0	32	16	53				15
1925	Lib.	14	11	56	3	42				2
1926	Lib.	14	12	54	2	43				3
1930	Con.	14	10	53	4	47				
1935	Lib.	12	0	32	12	52				16
1940	Lib.	12	1	40	10	51	1	6		3
1945	Lib.	12	2	37	9	46	1	17		
1949	Lib.	13	2	37	10	53	1	10		
1953	Lib.	12	1	40	10	53	1	7		
1957	Con.	12	10	50	2	45	0	5		
1958	Con.	12	12	57	0	38	0	5		
1962	Con.	12	9	47	2	42	1	10		1
1963	Lib.	12	7	47	5	47	0	6		
1965	Lib.	12	10	49	2	42	0	9		
1968	Lib.	11	10	55	1	38	0	7		
1972	Lib.	11	10	53	1	34	0	12		
1974	Lib.	11	8	48	2	41	1	11		
1979	Con.	11	8	45	2	36	1	19		
1980	Lib.	11	6	39	5	40	0	21		
1984	Con.	11	9	51	2	33	0	15		

1. Wartime Coalition.
2. Including three Liberal Unionists.

NEW BRUNSWICK

Election Year	Party Forming Federal Government	Total Seats	Conservative Seats	Conservative Votes (%)	Liberal Seats	Liberal Votes (%)	Other Seats	Other Votes (%)
1878	Con.	16	5	45	11	55		
1882	Con.	16	9	55	7	45		
1887	Con.	16	10	51	6	49		
1891	Con.	16	13	59	3	38		3
1896	Lib.	14	9	49	5	44		7
1900	Lib.	14	5	48	9	52		
1904	Lib.	13	6	49	7	51		
1908	Lib.	13	2	46	11	54		
1911	Con.	13	5	49	8	51		
1917	Con.	11	7[1]	59	4	41		
1921	Lib.	11	5	39	5	50	1[2]	11
1925	Lib.	11	10	60	1	40		
1926	Lib.	11	7	54	4	46		
1930	Con.	11	10	59	1	41		
1935	Lib.	10	1	32	9	57		11
1940	Lib.	10	5	43	5	55		2
1945	Lib.	10	3	38	7	50		12
1949	Lib.	10	2	39	8	54		7
1953	Lib.	10	3	42	7	53		5
1957	Con.	10	5	49	5	48		3
1958	Con.	10	7	54	3	43		3
1962	Con.	10	4	46	6	45		9[3]
1963	Lib.	10	4	40	6	47		13[4]
1965	Lib.	10	4	43	6	47		9[5]
1968	Lib.	10	5	50	5	44		6[6]
1972	Lib.	10	5	45	5	43		11[7]
1974	Lib.	10	3	33	6	47	1	20[8]
1979	Con.	10	4	40	6	45		15
1980	Lib.	10	3	33	7	50	0	17[9]
1984	Con.	10	9	53	1	32	0	15[10]

1. Including four Liberal Unionists.
2. Progressive.
3. Including 5 percent NDP and 5 percent Social Credit.
4. Including 4 percent NDP and 9 percent Social Credit.
5. Including 9 percent NDP.
6. Including 5 percent NDP and 1 percent Social Credit.
7. Including 6 percent NDP and 6 percent Social Credit.
8. Including 9 percent NDP, 8 percent independent and 3 percent Social Credit.
9. Including 16 percent NDP.
10. Including 14 percent NDP.

PRINCE EDWARD ISLAND

Election Year	Party Forming Federal Government	Total Seats	Conservative Seats	Conservative Votes (%)	Liberal Seats	Liberal Votes (%)	Other Seats	Other Votes (%)
1878	Con.	6	5	57	1	43		
1882	Con.	6	1	48	5	52		
1887	Con.	6	0	46	6	54		
1891	Con.	6	2	48	4	52		
1896	Lib.	5	3	49	2	51		
1900	Lib.	5	2	48	3	52		
1904	Lib.	4	3	51	1	49		
1908	Lib.	4	1	50	3	50		
1911	Con.	4	2	51	2	49		
1917	Con.[1]	4	2	50	2	50		
1921	Lib.	4	0	37	4	46		17[2]
1925	Lib.	4	2	48	2	52		
1926	Lib.	4	1	47	3	53		
1930	Con.	4	3	50	1	50		
1935	Lib.	4	0	39	4	58		3[3]
1940	Lib.	4	0	45	4	55		
1945	Lib.	4	1	47	3	49		4[4]
1949	Lib.	4	1	48	3	49		3[5]
1953	Lib.	4	1	48	3	51		1
1957	Con.	4	4	52	0	47		1
1958	Con.	4	4	62	0	38		
1962	Con.	4	4	51	0	44		5[6]
1963	Lib.	4	2	51	2	47		2[7]
1965	Lib.	4	4	54	0	44		2[8]
1968	Lib.	4	4	52	0	45		3[9]
1972	Lib.	4	3	52	1	41		8[10]
1974	Lib.	4	3	49	1	46		5[11]
1979	Con.	4	4	53	0	40		7[12]
1980	Lib.	4	2	46	2	47		7[13]
1984	Con.	4	3	52	1	41		7[14]

1. Wartime Coalition.
2. Including 12 percent Progressive.
3. Including 3 percent Reconstruction Party.
4. Including 4 percent CCF.
5. Including 2 percent CCF.
6. Including 5 percent NDP.
7. Including 2 percent NDP.
8. Including 2 percent NDP.
9. Including 3 percent NDP.
10. Including 8 percent NDP.
11. Including 5 percent NDP.
12. Including 7 percent NDP.
13. Including 7 percent NDP.
14. Including 7 percent NDP.

QUEBEC

Election Year	Party Forming Federal Government	Total Seats	Conservative Seats	Conservative Votes (%)	Liberal Seats	Liberal Votes (%)	Other Seats	Other Votes (%)
1878	Con.	65	45	56	20	40		4
1882	Con.	65	52	59	13	41		
1887	Con.	65	36	51	29	49		
1891	Con.	65	29	52	34	45		3
1896	Lib.	65	16	46	49	54		
1900	Lib.	65	8	44	57	56		
1904	Lib.	65	11	43	54	56		1
1908	Lib.	65	11	41	54	57		2
1911	Con.	65	27	49	38	51		
1917	Con.[1]	65	3[2]	25	62	73		2
1921	Lib.	65	0	18	65	70		12
1925	Lib.	65	4	34	59	59	2	7
1926	Lib.	65	4	34	60	62	1	4
1930	Con.	65	24	45	40	53	1	2
1935	Lib.	65	5	28	55	54	5	18[3]
1940	Lib.	65	1[5]	20	61	63	3[4]	17
1945	Lib.	65	2[7]	8	53	51	10[6]	41
1949	Lib.	73	2	25	68	60	3	15
1953	Lib.	75	4	29	66	61	5[8]	10
1957	Con.	75	9	31	62	58	4[9]	11
1958	Con.	75	50	50	25	46		4
1962	Con.	75	14	30	35	40	26[11]	30[10]
1963	Lib.	75	8	20	47	46	20[11]	34[12]
1965	Lib.	75	8	21	56	46	11[13]	33[14]
1968	Lib.	74	4	21	56	53	14	26[15]
1972	Lib.	74	2	17	56	49	16[17]	34[16]
1974	Lib.	74	3	21	60	54	11[19]	25[18]
1979	Con.	75	2	13	67	62	6[21]	25[20]
1980	Lib.	75	1	13	73	70	0	17
1984	Con.	75	58	50	17	35	0	15[22]

1. Wartime Coalition.
2. Including one Liberal Unionist.
3. Including 9 percent cast for Reconstruction Party.
4. Independent Liberals.
5. Independent Conservative.
6. Six Independents, one Independent Liberal, two Bloc Populaire Canadien, one Labor Progressive.
7. Including one Independent Conservative.
8. Three Independents and two Independent Liberals.
9. Two Independents and two Independent Liberals.
10. Including 26 percent Social Credit and 4 percent NDP.
11. Social Credit.
12. Including 27 percent Social Credit and 7 percent NDP.
13. Including nine Créditistes, one Independent Progressive Conservative and one Independent.
14. Including 18 percent Créditiste and 12 percent NDP.
15. Including 16 percent Créditiste and 8 percent NDP.
16. Including 24 percent Social Credit and 6 percent NDP.
17. Including 15 Social Credit and 1 Independent.
18. Including 17 percent Social Credit and 7 percent NDP.
19. Social Credit.
20. Including 16 percent Social Credit and 5 percent NDP.
21. Social Credit.
22. Including 9 percent NDP & 2 percent Parti nationaliste du Québec.

ONTARIO

Election Year	Party Forming Federal Government	Total Seats	Conservative Seats	Conservative Votes (%)	Liberal Seats	Liberal Votes (%)	Progressive Seats	Progressive Votes (%)	CCF — NDP Seats	CCF — NDP Votes (%)	Other Seats	Other Votes (%)
1878	Con.	88	62	52	26	47						1
1882	Con.	92	54	51	38	49						
1887	Con.	92	54	51	38	49						
1891	Con.	92	48	49	44	49						2
1896	Lib.	92	43	45	43	40					6[1]	15
1900	Lib.	92	56	50	36	50						
1904	Lib.	86	48	50	38	50						
1908	Lib.	86	48	51	37[2]	47					1[3]	2
1911	Con.	86	73[4]	56	13	43						1
1917	Con.	82	74[5]	62	8	34						4
1921	Lib.	82	37	39	21	30	24	28				3
1925	Lib.	82	68	57	11	31	2	9			1[6]	3
1926	Lib.	82	53	54	26[7]	39	2	4			1[8]	3
1930	Con.	82	59	54	22	44	1	1				1
1935	Lib.	82	25	35	56	43					1[9]	22[10]
1940	Lib.	82	25	43	57[11]	51						6
1945	Lib.	82	48	42	34	41				14		3
1949	Lib.	83	25	37	56	46			1	15	1[12]	2
1953	Lib.	85	33	40	51	47			1	11		2
1957	Con.	85	61	49	21	37			3	12		2
1958	Con.	85	67	56	15	33			3	11		
1962	Con.	85	35	39	44	42			6	17		2
1963	Lib.	85	27	35	52	46			6	16		3[13]
1965	Lib.	85	25	34	51	44			9	22		
1968	Lib.	88	17	32	64	46			6	21	1	1
1972	Lib.	88	40	39	36	38			11	22		1
1974	Lib.	88	25	35	55	45			8	19		1
1979	Con.	95	57	42	32	37			6	21		1
1980	Lib.	95	38	36	52	42			5	22	0	7
1984	Con.	95	67	47	14	30			13	21	1	2

1. Three McCarthyite, two Patrons of Industry, one Independent.
2. Including one Independent Liberal.
3. Independent.
4. Including one Independent Conservative.
5. Including twelve Liberal Unionists.
6. Independent Liberal.
7. Including two Liberal Progressives and one Independent Liberal.
8. Independent Liberal.
9. United Farmers of Ontario-Labor.
10. Including 12 percent for Reconstruction Party.
11. Including two Liberal Progressives.
12. Independent.
13. Including two percent Social Credit.

MANITOBA

Election Year	Party Forming Federal Government	Total Seats	Conservative Seats	Conservative Votes (%)	Liberal Seats	Liberal Votes (%)	Progressive Seats	Progressive Votes (%)	Labor — CCF — NDP Seats	Labor — CCF — NDP Votes (%)	Other Seats	Other Votes (%)
1878	Con.	4	3	50	1	50						
1882	Con.	5	2	47	3	53						
1887	Con.	5	4	51	1	49						
1891	Con.	5	4	53	1	47						
1896	Lib.	7	4	47	2	35					1[1]	18
1900	Lib.	7	3	48	4	52						
1904	Lib.	10	3	42	7	55						3
1908	Lib.	10	8	52	2	45						3
1911	Con.	10	8	52	2	45						3
1917	Con.[2]	15	14[3]	80	1	20						
1921	Lib.	15	0	24	1	11	12	44	1	6	1[4]	15
1925	Lib.	17	7	42	1	20	7	27	2	11		
1926	Lib.	17	0	42	11[5]	38	4	11	2	9		
1930	Con.	17	11	48	4[6]	37		4	2	11		
								CCF				
1935	Lib.	17	1	27	14[7]	41			2	19		13[8]
1940	Lib.	17	1	26	15[9]	48			1	19		7
1945	Lib.	17	2	25	10	35			5	32		8
1949	Lib.	16	1	22	12	48			3	26		4
1953	Lib.	14	3	27	8	40			3	24		9[10]
1957	Con.	14	8	36	1	26			5	24		14[11]
1958	Con.	14	14	57	0	22			0	20		1
								NDP				
1962	Con.	14	11	41	1	31			2	20		8[12]
1963	Lib.	14	10	42	2	34			2	17		7[13]
1965	Lib.	14	10	41	1	31			3	24		4[14]
1968	Lib.	13	5	31	5	41			3	25		3[15]
1972	Lib.	13	8	42	2	31			3	26		1
1974	Lib.	13	9	48	2	27			2	24		
1979	Con.	14	7	44	2	24			5	31		1
1980	Lib.	14	5	38	2	28			7	33		1
1984	Con.	14	9	43	1	22			4	27		

1. McCarthyite.
2. Wartime Coalition.
3. Including six Liberal Unionists.
4. Independent Liberal.
5. Including seven Liberal Progressives.
6. Including three Liberal Progressives.
7. Including two Liberal Progressives.
8. Including 6 percent Reconstruction Party.
9. Including one Liberal Progressive.
10. Including 6 percent Social Credit.
11. Including 13 percent Social Credit.
12. Including 7 percent Social Credit.
13. Including 7 percent Social Credit.
14. Including 4 percent Social Credit.
15. Including 2 percent Social Credit.

SASKATCHEWAN

Election Year	Party Forming Federal Government	Total Seats	Conservative Seats	Conservative Votes (%)	Liberal Seats	Liberal Votes (%)	CCF — NDP Seats	CCF — NDP Votes (%)	Progressive Seats	Progressive Votes (%)	Other Seats	Other Votes (%)
1908	Lib.	10	1	37	9	57						6
1911	Con.	10	1	39	9	59						2
1917	Con.	16	16[1]	74	0	26						
1921	Lib.	16	0	17	1	21			15	61		1
1925	Lib.	21	0	25	15	42			6	32		1
1926	Lib.	21	0	27	18[2]	57			3	16		
1930	Con.	21	8	38	11	47			2	12		3
1935	Lib.	21	1	19	16	41	2	21			2[3]	19[4]
1940	Lib.	21	2	14	12	43	5	29			2[5]	14
1945	Lib.	21	1	19	2	33	18	44				4[6]
1949	Lib.	20	1	14	14	44	5	41				1
1953	Lib.	17	1	12	5	38	11	44				6[7]
1957	Con.	17	3	23	4	30	10	36				11[8]
1958	Con.	17	16	51	0	20	1	28				1
1962	Con.	17	16	50	1	23	0	22				5
1963	Lib.	17	17	54	0	24	0	18				4[9]
1965	Lib.	17	17	48	0	24	0	26				2[10]
1968	Lib.	13	5	37	2	27	6	36				
1972	Lib.	13	7	37	1	25	5	36				2[11]
1974	Lib.	13	8	36	3	31	2	32				
1979	Con.	14	10	41	0	22	4	37				1
1980	Lib.	14	7	40	0	24	7	36				
1984	Con.	14	9	42	0	18	5	38				

1. Including seven Liberal Unionists.
2. Including two Liberal Progressives.
3. Social Credit.
4. Including 16 percent Social Credit.
5. One Unity, one Unity Reform.
6. Including 3 percent Social Credit.
7. Including 5 percent Social Credit.
8. Including 10 percent Social Credit.
9. Including 4 percent Social Credit.
10. Including 2 percent Social Credit.
11. Including 2 percent Social Credit.

ALBERTA

Election Year	Party Forming Federal Government	Total Seats	Conservative Seats	Conservative Votes (%)	Liberal Seats	Liberal Votes (%)	Progressive Seats	Progressive Votes (%)	Social Credit Seats	Social Credit Votes (%)	Other Seats	Other Votes (%)
1908	Lib.	7	3	44	4	50		.				6
1911	Con.	7	1	43	6	53						4
1917	Con.[11]	12	11[1]	61	1	36						3
1921	Lib.	12	0	20	0	16	11	57			1[2]	7
1925	Lib.	16	3	32	4	26	9	32				10
1926	Lib.	16	1	32	3	24	11	39			1[2]	5
1930	Con.	16	4	34	3	30	9	30				6
1935	Lib.	17	1	17	1	21			15	48		14[3]
1940	Lib.	17	0	13	7	38			10	35		14[4]
1945	Lib.	17	2	19	2	22			13	37		22[5]
1949	Lib.	17	2	17	5	35			10	37		11[6]
1953	Lib.	17	2	15	4	35			11	41		9[7]
1957	Con.	17	3	28	1	28			13	38		6[8]
1958	Con.	17	17	60	0	14			0	22		4[9]
1962	Con.	17	15	43	0	19			2	29		9[10]
1963	Lib.	17	14	45	1	22			2	26		7[12]
1965	Lib.	17	15	47	0	22			2	23		8[13]
1968	Lib.	19	15	50	4	35			0	2		12[14]
1972	Lib.	19	19	57	0	25			0	4		13[15]
1974	Lib.	19	19	61	0	25			0	3		11[16]
1979	Con.	21	21	66	0	22			0	1		11[17]
1980	Lib.	21	21	66	0	21			0	1		12[18]
1984	Con.	21	21	69	0	13						18[19]

1. Including four Liberal Unionists.
2. Labor.
3. Including 13 percent CCF.
4. Including 13 percent CCF.
5. Including 18 percent CCF.
6. Including 9 percent CCF.
7. Including 7 percent CCF.
8. Including 6 percent CCF.
9. Including 4 percent CCF.
10. Including 9 percent NDP.

11. Wartime Coalition.
12. Including 7 percent NDP.
13. Including 8 percent NDP.
14. Including 9 percent NDP.
15. Including 13 percent NDP.
16. Including 9 percent NDP.
17. Including 10 percent NDP.
18. Including 10 percent NDP.
19. Including 14 percent NDP.

BRITISH COLUMBIA

Election Year	Party Forming Federal Government	Total Seats	Conservative Seats	Conservative Votes (%)	Liberal Seats	Liberal Votes (%)	CCF — NDP Seats	CCF — NDP Votes (%)	Social Credit Seats	Social Credit Votes (%)	Other Seats	Other Votes (%)
1878	Con.	6	6	89	0							11
1882	Con.	6	6	83	0	11						6
1887	Con.	6	6	87	0	13						
1891	Con.	6	6	72	0	28						
1896	Lib.	6	2	51	4	49						
1900	Lib.	6	2	41	4	49						10[1]
1904	Lib.	7	0	39	7	49						12[2]
1908	Lib.	7	5	47	2	36						17[3]
1911	Con.	7	7	59	0	37						4[4]
1917	Con.	13	13	68	0	26						6[5]
1921	Lib.	13	7	48	3	30					3[6]	22[7]
1925	Lib.	14	10	49	3	35					1[8]	16[9]
1926	Lib.	14	12	54	1	37					1[10]	9[11]
1930	Con.	14	7	49	5	41					2[12]	10[13]
1935	Lib.	16	5	25	6	32	3	34			2[14]	9[15]
1940	Lib.	16	4	31	10	37	1	28			1[16]	4[17]
1945	Lib.	16	5	30	5	28	4	29		2	2[18]	11[19]
1949	Lib.	18	3	28	11	37	3	31		1	1[20]	3
1953	Lib.	22	3	14	8	31	7	27	4	26		2
1957	Con.	22	7	33	2	21	7	22	6	24		
1958	Con.	22	18	49	0	16	4	25	0	10		
1962	Con.	22	6	27	4	27	10	31	2	14		1
1963	Lib.	22	4	23	7	33	9	30	2	13		1
1965	Lib.	22	3	19	7	30	9	33	3	17		1
1968	Lib.	23	0	20	16	42	7	33	0	5		
1972	Lib.	23	8	33	4	29	11	35	0	3		
1974	Lib.	23	13	42	8	33	2	23	0	1		
1979	Con.	28	19	45	1	23	8	32				
1980	Lib.	28	16	42	0	22	12	35				1
1984	Con.	28	19	47	1	16	8	35				

1. Labor.
2. Including 4 percent Socialist, 8 percent Independent.
3. Including 7 percent Socialist and 10 percent Independent.
4. Including 3 percent Socialist.
5. Including 5 percent Labor.
6. Two Progressives and one Independent.
7. Including 9 percent Progressive; 5 percent Labor; 5 percent Socialist; 2 percent Independent.
8. Independent.
9. Including 6 percent Labor and 6 percent Progressive.
10. Independent.
11. Including 7 percent Labor.
12. One Independent; one Independent Labor.
13. Including 6 percent Independent Labor.
14. One Reconstruction; one Independent.
15. Including 7 percent Reconstruction.
16. Independent.
17. Including 3 percent Independent.
18. One Independent CCF; one Independent.
19. Including 5 percent Labor Progressive.
20. Independent.

THE TERRITORIES

Election Year	Party Forming Federal Government	Total Seats	Conservative Seats	Conservative Votes (%)	Liberal Seats	Liberal Votes (%)	Other Seats	Other Votes (%)
1887	Con.	4	4	69		31		
1891	Con.	4	4	81		19		
1896	Lib.	4	1	44	3	46		10[1]
1900	Lib.	4	0	45	4	55		
1904	Lib.	11	4	43	7	57		
1908	Lib.	1	0	11	1	40		49[2]
1911	Con.	1	1	61	0	39		
1917	Con.	1	1	54	0	46		
1921	Lib.	1	1	51	0	48		1[3]
1925	Lib.	1	1	59	0	41		
1926	Lib.	1	1	56	0	44		
1930	Con.	1	1	60	0	40		
1935	Lib.	1	1	56	0	44		
1940	Lib.	1	1	54	0	46		
1945	Lib.	1	1	40	0	0		60[4]
1949	Lib.	1	0	0	1	49		51[5]
1953	Lib.	2	0	27	2	54		19[6]
1957	Con.	2	0	41	2	59		
1958	Con.	2	1	49	1	50		1[7]
1962	Con.	2	1	47	1	46		7[8]
1963	Lib.	2	2	54	0	42		4[10]
1965	Lib.	2	1	45	1	52		3
1968	Lib.	2	1	47	1	48		5[11]
1972	Lib.	2	1	39	0	30	1	30[12]
1974	Lib.	2	1	39	0	28	1	33[13]
1979	Con.	3	2	37	0	33	1	30[14]
1980	Lib.	3	2	32	0	37	1	31[15]
1984	Con.	3	3	47	0	25	0	28[16]

1. Independent.
2. Independent.
3. Independent.
4. Including 28 percent CCF and 32 percent Labor Progressive.
5. Including 17 percent CCF and 34 percent Independent.
6. Including 14 percent Social Credit.
7. Including 1 percent Independent Progressive Conservative.
8. Including 7 percent Social Credit.
9. Wartime Coalition.
10. Including 4 percent Social Credit.
11. Including 5 percent NDP.
12. Including 30 percent NDP thereby winning one seat.
13. Including 33 percent NDP thereby winning one seat.
14. Including 29 percent NDP thereby winning one seat.
15. Including 31 percent NDP thereby winning one seat.
16. Including 24 percent NDP.

COMBINED ELECTION RESULTS

Election Year	Party Forming Federal Government	Total Seats	Conservative Seats	Conservative Votes (%)	Liberal Seats	Liberal Votes (%)	Progressive Seats	Progressive Votes (%)	CCF — NDP Seats	CCF — NDP Votes (%)	Social Credit Seats	Social Credit Votes (%)	Créditiste Seats	Créditiste Votes (%)	Reconstruction Seats	Reconstruction Votes (%)	Other Seats	Other Votes (%)
1878	Con.	206	140	53	65	45											1	2
1882	Con.	211	138	53	73	47												
1887	Con.	215	128	51	87	49												
1891	Con.	215	122	52	91	46											2	2
1896	Lib.	213	88	46	118	45											7	9
1900	Lib.	213	81	47	132	52												1
1904	Lib.	214	75	47	139	52												1
1908	Lib.	221	85	47	135	51											1	2
1911	Con.	221	134	51	87	48												1
1917	Con.	235	153[2]	57	82	40												3
1921	Lib.	235	50	30	116	41	65	23									4	6
1925	Lib.	245	116	46	99	40	24	9									6	5
1926	Con.	245	91	45	128	46	20	5									6	4
1930	Lib.	245	137	49	91	45	12	3									5	3
1935	Lib.	245	40	30	173	45			7	9	17	4			1	9	7	3
1940	Lib.	245	40	31	181	51			8	8	10	3					6	7
1945	Lib.	245	67	27	125	41			28	16	13	4					12	12
1949	Lib.	262	41	30	193	49			13	13	10	4					5	4
1953	Lib.	265	51	31	171	49			23	11	15	5					5	4
1957	Con.	265	112	39	105	41			25	11	19	7					4	2
1958	Con.	265	208	54	49	34			8	9		3						
1962	Con.	265	116	37	100	37			19	14	30	12						
1963	Lib.	265	95	33	129	42			17	13	24	12						
1965	Lib.	265	97	32	131	40			21	18	5	8	9	5			2	
1968	Lib.	264	72	31	155	45			21	17		1	14	5			1	1
1972	Lib.	264	107	35	109	38			31	18	15	8					2	2
1974	Lib.	264	95	35	141	43			16	15	11	5					1	1
1979	Con.	282	136	36	114	40			26	18	6	5						1
1980	Lib.	282	103	33	146	44			32	20		2					1	2
1984	Con.	282	211	50	40	28			30	19		1					2	2

(Handwritten marginal annotations next to the last rows: "Clark — 1979", "Trudeau — 1980", "Molroney — 1984")

Printed in Canada

g